OXFORD STUDIES IN AFRICAN AFFAIRS

General Editors
JOHN D. HARGREAVES *and* GEORGE SHEPPERSON

THE CHRONOLOGY OF ORAL TRADITION

QUEST FOR A CHIMERA

THE CHRONOLOGY OF ORAL TRADITION

QUEST FOR A CHIMERA

BY

DAVID P. HENIGE

CLARENDON PRESS
OXFORD
1974

Oxford University Press, Ely House, London W. 1

GLASGOW NEW YORK TORONTO MELBOURNE WELLINGTON
CAPE TOWN IBADAN NAIROBI DAR ES SALAAM LUSAKA ADDIS ABABA
DELHI BOMBAY CALCUTTA MADRAS KARACHI LAHORE DACCA
KUALA LUMPUR SINGAPORE HONG KONG TOKYO

ISBN 0 19 821694 7

Printed in Great Britain by
Richard Clay (The Chaucer Press), Ltd,
Bungay, Suffolk

Preface

LIKE many pieces of research, this study as now constituted differs considerably from the original formulation of the problem. Research was begun with the hope, perhaps even the expectation, that a degree of exactitude could be brought to the study of pre-colonial African chronology through the application of techniques developed from a comparative study of the recollection of the duration of the past in both African and non-African societies and from the use of independent data.

As patterns of this recollection became more clear and, more importantly, as the nature and extent of the chronological data with which the historian of oral societies must work emerged, I realized that my initial aim was at best quixotic, at worst naïve. The task then became one of attempting to explain the causes and mechanisms of this unpleasant reality.

The resulting analysis inevitably emphasizes the deficiencies of the chronological content of 'traditional' accounts, both in their oral and in their newly literate forms. Nevertheless, I wish to stress at this point as well as throughout this study that my intent is not to demean the importance of these accounts as historical sources—to do so would be gratuitous and intellectually arrogant. Rather, my purpose is to stress the necessity of properly interpreting retroactive conceptions of the duration of the past in non-calendrical societies, particularly the contexts and the motivations which often prompted the development of this aspect of traditional accounts. At the same time I hope to suggest some ways in which this interpretation can be most effective.

In this task a broad comparative approach can be illuminating in so far as it can disclose patterns which would be invisible if the focus were more narrow. The first two chapters discuss in detail the nature of these patterns, the likely circumstances of their occurrence, and their implications for the chronology of pre-colonial Africa. Some reasons why these distortions occur are next discussed. In many ways Chapter III is the most important of the entire study for an understanding of the reasons for the defective quality of much of the chronological content of tradition. Still, despite the protean nature of the data, there seems to be a feeling among many Africanists that the past of African societies can somehow be quantified and rendered susceptible to statistical analysis. A major premiss of this study is that such exercises will be, with very few exceptions, fruitless. Even worse they will at the same time be misleading because the method will lend to the data the appearance of validity beyond that which they often possess.

The methodology developed in the first four chapters is applied in Chapters V and VI to two dissimilar corpora of traditional evidence. In many ways, perhaps most notably in the levels of literacy and of feedback, the Fante and Asante stool traditions are not 'typical' of many of the traditions of sub-Saharan societies. Even so, the chronological content of these traditions is in no small way reminiscent of many other African societies. The analysis of Fante and Asante traditions is therefore offered without apology but not without the reminder that every body of tradition will present both unique and representative problems to the historian.

ii

It is a pleasant duty to be able to offer at long last my appreciation to those who have offered guidance and assistance from the inception of the research to its conclusion. First thanks must go to my adviser Jan Vansina who initially encouraged me to turn to this piece of research at a time when I doubted whether its utility was as great as my interest in it. His continuing astute counsel was freely available until the last word had been written and rewritten and any expression of gratitude cannot but be inadequate.

To Professors Steven M. Feierman and John R. W. Smail, whose often very different commentary helped to bring needed perspective and coherence to this work, I also express my appreciation. At various times my colleagues Joseph C. Miller, Joseph Paul Irwin, and James W. Brown also read all or part of the present study and I appreciated their candour more than they may have surmised.

No small number of libraries, archives, and research institutions have responded to what must have at times seemed endless demands on their patience. In this respect I must thank Mrs. Jacqueline Kelly and Linda Alexander of the Interlibrary Loan Division of the University of Wisconsin Memorial Library, with whom I have accrued a heavy debt over the years. The staffs of the Public Record Office, Institute of Historical Research (University of London), Royal

Commonwealth Society, and the Society for the Propagation of the Gospel, all in London, and the Bodleian Library, Oxford, were invariably gracious in complying with my requests.

While I was in Ghana Mr. Kofi Kafe, Assistant Librarian of the Balme Library, University of Ghana, facilitated my use of the Furley Collection housed there. Messrs. J. K. Dapah, Assistant Archivist, National Archives of Ghana, Accra, and J. A. Danquah and George Jackson of the National Archives of Ghana, Cape Coast, and their staffs suffered with an exemplary patience through my demands and I am most grateful.

Many others contributed in no small measure to the completion of the research task. Foremost among these was Douglas Jones of the School of Oriental and African Studies, University of London, who provided not only a most generous and congenial hospitality during my second stay in London but also contributed stimulating observations on the state of my research as it was then. I benefited from his role as 'devil's advocate' as much as he enjoyed it. Professor H. A. Lamb, Head of the Department of History at the University of Ghana, and his wife Venice, provided crucial support at a time when it was most needed. Albert van Dantzig of the University of Ghana History Department very kindly and graciously assisted me with his unparalleled knowledge of Dutch activities on the Gold Coast, in translating several Dutch sources, and in suggesting informants in Cape Coast and Elmina. Jarle Simensen provided both friendship and keen intellectual *camaraderie* during my stay in Ghana.

My research abroad was sponsored by a Fulbright-Hays Fellowship, for which I am grateful. Needless to say, however, the conclusions embodied in this work are entirely my own and do not necessarily represent in any way those of the U.S. Office of Education.

My journey to this particular point has been an embarrassingly slow one. It began only after several years of what can best be described as an eminently forgettable limbo. Beginning this work entailed a drastic change in the life habits of my family. They have borne the change and some of the concomitant vicissitudes perhaps better than I have myself. Their having done so has made this work possible and I am indeed more grateful than I can say.

Contents

List of Tables

List of Figures

List of Abbreviations

AHS	*African Historical Studies* (Boston)
BEFEO	*Bulletin de l'École Française de l'Extrême-Orient*
BIFAN	*Bulletin de l'Institut Fondamental* [*Français*] *d'Afrique Noire*
CAH[2]	fascicles in revised edition of the *Cambridge Ancient History*, volumes I and II
CCA	Chief Commissioner, Ashanti
CCP	Commissioner, Central Provinces
CSSH	*Comparative Studies in Society and History*
CWP	Commissioner, Western Provinces
EJ	Elmina Journal transcription in Furley Collection
FC	Furley Collection, Balme Library, University of Ghana
GNQ	*Ghana Notes and Queries*
HCIP	*History and Culture of the Indian People*
IAS	Institute of African Studies, University of Ghana
JAH	*Journal of African History*
JAOS	*Journal of the American Oriental Society*
JASB	*Journal of the Asiatic Society of Bengal*
JCS	*Journal of Cuneiform Studies*
JHSN	*Journal of the Historical Society of Nigeria*
JNES	*Journal of Near Eastern Studies*
JPS	*Journal of the Polynesian Society*
JRAI	*Journal of the Royal Anthropological Institute*
JRAS	*Journal of the Royal Asiatic Society*
NAG	National Archives of Ghana, Accra
NAG/CC	National Archives of Ghana, Cape Coast
NBKG	Archief van de Nederlandische Bezittingen ter Kuste van Guinea
SNA	Secretary for Native Affairs, Gold Coast
T70	Treasury Papers, African Companies, Public Record Office, London
UJ	*Uganda Journal*

Introduction

What does chronology contribute to the wisdom of Socrates or the brilliance of Themistocles?[1]

Il n'est pas exagéré de dire qu'une datation exacte en histoire est aussi importante qu'une mesure exacte en physique.[2]

I STATEMENT OF THE PROBLEM

THE historian of Africa will recognize these sentiments as opposite extremes for his purposes—the one an unhistorical attitude, the other an unattainable ideal. The study of datation, once an end in itself, remains an indispensable tool to the historian in his analysis of the past. The achievements of Socrates and Themistocles would be less explicable if they could not be placed in proper temporal context. If one accepts the thesis that the main concern of the historian is to explain why things happened, an understanding of the sequence of actors and events within and between societies is necessary in order to postulate causal relationships.

Concomitantly, however, it is becoming increasingly apparent that it is quixotic to anticipate the possibility of arriving at any extensive exact dating for most of sub-Saharan Africa before the nineteenth century. This hope has too long beguiled historians, many of whom have been too naïve in their acceptance of chronological exactitude and too convinced that such exactitude is possible or even necessary in the study of pre-colonial African history. Yet when the historian asks chronological questions from oral tradition he is in most cases seeking information that these sources were never designed to provide. The memory of the past in oral societies seldom included its abstract quantification. Traditional accounts were

[1] Eunapius, a fourth-century A.D. historian, commenting on the work of Dexippus, a predecessor. K. Müller (ed.), *Fragmenta Historicorum Graecorum* (5 vols., Paris, 1841–70), iv. 12, quoted in A. Momigliano, 'Time in ancient historiography' in *History and the concept of time*, Beiheft 6 (1966) to *History and Theory*, p. 16.

[2] I. Meyerson, 'Le temps, la mémoire, l'histoire', *Journal de Psychologie normale et pathologique*, 53 (1956), 337.

designed to develop and transmit those aspects of the past which were deemed important, and absolute dating was never, nor could ever be, one of these. In this sense, while this study is concerned with the nature and scope of the evidence available for assessing the duration of the past of oral societies, it is no less concerned with the response of oral traditional accounts to the demands placed upon them and of the interpretations made of these responses.

The evidence presently available to historians and anthropologists interested in African societies consists essentially of the content of oral tradition. The term 'oral tradition' is a peculiarly vague one and susceptible to a host of ambiguous interpretations. The most thorough taxonomy constructed to date lists six broad categories, with several sub-divisions in each.[3] Additionally, there are distinctions to be made between traditions and testimonies, between official and unofficial traditions, and between individual and consensual accounts. For the purposes of this study the term 'oral tradition', unless specifically qualified, refers to that corpus of orally transmitted material which addresses itself specifically to recounting the past. This implies in most instances some attempt at assigning some form of duration and sequence to events over a period of time exceeding three generations, that is, a length of time beyond the maximum limits of personal testimony and experience. In this sense, poetry, heroic recitations, folk-tales, and like forms of oral art are excluded since they are essentially unconcerned with duration and sequence.

All forms of oral tradition have their strengths and their weaknesses, but it is generally recognized that their greatest deficiency is an inability to establish and maintain an accurate assessment of the duration of the past they seek to recount.[4] Some would consider them timeless and therefore ahistorical.[5] Regardless of this weakness, however, the body of oral tradition, real and potential, represents, together with archaeology and linguistics, nearly all that the

[3] J. Vansina, 'Once upon a time: oral traditions as history in Africa', *Daedalus* (Spring 1971), 450–1.

[4] See, for example, M. I. Finley, 'Myth, memory and history', *History and Theory*, 4 (1965), 285–6; Hélène d'Almeida Topor, 'Rigueur historique et imprécision de la tradition orale', *Bulletin de l'Institut Supérieur de Bénin*, 11 (Oct.–Nov. 1969), 47; J. Vansina, *Oral tradition* (Chicago, 1965), 102; A. K. Forbes, *Râs Mâlâ. Hindoo annals of the province of Goozerat in western India* (London, 1924), 265; G. I. Jones, 'Time and oral tradition, with special reference to Eastern Nigeria', *JAH* 6 (1965), 153; J. Ki-Zerbo, 'The oral tradition as a source of African history', *Diogenes*, 67 (Fall 1969), 118–20.

[5] Finley, 'Myth, memory and history', 286–7.

historian of sub-Saharan Africa has to work with in his efforts to understand the more remote past.

The task of recovery and assessment is an urgent one, for this body of oral evidence is disappearing quickly as literacy and the acceptance of its concomitants sound a death knell for the few 'pristine' oral traditions that remain.[6] The investigator, under these circumstances, is not justified in rejecting any oral traditions that he encounters, but must work and rework them with an increasing sophistication and critical sense.

II DISTORTIONS OF THE DURATION OF THE PAST

This study is intended to be an analysis of the chronological content of traditional accounts, whether still oral or already committed to writing. It will concern itself with three aspects of this problem:

(a) the patterns in which the concept of the duration of the past have been distorted

(b) the circumstances which have influenced the need for and the shape of this manipulation

(c) an assessment of the limitations of the resulting chronological data with which the historian of pre-colonial sub-Saharan Africa must work.

By definition, the chronological content of oral tradition encompasses those aspects of traditional accounts which may be useful in assessing the duration of the past and the sequence of events within it. The most important and most obvious of these indicators are the units by which a society remembers or measures its past. In those societies possessing calendars or other practical mnemonic devices it is possible to determine with reasonable accuracy the length of a period of time. Few African societies fall within this category, however, and so we must deal with other devices for the mensuration of the past. For societies in which a form of hereditary or at least centralized government existed one conception of the duration of the past will amost always be measured in terms of the reigns of the rulers of the state.[7] These reigns are usually seen as representing

[6] A. D. Roberts, *Recording East Africa's past* (Nairobi, 1968), 2; P. D. Curtin, 'Field techniques for collecting and processing oral data', *JAH* 9 (1968), 369.

[7] I assume throughout this work that each society preserves several perceptions of its past and of the events and duration within it. On this point, see especially B. S. Cohn, 'The pasts of an Indian village', *CSSH* 3 (1960/1), 241–9 and M. Fikry-Atallah, 'Wala oral history and Wa's social realities' in R. M. Dorson (ed.), *African folklore* (Garden City, N.Y., 1972), 237–53.

generations as well. In other words, the typical royal genealogy is also an ascendant one, with no collateral rulers acknowledged. In many African societies the institutions of age grades or age sets have been useful in establishing chronological parameters. An analysis of age grade systems may usually proceed on the same principles that are used for evaluating genealogies and kinglists, since age grades or sets represent a non-biological 'generation' of more or less conventional length. Specific attention, therefore, will not be devoted to age grade and age sets as chronological tools, and the reader is referred to the growing body of literature concerned with the use of age grades and age sets in developing chronological parameters.[8]

In cultures where descent groups rather than centralized institutions are the cement of unity, genealogies are usually the most common expression of social relationships and control. These will then tend to reflect relevant social truths rather than abstract historical ones. As a result these genealogies are usually quite shallow and their chronological value is minimal, although, because of their lack of depth, at least obviously so. Although the dichotomy between 'state' and 'stateless' societies and the way they measure their past is in many ways a simplistic one which admits of exceptions to both its parts, the general pattern is distinct enough, in our area of interest, to justify restricting any analysis to those societies which possessed some recognizable form of central control or mnemonic devices for remembering the past. For it is clear that it was in these societies that the greatest effort was made to create or remember a continuous past, from the most remote period to the present.

In kinglists where filiations are not included some assessment of the period allegedly covered can be made by an analysis of the succession system. Inferences have been made from such an analysis regarding the expected mean length of reign. This approach has obvious weaknesses. It assumes that the concept of 'average' has real relevance in historical reality. It further assumes that the succession system under study has not undergone changes from its inception. Finally, it presupposes that the kinglist/genealogy itself is accurate.

It may be useful to summarize very cursorily the chronological

[8] The most useful of these are Y.-D. Person, 'Classes d'âge et chronologie', *Latitudes*, sp. no. (1963), 68–83; S. Saberwal, 'The oral tradition, periodization, and political systems', *Canadian Journal of African Studies*, 1 (1967), 155–62 [Embu of Kenya]; A. H. Jacobs, 'The chronology of the pastoral Maasai', *Hadith*, 1 (1968), 10–31; E. Isichei, 'Historical change in an Ibo polity', *JAH* 10 (1969), 421–38; G. Muriuki, 'Chronology of the Kikuyu', *Hadith*, 3 (1971), 16–27.

aspects of traditional accounts which will be analysed in greater detail in Chapters I and II. The most common technique currently used by African historians to establish chronological bases for the precolonial period is the analysis of synchronistic references in traditional accounts. Mention of events or individuals from outside the tradition's own cultural milieu offers an opportunity to attempt the reconstruction of a rudimentary relative chronology. The use of synchronisms has met with mixed success. They have proved fruitful in many cases but they have also, for example in the interlacustrine area, been found wanting.[9] Synchronisms appearing in an oral tradition should never, of course, be rejected out of hand. None the less, a synchronism may not be the innocuous and independent datum it is often assumed to be. More than any other kind of evidence the isolated synchronism is subject to the limitations imposed upon it by other data. The temptation to use a small number of synchronisms many generations back in time as bases for structuring relative chronologies is one that cannot be resisted too strongly.

Telescoping may occur in a tradition for many reasons. In most cases it will occur when the duration of the past loses its relevance for the present. Only those past events which influence the present will be remembered. Generally these relate to the 'migration' to and settlement of the area, which encompassed land rights, and the legitimation of the ruling dynasty or social order. All of these can be, and usually are, remembered in a fashion which is not objectively quantifiable. In telescoping, whole epochs, such as the creation and development of the polity, may be remembered by a single archetypal figure.

Another and more purposeful form of telescoping is the omission of 'usurpers' and periods of foreign rule or natural or political cataclysm. 'Usurper' is a fluid and extremely relative term that is usually defined by the political circumstances attending the transmission of the tradition. Because of this the period of usurper rule can encompass a large part of the past, particularly when the reigning dynasty or most prominent lineage is of comparatively recent origin, or where the office of king is surrounded by a ritual complex

[9] D. W. Cohen, 'A survey of interlacustrine chronology', *JAH* 11 (1970), chart opp. 190 and 192–4, is a good example of the way synchronisms go awry after more than a few generations back, especially when the genealogical data are suspect. For the interlacustrine kinglists, see below, Chapter III, and D. P. Henige, 'K.W.'s Nyoro Kinglist: oral tradition or applied research?', *JAH* (forthcoming).

which may inhibit every incumbent from meriting inclusion in an oral kinglist because he did not undergo the complete ritual sequence.[10] Traditions also tend to 'forget' those rulers who failed to die in office or whose reigns were inglorious. These are two examples of what various societies might tend to regard as usurpers. A third and larger class includes those whose lineal legitimacy has, often only retrospectively, proved unacceptable.

As a distorting process, lengthening is much more widespread than telescoping, particularly among those societies that form the major interest of this study. In many ways lengthening is the obverse reflexive of telescoping in that it often represents a belated effort to compensate for earlier telescoping. Like telescoping it can be judged best with reference to the ambiences in which it arose and ultimately was transmitted. It is important to remember that often these would be identical. We cannot often trace the development of a tradition in its pre-literate context, but the assumption that it arose in response to actual events, that it was transmitted without regard to attendant exigencies, and that it was finally ossified in a written form that substantially encapsulated its form and spirit throughout its life is not an uncommon one. The premiss here, however, is that traditions are primarily seen and used as political symbols, and like the whole array of political symbolism, they serve specific purposes at particular times—primarily purposes of legitimation. In these circumstances the content of oral traditions continually underwent modification as necessity required.

This process can nowhere be seen more clearly than in an analysis of the circumstances under which artificial lengthening of genealogies and kinglists has occurred. J. H. Plumb has described three of these situations in the following terms: '. . . it is interesting, if not surprising, that outbreaks of genealogical fever occur most frequently when new classes are emerging into status, a new faction pushing its way into an ancient aristocracy, or when the established ruling classes feel threatened by the *nouveaux riches*.'[11] A fourth circumstance which encourages flights of genealogical fancy is the imposition of some form of foreign control and the often concomitant introduction of literacy. Some of the greatest historical works of antiquity were

[10] When used generically in this study 'kinglists' refers to both unfiliated lists of rulers and royal genealogies. The context will indicate which, if only one, is intended.

[11] J. H. Plumb, *The death of the past* (Boston, Mass., 1971), 31–2.

written during periods of foreign domination and with the expressed purpose of portraying the historians' peoples in a way at once palliative to their lost sovereignty and impressive to their new rulers. The works of Josephus, Berosus, and Manetho, all claiming chronological precedence for their respective subjects, are three of the most important examples of this genre in classical antiquity.[12]

The discovery of hitherto unsuspected antiquity as a response to the loss of sovereignty is more widespread, however. Whatever their ultimate origin, the traditions of most African societies were first recorded in the early period of European rule. It is not idle to speculate how differently these traditions might have developed if this domination had not so often taken forms which required the legitimation of the elements ruling at the time of its imposition. The imperial powers established 'indirect rule' most successfully in those areas which had a ruling structure both easily identifiable and putatively ancient. Respect for proclaimed antiquity was one of the conquerors' more obvious attitudes. What effect did this bias have on the accounts they received of their new subjects' past?

Lengthening of a genealogy or kinglist may be indicated in several ways. The least obvious, apparently, is through the assumption that each reign also represents a generation; but there are other forms as well. Euhemerism, or the inclusion of gods and heroes as human rulers, occurs commonly both in African traditions (e.g. the Bacwezi and the early Oyo *alafin*) and non-African ones. Indeed, only in the past few centuries has the mythological chaff been separated from the historical wheat even for ancient Greece.[13] A more direct means for increasing the the duration of the past is through the wholesale invention of fictive rulers; perhaps Geoffrey of Monmouth was the most blatant, but at the same time most successful, practitioner of this art.[14] This imaginative legerdemain may be accomplished in several

[12] J. W. Johnson, 'Chronological writing: its concepts and development', *History and Theory*, 2 (1962), 126–7. For Josephus, see his *Flavius Josephus against Apion*, I. i-xi, and preface to his *The Antiquities of the Jews*. For Manetho, see J. Marquart, 'Chronologische Untersuchungen', *Philologus*, Supplement to Vol. 7 (1899), 637–56, 657–93. For Berosus, see P. Schnabel, *Berossus und die babylonisch-hellenistische Literatur* (Berlin, 1923), 77–9.

[13] For Isaac Newton as a euhemerist, see F. E. Manuel, *Isaac Newton, historian* (Cambridge, Mass., 1963), 119–21, 214–16.

[14] See T. D. Kendrick, *British Antiquity* (London, 1950), 34–7, 65–85, for a discussion of the influence of Geoffrey of Monmouth's work into the seventeenth century. Significantly its impact intensified under what Kendrick called 'the Tudor cult of history', that is, when the Tudors, a dynasty of Welsh (i.e. 'Briton') descent, were ruling. S. Anglo, 'The *British History* in early Tudor propaganda',

ways. In societies where rulers are named on a cyclical basis it has proved tempting to add on a cycle or two, thereby impressively increasing the time-depth of the dynasty at a single stroke.[15] Sometimes these fictive early rulers were added to provide legitimation for later rulers. Lengthening can be effected by the inclusion of toponyms, eponyms, and patronyms as rulers. Usually this group of fictive rulers will be detected after a researcher becomes familiar with the *mores* and lexicography of his particular society.

Another, and less easily detectable, means of lengthening a kinglist is simply to include contemporaneous contenders as consecutive rulers. In this way 'pretenders' and 'usurpers' are used retroactively even though they have have been unsuccessful in their own time. If some of these contenders, although unsuccessful themselves, became progenitors of later, more successful, rulers or lineages, the need to include them becomes overwhelming. This may be seen as the polar opposite of the elision of usurpers already discussed. Obviously, different sets of circumstances require different responses.

Rotational and promotional systems, which allow various segments of a society to participate in the ruling office, are common in Africa. Rotational systems in practice have never been perfectly regular, although they may, through tradition, become retrospectively so. The manipulation of rotational kinglists has chronological implications. As it happens, the alternative possibilities have opposite ramifications. Those succeeding out of order may be eliminated, thereby reducing the depth of the list. On the other hand it may be thought more useful to add to the list those who should have succeeded but were prevented from doing so. These two responses have occurred with about equal frequency in regularizing rotational patterns, but once the probability of manipulation is recognized detailed investigation may determine which is the more likely in any given case.

Other elements of a tradition have less direct and profound chronological implications, but are important in their roles as indicators of possible anomalies. This group includes the widespread incidence of the Moses-in-the-bulrushes theme in traditional accounts, the general lack of remembered multiple reigns, and the excessively

---

Bulletin of John Rylands Library, 44 (1961), 17–48, discusses the political utility of Geoffrey to the Early Tudors.

[15] For Burundi, see J. Vansina, 'Note sur la chronologie du Burundi ancien', *Bulletin des Séances de l'Académie royal des sciences d'Outre-Mer*, N.S. 13 (1967), 430–3. For Karagwe, see R. Berger, 'Oral traditions in Karagwe', paper given at the East African Institute for Social Research, June 1963, 3–4.

long reigns often accorded to the founders and early rulers of a dynasty. The Moses theme, when it occurs in the early period of a dynasty's history, corresponds to the Culture Hero of the anthropologists. Its appearance later in a genealogy may indicate a dynastic change or a period of interregnum which has been distinguished through personification. Impossibly or improbably long reigns may likewise be seen as signposts of legendary periods, for this is a common mechanism by which traditional accounts separate what they regard as historical from what they see as legendary or mythical.

Regnal and generational length averages have long interested historians and chronographers. At least as far back as the fifth century B.C. Greek historians applied the concept of average generation to unknown periods of early Greek 'history' in an effort to provide sequence and an acceptable temporal perspective. Historians of Africa have not failed to pursue this theme. Scholars attending the SOAS Conference on African Chronology in 1966 devoted more attention to an effort to establish viable average regnal and generation lengths than to any other technique except the use of synchronisms.[16] The concept of average is an intriguing one, as the reliance on it by historians of all cultures amply attests. But the application of the concept will generally be fruitless unless it is so carefully controlled as almost entirely to lose any extrapolative or didactic value. Furthermore, the quality of the African data militates against their effective use.

III THE UTILITY OF THE COMPARATIVE APPROACH

It is often argued that the African experience and the evidence which documents it were unique. The corollary argues that the best way to assess any aspect of a society, including its traditions, is through a prolonged exposure to its cultural values. In Collingwood's words, 'the historian who studies a civilisation other than his own can apprehend the mental life of that civilisation only be re-enacting that experience for himself'.[17] It is a continuing presumption throughout this study that such exposure can be of inestimable value in the interpretation of data. Nevertheless, this analysis and interpretation can be carried out most effectively when it is assumed that the data can

[16] For a discussion of regnal and generation lengths in Africa, see D. H. Jones, 'Problems of African chronology', *JAH* 11 (1970), 166–8.

[17] R. G. Collingwood, *The idea of history* (London, 1946), 163. See also ibid. 282–4.

be analysed at two discrete levels—one unique, the other representative. The uniqueness implies a *combination* of specific circumstances in one society that occurs in no other. The representativeness assumes that few of these circumstances are of themselves unique and that their operation can be most effectively analysed by reference to similar cases in other ambiences. In other words, the profound but narrow perspective must be supplemented by a wider, if necessarily shallower, one. Principles or even patterns are seldom discerned through a micro-approach, where all appears in isolation. The factors that operated on what actually happened, as well as on the genesis, transmutations, and final disposition of the evidence are not significantly different on this level of analysis for Africa than they have been for much of the rest of the world. In this sense this study is explicitly comparative. The problem of pre-colonial African chronology is at a juncture where the placing of the African data into a comparative frame of reference can be a fruitful exercise. It is particularly important that this should be broad enough to provide the widest possible perspective in the hope that broad patterns, invisible to a more narrow focus, will emerge.

The SOAS Conference of 1966 took the first important steps in this direction by introducing the comparative concept to the study of African chronology and by formulating an array of conceptual tools. Nevertheless the results of the Conference were not as encouraging as had been expected.[18] This was partly because of the great disparity, qualitatively and quantitatively, in the evidence, which was mainly based on the available oral traditions for the different cultural units adopted by the Conference. Partly, too, the lack of concrete results may be attributed to the fact that the conceptual framework was not broad enough in its comparative aspects. Although a modicum of non-African materials was introduced into evidence, these data were too few in number and too limited in scope for significant analysis. In being forced to grapple with the African data without recourse to a broader spectrum of information, the Conference inevitably fell short of its expected goals. The present study hopes to carry forward the work of the Conference in this respect by introducing a larger body of non-African material to the study of the African data.

This comparison will be made on two levels. Evidence from those areas whose concept of the duration of their past developed late,

[18] Jones, 'Problems', 161.

such as Oceania and the Native States of India, will be analysed in search of common patterns. Secondly, those areas blessed with contemporaneous records will be studied in order to determine whether the patterns which developed there compare to those of the first instance. These latter areas will be compared, with, it is hoped, due allowance for cultural differences, to those whose evidence for their past consists primarily of oral materials.

Such an approach has weaknesses as well as strengths. It will be argued that because of cultural dissimilarities, for instance, any comparison would be between, as it were, apples and oranges. Of necessity there will be a bias throughout much of this work towards accepting documented material as, *ipso facto*, more valuable as evidence of chronology than oral data. Because of this it may be argued that the quantitative data lack true randomness. In fact the materials used in Chapter IV will be drawn from as complete a range of the total population of such data as possible, and the use to which other kinds of data are put will, it is hoped, allay some of these doubts.

Some of the fundamental biases, however, cannot be altered. My underlying assumption is that one's view of the past, including its duration, is more the product of the exigencies of the present than of a dispassionate desire to portray past events as they actually occurred. It may well be true, as Louis Halphen observed, when speaking of the craft of the trained historian, that 'l'objectif le plus immédiat de l'histoire est de sauver de l'oubli les *faits* du passé', but even under the most ideal circumstances this involves a selection process which is influenced by the historian's present.[19] Nor, of course, do first objectives in principle remain first objectives in practice; the past is too often regarded as a malleable symbolism. The hope here is to suggest what forms this manipulation of one type of the remembrance of the past is likely to have taken, and in what circumstances it is likely to have occurred.

V FANTE AND ASANTE TRADITIONS

This study is bipartite in structure and approach. Although its components are dissimilar in both mode of analysis and breadth of focus, they should be viewed as complementary in so far as Chapters V and VI, dealing with Fante and Asante traditions, are intended to serve as a case study embodying the principles of analysis discussed

[19] Halphen, *Introduction à l'histoire* (Paris, 1946), 12.

in Chapters I to IV. Such a microcosmic analysis illustrates how individual societies and their traditions can be both representative on one level and unique on yet another.

In many ways neither the Fante nor the Asante are typical of other African societies. Both, but particularly the Fante, have a long history of literacy and a propensity to reject traditional values in favour of western ones. At the same time this allows the historian to chart the ways in which these factors influenced the development and disposition of the traditional past. It is important to understand both the desire to incorporate non-traditional data into oral materials and the tortuous mechanisms involved in this process. The extensive documentation available for the Fante for a period of three centuries provides the opportunity to trace events as they occurred as well as the development of the traditional accounts of them

Another reason that the Akan-speaking area was chosen for analysis was that it offered the opportunity to study a matrilineal succession system. This complements the comparative data, which contain very little material from matrilineal systems. It was hoped that some firm patterns would emerge from this analysis. Unfortunately, eligibility in the stool in the Akan system was so wide and kinship terminology so inexact that few conclusions regarding possible chronological differences in the behaviour of patrilineal and matrilineal systems are possible. This difficulty was aggravated by the fact that whatever genealogical data are available for Fante and Asante stools seem to be in large measure a response to British desires for regularity and are not based on traditional sources, which seldom thought genealogically at all.

But the most serious difficulty in dealing with all aspects of Fante and Asante stool traditions is in understanding and evaluating the impact of feedback from extraneous sources. The process of incorporating written or printed materials into oral accounts is over a century old in the Fante areas of southern Ghana. But neither the mechanisms nor the patterns of this assimilative process were markedly different from those in other parts of Africa, nor ideed from those examined for other areas of the world. The diligence and alacrity with which traditional Fante informants incorporated extraneous printed matter into their accounts underscore the importance of analysing a tradition for feedback as a necessary first step, even before attempting to assess the value of its chronological content.

The role that indirect rule served in creating or maintaining the need for many traditions, while at the same time resulting in particular kinds of distortion, can be clearly seen in an analysis of those kinds of circumstances which produced the need for legitimation. A study of the Fante and Asante traditions strongly illustrates this thesis. The British colonial government in the Gold Coast established a hierarchy of chiefs to serve as insulators for and disseminators of British colonial policy. The structure of this hierarchy was loosely based on existing indigenous political forms. Nevertheless its implementation, with more rigidly formal British standards, created conditions peculiarly suitable for the political use of oral tradition. This propensity was aggravated when the British came to accept stool disputes as intrinsic realities of Akan political life and sought only to adjudicate them on broadly consistent principles. As a result 'new' lines came to rule in several Fante stools, and with them came new traditions. For the basic assumption—that incumbency dictated the tenor of oral accounts of the past—remained unchanged. Many Fante and Asante stool traditions changed more rapidly because the 'legitimacy' of their proponents was constantly, and often successfully, being challenged.

In several other ways Fante and Asante traditions support the premiss that contingencies peculiar to a given society usually serve to reflect broader patterns. For example, the policy among the Akan to eliminate destooled chiefs from their *adae* ceremony amounted in effect to institutionalized telescoping since these names would be quickly forgotten. The claim that the incidence of destoolment in pre-colonial times was markedly less than during the colonial period is seriously compromised by the contemporaneous evidence available for the nineteenth century. This is a basis for arguing that destoolment in earlier times was as common as in this century. Certain 'epochal' events in Asante and Fante traditions, such as the overthrow of Denkyira by the Asantehene Osei Tutu *c.* 1701, or the erection of the various European trading castles along the coast in the seventeenth and eighteenth centuries, have come to provide fixed points—*termini ante quos*—for the beginnings of many Asante and Fante traditions. They have become, in their own way, charters legitimizing the paramountcy or prestige of certain stools through their alleged participation in these events.

Despite the evidential handicaps under which he must labour, the historian of Africa is perhaps more fortunate than historians of other preliterate societies. No African society existed in the same kind of isolation that confronts the student of Polynesian and Melanesian cultures. Most African societies' interpretations of their own past can be supplemented by data from neighbouring societies—often from contemporaneous written sources. Nor has the problem of feedback, though unquestionably alarming and becoming more so, completely eliminated the possibility of working with uncontaminated oral traditions as it has, for example, in northern India. But the incessant pressures of modernization and the concomitant spread of literacy means that this respite is a brief one.

V THE IMPLICATIONS OF DIFFERING CONCEPTS OF TIME AND DURATION

Our own conditioning to the exactitude of the calendrical measurement of time too often inhibits our ability to appreciate that such precision is not universal and that many societies have, or at least had until recently, much less exact and less mensurable concepts of time. This propensity has been described well by Finley: 'We are in thrall to the highly sophisticated conception of time as a measurable continuum, a concept which is largely meaningless for ordinary human purposes . . . Duration of time, if it is a consideration at all, which is not always the case, is not experienced as a measurable quantity, but as an associative or emotional quality.'[20] In short, we transfer our own calendrical biases to societies in which the past is neither lineally conceived nor even approximately measurable. In doing so we often assume that these societies have remembered their past 'calendrically', that is, lineally, sequentially, and even chronometrically. In fact, achronicity is one of the concomitants of an oral non-calendrical society.

It is not necessary to discuss in detail the cosmological, cyclical concepts of the past that are characteristic of non-calendrical societies. This has been done in comprehensive detail.[21] Recently several studies have been devoted to the concept of time in African societies.[22] While the thrust and conclusions of these studies vary

[20] Finley, 'Myth, memory and history', 293.

[21] M. P. Nilsson, *Primitive time-reckoning: a study in the first development of the art of counting time among the primitive and first culture peoples* (Lund, 1920).

[22] e.g. T. O. Beidelman, 'Kaguru time reckoning: an aspect of the cosmology of an east African people', *Southwestern Journal of Anthropology*, 19 (1963), 9–20; J. Faublée, 'Espace et temps dans la tradition malgache', *Revue de Synthèse*, 55/6 (1969), 297–327; A. Hulstaert, 'Le temps pour les Mongo', *Bulletin des Séances de l'Académie royale des sciences d'Outre-Mer*, N.S. 15 (1969), 227–35;

in many of their details they agree that, for whatever reason, it is impossible for these societies to recall with even approximate accuracy the duration of the past because, in most cases, it was irrelevant for them even to attempt to do so. A similar conclusion, although on rather different grounds, was recently reached by John Mbiti in a study of African religious concepts.[23] Because the past, when remembered at all, is calculated by natural phenomena and human life spans, Mbiti observes that 'numerical calendars are both impossible and meaningless in traditional life'.[24] More germanely, Mbiti argues that time in traditional societies is 'two-dimensional' with 'a long past, a present and virtually no future' and that 'time has to be experienced in order to make sense or become real'.[25] In these terms the past, though known to have existed, is impossible to measure, although it may be an exaggeration to characterize it as 'the graveyard of [present] time' once it has been 'used up'.[26] Although Mbiti tends to extrapolate transcending principles from insufficient data in much of his work, it will become clear that here at least his arguments are valid.[27]

When traditional societies were confronted with demands from the calendar-oriented colonial authorities they could only respond in terms foreign to their own cultural milieu. The plaint of the Asantehene Osei Bonsu (*c.* 1801–24) to the Bowdich mission in 1817 vividly encapsulated this dilemma. When Osei Bonsu requested his retroactive annual stipend from the British authorities, they produced a set of figures which he disputed. When challenged to defend his own position he lamented that 'white men know how many months pass, how many years they live, and they know this, but they won't tell me'.[28] Osei Bonsu recognized his limitations in this area. Regrettably

---

F. N'Sougan Agblemagnon, 'Du temps dans la culture "Ewe" ', *Présence Africaine* (1957), 222–32; M. Bekombo, 'Note sur le temps; conceptions et attitudes chez les Dwala', *Ethnographie*, 60/1 (1966), 60–4. For other literature on the concept of time reckoning, see bibliography.

[23] J. S. Mbiti, *African Religions and Philosophy* (London, 1969).

[24] Ibid, 21.

[25] Ibid. 17.

[26] Ibid. 23.

[27] R. Horton, 'African traditional thought and western science', *Africa*, 37 (1967), 50–71, 155–87, is a perceptive and thought-provoking article on the problems of inter-cultural interpretation. Pages 173–5, 176–8 are particularly relevant to the present study.

[28] Quoted in Thomas E. Bowdich, *Mission from Cape Coast Castle to Ashantee, with a statistical account of that kingdom and geographical notices of other parts of the interior of Africa* (London, 1819), 48.

his candour has not often been emulated. The following study hopes to demonstrate the implications for chronology of the circumstances and responses which attended this confrontation of 'timeless' societies with those with calendrical biases.

CHAPTER I

The Shape of the Past: History as Present Politics

> All Nations, before they began to keep exact accounts of the Time, have been prone to raise their Antiquities. And this humor has been promoted by the contentions of Nations about their originals [*sic*][1]

THIS chapter will discuss the range of chronological distortions that can occur when dealing with kinglists, genealogies, and other putative indicators of the duration of the past in oral societies. The problem of extended father/son succession, however, will be reserved for more extended discussion in the next chapter because of its widespread occurrence and its direct and profound chronological ramifications. The problems discussed in this chapter have varying direct chronological implications but each of them bears directly on the ways societies have viewed and used their past.

I SYNCHRONISMS

In the last decade the use of synchronisms to help determine the time-depth of African societies has increased dramatically.[2] This trend is likely to continue and even accelerate with the realization that collecting as many traditions as possible from a given society is an important means of comparing, controlling, and assessing oral data. Synchronisms are seen as particularly valuable for establishing chronological bases because they appear to be relatively value-free and therefore more worthy of credence. Their appearance in traditions often has an aura of spontaneity and as a result historians do not always recognize the possibility of their having chronological biases. The Assyrian case discussed below suggests, however, that this kind of extemporaneity itself can be disadvantageous.

[1] Isaac Newton, *The chronology of ancient nations amended* (London, 1728), 43.

[2] For a survey of the problems and potentialities of the use of synchronisms for pre-colonial Africa, see Jones, 'Problems of African chronology', 170–2.

Essentially there are four types of synchronisms:

I. Intra-societal tie-ins. Clan and lineage traditions and genealogies may often corroborate the existence and sequence of rulers mentioned in 'official' genealogies. Since non-royal genealogies are usually shallower than royal genealogies this kind of synchronism will most often be confined to the more recent past and add little to dates available from other sources. However, they often can serve as indicators of distortions and telescoping in the 'official' lists.

II. Tie-ins with events or personalities from neighbouring societies.[3]

III. References in tradition to astronomical phenomena which are theoretically identifiable and datable. For Africa these are usually solar eclipses.

IV. References in tradition to events in a literate society or, conversely, mention in written records of events in an oral society which may also be mentioned in that society's traditions.

For Africa the first two types are much more common than the others but tie-ins can only supply relative chronologies between their societies. Even a fully authenticated synchronism of this kind will perforce be only as useful as the weakest of the chronological frameworks of which it is a part. The last two types of synchronism can provide the historian of Africa with his *summum bonum*—absolute dating. But in most instances this will only be the reward of perseverance, imagination, and good fortune. The utility of eclipse references for African chronology has been fully discussed elsewhere.[4] It only remains to reiterate that eclipses are extremely variable in appearance and it is important to secure as exact a description as possible from traditional accounts, which are seldom even adequately descriptive.

The author of the latest survey of ancient Near Eastern chronology which is based largely on synchronisms and tie-ins, and which has been subjected to several decades of intense scrutiny, still finds it necessary to point out the danger of 'obscuring the ever present element of uncertainty' and observes that 'only the solution which

[3] In conformity with the terminology of the 1966 SOAS Conference on African chronology and its *JAH* number I shall refer to this kind of synchronism as a tie-in, thus distinguishing it further from types III and IV.

[4] Richard Gray, 'Eclipse maps', *JAH* 6 (1965), 251–62; idem, 'Annular eclipse maps', *JAH* 9 (1968), 147–57.

appears to be the most probable at the moment of writing [i.e. the so-called "middle chronology"] can be given'. Consequently he warns that 'a picture [may be] drawn in bolder and surer outline than the evidence justifies'.[5] This classic example of the study of tie-ins and synchronisms still remains at this uncertain stage because, in fact, synchronisms often are neither trouble-free nor value-free. As a result, attempts to utilize tie-ins and synchronisms have resulted in some of the most ingenious, impassioned, and provocative argumentation in the literature.[6]

A basic problem in working with synchronisms is deciding how much weight should be assigned to a single synchronism or tie-in. More than any other datum, an isolated synchronism or tie-in should be subjected to every canon of historical criticism before it is accepted as a base line for postulating related chronologies. Much, of course, depends on the nature and quality of the source(s) which contains the tie-in. For example, the Sargon Chronicle, composed in the neo-Babylonian period, has a colophon, no more than an *obiter dictum*, which states that 'Ilushuma was king of Assyria in the time of Sumuabum [first ruler of the First Dynasty] of Babylon'.[7] No

[5] W. C. Hayes, M. B. Rowton, and F. H. Stubbins, 'Chronology: Egypt, Western Asia, the Aegean Bronze Age', Chapter VI [in fascicle form] of the revised edition of Vols. I and II of *Cambridge Ancient History* (hereafter *CAH*²), 23–4.

[6] Among the numerous examples, see especially F. E. Pargiter, 'Ancient Indian genealogies and chronology', *JRAS* (1910), 25–53; S. N. Pradhan, *The chronology of ancient India* (Calcutta, 1929), *passim*; J. Vansina, 'The foundation of the kingdom of Kasanje', *JAH* 4 (1963), 355, 371–2; D. B. Birmingham, 'The date and significance of the Imbangala invasion of Angola', *JAH* 6 (1965), 143–52; A. Goetze, 'On the chronology of the second millennium B.C.', *JCS* 11 (1957), 53–9; idem, 'The problem of chronology and early Hittite history', *Bulletin of the American Schools for Oriental Research*, 122 (1957), 18–20. Pargiter and Pradhan are examples of the use of type I and II synchronisms or tie-ins, Goetze's articles are examples of type III, and, indeed, much of the debate over the 'high', 'middle', and 'low' chronologies for the ancient Near East has been based on the results of astronomical observations carried out in the reign of Ammisaduqa, ruler of Babylon in the seventeenth century B.C. For an introduction to the problem, see M. B. Rowton, 'The date of Hammurabi', *JNES* 17 (1958), 97–111. The Vansina–Birmingham debate revolves around the identity of a Portuguese official in Angola mentioned in Imbangala traditions. See on this now, J. C. Miller, 'The Imbangala and the chronology of early central Africa', *JAH* 13 (1972), 569. The problem of synchronisms in Polynesian traditions is bound up with the father/son succession problem and will be dealt with in Chapter II.

[7] J. B. Pritchard, *Ancient Near Eastern texts relating to the Old Testament* (Princeton, N.J., 1955), 267. L. W. King, *Chronicles concerning early Babylonian kings, I, Introductory chapters* (London, 1907), 115–33, 136. See Appendix A for a fuller discussion of the Assyrian King Lists.

other extant source confirms this contemporaneity. Nor have records become available that explicitly contradict it. But the weight of available indirect chronological evidence indicates that such synchronism is highly unlikely. The acceptance of this tie-in would impeach the middle chronology date for Hammurabi (1792–1750 B.C.) if the rulers of his dynasty are interpreted as reigning without intermission. It is probable that Sumuabum's successor was not his son, but no further inferences can be drawn regarding their relationship.[8] To accept the Ilušuma–Sumuabum synchronism necessarily entails either the acceptance of an earlier date for Hammurabi or the postulating of an interregnal period after Sumuabum of at least fifty years.[9] A date of 1848 B.C. is astronomically available for Hammurabi's accession, so this putative contemporaneity of Ilušuma and Samuabum forms one of the buttresses for the 'high chronology' argument. But little other evidence favours accepting this date. The preponderance of available evidence, then, strongly suggests that this isolated synchronism of apparently late provenience is not a dependable one. If, however, the wealth of supplementary data indicating this unreliability were not available, it is likely that the Ilušuma–Sumuabum tie-in would serve as one of the keystones for erecting a chronological framework for the ancient Near East. This example illustrates briefly the difficulties that can arise when a procrustean bed of chronological conformity is constructed on the basis of a single unverified tie-in or synchronism.

A recurring problem in working with one-way tie-ins is the repetition of the same or similar names in kinglists and genealogies. The constant use of a few royal names among the Hittites, Kassites, and rulers of Iamkhad (Aleppo) in the second millennium B.C. has proved to be one of the most thorny problems in trying to establish and

[8] For the relationship of Sumuabum and his successor Sumulael, see below, p. 73. The necessity to avoid extended discussion of many of the cases cited in this study may often render the context less lucid than desirable. For a broader perspective on the chronology of the ancient Near East for the time of Hammurabi the reader is referred to Rowton, 'Date', and Hayes *et al.*, 'Chronology'.

[9] In fact some evidence indicates that a brief interregnum may have occurred during this period, but it almost certainly could have been no longer than fifteen years. For the arguments, see H. Lewy, 'Assyria, *c.* 2600 to 1816 B.C.', fascicle in *CAH*², 31, and F. Cornelius, 'Chronology. Eine Erwiderung', *JCS* 12 (1958), 102, who favour a longer interregnum, and D. Oates, *Studies in the ancient history of northern Iraq* (London, 1968), 28n., and S. D. Simmons, 'Early Old Babylonian tablets from Harmal and elsewhere', *JCS* 14 (1960), 87, who favour a shorter one. The indirect synchronisms adduced by Simmons strongly support his argument. See also T. Jacobsen, *The Sumerian king list* (Chicago, 1938), 193.

maintain viable synchronisms for the ancient Near East during this period.[10] Similarly, those who have undertaken the sisyphean task of attempting to reconstruct the Puranic chronologies into a coherent chronological framework have been faced with a multiplicity of similar royal names.[11] In this latter case, the problem may have been a blessing in disguise for those attempting this task, since it permitted the kind of interpretational flexibility which was clearly required to co-ordinate these particularly refractory legendary materials.

This problem will be a familiar one to Africanists. The similarity of the names of the rulers of the Senegambian states is one example.[12] A more obvious instance is the recurrence of certain names like Ntare and Ruhinda among the rulers of the interlacustrine states. The identity of the ruler of Nkore who earned the sobriquet of *kiitabanyoro*, for instance, has aroused considerable attention—attention stimulated by the fact that Nkore traditions offer no fewer than four Ntares from which to choose.[13] Which Ntare is chosen has further implications for interlacustrine chronology as secondary and tertiary tie-ins are affected. The similarity of the names of the Asantehenes Osei Tutu (*c.* 1690–1712/17) and Osei Tutu Kwamina (*c.* 1801–24) has resulted in much confusion in Asante stool traditions.[14]

The third major problem to be considered regarding synchronisms in kinglists and royal genealogies is that of the 'staggering' of generations over time. Here the historian's task is a delicate one. In the last analysis, *in situ* circumstances will determine his parameters of choice,

[10] For the Hittites, see A. Goetze, 'The predecessors of Šuppiliiumaš of Hatti', *JAOS*, 72 (1952), 67, H. G. Güterbock, 'The predecessors of Šuppiliiumaš again', *JNES* 29 (1970), 73–7, and O. R. Gurney, 'Anatolia, *c.* 1600 to 1380 B.C.', fascicle in *CAH*², 15–19. For the Kassites, see J. A. Brinkman, review of C. L. Woolley, *Ur: the Kassite period and the period of the Assyrian kings*, in *Orientalia*, N.S. 38 (1969), 320–7, and A. Goetze, 'The Kassites and Near Eastern chronology', *JCS* 18 (1964), 97–101. For Yamkhad, see J.-R. Kupper, 'Northern Mesopotamia and Syria', fascicle in *CAH*², 33–4, and S. Smith, 'Yarim-Lim of Yamhad', *Rivista degli studi orientali*, 32 (1957), 179–80.

[11] F. E. Pargiter, 'Ancient Indian genealogies', 15–16.

[12] For this, see S. M. Cissoko, 'Civilisation Wolof-Sérère', *Présence Africaine*, 62 (1967), 125–9, 146–7, and A. Teixeira da Mota, 'D. João Bemoim e a expedição Portuguesa ao Senegal em 1489', *Boletim Cultural de Guiné Portuguesa*, 101 (1971), 100–3.

[13] R. Oliver, 'Ancient capital sites of Ankole', *UJ* 23 (1959), 57, 59; S. R. Karugire, *A history of the kingdom of Nkore in western Uganda to 1896* (Oxford, 1971), 57, 59, 60. J. A. Meldon, 'Notes on the Bahima of Ankole', *Journal of the African Society*, 6 (1906/7), 242, shows Ntare Kiitabanyoro as the second of four Ntares; A. G. Katate, 'Abababe b'Ankole', typescript in Center for Research Libraries, Chicago, 56–8, 60.

[14] See Chapter VI.

but a survey of possibilities may none the less be appropriate. The basic question is: How much staggering can be accepted before a putative synchronism must be considered untenable? The response to this will vary as the circumstances of the kinglist or genealogy vary. If the tie-in is between two societies with similar succession practices or, even more to the point, if the genealogies purport to derive from a common ancestor, then acceptable tolerances must be close.[15] Much of the Maori genealogical past traditionally derives from ancestors who were said to have arrived in New Zealand at the same time—the time of the 'Great Fleet', which has been dated to *c.* 1350. But the genealogies from these ancestors vary markedly in their generational length.[16] The maximal discrepancies are unacceptable, given the level of probabilities the historian must work with.[17] Similarly, two Hawaiian genealogies springing from a common ancestor show sixty-one and forty-seven generations respectively.[18] Again, the balance of probabilities renders it unlikely that both are accurate.

Of course, a hypothetical genealogy from a common ancestor entirely through eldest sons will diverge quickly and widely from a similar genealogy entirely through youngest sons, particularly in social ambiences like Africa and Polynesia in which royal polygyny was common. On the other hand, the historian will usually find it impossible to ascertain such details for the materials he analyses, and so in the absence of data the assumption must be that the generational circumstances of compared genealogies are similar. The choice then becomes to reject either the synchronism or the genealogy. Only specialized knowledge can, in most cases, dictate which option to exercise. Thus, the astronomical synchronisms available for inter-

[15] The ruling lineages of many of the early Irish states claimed descent from sons of their fifth- or sixth-century founders. An extensive analysis of the copious genealogies available for the next five centuries might indicate probabilities more closely. The raw materials for such a study are in M. A. O'Brien (ed.), *Corpus Genealogiarum Hiberniae* (Dublin, 1962), but only a specialist could perform this useful but complex task. For staggering in early Irish genealogies, see J. V. Kelleher, 'The pre-Norman Irish genealogies', *Irish Historical Studies*, 16 (1968), 144–5.

[16] D. R. Simmons, 'A New Zealand myth: Kupe, Toi and the "Fleet" ', *New Zealand Journal of History*, 3 (1969), 28–9.

[17] R. W. Halbert and J. B. W. Roberton, 'Chronology of Maori tradition', *Historical Review* (Whakatane), 11/12 (Dec. 1963), 194.

[18] K. P. Emory, 'Development of a system of collecting, alphabetizing, and indexing Polynesian pedigrees. II. The Bishop Museum Polynesian Pedigree Collection', a paper given at the World Conference on Records and Genealogical Seminar, Salt Lake City, 5–8 Aug. 1969, p. 3.

lacustrine history no longer seem sound enough to preclude the hypothesis—a hypothesis supported by other considerations as well—that the genealogical filiations of several kinglists of the area are too ascendant.[19] But other circumstances may require the opposite choice.

When synchronisms occur between cultures with different succession systems the acceptable level of staggering will expectedly correlate with the degree of difference in these systems. Ultimogeniture seems to have been practised regularly in Burundi, in contrast to its neighbours.[20] Hence a given span of time will be covered by fewer generations in Burundi, perhaps by only half as many if we are able to project ultimogenitural practices back to the foundation of the dynasty. In most cases, however, allowable tolerances would more likely fall into the 10 per cent to 20 per cent range. It is important that all measurements be made on the shortest possible scale between known points of unconfirmed oral data. For example, interlacustrine chronologies stretch back about fifteen generations before 1900 but well-established tie-ins can be traced back to *c.* 1800. So, even if the 1520 (?) and 1680 eclipse synchronisms are not taken into account, all staggering must be measured against a scale of 10/11 generations rather than 15.

Lest the historian feel that an equivalency of generations in compared genealogies is evidence of the validity of both the tie-in and the genealogy, it should be noted that this equivalency may be an artificial one.[21] Genealogies have often been manipulated to create just this kind of 'grid effect'. The Spartan dyarchy was conceived of as originating with the twin sons of Aristodemos, who was represented as the great-great-grandson of Heracles. Greek annalists and historians of the sixth and fifth centuries B.C. felt obliged to support this myth of origin by providing an equal number of generations for each ruling line down to their own times.[22] Unfortunately the kinglists available to them showed the Eurypontid dynasty as shorter than the Agid dynasty. Even though Agis had been recognized as the elder

[19] For the discrepancies, see Cohen, 'A survey', chart opp. 190, 187–94.

[20] Vansina, 'La Chronologie du Burundi ancien', 440–2.

[21] See, for instance, H. F. Morris, *A history of Ankole* (Kampala, 1962), 23–4, for an assumption of telescoping because the genealogies of Buhweju were slightly shorter than those of Bunyoro.

[22] M. Miller, *The Sicilian colony dates: Studies in Chronolography*, I (Albany, N.Y., 1970), 174–5; F. Mitchell, 'Herodotus' use of genealogical chronology', *Phoenix*, 10 (1956), 51–2. These and other aspects of the Spartan kinglists are discussed in Appendix C.

'twin', this discrepancy was not wholly acceptable to the classical authors. As a result of efforts to bring the two lines into genealogical conformity several of the earlier names on the Eurypontid list are suspicious in form, one actually being a title rather than a proper name.[23] Still, in the late fifth century B.C. the Eurypontid line was shorter by one name and, sometime after Herodotus wrote, a certain Soös was introduced into the Eurypontid genealogy.[24] Certainly Soös, and probably other names, were early interpolations—'anecdotal kings'—attempting to bring the length of the Eurypontid genealogy into exact generational conformity with the Agid pedigree.[25] This final interpolation created the desired symmetry between the two dynastic lists, which now stretched in unbroken and serene descent through sixteen generations from the 'twin' founders to the two kings at the turn of the fifth century.[26] This grid system had been developed on the basis of a few tie-ins known from literary sources. Once the construction was complete and the grid effect whole and entire, new synchronisms were inferred from the generational contemporaneity established by the grid system itself.[27] The exercise had come full circle.

The genealogies of pre-Islamic Arabia illustrate a closely analogous process. The Arab approach to the early history of the peninsula has been aptly described as 'bound by a hypertrophied clan consciousness, an emotional overbearance of genealogy and blood kinship, and a complete lack of rational curiosity'.[28] Groupings occurred on the basis of kinship and common ancestry. The further back the common ancestor could be traced, the larger the group.

[23] K. M. T. Chrimes, *Ancient Sparta* (Manchester, 1949), 337; G. L. Huxley, *Early Sparta* (London, 1962), 20.

[24] D. W. Prakken, 'A note on the Megarian historian Dieuchidas', *American Journal of Philology*, 62 (1941), 348–51; A. R. Burn, 'Early Greek chronology', *Journal of Hellenic Studies*, 69 (1950), 71; W. Den Boer, *Laconian studies* (Amsterdam, 1954), 15, 22, 88; Chrimes, *Ancient Sparta*, 337–8, 344; Huxley, *Early Sparta*, 20; Prakken, *Studies in Greek genealogical chronology* (Lancaster, Pa., 1945), 91–3; E. N. Tigerstedt, *The legend of Sparta in Classical Antiquity* (Stockholm, 1965), 23.

[25] Miller, *Sicilian colony dates*, 175.

[26] For the results in tabular form, see, e.g., Prakken, 'Herodotus and the Spartan kinglists', *Transactions of the American Philological Association*, 71 (1940), 471; Den Boer, *Laconian studies*, 65–6; Chrimes, *Ancient Sparta*, 334.

[27] Den Boer, 'Political propaganda in Greek chronology', *Historia*, 5 (1956), 171, 175.

[28] J. Obermann, 'Early Islam' in Robert C. Dentan (ed.), *The idea of history in the ancient Near East* (New Haven, Conn., 1955), 242.

Thus all social and political relationships had genealogical premisses.[29] In pre-Islamic times, when writing was virtually unknown, these traditions were very fragmentarily preserved through poetry. It was only during the political strife of the early Caliphate that an extensive genealogical framework for early Arabia was devised and written down.[30] Then genealogists, with the example of the Koran to inspire them, began to trace tribal genealogies back to Nūh (Noah). The newly created genealogies primarily were used as partisan political tools which were resorted to when tribal strife threatened. For instance, when, in the years following the death of Muhammad, the northern and southern tribes of the peninsula warred against each other, the northern tribes (or Maʿadds) 'found that the new genealogies rendered their racial superiority over the tribes of Yemen part of God's plan of salvation; only *they* were linked by an exclusive nexus of blood kinship with Ishmael and Abraham, the founder of monotheism, and true precursor of Mohammed'.[31] The Yemenis were not slow to respond with their own genealogical arsenal.[32] The final products of this genealogical jousting were genealogies which traced each of the two tribal confederations back to common ancestors—ʿAdnān for the northern tribes and Qaḥṭān for the southern tribes. These ancestors were in turn grafted on to Koranic genealogies at a point suitably ancient.

The process by which this was done is revealing. The materials with which the seventh- and eighth-century genealogists had to work were both fragmentary and contradictory. Consequently, the alleged ancestry of the Quraysh, Muhammad's family, was used as the yardstick for all the other tribal genealogies. Naturally, the Prophet's genealogy was the most complete and impressive available and the others, when measured against it, were found wanting. To facilitate suspected or desired synchronisms it then became necessary to create a legion of 'dummy ancestors'.[33] This was accomplished by doubling

[29] These same principles still apply among the pastoral northern Somali and can be studied in the writings of I. M. Lewis, e.g. 'Historical aspects of genealogies in northern Somali social structure', *JAH* 3 (1962), 37–43, and his 'Literacy in a nomadic society: the Somali case' in Jack Goody (ed.), *Literacy in traditional societies* (Cambridge, 1968), 272–3.

[30] W. R. Smith, *Kinship and marriage in early Arabia* (2nd ed., London, 1903), 6–11; Obermann, 'Early Islam', 287–9, 301–5.

[31] Obermann, 'Early Islam', 304. Emphasis in original.

[32] A. Fischer, 'Kahtān', *Encyclopaedia of Islam*, III. 630; G. Levi della Vida, 'Nizar', ibid. III. 939–41.

[33] Smith, *Kinship and marriage*, 11.

known names and by using eponyms and other available proper names of no apparent genealogical significance.[34] The result, after three centuries of manipulation, was an impressively detailed and internally coherent body of genealogical data.[35]

The extensive manipulation of genealogies for the purpose of synchronistic symmetry was a task which could not have been carried out in an oral society. Indeed, its need would not have been perceived. The preceding discussion nevertheless becomes relevant when we recall that much of the genealogical oral traditions available for Africa are the products of an era of at least restricted literacy. Roland Oliver's description of the evolution of Nyoro and Nkore oral traditions shows how these came to full flowering only in the twentieth century and partially as a response to the publication of Ganda oral traditions by Roscoe and Kaggwa.[36] Other instances are not lacking but discussion of them will be deferred to Chapter III, which deals with the relationship of the nature and content of oral traditions to the circumstances of their creation and transmission. The interlacustrine example is cited here because it illustrates the folly of dismissing the possibility of synchronistic distortions from African oral traditions and because the genealogical fabric of the entire interlacustrine area bears interesting resemblances, at least in form, to that of pre-Islamic Arabia.

These are some of the points to bear in mind when analysing both isolated and genealogical-based tie-ins, as well as with those kinds of synchronisms which are inter-cultural or partly extra-traditional. Only synchronisms which survive this kind of rigid analysis should be considered as acceptable data by the historian of pre-colonial Africa.

[34] For a discussion of the major inconsistencies and interpolations, see Smith, *Kinship and marriage*, 11–19.

[35] These genealogical data are fully set forth in F. Wüstenfeld, *Genealogische Tabellen der arabischen Stämme und Familien* (Göttingen, 1852), *passim.* For a discussion of the retrospective manipulation of the earliest parts of the Anglo-Saxon royal genealogies in order to achieve 'a recognized standard length' for all of them, see K. Sisam, 'Anglo-Saxon royal genealogies', *Proceedings of the British Academy*, 39 (1953), 326–8.

[36] R. Oliver, 'The traditional histories of Buganda, Bunyoro and Nkole', *JRAI* 85 (1955), 111–17. See also J. Beattie, *The Nyoro state* (London, 1971), 57–61, and Henige, 'K.W.'s Nyoro Kinglist'.

II TELESCOPING

It has long been recognized that, in most societies where kinship is the primary means of social and political control, genealogies are likely to be foreshortened. In these segmentary genealogies only the first few founding generations and the most recent four to six legitimizing generations are remembered. Since the purpose of these genealogies is both to reflect and to justify current social patterns based on kinship considerations, it serves no purpose to preserve the memory of useless ancestors. Such genealogies tend to remain approximately the same length over time, but their components change constantly; relevance and utility are the guiding principles. The classic African example of the process of this 'structural amnesia' is that of the Tiv as described by the Bohannans.[37] After the Tiv genealogies were recorded in the early colonial period, the British naturally expected the details to remain constant, with additions as time passed. The Tiv, however, claimed, as time passed, that the earlier genealogies were incorrect; indeed, from their own perspective they were.[38] Other examples of this kind are quite common, but since it is obvious that, where structural amnesia has been the guiding principle of a society's recollection of the past, these genealogies have no value for determining the *duration* of the past, further attention to them is unnecessary.[39]

Institutionalized telescoping in dynastic societies does occur, and will be discussed very briefly at the end of this section. Generally, however, telescoping in dynastic societies assumes more varied and subtle shades. The processes are more subtle because they are not formally designed as mechanical ways of forgetting the past. Though their application is conscious it is usually haphazard as well. Like the Tiv, Nuer, and other kinship-oriented cultures, the traditions of

[37] J. A. Barnes, 'The collection of genealogies', *Rhodes–Livingstone Journal*, 5 (1947), 48. P. Bohannan, 'Concepts of time among the Tiv of Nigeria', *Southwestern Journal of Anthropology*, 9 (1953), 251–62; L. Bohannan, 'A genealogical charter', *Africa*, 22 (1952), 301–15. See also M. Crowder, 'Genealogy and the Tiv', *Nigeria Magazine*, 63 (1959), 282–301.

[38] L. Bohannan, 'A genealogical charter', 314.

[39] E. E. Evans-Pritchard, *The Nuer* (Oxford, 1940), 94–138; Jones, 'Time and oral tradition', 153–60; E. Leach, *Political systems of highland Burma* (London, 1954), 127; H. and C. Geertz, 'Teknonymy in Bali: parenthood, age-grading and genealogical amnesia', *JRAI* 94 (1964), 94–108; I. Mayer, 'From kinship to common descent: four-generation genealogies among the Gusii', *Africa*, 35 (1965), 366–84.

monarchical societies are designed for legitimation. This implies that kinglists and royal genealogies must assume specified patterns designed to appear uncontaminated and symbolically potent. This often necessitates the expunging of 'usurpers', interregna, and periods of foreign rule from the traditions, for each of these can be interpreted as disturbing what is viewed as a halcyon past.

The propensity to telescope kinglists (but not necessarily generations) in this manner is widespread. What interests us here are the forms that these concepts may take and the impact they may have on the telescoping process. The concept of usurper is a particularly fluid one. Not only does it vary from one type of society or succession system to another but it will also vary through time within the same polity. Broadly defined, a usurper is a ruler whose claim to office was, or was retrospectively held to be, inferior and illegitimate. Most often this illegitimacy is a lineal or juridical one. Sometimes this illegitimacy is only perceived later as, for instance, succession practices change or old lineages lose eligibility and new ones rise in their place.

Modifications of varying importance often occur in succession systems which endure for several centuries. Such changes can have direct chronological implications. This aspect will be discussed at greater length later. Such changes also result in rulers who succeeded under previous practices being regarded as usurpers. The case of Macbeth illustrates this point. Succession to the Scottish throne in the eleventh century followed the usual Celtic conventions. That is, succession was not lineal but rotated in no very systematic way among eligible royal males, with a bias towards ability and seniority. Succession usually fell to a brother or cousin of the late ruler. There was no instance of direct lineal succession to the Scottish throne for the fifteen reigns between the unification of the Scots and Picts in 844 and the death of Malcolm II in 1034.[40] This was wholly in character with the Celtic law of tanistry as particularly manifested in the Irish states of the same period. But by Macbeth's time these succession practices were coming under siege as the principles of lineal descent and primogeniture, with their concomitant strengthening of the royal power, were gaining adherents, particularly among those who had been exposed to English or Continental political culture. Malcolm II was succeeded by his grandson Duncan. This was in direct

[40] J. H. Stevenson, 'The law of the throne—Tanistry and the introduction of the law of primogeniture', *Scottish Historical Review*, 25 (1927/8), 3.

contravention to both the principles of collateral succession and seniority, for Duncan was described as still 'at an immature age' at the time of his death six years later.[41] Macbeth, who slew and succeeded Duncan, had a dual claim to the Scottish throne under the existing succession rules. He was probably the nephew of Malcolm; furthermore his wife was the granddaughter of an earlier ruler.[42] Macbeth ruled for seventeen years but was eventually slain by Malcolm III, the son of Duncan. In this effort Malcolm was supported by the English, who tended to regard many things Celtic, including their succession practices, as somewhat uncivilized. None of the contemporary annalistic accounts of Macbeth's accession, reign, and death spoke of him as a usurper.[43] His claims to the Scottish throne were regarded as superior to those of his predecessor and his regicidal act was in the best traditions of the Celtic political system.

The principle of lineal descent did not triumph completely with Malcolm III's accession, since he was succeeded by his brother and then by his four sons.[44] The first of these was killed in battle against his uncle, and the next two died *sine prole*, but the last, David I, left the throne to his grandson. With the latter's reign the Celtic principle of collateral succession vanished from Scotland and lineal succession replaced it, although it was not the 'eldest' line that secured the throne.[45] Each of the four brothers, though eligible under Celtic succession conventions, chose to emphasize his claims to the throne as a son of Malcolm III. It therefore became necessary to justify Malcolm's own accession as a son of Duncan. Ineluctably, this characterized Macbeth as a usurper who had broken the 'direct line' of succession. Later Scottish chroniclers and historians saw Macbeth as a usurper.[46] Malcolm III in his turn became more than a successful

[41] The Annals of Tigernach, quoted in N. K. Chadwick, 'The story of Macbeth', *Scotch Gaelic Studies*, 6 (1947), 195. None of the other chronicles mentions his youth. In any case he was a generation younger than Macbeth genealogically. See also J. Fergusson, *The man behind Macbeth* (London, 1967), 82–3.

[42] A. O. Anderson in a note to Stevenson 'Law of the throne', 377; G. Donaldson, *Scottish kings* (London, 1967), 12–13; A. O. Anderson, *Early sources for Scottish history, A.D. 500 to 1286* (2 vols., London, 1922), I, 579–80.

[43] 'The Annals of Tigernach', ed. W. Stokes, *Revue Celtique*, 17 (1896), 379, 398; Anderson, *Early sources*, 602, 604.

[44] Stevenson, 'Law of the throne', 6–12.

[45] Stevenson, 'The prince of Scotland', *Scottish Historical Review*, 22 (1924/5), 83–4.

[46] Anderson, *Early sources*, I. 600; Chadwick, 'Story of Macbeth', *SGS* 6 (1947), 189–211; 7 (1951), 1–25.

regicide; he became a symbol of legitimacy and was seen as 'recovering his paternal throne'.[47]

The case of Macbeth is exceptionally well documented, both in the facts of his time and reign, and for the transformation of his image from a ruler whose eligibility was unquestioned to that of usurper *par excellence*. In most oral societies a Macbeth would have been forgotten. Or, if remembered, he might have been attributed a reign of the briefest duration—just an unfortunate interlude. In fact, Macbeth's reign of seventeen years was longer than eleven of his fifteen predecessors. It would be fallacious to equate usurpers necessarily with short periods of rule.

Most cases of elided rulers involve collaterals and will be discussed in the next chapter. However, there are other categories of 'usurpers' as well. The most important includes those individuals who rule during periods of foreign hegemony. These may either be royals who secure office through the suzerain's favour, or governors from outside the society appointed to rule it. For obvious reasons periods of foreign dominance are prime candidates for the 'amnemonic' process. A polity's self-image usually requires a past free of such embarrassments. Those that are remembered, such as the Bunyoro occupation of Nkore, may themselves be telescoped into a period briefer than they in fact were.[48] That is, an extended period of foreign control may be interpreted in tradition as nothing more than a raid. The appearance of the Moses-in-the-bulrushes theme, discussed later, also may in some cases indicate such periods.

The propensity to disregard or disguise these periods is nowhere more clearly illustrated than by the Assyrian King Lists. The official lists of Assyrian rulers were composed in the eleventh to seventh centuries B.C., but dealt with events which had occurred over a millennium before.[49] When they were committed to their final and 'official' form Assyria was the dominant power in the ancient Near East. But this had not always been so. Before the fourteenth century B.C., except for a brief period at the end of the nineteenth century, Assyria had been either a minor and localized, but independent,

[47] G. Buchanan, *The history of Scotland* (4 vols., Glasgow, 1827), I. 336. Buchanan wrote in the sixteenth century.

[48] Katate, *Abagabe b'Ankole*, 63–9; Morris, *History of Ankole*, 10–11.

[49] I. J. Gelb, 'Two Assyrian King Lists', *JNES* 13 (1954), 209–10; A. Poebel, 'The Assyrian King List from Khorsabad', *JNES* 1 (1942), 250–1. See Appendix A for a fuller analysis of the Assyrian King Lists.

state, or under the control of stronger neighbours.[50] Before the twentieth century Assyria was under Akkad and Ur III and during the eighteenth and seventeenth centuries it fell under the domination of the Hurrian state of Mitanni to the north. Later it was briefly under the control of the Kassites of Babylonia. Inscriptions of a few rulers of Assyria of this earliest (Akkad–Ur) period have been discovered. None of the individuals known from these inscriptions to have ruled Assyria appears in the Assyrian King Lists. One of them, Zāriqum, is known to have governed Assyria for Ur III from before 2048 B.C. to after 2042 B.C., a period the King Lists claim to include.[51] Two governors under Akkad likewise found no place in the official King Lists.[52]

These are instances of foreign appointees ruling Assyria but some rulers of the indigenous dynasty who served at the pleasure of their Hurrian and Kassite overlords were also omitted. From extraneous sources we know that the son and grandson of Išme-Dagan I (*c.* 1783–*c.* 1743) ruled Assyria after him, apparently under the suzerainty of Mitanni.[53] There is a further record of one Puzur-Sin expelling a 'man of foreign seed, of non-Assyrian flesh' and ruling in his stead, but neither he nor the unnamed ruler he replaced (who may have been one of Išme-Dagan's descendants mentioned above) is known from the King Lists.[54] Two later rulers in the fifteenth century, when Assyria was under the Kassites, have also been omitted, presumably because they, too, were nominees of a foreign overlord.[55] Thus the fragmentary epigraphic evidence currently available has uncovered no fewer than eight rulers of Assyria which were omitted from the official King Lists.

The Assyrian King Lists show eight 'sons of nobodies', that is, rulers without the usual filiations. These eight can certainly be regarded as usurpers in the classical sense, even though one of them

[50] All dates in this study referring to the second millennium B.C. ancient Near East are those of the so-called 'middle' chronology (Hammurabi, 1792–1750), which is the most probable of the three chronologies offered by specialists in that field.

[51] W. W. Hallo, 'Zāriqum', *JNES* 15 (1956), 220–5.

[52] Lewy, 'Assyria, *c.* 2600–1816 B.C.', 20.

[53] B. Landsberger, 'Assyrische Königsliste und "Dunkles Zeitalter"', *JCS* 8 (1954), 32.

[54] Ibid. H. Lewy, 'On some problems of Kassite and Assyrian chronology', *Mélanges Isidore Lévy* [*Annuaire* de l'Institut de Philologie et d'Histoire Orientales et Slaves, 13(1953)], 264; idem, 'Assyria, *c.* 2600–1816 B.C.', 23–4.

[55] Lewy, 'Some problems', 279–82.

allegedly founded the dynasty which was to rule Assyria for a millennium and under which the Assyrian King Lists were composed. Interestingly, six of these eight 'sons of nobodies' were credited with reigns of zero-value years and the other two with reigns of only six years each.[56] Seven of these usurpers are alleged to have ruled in succession. All eight usurpers fall within a thirteen-king span in the King List and ruled during the same confused period in Assyrian history in which the descendants of Išme-Dagan ruled. Their inclusion at this point may reflect the confusion of the compilers as they sought to span the lacunae caused by the exclusion of these undoubted rulers. But still they found it difficult to credit these usurpers with regnal lengths sufficient to cover the period in question, even though one of them was the acknowledged founder of the ruling dynasty.[57]

The patterns of the Assyrian King Lists clearly indicate how official kinglists can, indeed must, given their purpose, eliminate rulers. For our purposes it is immaterial whether the eliminated rulers are members of the dynasty or not. Their reigns occupy historical time and their omission prevents the historian from accurately assessing the dimensions of this historical time.

Similar examples in Africa are not difficult to find. An early nineteenth-century observer claimed that the Asante 'did not speak of the death of a former king, or of the person likely to succeed to the throne, on pain of death; consequently it is not very easy to trace their history'.[58] A study of the eighteenth-century succession in Asante confirms this observation.[59] According to Asante stool histories only a handful of the thousands of stoolholders mentioned failed to die a natural death on the stool. In this way they either omit nearly all the stoolholders who were killed in battle or destooled or disguise the untimely ends of some of the rulers they mention. Consequently they are of little value as chronological tools.[60]

[56] Poebel, 'Khorsabad', 86–8, 460–5.

[57] To account for his zero-value reign Poebel, 'Khorsabad', 466–7, has speculated that Adasi (the usurper/dynasty-founder referred to) was either a very old man on his accession and died almost immediately, or that he served as a transitory figurehead and was deposed and succeeded by his son, once the 'revolution' was secure. Now see also W. W. Hallo and W. K. Simpson, *The ancient Near East: a history* (New York, 1971), 115.

[58] W. Hutton, *A voyage to Africa* . . . (London, 1821), 313.

[59] M. Priestley and I. Wilks, 'The Ashanti kings in the eighteenth century: a revised chronology', *JAH* 1 (1960), 89–90.

[60] For a fuller analysis of the effects of destoolments for Asante chronology, see Chapter VI.

According to a Nyoro historian no *mukama* (ruler) of Bunyoro who ruled for less than nine years (with a few stated exceptions) was worthy of remembrance.[61] Even though this claim is not likely to be literally true it can easily be seen that, given the likely mean regnal length for Africa, such a policy would result in the omission of any number of *bakama*. In cases like the interlacustrine area, where the traditional chronology is tightly welded to a genealogical framework with supplementary astronomical data, these kinds of omissions *may* not result in a truncated time-depth.

Among the Imbangala of Angola the king had to pass through a circumcision camp as the final step in a long series of rituals. Since this procedure was regarded by the Imbangala as the prelude for choosing a new ruler each king would try to postpone this rite and doubtless many of the stronger ones were able to do so. However, the Imbangala reckoned as kings only those who had performed this ceremony—it was the essence of kingship as it were. Only a very few of the Imbangala *kinguri* who did not perform this final ceremony are included in oral kinglists, mostly those who ruled in the last half of the nineteenth century. Furthermore, the Imbangala remembered regnal lengths only from the time that the circumcision ceremony was performed. The result of this peculiarity is that a total of fifty 'years' (equivalent to approximately twenty-five years) have been assigned to the twenty-eight *kinguri* who, as we know from Portuguese records, ruled from *c.* 1620 to 1911.[62] Here again, the circumscribed concept of kingship among the Imbangala prevents them from viewing the past as a lineal, mensurable concept.

In rotational succession systems rulers representing extinct lineages will often be forgotten when their legitimizing functions are no longer required.[63] Given the large number of this type of succession system

[61] J. A. Nyakatura, 'Abakama ba Bunyoro-Kitara', tr. by J. A. Rowe, typescript at Center for Research Libraries, Chicago, 55. For the *ekyebumbes*, or retroactive 'usurpers' in Nkore, see S. R. Karugire, 'Succession wars in the precolonial kingdom of Nkore', *Proceedings of the University of East Africa Social Science Council*, 1 (1969), 55–6. For more on the Bunyoro kinglists, see Chapter III and Henige, 'K.W.'s Nyoro Kinglist'.

[62] J. C. Miller, 'Kasanje kinglists—theories and facts: or, miscalculating African history?', paper presented at the Annual Meeting of the African Studies Association, Philadelphia, Pa., 8–11 Nov. 1972.

[63] One example of this type of structural amnesia, in Gonja, is discussed in J. Goody and I. Watt, 'The consequences of literacy' in J. Goody (ed.), *Literacy in traditional societies* (Cambridge, 1968), 33. The Gonja case can be documented because two lineages died out after the first traditions had been collected.

in Africa, this can be an important variation of this form of telescoping, but it is an extremely difficult one to document, either for African or non-African areas, simply because traditions without functions and without caretakers often will not survive. Cases of elision because of collateral suppression will be described in the next chapter.

The impact of interregna on the chronological past is impossible to measure. The documented occurrence of lengthy interregna, narrowly defined, is rather rare, although not unknown. Obviously, however, the occurrence of interregna can be at least loosely correlated with types of succession systems. Interregna are unlikely to occur often in societies with well-defined and longstanding succession practices, especially if these practices include the predesignation of heirs. Conversely, where the eligibility is broad or where a loose rotational system prevails—both commonplace in Africa—the probability of prolonged succession disputes increases.[64] Many African societies have obligatory interregnal periods during the obsequies of the deceased ruler. In short, despite the difficulties of assessing quantitatively the occurrence and significance of interregnal periods, they remain a factor affecting the duration of the remembered past.

A third way to telescope the past is to regard a single archetypal figure as the personification of an entire epoch of uncertain duration. Usually the epoch so represented is the period of the gradual coalescence of the state structure to a recognizable form. It is remarkable how many states, according to traditional accounts, were the creation of a single individual.[65] He is often represented as either a scion of a prestigious nearby dynasty, or as a hunter or warrior of such outstanding ability that he secures the allegiance of the people by his prowess and charismatic personality. A few states in history have arisen in this fashion, but not many; even Alexander the Great developed his empire from the strong Macedonian base established by his father.

[64] Interregna were common in Aboh, where rotational succession prevailed, after 1844 and probably before as well. K. O. Ogedengbe, 'The Aboh kingdom of the lower Niger, *c.* 1650 to 1900', unpublished Ph.D. dissertation, University of Wisconsin, 1971, 213–14. In fact Ogedengbe thinks the periods of interregnum may actually have been greater than the years of kingly rule. For a survey of African rotational systems, see Jack Goody (ed.), *Succession to high office* (Cambridge, 1966), 172–4.

[65] It is important to understand that this discussion does not refer to appanage states which are 'instant creations', but to 'conquest states' or states that developed independently.

Aboh traditions relate that the founder of their state was a dissatisfied Benin prince who fled from Benin and migrated to Aboh where he established new hereditary kingship where none had existed previously. Thus Aboh traditions compress the founding of their state into the compass of a single generation. In fact it appears that the migrants from Benin to Aboh, who admittedly paused at several points along the route, may have taken as long as 200 years to complete their journey.[66]

In similar fashion the Dyolof empire is said to be the creation of a single individual, Ndyadyan Ndyay. Before this accomplishment, however, he also had had time to found the state of Waalo and rule there for sixteen years.[67]

Lunda and Luba traditions seem to offer an even more extreme example of the telescoping of several centuries of state formation and growth into the span of a few generations. The Luba empire is seen in tradition as developing from a congeries of small chiefdoms into a large political entity under the reign of Kalala Ilunga or in that of 'Nkongolo' who represented the earlier, Songye period. In the next generation one of Kalala Ilunga's sons, Cibinda Ilunga, migrated to the Lunda country and established the Lunda state.[68] Nkongolo, Kalala Ilunga, and Cibinda Ilunga must be interpreted as archetypal examples of epoch personification. The epoch they personify seems to have been of unusually long duration. As early as the eighth century, 'the nucleus of some sort of state' existed near Lake Kisale in the core of the Luba area.[69] It is not unreasonable to assume that much of the development and expansion which occurred during the several centuries between this time and the time of the 'founders' Nkongolo, Kalala Ilunga, and Cibinda Ilunga, has been attributed to them alone.

The concept of the 'epoch-ruler' is not confined to Africa, of

[66] Ogedengbe, 'Aboh', 197–200, 205–6.

[67] V. Coifman, 'History of the Wolof state of Jolof until 1860, including comparative data from the Wolof state of Walo', unpublished Ph.D. thesis, University of Wisconsin, 1970, pp. 190–2, 214; B. Barry, *Le Royaume du Waalo le Sénégal avant la conquête* (Paris, 1972), 327–9. A. Wade (tr. and ed. V. Monteil), 'Chronique du Wâlo sénégalais (1186?–1855)', *BIFAN* 26 (1964), 454–61.

[68] For the traditional accounts of these events, see J. Vansina, *Kingdoms of the Savanna* (Madison, Wis., 1966), 70–80.

[69] M. Posnansky, 'Bantu genesis: archaeological reflexions', *JAH* 9 (1968), 10; Vansina, *Kingdoms*, 35; J. Nenquin, 'Notes on some early pottery cultures in northern Katanga', *JAH* 4 (1963), 29–32. Several of the 'civilizing heroes' discussed in H. Tegnaeus, *Le Héros civilisateur* (Uppsala, 1950), were doubtless epoch-rulers.

course, but is a universal one. The earliest Emperors of China were assigned reigns of Biblical proportions by early Chinese annalists and each was credited with the introduction of certain basic cultural elements.[70] 'King Arthur', at least as he was portrayed in later accounts, served as the personification of several centuries of Briton resistance to Anglo-Saxon encroachments. The epoch-ruler is the natural consequence of the inability of myth and tradition, which are essentially personality-oriented, to accommodate to change as a process over time. Consequently, changes that are known to have occurred are attributed to preterhuman 'founders' or 'ancestors'. In this process the single Hero replaces a chain of lesser mortals and centuries become generations.

Although the classic forms of structural amnesia have been developed by and from segmentary societies, some dynastic societies have deemed it expedient to limit the class of royals, regardless of the type of succession practised. This could be accomplished most satisfactorily by stipulating that only those within a restricted degree of consanguinity could be considered members of the royal 'clan'. This was the principle adopted by the Irish in the early Middle Ages. The *derbfhine* was the 'legal family' both for inheritance of personal property and to describe eligibility to the throne. The *derbfhine* consisted of an individual and his descendants or ancestors to and including the third generation. That is, it was a four-generation cohort. As each new generation grew to maturity it replaced the apical generation, which no longer was of any practical concern.[71] The *derbfhine* system was particularly relevant in view of the broad eligibility to the throne in Celtic societies. But similar systems can serve as mechan-

[70] F. Hirth, *Ancient history of China* (New York, 1908), 13–14; J. Macgowan, *A history of China from the earliest times to the present* (London, 1897), 4–17.

[71] The best analysis of the *derbfhine* system is J. Hogan, 'The Irish law of kingship, with special reference to Ailech and Cenél Eoghain', *Proceedings of the Royal Irish Academy*, 40, Section C, 3 (1932), 137–95. Recently D. O'Corráin, 'Irish regnal succession: a reappraisal', *Studia Hibernica*, 11 (1971), 7–39, has argued that the *derbfhine* principle was not explicitly regarded as controlling succession to the throne and cites several examples of rulers from beyond the parameters of the *derbfhine* succeeding. O'Corráin argues that nearness to the sources of power, that is, the throne, was 'the determining factor' in governing succession and concludes that 'to have once held the kingship . . . is sufficient claim and any succeeding member of the dynasty, regardless of how long his family and his segment had been excluded from the kingship, could scarcely be regarded as a usurper or intruder'. None the less, as O'Corráin points out, more than 90 per cent of Irish rulers fell within the *derbfhine* when elected. Perhaps the important point for our purposes is that, like rotational succession, the *derbfhine* principle, if indeed it was a principle, was governed by *Realpolitik*.

isms to control the proliferation of royals even in societies in which the succession to the throne itself was circumscribed. They restrict the distribution of the spoils of power, whether they be offices, booty, or other perquisites.

A variation of the *derbfhine* principle in its effect on the recollection of the past is what has been termed 'positional succession'.[72] Here, too, telescoping becomes inevitable. Offices in societies practising positional succession have particular but permanent titles attached to them. This title is usually the name of the first founder of the office. Upon assumption of the office an individual assumes the prescribed title/name and his own personal name is forgotten. Furthermore he personally identifies himself with the founder—in fact he becomes one with the founder. The office is a living organism because the present occupant is always identified with the founder-endower in a personal fashion.[73] Under these circumstances it becomes both impossible and quite irrelevant to recall the number of past office holders.

The effect of positional succession on the chronology of a titled office can be seen in a study of the *kinguri* title among the Imbangala. Imbangala traditions state that their migration from Lunda country to the Angolan hinterland occurred under a leader named Kinguri, inevitably a member of the Lunda royal house. But in fact the memory of Kinguri does not represent the memory of a single individual, as most interpretations have contended, but rather of any number of successive individuals holding the *kinguri* title. It is similar to Roman annalists referring to 'Caesar' and meaning, not Julius Caesar himself but the Emperor of the moment.

In fact Imbangala traditions do represent the migration as a long one, with several stops along the way. With the realization that the Kinguri referred to in these traditions is a title, not a person, it becomes obvious that this migration took many generations to effect. At the same time it implies a much earlier date for the establishment of the Luba–Lunda complex—an earlier date supported by other forms of evidence as well.[74] Positional succession has been

[72] I. Cunnison, 'History and genealogies in a conquest state', *American Anthropologist*, 59 (1957), 22–3.

[73] This description is simplistic and makes no pretence to include all the complexities of positional succession and its corollary perpetual kinship. For these, see Cunnison, 'History and genealogies', 20–31, and idem, *History on the Luapula* [Rhodes–Livingstone Papers, 21], 33–5.

[74] Miller, 'The Imbangala', 572–4.

most closely studied in central Africa, but it has occurred elsewhere as well. Several of the Fante stools, notably Upper Dixcove, came to have a single royal name/title attached to them. The four successor states of Mataram in Java each had a throne name which their rulers assumed on accession.[75] Several other examples could also be cited.[76] Positional succession, by whatever name, seems to be more common than the few cases actually studied in depth would imply. For our purposes it is important to remember that wherever it occurred in oral societies its natural concomitant was telescoping.[77] It can also be seen that the forms telescoping might be expected to assume because of positional succession are very similar to the epoch-ruler variation discussed above. Indeed, the Kinguri of Imbangala traditions *was* an epoch-ruler, but he became so because of very particular structural contingencies in Imbangala society.

This discussion of the means by which a society can telescope its past emphasizes the variety of both motives and mechanisms which have been brought into play. Much of the impetus for telescoping derives from the legitimizing and regularizing functions telescoping often serves. In this respect, the process of telescoping, more than that of artificial lengthening, seems more a response to factors inherent in the nature of the office of ruler. Unlike artificial lengthening, very few examples of telescoping can be considered as responses to external considerations.

III ARTIFICIAL LENGTHENING

The incidence of the artificial lengthening of kinglists and genealogies and the concomitant development of an exaggerated notion of the length of the past are much more common than telescoping. This is scarcely surprising, given both the nature of the polities we are

[75] H. J. de Graaf, *Geschiedenis van Indonesie* (The Hague, 1949), 483.

[76] The most bizarre variation of throne name/titles occurred in the Reuss principalities of Germany. *Every* male member of the ruling family was named Heinrich. In one line the ordinal sequence ran from the beginning of a century until the end; in the other lines the procedure varied, sometimes, for example, running from Heinrich I to Heinrich XXX and then beginning again. See A. H. M. J. Stokvis, *Manuel de généalogie et de chronologie de tous les états du globe* (3 vols., Leiden, 1888–93), III. 319–23.

[77] The factor of rotational succession seems to mitigate this uncontrolled telescoping. Once the Imbangala state was established, the practice of rotational succession to the *Kinguri* title was instituted. Each of the eligible lineages, in guarding its own rights, found it necessary to know the rotational sequence. Hence fewer names were forgotten. Miller, 'Kings and kinsmen', 69n. Ogedengbe makes a similar point for Aboh, 'Aboh', 63.

concerned with and the circumstances under which many oral traditions have been transmitted. Even more than telescoping, the process of artificial lengthening assumes many guises. Some of these forms are obvious, often egregiously so. Paradoxically, however, some of the most important forms of artificial lengthening are seldom recognized. The most important of these is the pattern of extended father/son succession, as it is remembered in tradition. This problem will be given special consideration in the next chapter.

The present discussion will limit itself to the several other means societies have used to elongate their perceived past. Sometimes this lengthening is quite unconscious and accidental. More often it is the result of exposure to what seems to be the universal propensity to revere antiquity for its own sake. The unconscious proclivity to extend the remembered past is implicit in those traditions which are designed to show that their societies settled on previously unoccupied land. That is, traditions often claim to recount the entire period of settlement in their area and they equate this period with the existence of the polity itself. This tendency is very common in Africa as well as in other areas whose pasts are remembered principally through tradition. The region most analogous to Africa in this respect is Polynesia. Almost without exception the traditions of the various island groups relate that when their genealogically claimed ancestors arrived the islands were unoccupied. The available archaeological evidence tends to show that the first settlement in most of the island groups occurred many centuries before the traditional chronology based on genealogical reckoning allows.[78] Since further radiocarbon

[78] See R. C. Suggs, 'Historical traditions and archeology in Polynesia', *American Anthropologist*, 62 (1960), 764–73, esp. 767, 772. Suggs's interpretation of the validity of genealogical reckoning as measured by its conformity to archaeological evidence differs markedly from that of the latest work on Polynesia, I. Goldman, *Ancient Polynesian society* (Chicago, 1971). Goldman argues that Suggs 'found that genealogical traditions and archeological findings were often in substantial agreement', xii. He cites three of Suggs's works, but not the one mentioned above. Goldman's conclusion is that 'the degree of conformity' between C14 dates and dates arrived at from genealogical reckoning is 'surprising', xiii, 573. Goldman's approach is certainly open to question. He invariably uses the longest genealogy available for each island in finding this 'surprising conformity'. For instance, for the Marquesas he uses a genealogy of 90 generations, although he admits that the ethnographer who originally collected it distrusted it. On the other hand Suggs, who did his major work in the Marquesas, used genealogies of about 40 generations because he considered them more reliable and representative, Suggs, 767. Another example of Goldman's questionable use of genealogical dating, for Easter Island, will be discussed below, pp. 88–9.

dating will probably push back even further the notional dates of first settlement, this divergence can only become greater. The agreement between the archaeological and traditional evidence for New Zealand is somewhat closer than for most of the other islands.[79] How close this agreement becomes depends partly on the interpretation of the archaeological data and partly on which genealogies are used and what average generational length is adopted.[80] For most of the other islands, however, no amount of flexibility in handling the evidence will permit any reasonable correlations.

The habit of co-opting the entire inhabited past into a polity's dynastic traditions will be a familiar one to Africanists. The pattern is particularly common in southern Africa. Most Tswana, Nguni, and Sotho genealogical traditions extend back 300–400 years.[81] In most instances these traditions assert that the group in question settled in uninhabited territory. However, archaeological investigations at several sites in the Transvaal and elsewhere indicate a continuous chronological sequence of occupation since at least the eighth century.[82] It would be superfluous to catalogue other African examples of this nature. In almost every case where archaeological data are available it can be shown that permanent settlement long antedated traditional chronology. It is, of course, quite natural for a group or a dynasty, in seeking to justify claims to land, to do so on the basis of *res nullius*. This reflexive lengthening has few chronological implications *per se*. It is merely an assumption become a dogma. As such, it is not often thought of as having duration, but simply existence. But the assumption is a seminal one. From it flow both the

[79] For a discussion of the Maori evidence, see W. Shawcross, 'Archaeology with a short, isolated time scale: New Zealand', *World Archaeology*, 1 (1969), 186–98. This article seems to involve a great deal of circular reasoning. L. M. Groube, 'Research in New Zealand Prehistory since 1956', in I. Yawata and Y. H. Sinoto (eds.), *Prehistoric Culture in Oceania* (Honolulu, 1968), 197, argues for a settlement date several centuries before the traditional date for the arrival of Toi. For more on Maori genealogies, see below, 85–6, 100–2.

[80] For examples of this dependency of archaeology of historical evidence for close dating, see H. L. Thomas and R. W. Ehrich, 'Some problems in chronology', *World Archaeology*, 1 (1969), 146–51.

[81] A. T. Bryant, *Olden times in Zululand and Natal* (London, 1929), *passim*; M. Legassick, 'The Sotho-Tswana peoples before 1800' in L. Thompson (ed.), *African societies in southern Africa* (London, 1969), 87–9 [and sources cited there], 100–4.

[82] N. J. van der Merwe and R. T. K. Scully, 'The Phalaborwa story: archeological and ethnographical investigation of a South African Iron Age group', *World Archaeology*, 3 (1971), 184, 187–8; B. Fagan, *Southern Africa* (London. 1965), 153–60; Legassick, 'Sotho-Tswana', 119–20.

need to lengthen the past and the ideological framework which permits this need to be satisfied.

The following discussion proposes to describe and briefly analyse the means through which the duration of the past is exaggerated, both consciously and unconsciously. The widespread incidence of artificial lengthening can often be attributed to a belated effort to flesh out a telescoped past. Sometimes this past suddenly becomes relevant as a society is exposed to the exigency of creating a remote past which sanctions the present. In many oral societies the remote past is of little concern beyond its essentially synchronic purposes of justifying land rights and lineage segmentation, and it is therefore forgotten. The development of certain exigencies caused, for example, by the imposition of indirect rule, required a reorientation of their own views of the past. Whereas telescoping may have once best suited their social and political relationships, a new view of the past now seemed desirable. There are other reasons, of course, for lengthening the past. These include, *inter alia*, the desire to create a priority of settlement, or to ensure lineage eligibility for high office, or simply to enhance prestige. None the less, much artificial lengthening is not the result of these kinds of conscious and motivated effort at legitimation but rather the product of a period of indifference and neglect. In these cases there is little hope of assessing the duration of the past with any exactitude. But, whatever the reasons for artificial lengthening, it will perforce assume one or more of several possible forms. A survey of artificial lengthening as a process and as a response will therefore serve to indicate areas of further concern.

Since there are several means of lengthening the perceived past, it is useful to catalogue them briefly before beginning a detailed discussion of them seriatim. For convenience, it is most appropriate to categorize these forms as mechanical processes. These include the following:

(*a*) contemporary rulers being remembered as successive
(*b*) inclusion of eponyms, toponyms, and patronyms as rulers; collectively, these may be referred to as spurinyms
(*c*) euhemerism
(*d*) the crediting of early rulers with exaggerated regnal lengths
(*e*) genealogical parasitism, or the imputation of filiation with earlier, prestigious dynasties
(*f*) inferring present succession patterns into the past

(*g*) the outright fabrication of rulers
(*h*) extended father/son succession (see Chapter II)

The mechanisms listed above vary widely in terms of their detectability and the consciousness of their application, which are correlated concepts. Probably only (*g*) and, to a lesser extent, (*a*) and (*b*) are the results of deliberate efforts to lengthen the past. All the other forms are simply matters of naïve or inaccurate perception or interpretation. All too often, as will become apparent, these errors of interpretation are those of observers rather than of the societies themselves.

a Contemporary Contenders as Successive Rulers

The propensity to list all remembered rulers and contenders in sequence is neither uncommon nor unnatural. The earliest known example of this phenomenon was the Sumerian King List, which was composed *c.* 2100 B.C. and purported to present a list of the dynasties that had ruled Mesopotamia up to that time.[83] For the Sumerians, a dynasty was not necessarily a succession of rulers of provable or claimed consanguinity, but rather a sequence of rulers of a city. The Sumerian King List showed, for the historical period, about 115 rulers with no indication that they ruled in other than consecutive order. They were grouped into 'dynasties' from several of the important Sumerian cities, such as Kish, Uruk, Ur, and Akkad, and the impression gained from the list is that the capital of Sumer moved from city to city as divine sanction vacillated. In fact, we know from other sources that most of the dynasties listed were contemporaneous with at least one of the others and that at times as many as five of the dynasties were ruling simultaneously.[84] The 'changing capital' recorded in the King List disguised this contemporaneity, a contemporaneity that must have been known to the compiler. The chronological distortion caused by this device was great. The time-span actually represented by the historical parts of the Sumerian King List was no more than 600 years. But the total period assigned by the list to the rulers of this period was over 1,900 years.[85]

[83] Jacobsen, *Sumerian king list*, *passim*; C. J. Gadd, 'The cities of Babylonia', fascicle in *CAH*^{2}, 16–17.

[84] Jacobsen, *Sumerian king list*, *passim*, esp. Charts I and II; W. J. Hayes *et al.*, 'Chronology', 48–60.

[85] The 600-year figure is based on the chronology in Gadd, 'Cities', and regards Gilgameš as the first unquestionably historical ruler. See Jacobsen, *Sumerian king list*, 91–127, for the actual list.

The most notorious example of this form of artificial lengthening, however, is not the Sumerian King List, but the structuring of ancient Egyptian history by the historian Manetho into thirty purportedly successive dynasties. Manetho wrote in the third century B.C. and obviously had recourse to the same or similar records that have since been used to impugn in part his dynastic structure itself and in whole the fashion in which he assembled it.[86] The acceptance of Manetho's reconstruction of Egyptian chronology would necessitate a date early in the sixth millennium B.C. for the unification of Upper and Lower Egypt and the beginning of I Dynasty.[87] This is partly because Manetho exaggerated the regnal lengths of many Pharaohs. For example he credited the builders of the three largest pyramids with reigns of 63, 66, and 63 years respectively, whereas the Turin Canon allowed them but 23, 8, and 18 (or 28) years.[88] Presumably Manetho felt obliged to credit them with reigns long enough to encompass a period he thought sufficient to construct these monuments. But far greater chronological disorder arose from the fact that Manetho arranged his thirty dynasties in consecutive order when, in fact, many of them were localized and contemporaneous, especially in the troubled Intermediate periods of the VIII–X Dynasties and XIII–XVII Dynasties. These two groups of dynasties ruled between *c.* 2181 and *c.* 2040 B.C. and *c.* 1786 and 1567 B.C. Manetho or his later redactors assigned these eight dynasties durations of 146, 409, 185, 453, 184 (484?), 284, 518, and 151 years.[89] Some of Manetho's later dynasties also ruled simultaneously so that, even though the duration he assigns each of them is fairly accurate, their true total span was shorter than a straightforward interpretation of his list would suggest.

The Sumerian King List and Manetho's account of the Egyptian dynasties are the archetypal examples of the results of treating as consecutive dynasties or rulers which were not so. In evaluating this aspect of the Sumerian King List Jacobsen speculated that the list was intended to be more than a simple enumeration of rulers. It was composed just after a period of foreign, 'barbarian', Gutian rule had ended and the dynasty under which it was composed (Ur III) claimed to rule all Mesopotamia. The King List was designed to show

[86] For Manetho, see Alan Gardiner, *Egypt of the Pharaohs* (Oxford, 1961), 46–7.

[87] Ibid. 61.

[88] Ibid. 80–2, 434.

[89] Ibid. 147–8, 437–8.

that 'Babylonia had always been united in a single kingdom with a single capital, so that two different cities could never have held the "kingship" simultaneously'.[90] The Ur III Dynasty sought to justify and bolster its own sovereignty over all the cities of Babylonia by stressing the concept of the indivisibility of a divinely guided kingship. This required that existing lists of rulers from various cities be assembled into one long, unified list. Only this device permitted the utilization of all the available source materials without inpeaching the overriding concept the Sumerian King List was designed to support.

These examples are archetypal, but scarcely unique. When Darius I was composing his Behistun inscription justifying and glorifying his assumption of the Persian crown he spoke of his nine ancestors who had ruled before him. He failed to mention that they had ruled in parallel lines during much of the period and that consequently these predecessors had spanned a period of only four to five generations.[91] The Assyrian King Lists provide yet another example of this technique, so widely used in the ancient Near East.[92]

It is apparent that this mechanism is an extremely important means of lengthening the dynastic past. It is often the polar opposite of telescoping by the elision of usurpers in so far as it will include contenders who never reigned instead of excluding actual rulers. Regrettably, the operation of this principle is exceedingly difficult to detect, and in most cases it will be quite impossible to do so. It is true that the omission of a ruler can often be discerned through the collation of variant traditions, but given the fragmentary nature of most oral data it usually will be impossible to detect contemporaneous contenders as such and thereby to place them outside the chronological framework.

[90] Jacobsen, *Sumerian King List*, 164.

[91] R. G. Kent, *Old Persian: grammar, texts, lexicon* (New Haven, Conn., 1950), 158–9; W. C. Benedict and E. von Voigtlander, 'Darius' Bisitun Inscription, Babylonian version, lines 1–29', *JCS* 10 (1956), 9.

[92] Hallo, 'Zāriqum', 220–1; for the application of this technique to Puranic chronology see, e.g., K. Venkatachela, *Chronology of ancient Hindu history* (2 vols., Gandhinagar, 1957). An important example of contemporaries being restructured into a 'dynasty', is discussed in R. T. Zuidema, *The Ceque system of Cuzco: the social organization of the capital of the Inca* (Leiden, 1962). Zuidema argues persuasively that 'contemporaneous [lineage] chiefs in Cuzco' were 'presented as belonging to a dynasty of ten rulers' by later informants in order to provide an explanation for the social structure of the kingdom which fitted Inca cosmological concepts, and that in fact Pachacuti, the ninth ruler in the kinglists, actually was the first Inca Emperor. Ibid. 206. See also pp. 12–15, 32–3, 36–7, 54–61, 122–31, 216–29.

Consequently, only a few reasonably probable African examples can be cited. Eleven lists of the *Citimukulus* of the Bemba of Zambia have been collected. This seems a large enough number to analyse for our present purposes. There are forty different names on these lists. Only one of these names is mentioned in all eleven sources. Six names (including three of the most recent five) are mentioned in ten of the lists. Fourteen names are mentioned in fewer than five of the sources. Eight of the names are mentioned only in one source.[93] The neighbouring Bisa, who claim that their own paramountcy was founded about the time the Bemba arrived in Zambia, aver that the Bemba 'often quote as chiefs the names of contenders'.[94] This may simply reflect Bisa dissatisfaction with their own, much shorter, list of paramount chiefs, but the evidence of the Bemba kinglists themselves lends credence to this allegation.[95] The fact that most of these kinglists, though collected over a period of thirty-five years, appear to be uncontaminated by feedback, does not invalidate the possibility that contenders are included. Many of these, for instance, could have disputed the paramountcy with several *citimukulus* over a long period of time and thereby impressed themselves on tradition as paramounts themselves. But their contemporaneity with other rulers would remain unaffected.

We know from French sources that two *braks* in the 1770s were competing contenders for the Waalo throne, although they are remembered in Waalo traditions as having ruled consecutively.[96] Whether these two individuals effectively did rule as *brak* in succession is problematical, but, in any case, tradition has forgotten their 'regnal' contemporaneity for the period covered by the French records. Most African polities had succession systems which fostered succession struggles or even continuous internecine strife among contenders. Waalo and the other Wolof/Serer states exemplify this

[93] A. D. Roberts, 'Chronology of the Bemba (N.E. Zambia)', *JAH* 11 (1970), 222–5.

[94] Vansina, *Kingdoms*, 89; Roberts, 'Chronology', 230; F. M. Thomas, *Historical notes on the Bisa tribe, Northern Rhodesia* (Lusaka, 1958), 4.

[95] Roberts, 'Chronology', 231, argues that the number of generations in the Bisa list implies a foreshortening of the Bemba genealogy. This may, of course, be true. There may have been fewer *citimukulus* for more generations. But a divergence of two generations in nine, particularly in view of the Bemba succession system, does not seem inordinate, since the Bisa generations would expectedly be shorter.

[96] L.-P. Raybaud, 'L'Administration du Sénégal de 1781 à 1784', *Annales Africaines* (1968), 168–70.

pattern. So, too, do the interlacustrine states, the Congo kingdom, and the states of the Mwene Mutapa complex. Unfortunately, the evidence currently available permits us to do no more than compare succession systems and kinglists in traditional areas with those for which we possess enough evidence to draw firmer conclusions. When this is done it becomes apparent that contemporaneous rulers are often remembered as successive. One of the greatest challenges facing the historian of Africa in his quest for closer and more probable chronological parameters is the detection of likely circumstances for this kind of chronological distortion in the society he studies.

b Spurinyms

The expansion of a kinglist through the inclusion of eponyms, toponyms, and patronyms is probably more common than the arrangement of contemporary rulers in succession. At least it is more easily detectable, which may account for its appearing more widespread. Usually, however, a close familiarity with the *mores* and vocabulary of a society is necessary in order to recognize the full extent of this technique. Often, of course, it is egregiously apparent that spurinyms have been added. Perhaps the most obvious example of all, at least when it is viewed retrospectively, is a list of Kuba rulers collected in 1908/9, which contained no fewer than 121 names.[97] The investigator who collected this impressive list admitted that it was 'rare' to find such a long kinglist in Africa, but maintained that this simply proved that the Bakuba were 'a remarkable people'.[98] Be that as it may, it cannot be gainsaid that the list itself is quite remarkable. Later investigation disclosed that the first 88 names on this list were nothing but spurinyms of all kinds—contenders, heirs-apparent, gods, eponyms, toponyms, and animals. These were apparently given to the original investigator quite at random, although the fact that all the spurinyms were at the beginning of the list while the last 33 names represented a reasonably accurate account of the Kuba kings may be significant.[99] The magnitude of this effort made it obvious that some kind of elongation had taken place; even so, it was only half a century later that more thorough

[97] E. Torday, *Notes ethnographiques sur les peuples communément appelés Bakuba ainsi que les peuplades apparentées—les Bushongo* (Brussels, 1911), 17–19.

[98] Ibid. 117.

[99] For an analysis of Torday's kinglist, see Vansina, *Geschiedenis van de Kuba van ongeveer 1500 tot 1904* (Tervuren, 1963), 350–3.

analysis of Kuba traditions identified precisely the forms this lengthening took.

The addtion of spurinyms is not always so apparent, although these accretions are usually added at the beginning of the list, as in the Kuba case. Spurinyms most often appear as lineage patronyms, deities, or toponyms. It is not always clear how these become transmogrified into rulers, but it is not unlikely that at a distance of several generations or even centuries, many proper names of early provenience were assumed to represent early rulers. This seems the most plausible explanation for the early genealogy of the First Dynasty of Babylon as presented in an inscription composed towards the end of the dynasty, that is, about the middle of the seventeenth century B.C. This genealogy contained twenty-eight names, of which the last nine are the first nine rulers of the dynasty.[1] However, the first fifteen names are either tribal names or toponyms.[2] In fact seven of these names are garbled versions of the seventeen kings 'who dwelt in tents' who appear at the apex of the Assyrian King Lists.[3] The editor of this genealogy sees these spurinymic elements as evidence that Hammurabi's descendants, long sedentary, retained 'a consciousness of tribal origin'.[4] It is particularly significant and minatory that this recollection was so easily and instinctively converted into a genealogical framework.

In fact it seems that the territorial structure of a state, like its myths, is often elaborated in genealogical terms. The ancestors of the north Welsh dynasty of Gwynedd were named in later genealogies after Welsh districts.[5] In exactly the same way, the name of the legendary first Pictish king was Cruithne, which means 'land of the Picts'. Cruithne was credited with seven sons; each had the name of

[1] J. J. Finkelstein, 'The genealogy of the Hammurapi dynasty', *JCS* 20 (1966), 95–6. A. Malamat, 'King lists of the Old Babylonian period and Biblical genealogies' in W. W. Hallo (ed.), *Essays in memory of E. A. Speiser* (New Haven, Conn., 1968), 165–8. A recent account of early Biblical history has argued that many of the names in the First Book of Chronicles are 'either blatantly geographical or connected with place names' while other names are 'mostly eponymous heads of clans', Sh. Yeivin, *The Israelite conquest of Canaan* (Istanbul, 1971), 11.

[2] Finkelstein, 'Genealogy', 97–8, 101–2.

[3] For the earliest part of the Assyrian King Lists, see especially F. R. Kraus, *Könige die in zelten Wohnten. Betrachtungen über der Kern der assyrischen Königsliste* (Amsterdam, 1965). See Appendix A below.

[4] Finkelstein, 'Genealogy', 99.

[5] N. K. Chadwick, 'Pictish and Celtic marriage in early literary tradition' *Scotch Gaelic Studies*, 8 (1955), 64.

a later Pictish province.[6] It is well known that nearly every city and region of ancient Greece had a god or a hero as a namesake. According to Geoffrey of Monmouth, each British city was named after a king or prince. Geoffrey certainly did not believe much of what he wrote about this early period. It was simply conventional that rulers became eponyms. It is no less conventional for eponyms in return to become rulers.

This discussion is not meant to imply that no ruler ever established towns or granted regions the honour of bearing his name—Alexander the Great would be the classic refutation of such a thesis. Rather it is meant to suggest that it has long been a pattern to assume that every prominent geographical feature must have had a namesake and every lineage or family must have had an apical ancestor who ruled at some remote period. Often such an assumption is purely reflexive and gratuitous and should be neither made nor accepted without independent supporting evidence.

c Euhemerism

Euhemerism is the belief that the contents of myths were real events and that the gods and heroes were living human beings who became deified as time passed. The Greeks, who believed that 'their heroic mythology was their ancestral history', are perhaps the classic example of euhemerism.[7] In practising euhemerism, Greek chronographers and annalists found it necessary to construct a chronological framework to accommodate these gods and heroes. This was the inevitable consequence of these beliefs. In this sense euhemerism operated in exactly the same way as spurinyms. The euhemeristic technique was also used in developing the vast fabric of pre-Patrician genealogies discussed at the end of this chapter. O'Rahilly succinctly described the advantages of euhemerism as a device for lengthening a genealogy: 'It is easy to apply; it enables the uncritical writer to

[6] H. M. Chadwick, *Early Scotland: The Picts, the Scots and the Welsh of southern Scotland* (Cambridge, 1949), 1–3; I. Henderson, *The Picts* (London, 1967), 35–6. For the massive use of eponyms to explain later place-names among the medieval German chroniclers, see F. L. Borchardt, *German antiquity in Renaissance myth* (Baltimore, Md., 1971), *passim*, esp. listing in index at pp. 342–3.

[7] M. P. Nilsson, *Cults, myths, oracles and politics in ancient Greece* (Lund, 1951), 12. This contains an excellent account of how the Greeks used their myths as serviceable political tools. For euhemerism among the Greeks, see P. Decharme, *La critique des traditions religieuses chez les Grecs des origines au temps de Plutarche* (Paris, 1904), 371–93; J. Seznec, *The survival of the pagan gods: the mythological tradition and its place in Renaissance humanism and art* (New York, 1953), 11–13.

fill up the historical vacuum he abhors; and it gives us the flattering notion that the records of our history reach back into the very remote past.'[8] As the memory of the pre-Christian Irish deities faded under the impact of several centuries of Christianity these names were no longer recognizable as pagan deities and became accepted as mortal rulers. Euhemerism died hard in the western world. Isaac Newton, when constructing his chronology of the ancient world, accepted *in toto* the framework of Greek mythology and built much of his otherwise carefully reasoned analysis on it.[9] It can scarcely be doubted that euhemerism is practised in some African societies, such as the Yoruba, that have highly developed pantheons.[10]

d Early Rulers and Long Reigns

Yet another form of lengthening is to credit the earlier rulers of a dynasty with unusually or impossibly long reigns. Examples of this procedure have occurred throughout historical time and space where dated kinglists exist. Again, the Sumerian kinglist has the dubious honour of inaugurating a distorting procedure. The antediluvian rulers described in the list all had incredibly long reigns. As the list approached the historical period the reigns become shorter and eventually the historical period and reasonable regnal lengths arrived simultaneously.[11] This correlation of regnal length to historicity is a rough one, but is supported by additional examples. The pattern is particularly widespread among the *vamśavalis*, or Indian chronicles, but stands in sharpest relief when one examines the *Rājataraṅgiṇī* of Kalhana. This chronicle of Kashmir was written in the twelfth century and is widely regarded as the finest, indeed only, example of critical historical literature from pre-Muslim India.[12] Even so, the account of Kashmiri rulers in the *Rājataraṅgiṇī* becomes historical only at the turn of the seventh century. This interpretation of its historical character is not based on the regnal lengths given

[8] T. F. O'Rahilly, *Early Irish history and mythology* (Dublin, 1957), 261.

[9] Manuel, *Isaac Newton*, 120–1.

[10] P. Morton-Williams, 'An outline of the cosmological and cult organization of the Oyo Yoruba', *Africa*, 34 (1964), 254–5.

[11] Jacobsen, *Sumerian king list*, 71–87; E. Sollberger, 'The rulers of Lagaš', *JCS* 21 (1967), 279. This aspect of the kinglist led Sollberger to label it 'a politico-satirical work'.

[12] A. L. Basham, 'The Kashmir Chronicle' in C. H. Philips (ed.), *Historians of India, Pakistan and Ceylon* (London, 1961), 57–9; U. N. Ghoshal, 'The dynastic chronicles of Kashmir', *Indian Historical Quarterly*, 18 (1942), 195–200.

earlier rulers, but it is strongly supported by this pattern. The average regnal lengths for the rulers of the three pre-historic dynasties are 48, 32, and 59 years, whereas the average regnal length for the historical period is less than 11 years.[13]

The Pictish kinglists contain about 60 names. The first 30 rulers, who were legendary, were alleged to have ruled about 1,000 years; the last 30, historical, rulers reigned only for about 300 years.[14] Early Japan, early Korea, the earliest Chinese Emperors, Macedon, Paekche, and the earliest Mesoamerican states are further examples of this process which often, as in Japan and Korea, was reflected by extended father/son succession patterns.

The problem also manifests itself in those areas of Africa which claim to possess dated kinglists. These are generally confined to west and north-east Africa. For instance, the Kano Chronicle exhibits this tendency to a marked degree.[15] The Bornu kinglists assign impossibly long reigns to several early rulers of Kanem.[16] The problem of long early reigns in Bono-Manso has been discussed elsewhere.[17] The tendency of modern researchers to follow the same practice is illustrated by Bieber's chronology for Kaffa. Bieber assigned the first 11 rulers 385 years while he allotted the last 9 only 122 years.[18]

Some lists which do not assign regnal lengths to each king none the less necessitate the application of a high regnal average to the entire list. Such is the case of the *buurs* of Dyolof before the dissolution of the 'empire'. Traditionally there were 12 *buurs* of Dyolof during the period, which, by traditional accounts, lasted about 350 years.[19] Yet their 30 successors ruled only 329 years.[20] For reasons

[13] Ghoshal, 'Dynastic chronicles', 203. For the problem of extended father/son successions in the *Rājataraṅgiṇī*, see Chapter II. For long early reigns in other Indian states, see R. J. K. Singh, *A short history of Manipur* (Imphal, 1965), 315–17, and S. Sinha, 'State formation and Rajput myth in tribal central India', *Man in India*, 42 (1962), 40–2.

[14] Chadwick, *Early Scotland*, 6.

[15] H. R. Palmer (tr.), 'The Kano Chronicle', *JRAI* 38 (1908), 58–70.

[16] H. R. Palmer, *Bornu Sahara and Sudan* (London, 1936), 90.

[17] C. Flight, 'The chronology of the kings and queenmothers of Bono-Manso: a revaluation of the evidence', *JAH* 11 (1970), 259–67. Flight seems to have fallen prey to the same propensity he was assessing since he proposes a 150-year period for the first 8 reigns and only 153 years for the next 12. See Chapter IV for a discussion of Flight's data.

[18] A. Orent, 'Refocusing on the history of Kafa prior to 1897: a discussion of political processes', *AHS* 3 (1970), 268.

[19] V. Monteil, 'Le Dyolof et al-Bouri Ndiaye', *BIFAN* 28 (1966), 605–6.

[20] Ibid. 606, where regnal lengths are discussed.

to be discussed later it is inadvisable to accept a regnal average of over 20 years for any part of Africa, whatever the succession system is alleged to have been. The acceptance of long early reigns for parts of Africa has been criticized.[21] But this criticism of specific cases could be stronger if the problem is viewed in the widest possible perspective. Alloting longer reigns to earlier, probably non-historical, rulers is, with the exception of extended father/son successions, the simplest and most direct way of effecting a prolongation of the past in areas with dated kinglists.

e Genealogical Parasitism

The beginnings of dynasties are often antedated by attaching them to other dynasties of alleged or demonstrably earlier dating. More than any other mechanism, this process emphasizes the wide utility of genealogies in societies whose interpretation of the past is personality-oriented. The Greeks demonstrated early the spectrum of uses to which genealogy could be put. When Macedon was beginning to wax powerful and its help was needed to help repel the Persian invaders, it was thought useful to provide the Macedonian royal house with a genealogical link with the Heracleids, Greece's most prestigious aristocratic group. A series of rulers was created, headed by one Perdiccas I, who allegedly was a Heracleid who had fled from Argos, of whose royal house he was a member.[22] This necessitated filling in more than two centuries of Macedonian rulers, but the Greek historians were equal to the task and some even pushed the Macedonian genealogy back a little further.[23] As other states on Greece's northern flank, such as Epirus, Thrace, and Thessaly, became powerful, similar genealogical origins were propounded for their rulers.[24] In like fashion the founders of Rome were genealogically tied to Troy, as were the Britons' rulers as imagined by Geoffrey of Monmouth. Imputing Trojan and early Roman genealogical

[21] For Bieber, admittedly an extreme and unimaginative example, see C. F. Beckingham and G. W. B. Huntingford (eds.), *Some records of Ethiopia, 1593–1646* (London, 1954), lvii–lviii.

[22] Herodotus, VIII. 137–9.

[23] S. Casson, *Macedonia, Thrace and Illyria* (London, 1926), 175–7; Ap. Dascalakis, *The Hellenism of the ancient Macedonians* (Thessaloniki, 1965), 97–146; idem, 'L'Origine de la maison royale de Macédonie et les légendes relatives de l'antiquité' in *Ancient Macedonia: papers read at the 1st International Symposium held in Thessaloniki, 26–9 Aug. 1968* (Thessaloniki, 1969), 155–61; Sp. Marinatos, 'Mycenaean elements within the royal house of Macedonia', ibid. 45–52.

[24] Nilsson, *Cults*, 98, 107–8.

origins to the Germanic tribes was also a popular pastime among the German chroniclers.[25]

With the spread of Christianity the Biblical genealogies replaced those of Greek and Roman mythology as cynosures. It became fashionable to connect newly converted peoples to Biblical patriarchs, usually through Japheth, one of the sons of Noah.[26] This justified both the necessity for and the fitness of their conversion. This particular usage was supplemented by the necessity to claim each new ethnic group, as its existence came to the attention of the church fathers, as an offshoot of the focal Biblical genealogies.

Nor was the utility of genealogies lost on the rulers of most of the ancient and medieval Indian dynasties. Most of these were of *mlechcha* or foreign origin. It became necessary for them to disguise these undesirable origins and claim *kśatriya* ancestry in order to legitimize their rule. The easiest way to do this was to claim affiliation with one of the Puranic dynasties.[27] This desire for legitimation was particularly strong among the early Rajput dynasties of northern India and, by association, with their modern successors.[28] It would be useless to cite specific examples of 'genealogical fever' in the Indian dynasties. These dynasties number in the hundreds and the fever reached pandemic proportions. It should be noted, however, that

[25] Borchardt, *German antiquity, passim.* G. R. Spohn, 'Armenien und Herzog Naimes', *Zeitschrift für bayerische Landesgeschicht*, 34 (1971), 185–210.

[26] For the utility of Japheth as a Biblical ancestor, see, among others, M. Chamchian, *History of Armenia* (2 vols., Calcutta, 1827), I. 4–6; M. Daxcuranci, *The history of the Caucasian Albanians*, tr. C. F. J. Dowsett (London, 1961), 1–5; J. W. Johnson, 'The Scythian: his rise and fall', *Journal of the History of Ideas*, 20 (1959), 254–7; T. Kendrick, *British Antiquity*, 70–1. For a survey of the many local Caucasian dynasts who traced their 'immemorial dynastic origins' to the Medes, the Assyrians, the Canaanites, the Parthians, King David, and even the Emperors of China, see C. Toumanoff, *Studies in Christian Caucasian history* (Georgetown, Md., 1968), 197–219, 257–9, 303–5, and idem, 'La noblesse géorgienne sa génèse et sa structure', *Rivista araldica*, 54 (1956), 260–73; E. M. Sanford, 'The study of ancient history in the Middle Ages', *Journal of the History of Ideas*, 5 (1944), 35–8; D. C. Allen, *The legend of Noah* (Urbana, Ill., 1949), 114–17.

[27] R. Thapar, 'Image of the barbarian in ancient India', *Comparative Studies in Society and History*, 13 (1971), 427–8; B. Stein, 'Early Indian historiography: a conspiracy hypothesis', *Indian Economic and Social History Review*, 6 (1969), 44–6, 51, 52–3, 58–9; D. C. Sircar, *Studies in the society and administration of ancient and mediaeval India*, I, *Society* (Calcutta, 1967), 45–6.

[28] D. C. Sircar, 'The Guhila claim of Solar origin', *Journal of Indian History*, 42 (1964), 381–7; idem, 'The Guhilas of Kiśkindha', *Our Heritage*, 11 (1963), 12–15; R. Niyogi, *The history of the Gāhadavālas* (Calcutta, 1959), 28–9. See also C. Mahoney, 'Dynastic drift: a process of cultural universalization', *Prof. K.A.N. Felicitation Volume in honour of his 80th birthday* (Madras, 1971), 89–107.

most of these exaggerated claims developed only as the dynasty became entrenched or, conversely, when it had fallen under the control of another dynasty.[29] They were political tools of the trade.

The post-Patrician Irish genealogies also reflect the tendency to ascribe genealogically appropriate origins to the smaller and more recent dynasties as political exigencies required. In the eleventh century the ruler of Osraige, hitherto a minor state, became the ruler of the *cóiced* [province] of Lagin (Leinster). This created the need to justify this turn of events by imputing a Laginian origin to the Osraige royal line—a reasonably simple task.[30] The Osraige example is only one of many, for the Irish annalists and genealogists seemed particularly adept at this kind of genealogical legerdemain. Indeed, the kaleidoscopic political fortunes of the island tested their abilities often.[31]

There are several prominent African examples of genealogical parasitism which bear close resemblance to the cases we have already discussed. Many interlacustrine states trace the origins of their dynasties to the Bacwezi. Doing so necessarily places their own formation at a period coeval with the disappearance of this legendary dynasty.[32] The traditional accounts of these states are usually very confused or very skeletal for this early period, and one of the few pieces of consistent and detailed information in them seems to be this tale of genealogical origin. In this respect it bears the character of a retrospective version that we noticed in the Irish case of Osraige/Lagin. Acceptance of genealogical filiation with the Bacwezi necessitates postulating a date several generations earlier than any other aspects of the traditional accounts warrant.

Another area of Africa victimized by genealogical fever has been

[29] A more detailed description of these processes for the genealogy of Jodhpur is now being prepared by the author but see also Appendix B. See also Chapter III for the effect of indirect rule on traditional genealogies.

[30] O'Rahilly, *Early Irish history*, 18–20.

[31] J. V. Kelleher, 'Early Irish history and pseudo-history', *Studia Hibernica*, 3 (1963), 113–27, discusses the purposes of the Irish genealogies and how these purposes governed their use and structure. See also O'Rahilly, *Early Irish history*, 15. The Dál Cais sept achieved the kingship of all Muma (Munster) by conquest in the late tenth century. To justify this new state of affairs a Dál Cais genealogy was constructed and grafted on to an appropriately legitimizing genealogy at a point early enough in time to avoid scrutiny. Kelleher, 'The rise of the Dál Cais' in E. Rynne (ed.), *North Munster studies* (Limerick, 1967), 234–5, 239–40, and O'Corráin, 'Irish regnal succession', 38–9.

[32] For the Bacwezi, see especially C. C. Wrigley, 'Some thoughts on the Bacwezi', *UJ* 21 (1957), 11–17.

western Nigeria. All the Yoruba states and Benin claim that the founders of their dynasties were members of the royal family of Ife, the Yoruba ancestor state.[33] Admittedly, the cultural and political cohesiveness of the Yoruba makes it easy to accept a circumscribed origin for most of these states. But most of the traditions trace them directly to one of the many (the number varies from seven to sixteen) sons of Oduduwa, the first ruler of Ife, or to his grandsons.[34] This has the advantage of allowing each of the crowned *obas* to admit to only a slight genealogical juniority to Ife. On the other hand, in many cases it unquestionably antedates the foundation of these states.

The Benin dynasty, traditionally founded from Ife, seemed itself to be a prolific progenitor of other dynasties. Several of the lower Niger states, such as Aboh and Onitsha, claim to have been founded by emigrating Benin princes.[35] Reconciling Aboh and Benin traditions requires the positing of a migration of about two centuries.

Lagos traditions also ascribe Benin origins to their dynasty. Serious chronological problems arise from this claim. The Lagos kinglists can be stretched back no further than *c.* 1650, whereas the Benin *oba* who Lagos traditions mention as contemporary with the migration must be dated about a century before this.[36] This discrepancy, like that for Aboh, could be accounted for if a migration of about 100 years is assumed in place of a 'conquest'. But at this point the migration solution as a filler for long periods of otherwise unaccounted time begins to assume the character of a *deus ex machina*.

A singularly large number of Zambezian dynasties claim that their founders were sons of Mwene Mutapas.[37] These claims necessitate a fifteenth- or sixteenth-century date for the foundation of these dynasties but in many cases a date as early as this is contradicted, or at least not supported, by whatever other evidence is available.

[33] R. S. Smith, *Kingdoms of the Yoruba* (London, 1969), 11.

[34] Ibid., 18 *passim*; E. A. Kenyo, *Yoruba natural rulers and their origin* (Ibadan 1964), 61–2.

[35] Ogedengbe, 'Aboh', 167–71; R. W. Harding, *The Dispute over the Obiship of Onitsha: Report of the Enquiry* (Enugu, 1963), 12–13.

[36] R. C. C. Law, 'The dynastic chronology of Lagos', *Lagos Notes and Records*, 2 (Dec. 1968), 51–2; J. U. Egharevba, *A short history of Benin* (Ibadan, 1960), 31. Law, 52, suggests that the Lagos list has been telescoped. This seems the least likely of several possible solutions. The earliest Lagos kinglist was recorded in 1853, that is, just after the assumption of British control. It would be interesting, perhaps enlightening, to learn more of the circumstances surrounding this transmission.

[37] E. A. Alpers, 'Dynasties of the Mutapa-Rozwi complex', *JAH* 11 (1970), 209–18.

It may be true that the kinglists of some of these states are 'deficient', but such a conclusion would partly be based on a presumption that the stated genealogical origins are acceptable.[38] For Maungwe Abraham estimated that seven generations spanned 270 years.[39] This made it possible to establish an early date for the foundation of the dynasty there, but this average seems too high to be maintained over such a long period, even for fraternal/consobrinal succession. The alternative, that many of these dynasties were not in fact founded by scions of the Mwene Mutapa dynasty, should also be considered.

A study of the problem of genealogical parasitism is important for more than its chronological implications. It most clearly illustrates the manifold uses to which very simple genealogical concepts can be put. 'Genealogical conquest' is almost as common as the more familiar types of subjugation. It cannot be emphasized too often that traditional societies are more personality-oriented than more technologically advanced and literate ones, although it is quite clear, even from the few examples cited, that literacy did not provide immunity. Genealogies can project perception beyond the circumscribed spatial and temporal boundaries within which most such societies perforce exist. Genealogies become all-purpose tools, substituting for an array of unavailable mechanisms for social and political regulation. As such, they are regarded, not as immutable abstractions, but as pragmatic and serviceable instruments readily adaptable to continuing exigencies.

f Inferring Present Succession Patterns into the Remote Past

The remote past is often seen as a quiet prelude to the more recent past and the present—undisturbed in its serenity by change. This implies, among other things, that the succession patterns of the present accurately reflect previous patterns. This is often, but not always, true. Changes in succession practices have obvious chronological import. Although traditional accounts almost always see such changes—when they are recognized at all—as proceeding from lineal to collateral succession, most often in fact this progression, where it can be documented, is precisely the opposite.

In the eleventh and twelfth centuries the Slavic states, which had

[38] Ibid. 213, referring to Manyika.

[39] D. P. Abraham, 'The principality of Maungwe', *NADA* 28 (1951), 83. The eighth, historical, generation lasted from 1889 to 1943 and thus supports Abraham's chronology. But it would be reckless to extrapolate from this single known example.

previously practised succession by seniority, began changing to the Germanic principle of primogeniture or lineal succession.[40] As a result the average regnal lengths increased. In Bohemia there had been twenty-three rulers from 905 to 1196, but only five in the next 110 years before the dynasty died out—a more likely eventuality in narrowly defined lineal systems.[41] A survey of the many Russian principalities for the same period illustrates a similar pattern.[42] In like fashion the Celtic succession conventions began to change in the eleventh and twelfth centuries, both in Ireland and in Scotland.[43] Most of the Irish states which endured into the Anglo-Norman period practised at least modified forms of primogeniture, and longer reigns resulted.

Succession practices, if not the principles governing them, changed in Benin and in Bornu from the sixteenth to the eighteenth centuries.[44] But most changes in succession in oral societies, once effected and maintained for several generations, are difficult to detect. Those elements benefiting from the changes will not be fain to preserve memories of earlier practices and will instead strive to obliterate all traces of antecedent norms.

The circumstances attending a change of succession conventions can be illustrated by a detailed analysis of the succession in Manya Krobo during the last century. Succession in the two Krobo states of south-east Ghana, Manya Krobo and Yilo Krobo, was patrilineal. Manya Krobo traditions claim that all Krobo was once united under their *konor* (paramount chief) and that Yilo Krobo was given to a relative of the ninth *konor* of Manya Krobo.[45] The last four *konors* of Manya Krobo have ruled since *c.* 1832 and the last three have succeeded lineally—son, nephew, son. Some Manya Krobo traditions give as many as twenty-one *konors*.[46] The official

[40] For Bohemia, see B. Mendl, 'Les derniers Přemyslides: la fin d'une dynastie Slave', *Revue Historique*, 179 (1937), 37. For Serbia, see V. Grumel, *La Chronologie* (Paris, 1958), 88–90.

[41] W. Wegener, *Die Přemysliden* (Göttingen, 1957), 3–14.

[42] Stokvis, *Manuel*, II. 334–41.

[43] See above, 28–30.

[44] R. E. Bradbury, 'Chronological problems in the study of Benin history', *JHSN* 1/4 (1959), 267; R. Cohen, 'The Bornu king lists' in J. Butler (ed.), *Boston University papers on Africa*, II, *African History* (Boston, Mass., 1966); idem, 'The dynamics of feudalism in Bornu' in ibid. 96–9.

[45] Testimony of Emmanuel Mate Kole, 15 Nov. 1903, National Archives of Ghana (hereafter NAG), ADM11/1/1117, Box 1.

[46] C. A. O'Brien to Secretary of Native Affairs, 18 Sept. 1904, NAG-

Manya Krobo version today is that succession in the past was 'usually' from father to son.[47] Most of the Krobo kinglists do not agree with each other but for our present purpose this is irrelevant and we shall assume that nineteen *konors* have ruled Manya Krobo to the present. What is more important is that, based on the assumption that succession in Manya Krobo has always been lineal, the arrival of the Krobos to their present location has been dated to about the fifteenth century.[48]

Early evidence indicates, however, that, until *c.* 1832, when a new dynasty seems to have acquired the stool, succession was not lineal. In 1892 Emmanuel Mate Kole I became *konor*. At the time his succession was disputed in Manya Krobo on the grounds that he was not the rightful successor.[49] However, Emmanuel Mate Kole was educated and a Christian and was therefore strongly supported by the British administration in the Gold Coast, which was anxious to suppress certain Krobo customs it regarded as obnoxious and uncivilized.[50] Opposition to Mate Kole continued, however, and in 1904 an inquiry was held into both Mate Kole's right to the stool and his claim to the suzerainty of Yilo Krobo.[51] During the inquiry Mate Kole testified that succession in Manya Krobo was from father to son. To bolster this argument he evidently went so far as to claim that he was his predecessor's son when he was actually his nephew.[53] After

ADM11/1/1115, Box 1; Addendum to Quarterly Report of Akuse District for quarter ending 31 Dec. 1901, SNA 24/02, NAG-ADM11/1/1098.

[47] Testimony of Mate Kole II obtained in 1971 by Irene Quaye, University of Ghana.

[48] N. A. Mate Kole [Mate Kole II], 'The historical background of Krobo customs', *Transactions of the Gold Coast and Togoland Historical Society*, I/4 (1955), 134, claimed that the settlement 'could not be much later than 1450' and that the ninth *konor* was ruling *c.* 1735. R. J. H. Pogucki, *Report on land tenure in Adangbe customary law* (Accra, 1955), 46–7, while not accepting lineal succession in the early period, nevertheless allows 20 to 25 years per reign. Working back from *c.* 1842, the notional date for the first *konor* would be 1467/1542.

[49] See miscellaneous correspondence in NAG-ADM11/1/1115, Box 1.

[50] Report of 1904 Inquiry, p. 5, NAG-ADM11/1/1115, Box 2; Alexander Williams, DC, Akuse to Colonial Secretary, 18 Mar. 1892, NAG-ADM1/9/4, pp. 252–3.

[51] SNA Hull minuted in 1903 that Mate Kole 'was not entitled to the position and he knew it; the Krobos also knew it', Minute dd 31 July 1903, SNA 374, NAG-ADM11/1/1115, Box 2.

[52] Report of 1904 Inquiry, p. 8. It should be noted that Mate Kole had been educated by the Basel missionaries and spoke and wrote excellent English.

[53] 'I may mention that while at Odumasi [capital of Manya Krobo], Mate Kole spoke and led me to believe that Sakité [the previous ruler] was his father, taking

extensive investigations in both Krobos the Commissioner of Inquiry concluded, doubtless somewhat tidily, that

I am strongly of the opinion that the law of succession in Eastern [Manya] Krobo is from brother to brother, the eldest son of the 1st wife succeeding first, then the eldest son of the second wife, then the eldest son of the 3rd wife, and then the 2nd son by the 1st wife, 2nd wife and 3rd wife, and so on, and failing brothers or on the exhaustion of brothers, to eldest son of eldest son by the 1st son, then other brothers as before.[54]

He also recognized that, since Mate Kole had already been on the stool for twelve years and, though not universally accepted, had the support of government, he should be allowed to retain the stool. But he urged that after Mate Kole's death the stool should revert to the proper line under the rules of collateral succession and that consequently 'Mate Kole's children [would] run an extremely slender chance of ever getting the stool'.[55] Mate Kole, however, outlived the effects of this recommendation and died only in 1939. He was succeeded by his son Fred Lawer Mate Kole, thereby solidifying the principle of lineal succession in Manya Krobo. In turn Mate Kole II still continues to rule, although there was considerable opposition to his succession, and will in turn certainly be succeeded by his own son.[56] Even in the literate ambience of southern Ghana the two Mate Koles have succeeded in outlasting the effects of previous succession practices and in creating in many quarters the impression that present succession patterns prevailed from the most remote time. In an oral society there can be little doubt that they would have outlived the very memory of these practices and that later succession patterns would have been inferred for the entire dynasty.[57]

The Manya Krobo example illustrates what is probably the course

---

it, I presume, that being new to this province I would not be likely to know', C. A. O'Brien to SNA, 18 Sept. 1904, ADM11/1/1115, Box 1. This may have been a misinterpretation on O'Brien's part of Adangbe customary kinship terms which had a different connotation from the narrowly biological one with which we are most familiar, but again the high level of Mate Kole's western education must be taken into account.

[54] Report of 1904 Inquiry, p. 4.

[55] Ibid. p. 5.

[56] See NAG-CSO381/32, *passim*; Dispatch 131 on 23 Feb. 1940, from Governor, Gold Coast to Secretary of State for Colonies, NAG-ADM1/2/256 and Dispatch 642 dd 7 Dec. 1939 from SS, Colonies to GGC, NAG-ADM1/1/519.

[57] This account of the change in Manya Krobo succession features since 1892 is a skeletal one and has omitted irrelevant details which illuminate but do not effect the long-term results of this change. A fuller analysis of the succession in both Krobos from *c.* 1860 to the present is being prepared.

most changes in succession practices follow. The evolution is gradual and may encompass several reigns or generations. By the time the change is completely effected, the memory of previous conventions has been eroded. Since most discernible succession changes have been from collateral to lineal succession, this means that in most cases the chronology of the polity, as measured by the reigns of its rulers, will be lengthened.[58] For instance, if we assume that fifteen *konors* reigned before *c.* 1832, and further assume that the rotational/fraternal succession patterns described by O'Brien prevailed throughout this period, then there were probably no more than three regnal generations. These could have been long generations of perhaps 40 to 45 years each. The resultant date for the establishment of the *konor*-ship would be *c.* 1700. This does not imply, of course, that the arrival of the Krobos did not antedate the establishment of the office of *konor*.[59]

It is not unlikely that over a period of centuries most succession systems change. Sometimes these changes will be sudden;[60] more often they will be gradual and imperceptible, but no less profound. By assuming *a priori* that the succession practices within the purview of direct or documented observation do not necessarily reflect these practices throughout historical time, the investigator may aid his understanding of both the dynamics of his society and the duration of its past.

g *Outright Fabrication*

When all else failed, chroniclers have not been loath to have recourse to the outright fabrication of genealogies, based principally on their own fertile imaginations. The most impressive examples of this technique were the pre-Patrician Irish genealogies and the Purānic genealogies of ancient India. The traditional view of early Irish history is found in the compilation known as *Lebor Gabála Érenn* (Book of the Conquest of Ireland). This work was begun about the eighth century and continued for several hundred years.[61] During

[58] The special case of father/son succession is discussed in the next chapter.

[59] Paul Isert, a practised observer who spent several years at the Danish settlements on the Gold Coast in the 1780s, described Krobo as 'une petite république qui peut mettre sur pied cinq cent hommes' into the field. P. E. Isert, *Voyages en Guinée et dans les îles Caraïbes en Amérique* (Paris, 1793), 272. This description suggests that the *konor*-ship, if established at that time, was something less than the paramountcy it later became. For Isert, see G. Nørregård, *Danish settlements in West Africa, 1658–1850* (Boston, Mass., 1966), 173–4.

[60] For instance, see the Ottoman case discussed in Chapter IV.

[61] O'Rahilly, *Early Irish history*, 193; Kelleher, 'Pre-Norman genealogies', 140.

this period constant changes were made to ensure that it presented a coherent and consistent picture of pre-Christian Ireland and one that fitted the era of its compilation as well. According to the *Lebor Gabála* there were several invasions of Ireland. The last of these was that of the Milesians from Spain and occurred *c.* 1500 B.C. The sons of Míl established the High Kingship at Tara and their descendants were still ruling when the *Lebor Gabála* was being written. The first few generations described in the genealogies of the *Lebor Gabála*, not surprisingly, consisted principally of eponyms.[62] Also, as we have seen, euhemerism played a part in the construction of these genealogies. The vast majority of the names in the *Lebor Gabála*, however, seem simply to have been born of the imagination of its compilers. The magnitude of their task and the fertility of their imagination in completing it are impressive. These mythical genealogies span about fifty-four generations up to the middle of the fifth century A.D. and contain hundreds of names of rulers and other personages.[63]

The Irish genealogists did their work well. Their genealogies were not replete with indications of their spuriousness. With the exceptions noted above, the names in the *Lebor Gabála* are not unusual. There are not an exceptional number of father/son successions. Few long reigns arouse the suspicions of the sceptic. As a result, the 'history' of Ireland as it was represented by the *Lebor Gabála* was accepted by scholars into this century. Only in the last fifty years has it come to be recognized that the *Lebor Gabála* was 'a palpable fabrication' and 'a work of deliberate fiction'.[64]

The Milesians of the *Lebor Gabála* in fact represented the Goidels, the last and most numerous of the Celtic invaders of Ireland. The Goidels invaded Ireland *c.* 50 B.C., more than a thousand years after the genealogical dates.[65] But the greatest falsification of the genealogies —and their greatest success—was the creation of a High Kingship of Ireland based at Tara. Recently it has been demonstrated con-

[62] O'Rahilly, *Early Irish history*, 195–8; Kelleher, 'Pre-Norman genealogies', 146.

[63] For a convenient, if streamlined, presentation of some of the early Irish genealogies, see Stokvis, *Manuel*, II. 233–7, 244, 247, 260–1.

[64] F. J. Byrne, 'The rise of the Uí Néill and the High-Kingship of Ireland', O'Donnell lecture delivered at University College, Dublin, 28 Nov. 1969, 2; O'Rahilly, *Early Irish history*, 193. The first doubts about the *Lebor Gabála* genealogies were expressed by E. Macneill, *Celtic Ireland* (Dublin, 1921), 25–42, and idem, 'The pre-Christian kings of Tara', *Journal of the Royal Society of Antiquaries of Ireland*, 57 (1927), 153–4.

[65] O'Rahilly, *Early Irish history*, 16–17, 194–5.

vincingly that, while a kingship did exist at Tara, any claims that this office was more than localized, at least before the ninth or tenth centuries A.D., are false.[66] The chroniclers thus succeeded in antedating the High Kingship by more than 2,000 years. The reasons for doing this are obvious when the circumstances of the compilation of the *Lebor Gabála* are scrutinized. The authors of the *Lebor Gabála* wrote under the aegis of the Uí Néill dynasties, which had risen from obscure origins in the fifth and sixth centuries to become the most powerful rulers in eastern and northern Ireland.[67] During the seventh to the tenth centuries the kingship at Tara was no more than the over-kingship of the Uí Néill, with the occupants of the office oscillating between the northern (Ailech) and southern (Mide) branches of the dynasty.[68] At no time during this period were the Uí Néill rulers able to claim effective suzerainty over the entire island, although they were unquestionably the most powerful dynasts in Ireland during most of the period. In their efforts to create an effective hegemony over the more than 150 states of the island the Uí Néills sought the aid of the monkish chroniclers. The result of their efforts was the concept of a High Kingship, created long before and in full flower by prestigious invaders. This High Kingship allegedly rotated among the various descendants of the two most important sons of Míl, but from the first century A.D. the list of High Kings was 'heavily weighted' in favour of the putative ancestors of the Uí Néills.[69] On the basis of the *Lebor Gabála* and similar works the Uí Néill could, and did, lay claim to Tara by virtue of ancestral rights instead of conquest, and at the same time argue that this right entailed, *pari passu*, the rule of all Ireland.[70]

The Purānic genealogies share many resemblances to the *Lebor Gabála* and its satellites. The eighteen Purānas or 'old narratives' were mostly composed between the fourth and seventh centuries

[66] D. Binchy, 'The passing of the old order', *Proceedings of the Congress of Celtic Studies* held at Dublin, 6–10 July 1959 (Dublin, 1962), 125–6, 131.

[67] 'The Uí Néill emerge into history like a school of cuttlefish from a large ink cloud of their own manufacture', Kelleher, 'History', 125.

[68] Ibid. 122.

[69] Ibid. 124n.

[70] The above interpretation is based primarily on Kelleher's articles because this accords better with what we know of the provenience and purpose of such genealogies elsewhere. Byrne, 'Rise', regards the early annalists and genealogists as having been somewhat less subject to Uí Néill influence. This difference of interpretation applies more to the existence of the High Kingship in the sixth and seventh centuries than to the pre-Patrician genealogies which both Kelleher and Byrne regards as fabrications.

A.D.[71] They dealt with several aspects of the Indian past, including accounts of the dynasties of the *kaliyuga* age, which traditionally began in 3102 B.C. The major dynasties of this period were divided into the five Solar and eight Lunar lines. The Solar dynasties were held to be descended from a son of Manu Vaivaśvata, while the Lunar dynasties claimed a grandson of Manu as their progenitor.[72] Other less important and shorter-lived dynasties were founded by Manu's nine other sons.[73] The Solar and Lunar dynasties, by Purānic reckoning, ruled northern India from *c.* 3102 B.C. up to the time the Purānas themselves were composed, but this discussion is limited to those dynasties alleged to have ruled in pre-Buddha times.

The longest kinglist (and genealogy?) contained 126 names down to the time of Buddha. Other dynasties of allegedly coeval origin, however, contained many fewer names.[74] The Bhārata war is the cardinal event in the Purānic accounts of this period. Interpretations of the materials in the various Purānas have placed the date of this war at various times between 2449 B.C. and the ninth century B.C.[75] The variant Purānic accounts have also allowed scholars, in their efforts to claim a greater antiquity for Hindu civilization, to equate Chandragupta Gupta (*c.* A.D. 320) with the Sandrocottos of the Greek records (i.e. Chandragupta Maurya, *c.* 325 B.C.) and concomitantly to push all other events of Indian history further back.[76] The Purānas are weak in their consistencies as well as in their inconsistencies, for all of them ascribed very extended patterns of father/son successions to their dynasties.

The effort to create some kind of order from this chaos began with the researches of F. E. Pargiter. Pargiter's efforts to reduce the wildly

[71] R. C. Majumdar *et al.* (eds.), *History and Culture of the Indian People*, III, *The Classical Age* (Delhi, 1954), 291–2, 298; R. Thapar, *A history of India* (Harmondsworth, 1966), I. 163.

[72] D. K. Ganguly, 'The Purānas and their bearing on the early Indian dynasties' in D. C. Sircar (ed.), *Bhārata war and Purānic genealogies* (Calcutta, 1930), 122–4.

[73] Ibid. 128–30, 134–6; F. E. Pargiter, *Ancient Indian historical tradition* (London, 1922), *passim.*

[74] D. C. Sircar, 'Nature of the Purānic genealogies' in idem (ed.), *Bhārata war*, 106–8. For Pargiter's explanation of some of these discrepancies, see his 'Ancient Indian genealogies and chronology', 9–11.

[75] D. C. Sircar, 'The myth of the Great Bhārata war' in idem, *Bhārata war*, 20–5; R. C. Majumdar, 'The Bhārata war' in ibid. 12–17. The earlier date is D. R. Mankad, *Purānic chronology* (Anand, 1951), passim; the latest date is that of H. Raychaudhuri, *Political history of ancient India from the accession of Parikshit to the coronation of Bimbisara* (Calcutta, 1927), 9–10.

[76] Mankad, *Purānic chronology*, 243–306.

variant Purānic accounts to a coherent whole displayed both erudition and perseverance, but was marked by reasoning that was sometimes ingenuous but more often ingenious.[77] The effect of Pargiter's work on subsequent Indian historiography has recently been assessed in the following terms:

> Pargiter's unfortunate attempt at making sense of the Puranas has produced an aftermath of wasted effort in the forms of several monographs in which able Indian scholars ingeniously juggle with king-lists, the names in which have little more historical validity than those of the legendary pre-Saxon kings recorded in mediaeval English chornicles.[78]

Indeed, several efforts in the past few years have assumed or argued the historical accuracy of the Purānic kinglists.[79] And what seems to be the present position of most Indian historians was expressed by a participant in a recent Seminar at the University of Calcutta on the Bhārata war and Purānic genealogies, when he asserted that 'it is absurd to suppose that the elaborate royal genealogies were all merely figments of imagination or a tissue of falsehood'.[80]

In sum, then, it may fairly be said that the Purānic genealogies and their portrayal of pre-Buddha India, despite all their artificial aspects, are still widely accepted by many scholars. The reasons why this is so are readily apparent. The Purānic genealogies provide an attractive framework for projecting Indian political civilization a full 2,500 years further back than other evidence will allow, at least for the geographical areas the Purānas describe. This is a fruit that Indian historical nationalism can scarcely be faulted for plucking.

[77] These include, in addition to the works already cited: 'Viśvāmitra and Vasiṣṭha', *JRAS* (1913), 885–904; 'Earliest Indian traditional "history",' *JRAS* (1914), 267–95; 'Viśvāmitra, Vasiṣṭha, Harīscandra and Sunahśepa', *JRAS* (1917), 37–67; 'Ancient Indian genealogies: are they trustworthy?' in Bhandarkar Oriental Research Institute (ed.), *Commemorative essays presented to Sir Ramkrishna Gopal Bhandarkar* (Poona 1917), 107–13; 'The northern Pañcāla dynasty', *JRAS* (1918), 229–48; 'Sagara and the Haihayas, Vasiṣṭha and Aurva', *JRAS* (1919), 353–67; *The Puranic text of the dynasties of the Kali age* (London, 1913).

[78] A. L. Basham, 'Modern historians of ancient India' in Philips, *Historians*, 291.

[79] e.g. *HCIP*, Vol. 1, *The Vedic age* (London, 1951); R. M. Smith, 'On the ancient chronology of India', *JAOS* 77 (1957), 116–29, 266–79; V. Pathak, *History of Kośala up to the rise of the Mauryas* (Delhi, 1963), 84–114 *passim*; Y. Mishra, *Early history of Vaiśālī* (Delhi, 1962), 4–7 *passim*.

[80] Ganguly, 'Purānas', 128. Of the participants in this only D. C. Sircar regarded the Bhārata war as legendary and the Purānic genealogies as worthless historical documents.

There are, of course, numerous other examples of this kind of genealogical fabrication, although none of them is as impressive as the Irish and Purānic genealogies. The Briton kings of Geoffrey of Monmouth, alluded to by Basham, are obvious examples. So, too, are the Danish, Norse, and Swedish genealogies in the early Scandinavian chronicles, and the Scottish rulers from 330 B.C. so fully described by Boece and Buchanan.[81]

Significantly, even those cases of fabrication which seem so flagrant retrospectively were long accepted as being fact. Too often the canons of historical criticism have been subordinated to the interests of national or ethnic pride. Less obvious cases of this kind of fabrication undoubtedly lie undiscovered. Many of them are probably undiscoverable, but this does not exonerate the historian from an investigation duly based on a healthy dose of scepticism.

IV MISCELLANEOUS AND MINOR CHRONOLOGICAL DISTORTIONS

In addition to the various factors which operate to telescope or lengthen the perceived past, there are two other facets of oral tradition which deserve mention, even though their chronological implications are usually minimal. These are the 'Moses-in-the-bulrushes' theme and the lack of multiple reigns remembered in oral tradition.

The Moses-in-the-bulrushes theme involves what is often called the 'culture hero'. The culture hero, like Moses, appears at a critical stage in a society's development as a kind of *deus ex machina*. Traditional accounts of culture heroes usually associate him with earlier periods of dynasties and explain his rather sudden appearance in a limited number of ways. Sometimes they speak of a period during which, for stereotyped reasons, his identity was hidden from all but a select few. In African traditions it has been more common to identify the hero as a son of a previous ruler sired when that ruler was *en voyage* in a neighbouring country. In either case the Moses returns in

[81] For the legendary Danish kings, see Saxo Grammaticus, *The first nine books of the Danish History of Saxo Grammaticus*, ed. O. Elton (London, 1893), cviii-cxv, 414–17; for legendary early Norse rulers, see H. H. Howorth, 'Harald Fairhair and his ancestors', *Saga-Book of the Viking Society*, 9 (1914/18), 10–15; for the Yngling dynasty in Sweden, Snorri Sturluson (ed. L. Hollander), *Heimskringla* (Austin, Texas, 1964), 14–44; for the Scottish rulers, see Buchanan, *History*, I. 153–231, whose account was based on Hector Boece's *Scotorum Historiae*, discussed in Chapter III. Some of the names in the Scandinavian king-lists are gods, heroes, and eponyms, but the majority seem to be outright fabrications.

due course, assisted by a felicitous combination of circumstances, to reclaim his patrimony and the dynasty carries on. This motif is too familiar, and its incidence too widespread, to require a detailed description.[82] What concerns us here are the implications the Moses-in-the-bulrushes theme has for chronology. This involves the effort to fathom the length of the period that the hero was 'lost' or 'in exile'. This in turn requires an investigation of what this penumbral period can mean in various circumstances.

The appearance of a culture hero early in a kinglist often can be interpreted as a sign of the advent of historicity. The traditional chronology of the Korean kingdom of Paekche is a case in point. The Korean chronicles assigned a date of 18 B.C. for the foundation of the state and described the first ruler as a son of the first ruler of Koguryo, a state to the north.[83] These chronicles are all of late provenience, some as late as the twelfth century.[84] An analysis of contemporaneous Chinese annals makes it clear that as late as the middle of the third century A.D. Paekche was 'no more than one of a great number of similar tribal units' in the area.[85] The same records show that some time in the next century Paekche coalesced into a state.

There were two Piryus in the traditional chronology of Paekche. One was identified as the non-reigning older brother of the first king of the state and the other was listed as the eleventh ruler of the dynasty and assigned the dates 304–44. That is, he was remembered as ruling at precisely the time when the kingdom actually came into existence. Significantly, the chronicles also relate that this Piryu did not directly succeed his father, but 'lived long [in fact 70 years] amongst the people.'[86] Gardiner regards this Piryu as the only Piryu in Paekche history and 'the real rounder' of the state.[87] The chroniclers evidently knew this, or at least were aware that this Piryu had played an

[82] For a survey of the Moses-in-the-bulrushes theme in the ancient world see O. Rank, *The myth of the birth of the hero and other writings*, ed. P. Freund (New York, 1964), 14–64.

[83] K. H. J. Gardiner, 'Some problems concerning the foundation of Paeckche', *Archiv Orientálni*, 37 (1969), 577. Gardiner's analysis is a superior one, which identifies all the chronological distortions of early Paekche history in the Korean chronicles and explains their purposes.

[84] Ibid. 562. For one of the most important of those chronicles, see Gardiner, 'The Samguk-sagi and its sources', *Papers on Far Eastern History*, 2 (Sept. 1970), 1–34.

[85] Gardiner, 'Some problems', 565.

[86] Ibid. 584n.

[87] Ibid. 586.

important role in the formative period of Paekche history. But they could not achieve the desired chronology by accepting this fact straightforwardly. Instead they created a duplicate Piryu, whom they associated with a fictitious founder of the kingdom. In addition they doubled some other names as well, created further names, and assigned improbably long reigns and genealogical filiations to the early legendary rulers. They were thereby able to add another 350 years to the duration of the state.[88] In order to accommodate both Piryus the chroniclers adopted the expedient of having the second Piryu disappear from public view for a long period and then return to 'reclaim' his ancestral throne. In this way he caricatured what he may well have done as the founder of the state. In the Paekche case the penumbral period of 'exile' represented the entire pre-polity period; in the traditional chronology this amounted to, as noted, about three and a half centuries.

We are fortunate that the traditional history of Paekche has been analysed so thoroughly. This kind of analysis has also been applied to few African dynasties. Kimera, the third *kabaka* of Buganda, at least in Ganda traditions, is remembered as returning from Bunyoro to succeed his grandfather.[89] Bunyoro traditions dispute this and claim that Kimera was the twin brother of the first *mukama* of Bunyoro sent to rule Buganda in subordination to Bunyoro. Buganda traditions have attempted to dispute this early coevality with Bunyoro by pushing their own independent history a few generations further back.[90]

The appearance of a culture hero early in a dynasty may, then, often indicate the actual founder of the dynasty. When he appears at a later point in the kinglist it may indicate a change in dynasty or the end of an interregnal period. A slight variation of the classic Moses theme occurs in the traditional accounts of Mulondo, the ninth

[88] Gardiner, 573–9. A good discussion of the appearance of what seems to have been a culture hero in Onitsha history is in R.N. Henderson, *The king in every man* (New Haven, Conn., 1972), 448–51, 468–9. See also R. C. C. Law, 'The Oyo empire: the history of a Yoruba state, principally in the period *c.* 1600 to *c.* 1836', Ph.D. thesis, University of Birmingham, 1971, for a discussion of the *alafin* Ofinran.

[89] J. Roscoe, *The Baganda: an account of their native customs and belief* (London, 1911), 215–16.

[90] M. Southwold, 'The history of a history: royal succession in Buganda' in I. M. Lewis (ed.), *History and social anthropology* (London, 1968), 143. Bunyoro traditions call Kimera (or Kato) the twin brother of the first *mukama* of Bunyoro, J. Beattie, *The Nyoro state* (London, 1971), 54.

kabaka of Buganda. Mulondo's father was killed in battle with the Banyoro, and Mulondo succeeded as an infant—a very unusual circumstance in Buganda.[91] The suspicion of a possible change of dynasty at this point is reinforced by the simultaneous introduction of a new succession pattern. After the reign of Mulondo fraternal succession became the norm and remained so for several generations, but before Mulondo's reign no brother was remembered as succeeding to the throne.[92] Similarly, at least two rulers of Rwanda are alleged to have returned from outside the kingdom to claim the throne—an almost certain indication of a dynastic change.[93] This theme seems to have been a common one in the interlacustrine area. Kyebambe I of Bunyoro allegedly returned from Nkore to succeed his aunt and carry on the dynasty.[94]

The chronological implications of such dynastic changes may be several. First, of course, there may be none at all. A dynastic change can occur and often has occurred in the same way as a more regular succession. On the other hand a change of dynasty can result in the gain of a generation if the first ruler of the new dynasty is disguised as the son of his predecessor. For it is certainly as likely that he was a generational contemporary of the ruler he succeeded.[95] Or, a dynastic change could mean, as it often has, the reasserting of independence after a period of foreign rule under a new, indigenous dynasty which fortifies its new positon by claiming relationship with the previous local dynasty. Under these circumstances the interregnum would

[91] Roscoe, *Baganda*, 217–18.

[92] Southwold, 'Royal succession', 139, rejects this possibility. In doing so he assumes that, if Mulondo represented a new dynasty it was a Bunyoro dynasty and, since fraternal succession was not known to be common in Bunyoro, it seems unlikely that the introduction of Bunyoro rule would result in fraternal succession in Buganda. Although Mulondo's father was killed in fighting the Banyoro, it is not necessary to assume that any new dynasty that might have succeeded in Buganda was in fact Nyoro. It could have been Ganda. Again, it may be presumptuous to argue that fraternal succession was rare in Bunyoro, given the admitted policy of Bunyoro traditions to excise *abakama* who ruled less than nine years. This is not to argue that Mulondo necessarily represented a new dynasty, but only to note that the objections to such an interpretation are not unanswerable.

[93] J. Vansina, *L'Évolution du royaume Rwanda des origines à 1900* (Brussels, 1962), 49–50, 51. For yet another example in Rwanda, see A. Kagame, *Un Abrégé de l'ethno-histoire du Rwanda* (Butare, 1972), 170–1.

[94] K. W., 'The kings of Bunyoro-Kitara', *UJ* 4 (1936), 83.

[95] In this regard I should point out that, when calculating generational averages in Chapter IV, I have arbitrarily assumed that a dynastic change represents one half-generation.

probably be of undeterminable duration, unless some strong synchronisms or absolute dates are available for both the last rulers of the old dynasty and the early rulers of the new one. Unfortunately, this last alternative to explain a Moses-in-the-bulrushes account in a tradition seems at least as likely as any of the others. New dynasties usually attempt to identify themselves genealogically with their predecessors. What better way to do so than to claim their founders as lost or exiled sons of earlier rulers?

The final weakness of the chronological content of oral tradition to be considered here is the almost total lack of multiple reigns remembered in tradition. This is scarcely surprising since a multiple reign is precisely the kind of detail that oral tradition cannot be expected to cope with or even to be concerned with. Multiple reigns are not common in any society. A tabulation of 328 dynasties drawn from the larger sample discussed in Chapter IV indicates an aggregate incidence of one multiple reign per 56 successions. This ratio increased in societies where succession to the throne is ill defined or eligibility broad, or where a group of small, weak states is dominated by a few large ones. The interlacustrine area satisfies both these requirements. It would therefore be reasonable to expect an incidence of multiple reigns somewhat greater than 1:56, but quite the opposite is true. A survey of 311 reigns in 21 states revealed only one multiple reign, and even that was a case of abdication and reaccession.

Later traditional accounts of the Wolof state of Waalo illustrate the difficulty traditional accounts have in grappling with the concept of multiple reigns. French records show that two *braks* alternated on the throne of Waalo from 1827 to 1840 in the following manner:

1827–30 Fara Penda Adam Sal (1)
1830–2 Kherfi Khari Daaro (1)
1832–3 Fara Penda Adam Sal (2)
1833–5 Kherfi Khari Daaro (2)
1835–40 Fara Penda Adam Sal (3)[96]

Compare this with the various traditional accounts of the same sequence:

(*a*) 1823–33 Fara Penda Adam Sal (1)
1833–6 Kherfi Khari Daaro (1)
1836–40 Fara Penda Adam Sal (2)[97]

[96] Barry, *Le Royaume du Waalo*, 265–87, 335.

[97] A. Wade, 'Chronique du Wâlo sénégalais', 494–5. This corrects the list in ibid. 466, which takes no account of Kherfi Khari Daaro's reign as an intrusion.

(*b*) 1827–30 Kherfi Khari Daaro
1830–40 Fara Penda Adam Sal[98]

(*c*) 1827–30 Fara Penda Adam Sal (1)
1830–3 Kherfi Khari Daaro
1833–40 Fara Penda Adam Sal[99]

Yoro Dyaw, who wrote about fifty years after these reigns and whose father had participated in the civil wars at a high level, recorded that Fara Penda Adam Sal's reign was interrupted only once for three years by Kherfi Khari Daaro.[1]

Thus none of the traditional accounts was correct, although none was wildly aberrant either. The version in Azan is the most nearly accurate, perhaps because it was the earliest collected and because Azan probably used French colonial records. Probably the greatest distortion that can occur when oral tradition attempts to handle multiple reigns is the jumbling of the sequence of reigns. But the difficulty traditional accounts have in handling multiple reigns illustrates in a very concrete way their limitations in dealing with the duration of the past in any detailed or objective manner.

This chapter has attempted to illustrate the various ways in which traditional accounts tend to manipulate or forget the duration of their perceived past. The emphasis has been on the mechanisms through which this distortion occurs.[2] The necessity for distortion and the

[98] F. Brigaud, *Histoire traditionnelle du Sénégal* (Saint-Louis, 1962), 72, which is based on the list of Samba Ndienne Bara Gaye.

[99] H. Azan, 'Notice sur le Oualo', *Revue Maritime et Coloniale*, 10 (1864), 356–60.

[1] R. Rousseau, 'Le Sénégal d'autrefois: une étude sur le Oualo', *Bulletin de la Comité des Études Historiques et Scientifiques de l'Afrique Occidentale Française* (1929), 152–6.

[2] In concentrating on internal mechanisms of distortion I have neglected the importance of the mechanisms of transmission, For instance, the question of consensual accounts may be important here. If we concede Horton's argument that 'a confession of ignorance' is 'intolerable' in a traditional society then we must consider the ramifications of consensual accounts in which there is proportionately more information to assimilate in a 'final' version. Horton, 'African traditional thought', 173. For instance one of the longest lists of Bemba *citimukulus* was recorded 'before an Assembly of the Bemba', Roberts, 'Chronology of the Bemba', 223. Presumably the probability of feedback (which is discussed in Chapter III) is likewise increased with consensual accounts. Some historians of African traditional materials such as Ogot and Webster have relied heavily on consensual accounts and it may prove fruitful to compare such work with data collected from individual informants. It may be that in some cases the whole is greater than the sum of the parts.

ability to effect it will be discussed at greater length in Chapter III. It will not escape the reader's attention that this discussion has been limited to oral tradition's conception of the duration and to a lesser extent the sequence of events in the more remote past. The strengths and weaknesses of oral traditional accounts for other aspects of the past have been rigorously excluded from this analysis.

CHAPTER II

The Problem of Extended Father/Son Succession

> Thus far I have spoken on the authority of the Egyptians and their priests . . . They led me into the inner sanctuary . . . and showed me a multitude of colossal statues, in wood, which they counted up, and found to amount to the exact number they had said . . . As they showed me the figures and reckoned them up, they assured me that each was the son of the one preceding him, and this they repeated throughout the whole line . . . and the number of them was 345.[1]

THE problem of extended (defined for our purposes as ten or more consecutive) father/son succession to royal office in traditional accounts deserves more extensive attention. The tendency to assume reflexively that a ruler is the son of his predecessor is nearly universal.[2] This assumption is not confined to the traditional accounts themselves, but has often been provided gratuitously by investigators dealing with them. It is not difficult to understand why this happens. Viewed idiosyncratically, an extended father/son succession pattern may not seem unusual. After all, it is the norm in most western societies today. As a result, many genealogies which had originally laid claim to being no more than ascendant genealogies have been transformed into kinglists.[3] Conversely, however, many kinglists have been constructed into ascendant genealogies simply because this seemed the natural thing to do. Whichever eventuality occurred, it is apparent that the chronological implications are profound.

[1] Herodotus, II. 142–3. For a discussion of this list and Herodotus' sources, see W. A. Heidel, 'Hecataeus and the Egyptian priests in Herodotus, book II', *Memoirs of the American Academy of Arts and Sciences*, 18 (1935), 71–110.

[2] One exception was Isaac Newton, who, when calculating his ancient chronologies and establishing average regnal lengths, noted that '. . . the Reigns of Kings are still shorter [than generations], because Kings are succeeded not only by the eldest son, but sometimes by their brothers, and sometimes they are slain or deposed . . .', *Chronology*, 54.

[3] See particularly the Indian cases cited below.

Fortunately, the extended father/son succession pattern is the chronological distortion most amenable to quantitative analysis. In order to determine the documented incidence of extended father/son successions, I surveyed 660 dynasties incorporating a total of 10,236 successions, including multiple reigns and usurpers. As far as can be determined, filial succession was the ideal or at least the preferred practice in nearly all of these dynasties. It also was the most common. It was arbitrarily decided to define 'extended' as ten or more consecutive father-to-son successions.[4] Dynasties of fewer than ten successions were excluded from this tabulation if all the successions within the dynasty were father/son but, for various reasons, excluding lack of filial heirs, the dynasty did not run to ten generations. On this basis the following examples of extended father/son succession were determined:

TABLE 1

Documented Extended Father/Son Successions

			Average Generation Length
Lippe[-Detmold]	15 successions	1196–1650[5]	30·3
Nassau-Weilburg	13 successions	1472–1866[6]	30·3
Nguyen of Hué	12 successions	1485–1777[7]	24·4
Ampurias	11 successions	931–1313[8]	34·9
France	11 successions	996–1316[9]	29·1
Brandenburg-Prussia	11 successions	1486–1786[10]	27·3
Foix	10 successions	1070–1391[11]	32·1
Ahoms of Assam	10 successions	1407–1644[12]	23·7
Denmark	10 successions	1534–1839[13]	30·5

[4] The number of nine consecutive father/son successions was about the same as the number of tens. Below nine, however, the incidence increased rapidly.

[5] O. Weerth, 'Zur Genealogie des lippischen Fürstenhauses', *Mitteilungen aus der lippischen Geschichte und Landeskunde*, 6 (1908), 81–98; W. Karl, Prinz von Isenburg, *Stammtafeln zur europäischen Staaten* (2 vols., Berlin, 1936–7), I. 143b–5; A. Fluviá y Escorsa, 'Genealogia de las casas soberanas', *Hidalguía*, 87 (1968), 288; 88 (1968), 417–22.

[6] A. W. E. Dek, *Genealogie van het vorstenhuis Nassau* (Zalbommel, 1970), 25–34, 48–55.

[7] Ton Thât Hân, 'Généalogie des Nguyen avant Gia-Long', *Bulletin de l'Association des Amis de Vieux-Hué*, 7 (1920), 295–328; L. Cadière, 'Tableau chronologique des dynasties Annamites', *BEFEO* 5 (1905), 110–17; R. Orband, 'Les Tombeaux des Nguyen', *BEFEO*, 14 (1914), pt. 7, 1–10.

[8] S. Sobreques i Vidal, *Els barons de Catalunya* (Barcelona, 1957), 13–21, 83–95; *Diccionari Biografic* (3 vols., Barcelona, 1969), II. 89.

Footnotes continued on opposite page.

The Ahom dynasty of Assam is the only doubtful case on this list. There the nature of the sources, and perhaps the low generational average as well, cast some doubt.[14] It is possible, however, that one or two of the other examples might prove to be less lineal than present evidence indicates.

In this regard it should be noted that in a previous analysis of extended father/son successions I erroneously included the First Dynasty of Babylon (*c.* 1894–1695 B.C.) and the counts of Brienne from *c.* 1020 to 1356.[15] In fact Brienne had only six consecutive father/son successions from *c.* 1090 to 1261. The earlier filiations have been proved doubtful and a new collateral succession has been discovered.[16] The case of the First Dynasty of Babylon is more complex. In the discussion of synchronisms the probability of an interregnum between the first two rulers of this dynasty was noted.[17] This probability is reinforced by the fact that none of the later genealogies of the dynasty provides any filiation between these two rulers.[18] The likelihood of an interregnal period, together with the fact that the filiations of all subsequent rulers is provided by the epigraphic sources for the dynasty, suggest that Sumulael, the second ruler of the dynasty was not the son of his predecessor even though several scholars have assumed a father/son relationship for them.[19] The inclusion of these two succession patterns in this earlier analysis demonstrates

---

[9] G. Sirjean, *Encyclopédie généalogique des maisons souveraines du monde* (1 vol. to date, Paris, 1959), I, cahier 3; J.-L.-A. Calmette, *Le Réveil capétien* (Paris, 1948), *passim.*

[10] Isenburg, *Stammtafeln*, I. 61–3.

[11] Stokvis, *Manuel*, II. 125; J. Juillet, 'Esquisse généalogique de la maison de Foix', *Bulletin de la Société ariégeoise des sciences, lettres et arts*, 21 (1965), 119–20.

[12] E. A. Gait, *A history of Assam* (3rd rev. ed., Calcutta, 1963), 85–125; N. N. Acharyya, *The history of mediaeval Assam* (Gauhati, 1966), 82–107.

[13] P. Lauring, *Reges Daniae: Danske kongen på mønter og medaljer* (Copenhagen, 1961), 31–67.

[14] Gait, *History*, 105–7, speaks of the confused and conflicting accounts in the chronicles for part of this period.

[15] D. P. Henige, 'Oral tradition and chronology', *JAH* 12 (1971), 378.

[16] Stokvis, *Manuel*, III. xi.

[17] See above, pp. 19–20.

[18] See D. O. Edzard, *Die 'Zweite Zwischenzeit' Babyloniens* (Wiesbaden, 1957), 122; Finkelstein, 'Genealogy', 103; Pritchard, *ANET* 271; Lewy, 'Assyria', 30–1; F. Cornelius, 'Chronology', 102.

[19] e.g. H. Frankfort *et al.*, *The Gimilsin Temple and the Palace of the Rulers at Tell Asmar* (Chicago, 1940), 124, and the latest survey of the Ancient Near East, Hallo and Simpson, *The ancient Near East: a history*, 100.

all too amply that the probability of father/son relationship can beguile even the most sceptical observer.

At least four other possible cases of extended father/son succession have been excluded from the present list. These are the ten rulers of Bithynia from *c.* 435 to 74 B.C., the ten rulers of Assyria from 971 to 773 B.C., the rulers of Judah, and the first thirteen Ottoman Sultans, who ruled from *c.* 1290 to 1603.

The Assyrian rulers were rejected principally because the genealogical evidence does not fit the known chronology. These Assyrian kings ruled from 971 to 773 B.C. This entails either accepting an average generational length of only 19·8 years over a ten-generation span, or postulating one or more collateral successions during the period. There are other instances, earlier in the Assyrian King List, where supplementary epigraphic evidence has shown the genealogies of the King List to be incorrect.[20] There is at present no direct evidence to support the suggestion of collateral succession during this period, but the possibility seems strong enough to justify omitting this succession of rulers from Table 1.[21]

To include the Bithynian kings would require accepting a father/son relationship between the first two rulers. This relationship has, in fact, often been assumed.[22] But Memnon, the classical historian who is our only source for this period of Bithynian history, stated only that 'when he [Doedalsus, the first known Bithynian ruler] died, Boteiras succeeded'.[23] Memnon, however, carefully called each of the later

[20] Poebel, 'Khorsabad', *JNES* 1 (1942), 483–4; 58–62, 68, 70, 88–9. For the period from Adasi to Aššur-nadin-ahhe II (*c.* 1700–1393) collateral succession was common but often disguised as father/son succession in the Assyrian King List. See B. Landsberger, 'Assyrische Königsliste und "Dunkles Zeitalter" ', *JCS* 8 (1954), 42–5. Landsberger argues that the number of father-to-son successions during this period should be reduced from the fifteen shown in the King List to only nine.

[21] A. T. Olmstead, *A history of Assyria* (New York, 1923), 74, called this sequence 'a group which for length of rule and for ability to transmit the succession without break has no rival'. Appropriately, Olmstead entitled the chapter dealing with these rulers 'Dark Centuries', reflecting the relative dearth of materials for the period. Miller, *Sicilian colony dates*, 143n., suggests that perhaps some rulers were omitted in this part of the King List. Collateral succession during the period is certainly likely, but here collateral succession seems more likely to have occurred among the rulers already included in the Lists.

[22] F. Sévin, 'Recherches sur les rois de Bithynie', *Mémoires de littérature tirés des registres de l'Académie des Inscriptions et Belles-Lettres*, 12 (1740), 336, and D. Magie, *Roman rule in Asia Minor* (2 vols., Princeton, N.J., 1950), I. 311.

[23] Memnon, xx, in Müller, *Fragmenta*, III. 536–7.

rulers the son of his predecessor.[24] In addition, the reigns of these first four rulers covered $156 + x$ years, since Doedalsus was already ruling in 435 B.C. and his third successor died in 279 B.C.[25] This is not an impossible four-generation/four-ruler span, but it would be highly exceptional. It suggests that collateral rulers or an interregnal period may have been omitted in later accounts.

The succession in the kingdom of Judah is often represented as having been perfectly lineal. Doing so necessitates regarding Athaliah (841–835 B.C.) only as Regent, whereas she was a reigning Queen.[26] In addition, the Biblical account of Joash, who succeeded Athaliah and was regarded as the son of her predecessor, is a typical Moses-in-the-bulrushes story.[27] The story of Joash in any case conformed to the interest of the author(s) of Chronicles to maintain the image of an unbroken and direct Davidic descent for the rulers of Judah.[28]

The Ottoman Sultans from *c.* 1290 to 1603 succeeded one another in a direct father/son succession, but with two minor deviations. There was a period of collegial rule from 1402 to 1413 when the sons of Bayazid I divided the empire and fought among themselves until only one son remained. Later (1444 and 1446) there were two instances of abdication and reaccession.[29] Admittedly these were only minor blemishes on the serene aspect of father/son succession, but since we are concerned with a pattern which traditional accounts almost always present as quite unblemished, it is desirable that the Ottoman example be excluded.

[24] Ibid. 537.

[25] J. Toepffer, 'Astakos', *Hermes*, 31 (1896), 135.

[26] Poebel, 'Khorsabad', 271n., was willing to ignore both the reign of Athaliah and the brief reign of Jehoahaz (609) in order to show a very extended father/son succession. Similarly, J. A. Montgomery, *A critical and exegetical commentary on the Books of Kings* (New York, 1951), 426–7, dated Joash's reign from the death of his father. For Athalian as reigning Queen for six years, see E. R. Thiele, *The mysterious numbers of the Hebrew kings* (Grand Rapids, Mich., 1965), 71, and J. Gray, *I and II Kings: a commentary* (London, 1964), 64–5, 680–2. For Jehoahaz, see ibid. 680–2. The Biblical account is certainly ambiguous. It speaks of Jehoahaz' rule, then states that his brother and successor, Jehoaichin, ruled 'in the stead of his father', 2 Kings 23: 30–4.

[27] 2 Kings 11: 1–4, 2 Chronicles 22: 11–12, 23: 1.

[28] See M. D. Johnson, *The purpose of the Biblical genealogies with special reference to the setting of the genealogy of Jesus* (Cambridge, 1969), 74–6, 81–2; D. N. Freedman, 'The chronicler's purpose', *Catholic Biblical Quarterly*, 23 (1961), 436–42; W. F. Stinespring, 'Eschatology in Chronicles', *Journal of Biblical Literature*, 80 (1961), 211.

[29] A. D. Alderson, *The structure of the Ottoman Dynasty* (Oxford, 1956), 54–8.

We have, then, a reasonably large body of documented data available for an analysis of the problem of extended father/son succession. These data strongly suggest that the probability of more than eight or nine such successions is extremely low.[30] This was not a random sample, but a comprehensive survey of the available universe of such successions.[31] Nor are the results particularly surprising. Even the most rigidly narrow succession systems, operating close to the ideal, must face, over a period of ten generations, a number of contingencies which will erode and perhaps shatter its symmetry.[32]

Thus, although it is obvious that every son has had a father, it seems much less obvious that not every individual need have had a son. A ruler may die before reaching the age of procreation, or, if he lives longer, he may still produce no sons. Polygyny will reduce this latter possibility, but it cannot eliminate it completely, since it is the male who determines the sex of the child.[33]

Surprisingly few chronicles have echoed an account of the last Viscount of Dax—'he left several daughters when he died, but no son'.[34] In this case the dynasty ended, and the Viscounty fell to Navarre. Medieval and early modern Europe was often kept in turmoil because rulers of desirable territories were constantly dying without male progeny, and so distant heirs of divers kinds fought over the estate. Serial monogamy was common in the noble houses of

[30] It is perhaps significant that Molly Miller, arguing from demographic evidence, has recently come to the same conclusion. She feels that it should be a 'guiding rule that any alleged run of more than ten inheritances without collaterals is either an ithagenic [ascendant] abstract from the complete [regnal] genealogy, or a fiction, or both', *Sicilian colony dates*, 143. For the bases of her conclusions, see ibid. 117–61.

[31] One group of successions omitted from this analysis is the British peerage. A few extended father/son successions occurred there but the narrowly lineal succession practices also resulted in a high rate of extinction among the peerage. See J. B. Burke, *Vicissitudes of families*, 3rd Ser. (2nd ed., London, 1863), 7–13; R. J. Beevor, 'Distinction and extinction', *Genealogist's Magazine*, 4 (1928), 59–62; S. P. Vivian, 'Some statistical aspects of genealogy', *Genealogist's Magazine*, 8 (1934), 482–9.

[32] A point made by Goody, *Succession*, 27. Elsewhere Goody discusses in greater detail the intrinsic difficulties in maintaining vertical (i.e. father/son) succession, Goody, 'Strategies of heirship', *Comparative Studies in Society and History*, 15 (1973), 3–20.

[33] That is, the *y* chromosome, necessary to conceive a male child, is transmitted only by the sperm, and a small percentage of males are not capable of transmitting a *y* chromosome. The lack of quantitative research done in this area and the possible differing effects between gene pools make it inappropriate to do more than indicate the existence of the problem.

[34] J. Jaurgain, *La Vasconie* (2 vols., Pau, 1898–1902), II. 58.

Europe, but it failed to provide a total solution to this problem. That polygyny itself cannot necessarily succeed in producing male heirs is strikingly apparent from the discussion of the Native States of India below.

Levirate marriage and classificatory kinship can mitigate these problems, but these institutions cannot cope with other threats to the serenity of the father/son succession. The most important of these is collateral ambition and usurpation. Succession systems which maintain the ideal that a son is the proper heir deprecate the succession of a collateral when a son is available. It seems unnecessary to add that this has had little effect in preventing such collaterals from seizing power whenever opportunity and ambition combined to make it possible. If the collateral ultimately proved successful, his predecessor might be forgotten; if he failed, he himself would be forgotten. Collateral suppression will be discussed more extensively below.

Ten generations will, under normal circumstances, span about three centuries. During such a period of time a polity will probably engage in several wars. Some of these wars will be won, others lost. Lost wars may result in a period of foreign rule which in turn may entail the temporary displacement of the ruling line by an amenable collateral or by an agent of the victorious power. Finally, ambiguous or changing modes of succession may result in power struggles and multiple reigns. These and other, less important, factors operate to erode the serene and undisturbed father/son or one ruler per generation succession pattern.

A study of the large number of documented cases outlined above reveals that their cumulative effect has been remarkably successful in preventing extended father/son succession. When one begins to examine traditional genealogies and kinglists, however, one discovers a remarkable increase in both the incidence of extended father/son successions and in their generational duration. Obviously, this is a most important problem because it can exert profound influence on the inferred time depth of a society. Regrettably, this pattern in traditional accounts has not often been recognized as anomalous, either by investigators of the societies who have adopted these patterns or by the societies themselves.[35] Nor have ascendant genealogies often

[35] Exceptions include Macneill, 'Pre-Christian kings of Tara', 154; Cohen 'Bornu King Lists', 76; A. L. Basham, 'The average length of the reign and generation in ancient India' in idem, *Studies in Indian History and Culture* (Calcutta, 1964), 81–3.

been recognized for what they usually are—simple legitimizing ancestral documents and not kinglists at all.[36] Much futile argumentation and naïve chronology have resulted. It is not possible to do more than indicate briefly here the widespread incidence and stereotyped nature of traditional father/son succession patterns and their interpretation. But a detailed and extended discussion of two of the most important areas of its occurrence will illustrate more clearly both the nature of this problem and the response to it.

After the Sepoy Mutiny of 1857 those rulers of Indian states who had supported the British Government were rewarded with *sanads* defining their relationship to the Government of India. These *sanads* recognized, *inter alia*, the right of adoption to the *gadi* (throne). It was recorded that the granting of the right of adoption was received 'with unrestrained rejoicing in every court'.[37] During the decade before the Mutiny no fewer than five Indian states had been absorbed into British India under the doctrine of lapse, that is, because there were no direct male heirs to these *gadis*.[38]

The response of the Indian princes to these *sanads* was appropriate; they correctly understood the implications of the right of adoption; it ensured the preservation of many of their states. Between 1857 and 1947 at least seventy Indian states found it necessary to adopt to the *gadi* in order to preserve their ruling lines.[39] Some of these found

[36] On this matter, see the discussion of the reconstruction of early Indian dynasties' from epigraphic evidence below.

[37] T. R. Metcalf, *The aftermath of revolt: India, 1857–70* (Princeton, N.J. 1964), 224.

[38] M. Maclagan, *'Clemency' Canning* (London, 1962), 32; *HCIP* IX, *British paramountcy and Indian renaissance* (Bombay, 1963), 58–77.

[39] Akalkot (1896)
Ali Rajpur (1881, 1891)
Alwar (1874, 1939)
Aundh (1848, 1902)
Bamra (1869)
Bansda (1862)
Baraundha (1870, 1886)
Baroda (1875)
Benares (1885, 1939)
Bijawar (1899)
Bikanir (1887)
Bobbili (1871)
Bundi (1945)
Charkhari (1880)
Chhatarpus (1854)
Daspalla (1913)
Datia (1857)
Dewas Junior (1892)
Dewas Senior (1861, 1899)
Dhar (1857, 1898, 1926)
Dhenkanal (1877)
Dholpur (1873, 1911)
Dinajpur (1865)
Ichalkaranji (1852, 1854, 1876)
Idar (1868, 1901)
Jaipur (1880, 1922)
Jaisalmir (1891)
Jamkhandi (1897)
Jassu (1860, 1889)
Jath (1892)
Jawhar (1865, 1865)
Jhabua (1894)
Jhalawar (1875, 1896)
Kalahandi (1881)

it necessary to adopt consistently. In fact the number 70 should be regarded as minimal. Not all the Indian states were included in this survey because sufficient information was not always available. Furthermore, the sources that were available were often reticent about the fact of adoption. For instance, one description of the ruling line of Karauli found it 'remarkable that the last eight rulers have all succeeded by adoption'.[40] Yet only four of the Karauli rulers are so designated in the official account of the state. Furthermore, the 70 states listed here include only those where the rubric 'adopted' was specifically applied to one or more successions. Cases of succession by brothers, cousins, grandsons, and uncles usually are not included. Fewer than half of all successions between 1857 and 1947 that were analysed were father/son. None the less a ruler adopted to the *gadi* was normally referred to as the 'son' of the previous ruler. Many of them, however, were as much as two generations younger than their predecessor, while others were of the same age or even older.

The pattern of sonless rulers was not confined to the post-Mutiny period alone. From 1760 to 1857 at least (and once again this is only a partial figure) 71 adoptions were recorded. So, for the last two centuries—the period where more or less contemporaneous evidence is available—the succession to the *gadis* of Indian states was not only not consistently father/son, it was consistently *not* so. This is in marked contrast to the evidence for the earlier period, for which we have, with few exceptions, only the records of the chronicles.

Kanker (1903, 1925)
Karauli (1854, 1869, 1869, 1875, 1886, 1927)
Kawardha (1874)
Khandpara (1905, 1922)
Khilchipur (1869)
Kolhapur (1866, 1870, 1884, 1941, 1947)
Korea (1899)
Kotah (1889)
Kulu (1892)
Limbdi (1907)
Lunawada (1867)
Maisur (1868)
Mandi (1913)
Miraj Junior (1899)
Mudhol (1900)
Nabha (1871)
Narsinghgarh (1895)
Nawanagar (1906, 1933)
Nayagarh (1889, 1890, 1897)
Nilgiri (1894)
Pal-Lahara (1913)
Panna (1903)
Partabgarh (1890)
Patna (1878, 1924)
Porbandar (1900)
Pudukottai (1886)
Ramdurg (1872)
Ratlam (1857)
Sailana (1895)
Setupati (1862)
Shahpura (1870)
Sitamau (1885, 1899, 1900)
Sunth (1872, 1896)
Talcher (1891)
Tripura (1909)
Wankaner (1860)

[40] Rajputana and Ajmer, *List of ruling princes, chiefs and leading personages* (Delhi, 1938), 116.

A survey of a few of the more obvious contrasts will serve to illustrate this point. In Banswara the first 13 successions were reputedly all father/son, but the last 8 included a brother and two 'distant relatives'.[41] The first thirteen rulers/generations allegedly ruled from 1529 to 1747, which allows an average of only 16·8 years per generation. In Bhavnagar the first 23 rulers succeeded in unbroken father-to-son succession according to the chronicles, but the last five (1852–1948) include a grandson and a brother.[42] The state of Chanda, which was conquered by the Marathas in 1751 and for which no contemporary records are available, shows father/son succession throughout its entire existence—nineteen ruler-generations.[43] Danta records showed 21 consecutive father/son successions to *c.* 1600 After *c.* 1600–1947 five brothers, a nephew, and an uncle succeeded among 19 successions.[44] Dungarpur showed 27 consecutive father/son successions, then two adoptions and a grandson in the last four successions.[45] Karauli, as noted, had eight adoptions in its last nine successions. However, all the previous 18 successions were considered to be father/son. These few examples are perhaps more stark in their contrasts than many of the other Indian states, but they are otherwise representative of the general pattern of the genealogies of the native states of India. This pattern is for India, as elsewhere, too consistent to be explained by alleging changed circumstances in the nineteenth and twentieth centuries. If anything, the advent of British overrule with its concomitant stability, provided circumstances more congenial to unbroken father/son succession than those which obtained in the earlier, more turbulent, period.

How, then, are we to explain, the distortions of the records? The chronicles of the Indian states conform to the broad pattern of Indian genealogical records already described with reference to the Purānic genealogies.[46] As always, genealogies continued to be the legitimizing force which enabled individuals and families to acquire and maintain sovereignty. Furthermore, 'primogeniture and impartibility' were seen as 'independent, causal variables'.[47] The presence of unbroken filial

[41] Rajputana and Ajmer, *List*, 21–22a.

[42] H. Wilberforce-Bell, *A history of Kathiawad* (London, 1916), 279–80; *Gujarat District Gazetteers: Bhavnagar* (Ahmedabad, 1968), 59–86.

[43] *Central Provinces District Gazetteers: Chanda* (Allahabad, 1909), 37–51.

[44] F. S. Master, *The Mahi Kantha directory* (2 vols., Rajkot, 1922), I. 155–61.

[45] Rajputana and Ajmer, *List*, 69–77.

[46] See above, pp. 61–3.

[47] R. G. Fox, *Kin, clan, raja, and rule: state-hinterland relations in pre-industrial India* (Berkeley, Calif., 1971), 81.

succession implied strength, power, prestige, and continuity, and furthermore indicated that the state had *always* been strong and united. Ruling collaterals, therefore, tended to be forgotten, for they contravened this principle.[48] Unfortunately this does not allow us to assume that the recorded rulers of Indian states represented generations and to calculate chronologies on this basis. For the chronicles were designed to uphold the standards of antiquity and prestige as well.[49] On this principle collaterals of the same generation may have been shown as fathers/sons in order to achieve the desired succession pattern and at the same time give an impression of venerable antiquity. All that can confidently be said is that the royal genealogy of perhaps every Indian state before *c.* 1800 is incorrect in its lineal regularity.

A similar tendency for earlier chronicles to presume father/son succession patterns for unknown periods is exemplified by Kalhana's *Rājataraṅgiṇī*. Just as all of the unlikely reign lengths in the *Rājataraṅgiṇī* are confined to the earliest period so, too, do extended father/son succession patterns fall entirely within this prehistoric period. Kalhana recorded only two fraternal successions among the first 54 rulers, but after A.D. 598 collateral successions became very common, even typical.[50]

The problems confronting the investigator of the ancient and early medieval Indian dynasties have been of a different order. The existence of many of the more obscure 'dynasties' has been postulated or reconstructed from as little evidence as a single inscription.[51] Such

[48] For an example of collateral suppression in a Rajput state, see Henige, 'Oral tradition', 380. See also G. Raychaudhuri, 'The early history of the Kachwāhas of Amber' in D. R. Bhandarkar (ed.), *B. C. Law Volume*, Pt. I (Calcutta, 1945), 683–94.

[49] Stein, 'Early Indian historiography', 51, 53, 56–9; A. M. Shah and R. G. Shroff, 'The Vahīvancā Bārots of Gujarat: a caste of genealogists and mythographers' in M. Singer (ed.), *Traditional India: structure and change* (Philadelphia, Pa., 1959), 50–2.

[50] *Kalhana's Chronicles of the Kings of Kashmir*, ed. M. A. Stein, 2 vols. (London, 1900–2), *passim*.

[51] It is not possible to cite all the examples of this tendency. Some representative samples include T. V. Mahalingam, 'The early Pallava genealogy and chronology', *Proceedings of the 26th International Congress of Orientalists held at Delhi, 1964* (Delhi, 1969), 693–9; M. Rama Rao, 'New light on the Visnukundins', *Proceedings of the Indian History Congress*, 27 (1965), 78–82; B. R. Gopal, 'The Sindas of Reñjeru', *Journal of Ancient Indian History*, 2 (1968/9), 84–93; D. Sharma (ed.), *Rajasthan through the ages* (1 vol. to date, Bikanir, 1966), I. 693–7, 756 *passim*; C. Krishnamurthy, 'Some minor dynasties of the Kolar district (1179–1338 A.D.)' in *Prof. K. A. Nilakanta Sastri Volume*, 72–83; A. V. N. Murthy,

inscriptions commonly involve grants of land or religious endowments and invariably supply an ascendant genealogy for the grantor. These genealogies seldom claim to be more than just that—genealogical validation of the inscriber's right to make the grant. Although his direct ancestors will usually be called rulers, there is seldom the claim that they were the only members of his family to rule. That is, these inscriptions were designed neither as historical documents nor as kinglists. Surprisingly often, however, they have been interpreted as both. As a result the evidence of various inscriptions of a given 'dynasty' have been manipulated and juxtaposed to create dynastic successions which almost certainly never took place. The dating of the dynasties themselves as well as of the rulers within them has then been calculated on the basis of the results of this manipulation. There is no doubt that many of these ruling families existed, but the dating and morphology of their 'dynasties' have often been the product solely of the syndrome that sons consistently succeeded their fathers in office.

The eagerness to make this assumption is also apparent in the studies of those dynasties for which the abundance of epigraphic evidence forbids the free use of the juxtaposition of ascendant genealogies. A recent study of a south Indian 'dynasty', for instance, states that 'Alagiyaśena . . . may be taken as the son of Kopperuñjinga, since chronologically he seems to succeed him'.[52] In fact all that is known is that Alagiyaśena was of the same family as Kopperuñjinga and seems to have ruled in the same area as Kopperuñjinga, and died 32 years after him. Hence it cannot even be inferred that he succeeded Kopperuñjinga, and the assumption that Kopperuñjinga and Alagiyaśena were father and son is absolutely without foundation. Indeed, there is no evidence that these two rulers and their single known 'successor' formed any kind of a dynasty at all.

The Eastern Gaṅga dynasty of Vengi is more fully documented than Kopperuñjinga's 'dynasty', and it unquestionably existed for several centuries as a ruling family. Even so, there are lacunae in the epigraphic data, and several assumptions regarding the dynasty's regnal genealogy have been made without factual support. It has been assumed, for example, that 'Narasimha IV was succeeded by

The Sevunas of Devagiri (Mysore 1971). The tendency to create a dynasty from a single inscription is exemplified in N. Venkata Ramanayya, *The Chalukyas of L(V)ēmulavāḍa* (Hyberabad, 1953), 35–7n.

[52] M. Arokiaswami, 'The Pallava Nayaks of Kōrtāmpet', *JASB*, 4th Ser. 5 (1963), 29.

his son Bhandudeva IV in or sometime before A.D. 1414'.[53] All that is certain, however, is that Narasimha IV was ruling as late as 1402 and that Bhanudeva IV was already ruling in 1414.[54] Again, the assumption that no collateral could have intervened is not warranted by the present state of the evidence.

The desire to strain scattered epigraphic evidence to cover all contingencies is further demonstrated by recent studies of the Maitraka dynasty, which ruled in western India from the fifth to the eighth centuries.[55] Succession in the dynasty was often fraternal. There were at least nineteen rulers in eleven generations. Between 589 and 616 only one ruler is known. This is Śiladitya I, whose only known dates are 606 and 612. There is thus a seventeen-year gap between his first known date and the last known date of his assumed predecessor, his father Dharaśena. Historians of the dynasty have assumed either that Dharaśena ruled until just before 606 or that Śiladitya I succeeded soon after 589.[56] Again the possibility of intervening rulers has been ignored.

The efforts of the various chroniclers to create lineal dynasties of great antiquity is not surprising, since they were panegyrists first and historians later, if at all. The propensity of contemporary Indian historians to emulate this unhistorical approach is harder to explain. What is of particular interest here is that many of these 'dynasties' have been the product of this presumed father/son succession pattern. The corpus of epigraphic evidence for any dynasty is potentially expandable and the discovery of new inscriptions will in many cases result in the necessity of accepting collateral rulers.[57] Unlike many early Indian dynasties, the genealogy of the Yadava dynasty of Devagiri is known from two independent sources. The first is the body of inscriptions available for the whole of the dynasty. The other

[53] *HCIP* VI, *The Delhi Sultanate* (Bombay, 1960), 363.

[54] Ibid. 428.

[55] The latest account of the Maitrakas is *Gujarat District Gazetteers: Bhavnagar*, 48–55.

[56] D. Devahuti, *Harsha: a political study* (Oxford, 1970), 47, somehow makes both these assumptions.

[57] For an excellent discussion of some of the problems facing the historian of early India, see B. C. Sen, 'Early Indian approach to history and some problems of its reconstruction', *Journal of the Bihar Research Society*, 54 (1968), 1–15. Sircar, *Indian epigraphy* (Delhi, 1965), 11–13, shows how the existence and significance of a fifth-century Gupta ruler was only gradually discovered between 1838 and the present, as new epigraphic evidence came to hand. Sircar properly emphasizes that our knowledge of this ruler is still in flux, and will always remain so, as new discoveries can always be expected.

is the *Vratakhanda*, the introductory portion of the legal treatise *Caturvargacintāmaṅi* composed in the late thirteenth century by the minister Hemādrī.[58] As usual, the genealogies in both sources trace the origin of the family to Purānic heroes, in this case through about 60 generations. Dridhaprahara, who began to rule *c.* 860 by genealogical reckoning, is usually considered to have been the first historical ruler of the dynasty. Of the 23 rulers from *c.* 860 to 1185, seven are known only from the *Vratakhanda.* They are ignored in later inscriptions and none of their own inscriptions has yet come to light.[59] Conversely, two of the rulers of the dynasty known from epigraphic evidence were ignored by Hemādrī.[60] In other words, the structure of the Yadava dynasty, as presently known, is a combination of epigraphic and chronicle evidence and neither of these two sources provides a complete picture. All of the rulers omitted were collaterals, but not all of them were short-lived rulers.

Likewise new epigraphic discoveries have brought to light several previously unknown rulers of Cambodia. Two of these intervened between a father and son and until this new evidence became available it was, not unnaturally, assumed that the son had directly succeeded the father.[61] The assumption rested on the fact that later ascendant genealogies did not include these collaterals.[62] The genealogies of the Kadamba dynasties of the western Deccan underwent considerable change between the first study of them in 1931 and more recent studies. And again the change was from a very lineal profile to a more collateral one.[63]

The reconstructed genealogies of the Indian dynasties from the beginning of the Purānic era to the suppression of the native states after independence assume two very distinct patterns. These patterns are not related to the type of succession or to the political circumstances of the period during which a dynasty ruled. Rather

[58] For Hemādrī, see G. Yazdani, *The early history of the Deccan* (2 vols., London, 1960), II. 570, and P. V. Kane, *The history of Dharmaśastra literature* (5 vols., Poona, 1930–62), 1. 354–9.

[59] O. P. Verma, *The Yādavas and their times* (Nagpur, 1970), 21–3, 42–9, 367–8; idem, 'A discrepancy in the Yādava genealogy', *Nagpur University Journal* [Humanities], 16 (1965), 32–6.

[60] Verma, *The Yādavas*, 367–8.

[61] L. P. Briggs, *The ancient Khmer empire* (Philadelphia, Pa., 1951), 205, and earlier works cited there.

[62] Ibid.

[63] Cf. G. M. Moraes, *Kadamba Kula* (Bombay, 1931), 93, 167, with B. R. Gopal, 'The Kadambas of Hangal', *Journal of Karnatak University* [Dharwar], *Social Sciences*, 3 (1967), 99–115, and 'The Kadambas of Goa', ibid. 4 (1968), 164–77.

they are related to the amount and type of contemporaneous evidence available for them. Those dynasties for which little or no such evidence is available assume very simplistic, narrowly lineal forms—father succeeded son in regular, almost monotonous, fashion. Whenever these dynasties entered a period for which more detailed evidence existed this pattern tends to change abruptly.[64] Those dynasties for which abundant contemporaneous evidence is available, including several of the more prominent medieval dynasties and those Rajput states in constant contact with the Mughal court, show more variegated succession patterns. In fine, there is not a single indisputable case of extended father/son succession in Indian history even though Indian traditional accounts are replete with them.

The past of Polynesia is more dependent on genealogies than that of any other area of the world. Genealogies of prodigious length and complexity have been recited.[65] Inevitably the duration of the Polynesian past has been calculated by genealogical reckoning. The value to be attached to these genealogies depends on a variety of circumstances, as well as the limits the investigator is inclined to place on the human memory. In evaluating such recitations, however, the following aspect of Polynesian political thought should be considered:

> The Polynesians regarded the growth of power as a natural thing, . . . and assumed power to be the greater the longer it had been exercised. The mere passing of time was thus a power factor, both the time an individual had held office and the time a long row of ancestors had held office before. The importance of an office increased from generation to generation, for power, if not checked by a superior power, grows incessantly.[66]

Some of these genealogies, particularly those of the Maori of New Zealand, have been scrutinized in great detail. Some authorities find them consistent among themselves and with other traditions.[67]

[64] e.g. the account of the ruling line in the state of Korea in India: 'The direct line [1,800 years old] became extinct in 1897' and the succeeding chief was 'a collateral relative of the late chief', *Central Provinces District Gazetteers: Chattisgarh Feudatory States* (Bombay 1909), 296. In Bashahr the chronicles related 121 consecutive father/son successions before *c.* 1890, when two successive generations died before acceding to the *gadi* and the direct line suddenly became extinct. *Punjab State Gazetteers: Simla Hill States* (Lahore, 1908), s.v. Bashahr, 5.

[65] E. Best, *The Maori school of learning* (Wellington, 1923), 5, spoke of a recitation which lasted three days and included more than 1,400 names.

[66] F. Steiner, *Taboo* (Harmondswoth, 1967), 38. Note how this echoes the sentiments of George Mackenzie cited on p. 117.

[67] The leading exponent of this school of thought is J. B. W. Roberton, whose views are expressed in the following articles: 'The role of tribal tradition in New

Other scholars, however, have found them wanting in this respect.[68] Many of the Maori genealogies are obviously contradictory, especially those which claim to trace their lines back to common ancestors who allegedly arrived at the time of the 'Great Fleet'. This epochal event has been dated on the basis of genealogical reckoning of the most dubious nature to *c*. 1350. In large measure the question of the validity of many Maori genealogies depends on whether they are accepted as uncontaminated relics from pre-colonial times or whether they are seen as emerging in the last part of the nineteenth century in response to the exigencies created by British rule. Maori genealogies, then, will be discussed in Chapter III which discusses the influence of literacy and indirect rule on genealogies and kinglists.

Many Polynesian genealogies, unlike those of the Maori, claim to be, or have been assumed to be, kinglists as well. In this guise they can be evaluated on very different terms. The origin of the Tu'i Toga line in Tonga has usually been dated to the tenth century on the basis of genealogical reckoning, which allots one ruler to each 25-year generation.[69] Attention has been devoted to Tongan genealogies elsewhere.[70] It needs only to be repeated here that there are no adequate reasons to assume a father/son succession pattern occurred in the Tu'i Toga line in pre-contact Tonga.

Tonga is by no means an isolated example of the willingness to accept extended father/son succession patterns for early Polynesia. Buck, in collecting traditions from Mangareva, stated that 'direct father-to-son succession' to the senior line occurred from the twenty-first generation before 1900.[71] Indeed the system truly worked to

---

Zealand prehistory', *JPS* 66 (1957), 247–63; 'The significance of New Zealand tribal tradition', *JPS* 67 (1958), 39–57: 'Genealogies as a basis for Maori chronology', *JPS* 65 (1956), 45–53; 'The evaluation of Maori tribal tradition as history', *JPS* 71 (1962), 293–309. See also P. Te Hurinui, 'Maori genealogies', *JPS* 67 (1959), 162–5.

[68] Notably Simmons, 'A New Zealand myth', 14–31, but also R. Piddington, 'A note on the validity and significance of Polynesian traditions', *JPS* 65 (1956), 200–3; A. Sharp, 'Maori genealogies and canoe traditions', *JPS* 67 (1958), 37–8 and idem, 'Maori genealogies and the "fleet"', *JPS* 68 (1959), 12–13; Kelly, 'Some problems in the study of Maori genealogies', *JPS* 49 (1940), 237.

[69] Twenty-five years per generation is the standard figure for Polynesian genealogies. This may be somewhat high for Polynesia, but not by more than two or three years per generation. Given the questionable worth of much of the genealogical data it is unnecessary to discuss the merits of the various generational lengths applied to Polynesia.

[70] Henige, 'Oral tradition', 380–1.

[71] P. H. Buck (Te Rangi Hiroa), *Ethnology of Mangareva* (Honolulu, 1938), 18.

perfection, for the 'law of male primogeniture operating through successive generations made the first-born of the first-born' the chief or family head.[72] In the 1830s French missionaries arrived in Mangareva and after that date detailed contemporaneous records become available.[73] Te Ma-puteoa, the chief of Mangareva when the first missionaries arrived, had succeeded, not his father but his grandfather.[74] He therefore represented two regnal generations, although he ruled only about 25 years. Te Ma-puteoa died in 1857 and was succeeded by his son Joseph Gregorio II, who died eleven years later 'without leaving [male] progeny'.[75] As a result, the royal line, which had allegedly sustained itself by father/son successions for several centuries, became extinct because 'in Mangareva the sceptre never falls to the female line'.[76]

In Rarotonga the royal genealogy is almost completely ascendant through 25 generations up to 1900.[77] The one exception occurred in the eleventh generation. The tenth ruler, defeated by his brother, in turn became ruler of a small group on the island. The genealogy of this latter group showed only eight generations between him and the ruler in 1823, whereas in the main group there were 13 generations for the same period.[78] Gill explained this discrepancy by assuming that 'one or two links in the [shorter] genealogy are irrevocably lost, owing to the perpetual slaughter of their leading men'.[79] Yet 'strangely enough' (as Hill says) two sons and two daughters of the chief in 1823 ruled in succession until at least 1868.[80]

The succession of rulers in Uvea (Wallis) and in Futuna in the

[72] Ibid. 157.

[73] The major sources for Mangareva traditional history are H. Laval, *Mangareva: l'histoire ancienne d'une peuple Polynésien* (Brain-le-Comte, 1938), and idem, *Mémoires pour servir à l'histoire de Mangareva*, eds. P. O'Reilly and C. W. Newbury (Paris, 1968). Laval arrived in Mangareva in 1834 and remained until 1871.

[74] Buck, *Mangareva*, 91–6; Laval, *Mémoires*, cxxxix. None the less Te Maputeoa's father is included in the royal genealogy as if he had ruled his allotted 25 years.

[75] Laval, *Mangareva*, 59; idem, *Mémoires*, 578.

[76] Ibid.

[77] W. W. Gill, 'The genealogy of the kings of Rarotonga and Mangaia, as illustrating the colonisation of those islands and the Hervey group', *Annual Report of the Australasian Association for the Advancement of Science*, 2 (1890), 628–31. The genealogies had been collected in 1867/8.

[78] Ibid. 631–2.

[79] Ibid. 629.

[80] Ibid. 628.

nineteenth century also showed a greater divergence from lineality than for early periods. Futuna was divided into two parts, Tua and Sigave. From 1800 to *c.* 1865 there was a total of seven successions in these two lines. None of them was a direct father/son succession.[81] A similar fragmented succession pattern occurred in the neighbouring island of Uvea, with several multiple reigns in the late eighteenth and early nineteenth centuries.[82]

Scholars have not only accepted the traditional statements of long father/son successions in the pre-contact period, but have inferred them even where the traditional evidence did not warrant doing so. The most recent study of Easter Island is a case in point.[83] There are several extant kinglists of Easter Island, the earliest dating from 1867. There seem, however, to be only four independent lists; all the others are derivative. These four lists contain 23, 30, 32, and 57 names.[84] Métraux found that the longest kinglist was inflated by the conventional methods of euhemerism and by including priests and other intrusive names.[85] Nevertheless, Goldman, in attempting to correlate the archaeological and genealogical evidence for the date of the settlement of Easter Island, suggests that a C14 date of A.D. 386 ± 100 is 'consistent' with the traditional evidence. In arriving at this conclusion he argues that allowing the usual 25 years for each generation gives a total of 1,425 years, which, subtracted from 1860, places the first occupancy at A.D. 435, remarkably close indeed to the radio-carbon date.[86] He not only has taken the longest, most aberrant, genealogy available, but inferred from it a one-ruler-per-generation succession—a commonplace among Oceanists.

The American naval officer who collected this longest kinglist during a brief visit in 1886 nowhere claimed that it represented an

[81] A.-C.-E. Caillot, *Mythes, légendes et traditions des Polynésiens orientales* (Paris, 1914), 312–13; E. G. Burrows, *Ethnology of Uvea* (Honolulu, 1937), 18–19; J. Henquel, 'Histoire ancienne de Wallis des origines à 1836', *Bulletin de l'Information du Territoire des îles Wallis et Futuna*, 29 (Jan. 1967), 16–17.

[82] Burrows, *Ethnology of Futuna* (Honolulu, 1936), 18–19.

[83] I. Goldman, *Ancient Polynesian society*, 93–121.

[84] An analysis of these kinglists and their common features is in A. Métraux, *Ethnology of Easter Island* (Honolulu, 1940), 89–94.

[85] Ibid. 91–2.

[86] Goldman, *Ancient Polynesian society*, 99. Goldman, 111, admits that Métraux considered this longest list inaccurate but he finds it 'so close to the radio-carbon date of earliest occupancy, as to invite belief in it'! For an African attempt to correlate archaeological and genealogical dateage, see M. Wilson, 'Reflections on the early history of north Malawi' in B. Pachai (ed.), *The early history of Malawi* (London, 1972), 138–40.

ascendant genealogy.[87] In fact, although he specified that descent among the lesser chiefs was from father to son, he stated only that the *kingship* was 'hereditary in his [the founder's] family'.[88] Easter Island had a particularly chequered history in the nineteenth century and the accounts of the genealogical filiations of some of its last rulers are confused. It seems, however, that the last king was the cousin of his predecessor.[89] Furthermore, this ruler died at the age of twelve leaving no male heir and, as in Mangareva, the kingship was allowed to end.[90] Métraux felt that the shortest kinglist of 23 names contained only 18 generations.[91] Easter Island traditions also specify that kings abdicated on the marriage of their eldest sons.[92] Such a practice would scarcely foster a continuous father/son succession.

It is apparent that in Polynesia, as in the native states of India, succession patterns in the historical period have been markedly different from what they allegedly had been in the traditional period. There were factors operating in some parts of Polynesia during the eighteenth and nineteenth centuries that might have militated against serene lineal succession. This was particularly true for Easter Island, where Peruvian slavers nearly depopulated the island. But many of the deviations from a father/son pattern, particularly premature royal deaths, cannot be attributed solely to the intrusion of these new factors. Rather, the traditional evidence must be questioned.

Although Polynesia and the native states of India showed a high concentration of extended father/son successions in their accounts of the past, this pattern is by no means confined to these areas. Herodotus' account of the Egyptian priests, although exaggerated, is reflected in other Egyptian sources. A list of 60 Memphite priests dating from *c.* 750 B.C. has been preserved. According to this list each priest was the son of his predecessor.[93] This list of priests provides some useful internal chronological information which indicates that the first priest on the list ruled under XI Dynasty, that is *c.* 2100 B.C. Several

[87] W. J. Thomson, 'Te Pito te Henua or Easter Island', *Annual Report* of the U.S. National Museum for 1889, 534.

[88] Ibid. 473.

[89] Métraux, 'The kings of Easter Island', *JPS* 46 (1937), 41.

[90] Métraux, *Ethnology*, 92.

[91] Ibid. 93.

[92] Métraux, 'Kings', 51–2.

[93] For the list, see L. Borchardt, *Die Mittel zur zeitlichen Festlegung von Punkten der ägyptischen Geschichte und ihre Anwendung* (Cairo, 1935), 99–100; idem, 'Ein Stammbaum memphitischer Priester,' *Sitzungberichten der preussische Akademie der Wissenschaften*, Phil.-hist.Kl. 24 (1932), 618–22.

Pharaohs are included in the list, which allows some synchronisms to be made. The results are not encouraging for accepting a straight father/son succession pattern. It is evident that some of the names in the early part of the list actually represent collateral rulers.[94]

Chronicles of late provenience have a penchant for claiming extended father/son successions for the earliest and unknown parts of the dynasty(ies) they treat. The Burmese chronicles assigned a suitably early date of 2666 B.C. for the foundation of Arakan. This was more easily accomplished by showing a nearly perfect father/son succession until the time of the last dynasty, which was founded in 1404. The need to establish this pattern was so strong that the chronicles show 22 generations between 1191 and 1276, including five generations between 1205 and 1210.[95]

Evidence for the proto-history of the Persian Gulf principalities of Lār and Hormuz comes solely from later chronicles. Detailed information on Hormuz only begins *c.* 1200. Succession to the throne after that time was confused and collateral. Before *c.* 1200, however, the chronicles recorded a straight father/son succession for eight generations.[96] This is not an impossibly high figure, of course, but it is highly out of character with the later succession patterns. Lār provides the more sharply defined dichotomy we have come to expect. According to the chronicles the first 25 rulers ruled in an unbroken father/son succession.[97] The succession pattern after *c.* 1200 shows several departures from this ideal, although the recorded succession still remained much more regular than in neighbouring Hormuz.[98] It

[94] L. Bull, 'Ancient Egypt', in Dentan, *Idea of History*, 10–11. There are seven generations of priests covering a period of only about sixty years, if one accepts the Pharaonic synchronisms included in the list. Bull argued that 'it is obvious that in the course of centuries certain of the royal names have become associated incorrectly with particular priests, but such errors do not necessarily throw suspicion on the general reliability of the Memphite genealogy'. Ibid. 11. Given a choice between accepting the synchronisms or the father/son morphology of the genealogy, I would unhesitatingly opt for the former. Neither may be correct, of course, but the synchronisms are *more* likely to be accurate than the genealogy.

[95] A. P. Phayre, *History of Burma . . .* (London, 1883), 292–304.

[96] A. Faroughy, *Histoire du royaume de Hormuz depuis son origin jusqu'à son incorporation dans l'empire persan de séfévis en 1622* (Brussels, 1939), 51–51b, 103.

[97] J. Aubin, 'Références pour Lār médiévale', *Journal Asiatique*, 243 (1955), 492. The last seven rulers before *c.* 1200 were alleged to have spanned the period from *c.* 715 to *c.* 1200. Aubin rejects this as literally true, but accepts the probability of long father/son reigns during this period, adding that 'the length of the reigns [and] the direct filial succession are signs of stability', ibid. 495.

[98] Ibid. 493–5.

must be remembered, however, that there is less contemporaneous evidence available for this period of Lār history than for Hormuz, an important entrepôt, and the Lār chronicle is of late date (middle of the sixteenth century). It may be significant that none of the kings who ruled nearest the time the chronicle was composed directly succeeded his father.[99]

Further examples of this kind could be cited almost *ad infinitum*. This would only serve to emphasize by repetition and variation a theme which is already apparent.[1] And at this point the reader may feel that Pelion has already been piled on Ossa. If so, he will be apprehending correctly one of the purposes of this chapter. The importance for chronology of false extended father/son succession patterns, their widespread occurrence, and their uncritical acceptance by scholars make it of paramount importance that the problem be dealt with in great, if sometimes burdensome, detail. The purpose here has not only been to indicate the widespread incidence of this particular problem but also to emphasize that claims of extended father/son succession have occurred almost invariably under particular circumstances. The dichotomy between alleged succession patterns in given societies in earlier and in later times is sharp and significant, and cannot be emphasized too strongly.

At present much of the chronology of pre-colonial Africa is based on genealogical reckoning, which often accepts extended father/son succession patterns. Nowhere is this more obvious than among the south-east Bantu (Nguni, Sotho, and Tswana). Perhaps more than anywhere else in Africa the pre-colonial history of this region hangs on a genealogical scaffolding.[2] From these genealogies the dates of entry into the area and the establishment of the various polities there have been inferred.[3] The south-eastern Bantu genealogies are

[99] Ibid. 494–5.

[1] The following list, however, may serve as an index of the stereotypical nature of this problem throughout historical time and space: C. Toumanoff, 'Chronology of the kings of Abasgia and other problems', *Le Muséon*, 69 (1956), 75n.; E. Taqaishvili, 'Les Sources des notices du Patriarche de Jérusalem Dosithée sur les rois d'Aphkhazie', *Journal Asiatique*, 210 (1927), 358; H. Burney, 'Discovery of Buddhist images with Deva-nágari inscriptions at Tagoung, the ancient capital of the Burmese empire', *JASB* 5 (1836), 160–4; Kachorn Sukhabanij, 'Proposed dating of the Yonok-Chiengsaen dynasty', *Journal of the Burma Research Society*, 43 (1960), 60–1.

[2] See Bryant, *Olden times in Zululand and Natal*, *passim*, and works by L.-P. Breutz cited in the bibliography.

[3] e.g. M. Wilson 'The Nguni people' and 'The Sotho, Venda and Tsonga' in

ascendant. In these societies fission often replaced usurpation as an outlet for collateral ambition. Younger sons and unsuccessful contenders migrated to new areas and established new dynasties. In theory, then, each chiefly genealogy would be lineal—collaterals never ruled, they just moved away. Succession disputes were endemic in early south-eastern societies.[4] As a result secession was unquestionably a frequent occurrence, at least while further land remained available.[5] Schapera analysed 107 such disputes in eight Tswana chiefdoms of the nineteenth and twentieth centuries.[6] The great majority of these disputes were between closely related contenders for the chiefship. Schapera pointed out that 'theoretically [these disputes] should not have occurred for . . . the Tswana have well-defined rules of succession and do not habitually select a new chief from among several candidates all considered equally eligible'.[7] That these disputes nevertheless did occur in such abundance despite such rules should be instructive for other south-eastern Bantu societies.

The nineteenth century is often regarded as a particularly turbulent period in southern Africa. Doubtless the scale of warfare and disputes increased, but reports of inter-group squabbling are prominent in traditional accounts of the early period as well.[8] It seems unnecessary to assume that the succession patterns of the nineteenth century were wildly aberrant from the earlier 'norms'.[9] Scholars working with south-eastern Bantu traditions have recognized that many of the

---

M. Wilson and L. Thompson (eds.), *Oxford history of South Africa*, I, *South Africa to 1870* (Oxford, 1969), 85–95, 133–7; Legassick, 'The Sotho-Tswana peoples', 98–104; S. Marks, 'The traditions of the Natal "Nguni": a second look at the work of A. T. Bryant' in ibid. 140–1; Bryant, *Olden times*, *passim*; M. Wilson, 'The early history of the Transkei and Ciskei', *African Studies*, 18 (1959), 175–6.

[4] Wilson, 'The Sotho, Venda and Tsonga', 156–8; Legassick, 'Sotho-Tswana peoples', 98–9; W. D. Hammond-Tooke, 'Segmentation and fission in Cape Nguni political units', *Africa*, 35 (1965), 152–64.

[5] P.-L. Breutz, 'Tswana tribal governments today', *Sociologus*, 8 (1958), 146, estimated that the number of Tswana chiefdoms had doubled in the previous seventy years because of secession.

[6] I. Schapera, 'Kinship and politics in Tswana history', *JRAI* 93 (1963), 159–73.

[7] Ibid. 162.

[8] Marks, 'Traditions', 128, observes that in the nineteenth century 'rules of succession were honored in the breach rather than in the observance'. Our information for earlier periods simply does not allow us to assume that these 'rules' were more often observed then.

[9] Wilson, 'The Nguni people', 95; Bryant, *Olden Times*, *passim*.

genealogies are too simplistic.[10] At the same time they seem to feel that the generational counts are correct or nearly correct and that distortions in these genealogies have resulted from collateral rulers being omitted.[11] The traditional chronology of the south-eastern Bantu at present rests on this assumption.

The most recent student of Bryant's work has characterized him as being 'over-cautious' in the limited credence he was willing to place in the genealogies he so assiduously collected.[12] Some of Bryant's reasons for questioning the accuracy of these genealogies are certainly unacceptable.[13] None the less, he may well have been right in his scepticism, if for the wrong reasons. Likewise, Bryant's assigning of 18 years per reign and 30 years per generation has been misinterpreted.[14] In making these calculations Bryant in effect was suggesting that each five generations in the genealogies he studied represented only three generations because collateral rulers had been remembered as successive. No final explication of this matter is possible, but perhaps the real profile of south-eastern Bantu genealogies lies somewhere between the extremes represented by Bryant on the one hand and modern scholars on the other. The bases of Bryant's distrust can be rejected, but his scepticism remains valid.[15]

Unfortunately it is easier to impeach the widespread incidence of extended father/son succession than to determine the precise chronological implications of this distortion. In any given case an ascendant genealogy/kinglist can represent any of three possibilities:

(*a*) it can be an accurate record of the succession
(*b*) it can accurately reflect the number of generations but not the number of rulers

[10] Legassick, 'Sotho-Tswana', 100; Marks, 'Chronology from genealogical evidence: the south-eastern Bantu', paper presented at 1966 SOAS Conference, 15.

[11] Ibid.; Legassick, 'Sotho-Tswana', 100.

[12] Marks, 'Traditions', 128.

[13] Bryant felt that the 'slipshod methods of thought customary among these peoples, . . . their innate credulity, their tendency to exaggerate, and their utter disregard for exactitude in details' made it impossible to accept their traditions. *Olden Times*, 30. Evidently Bryant had never read his Geoffrey of Monmouth, John Fordun, or Hector Boece.

[14] Marks, 'Traditions', 128, credits Bryant with 'allowing only eighteen years to an average *generation*' (emphasis added). But see Bryant, *Olden Times*, 31.

[15] It should be pointed out that the limits of extended father/son succession seriously affect the received genealogies of most of the interlacustrine states. Discussion of this point has been deferred to the future, but see Chapter III for a discussion of the kinglist of Bunyoro.

(*c*) it can accurately reflect the number and sequence of rulers but not the number of generations spanned by them

Obviously these alternatives are not equally probable. The foregoing discussion has illustrated that the first alternative is extremely unlikely. The second and third alternatives, however, are equally possible in any given instance in the absence of further data. An ascendant genealogy can be nothing more than a legal document purporting only to list royal ancestors in the direct line. This was true for most of the Indian epigraphs and for Rwanda, Nkore, and other interlacustrine states, as well as for the Spartan kinglists.[16] In cases where this can be proved true, construing the ascendant genealogy into a kinglist will not significantly distort the chronology since the dynastic generations will be the same—perhaps even fewer, if the apical ancestor in the ascendant genealogy represented a new line. Under these circumstances it is advisable to regard the names in the genealogy, not as the names of individual rulers, but as names of generations—each name collectively representing the one or more individuals who may have ruled in that generation.

Conversely, an ascendant genealogy, which *claims* to be a kinglist as well, often is practising collateral suppression. Collateral suppression can be defined in two ways. First, it may be the suppression of all collateral rulers from a kinglist or genealogy. Or it may be the suppression of the *concept* of collaterality by incorporating all known rulers, including collaterals, but deeming them to be lineal. Instances of both forms of collateral suppression are all too common and it is therefore impossible to do more than urge that an ascendant genealogy which consciously alleges to be a complete kinglist tentatively be rejected as such while efforts are made to determine whether rulers are missing from the genealogy, or whether father/son relationships in it actually disguise collaterality. At the same time it need scarcely be emphasized that an ascendant genealogy which does not claim to be more than that should under no circumstances ever be treated as a kinglist.

[16] For Rwanda, compare A. Kagame, *La Notion de génération appliquée à la généalogie dynastique et à l'histoire du Rwanda des Xe-XIe siècles à nos jours* (Brussels, 1959), with Vansina, *L'Évolution*, and idem, 'The use of oral tradition in African culture history' in C. Gabel and N. R. Bennett (eds.), *Reconstructing African culture history* (Boston, Mass., 1967), 62. For an excellent analysis of the legitimizing importance of 'the prestige [ascendant] line', see J. J. Fox, 'A Rotinese dynastic genealogy' in T. O. Beidelman (ed.), *Translation of culture* (Tavistock, 1971), 37–45, 69–71.

CHAPTER III

Literacy, Indirect Rule, and the Political Role of Antiquity in Oral Tradition

> The most retentive memory is weaker than the palest ink.[1]
>
> . . . the line of succession that became official [in Mangareva] was that of the holder of the title when European culture [i.e. rule] made its advent and prevented the making of further adjustments.[2]

I ORAL TRADITION AS A RESPONSE TO STIMULI

LIKE other historical sources oral traditions arose in response to a broad range of stimuli. The exigencies which had the greatest impact on the chronological content of historical traditions were usually external to the oral society and were related to the advent of literacy and the adaptation to foreign culture and indirect rule. These are interwoven factors. For instance, missionary activity introduced at least limited literacy to oral societies while the imposition of western political domination, particularly in the forms of indirect rule, prompted the ruling elements of many societies to tailor traditional accounts of the past to make them correspond to their new rulers' respect for antiquity. In this task they utilized their newly acquired literacy to broaden the possibilities for elaborating and synthesizing older oral traditions.

These new forms of the traditions often came from older accounts, caught and ossified in written form at a particular point in their development. Sometimes, though, they were new traditions fabricated to take advantage of new opportunities. In either case, however, the transcribed accounts would often be refined and elaborated after their initial transmission into written form as new information became available and new circumstances developed. This post-literate dynamic can be seen as a documentable extension of a similar process of continuous development which obtained the tradition's

[1] S. G. Champion, *Racial proverbs* (New York, 1931), 365.

[2] P. Buck, *Ethnology of Mangareva*, 157.

non-literate period as well, as tellers adapted it to changing circumstances.

It is impossible to detect the forms that these earliest changes might have taken, but changes in the chronological content of these traditions which occurred after the advent of literacy often took the form of coalescing variant accounts into a single standardized version. The more coherent, more circumstantial, and more consistent results were more readily accepted. Traditional chronologies which seemed to fit into a coherent and persuasive pattern were accepted, *ipso facto*, as more valid accounts of the past because they corresponded more closely to the biases of their literate interpreters.

The principal mechanism by which the contents of oral traditional accounts were adapted to form new coalesced traditions may be called 'feedback'. Feedback may be defined as the co-opting of extraneous printed or written information into previously oral accounts. This process occurred very widely, if not always obviously, and its prevalence emphasizes the extent to which newly literate societies recognized the truth of the Chinese proverb quoted above.

At the same time that literacy permitted the incorporation of new materials into oral accounts the imposition of indirect rule provided cogent reasons which influenced the way oral historians exploited this new opportunity. Most kinglists and royal genealogies are political tools—those that have not proved useful in this regard are often rejected and forgotten—and the circumstances of indirect rule provided an ideal ambience for their use. The fact that objective quantification of the past, which had not been an intrinsic part of most traditions, now became important meant that the chronological aspects of traditional accounts would be those most affected by feedback to make them conform to the expectations of the new colonial rulers, who almost universally professed to revere antiquity.

The examples discussed in this chapter illustrate that the manipulation of the past, and particularly of the concept of its duration, has not been confined to newly literate societies. The written Scottish and Rajput genealogies, for instance, demonstrate that the antiquity of the past has often been distorted by literate historians as a means of attempting to preserve sovereignty, or a favoured position of dependence, or simply to maintain the *status quo*. Both the Bunyoro and Scottish traditions discussed in greater detail in this chapter responded to political exigencies by elaborating the antiquity of their royal lines, even though the methods used and the chronological reasoning of these two responses differed from each other.

II FEEDBACK: THE EFFECT OF LITERACY ON THE CHRONOLOGY OF ORAL TRADITION

The impact of literacy, and of its concomitant feedback, on the traditional accounts of previously oral societies is critical to an assessment of the chronological value of these accounts. The following discussion is intended only to note the variegated and widespread incidence of the phenomenon of feedback and to suggest some implications for historians who must use traditions of this kind.

The 'sheer magic' of literacy in influencing oral traditions is clearly seen in many of the Polynesian traditions.[3] The introduction of Christianity in the early nineteenth century had important effects on the traditions of many of the island groups. Sometimes, when Catholic and Protestant missionaries were competing for the souls of a particular polity, the traditions of those political groups which had espoused the victorious faith prevailed. This occurred, for example, in Tonga, where Jioaji Tupou I, who supported the Protestant missionaries, managed, after several decades, to unite the several islands of the Tongan group under his own rule.[4] The Catholics had labelled Tupou a usurper. The Protestant Tongans countered by claiming that the Tu'i Toga line, the most ancient and sacred of the several royal lines in the islands, but opposed to Tupou, had become tainted with servile blood.[5] In the ensuing civil war between the adherents of the two faiths the Protestant forces triumphed. As a consequence, the Tu'i Toga line was allowed to die out and some subsequent traditions of the Tu'i Togas retained the probably apocryphal story of its contamination.[6]

[3] G. S. Parsonson, 'The literate revolution in Polynesia', *Journal of Pacific History*, 2 (1967), 44. Ibid. 44–50, and the sources cited there provide a good survey of the impact of literacy on preliterate Polynesian society. For the enthusiastic response of the Maori to literacy, see C. J. Parr, 'A missionary library: printed attempts to instruct the Maori, 1815–1845', *JPS* 70 (1961), 437–9; idem, 'Maori literacy, 1843–1867', *JPS* 72 (1963), 211–13, 232; J. M. B. Owens, 'Christianity and the Maoris to 1840', *New Zealand Journal of History*, 2 (1968), 35.

[4] A. A. Koskinen, *Missionary influence as a political factor in the Pacific islands* (Helsinki, 1953), 121–2.

[5] T. West, *Ten years in south-central Polynesia* (London, 1865), 54–8, 395–6.

[6] B. H. Thomson, *Diversions of a prime minister* (Edinburgh, 1894), 292–4, 307–8; West, *Ten years*, 55.

On Samoa, Tahiti, and other islands the ubiquitous political strife assumed religious guises as well.[7] Traditions were used by contending parties to support and justify their positions, but in reality these contents, in the nineteenth century, were often decided by the influence and power of the missionaries and the support they could obtain from their respective countries' peripatetic naval squadrons. The influence of these events on the traditions of the Polynesian islands can sometimes be documented, although most often only that strain of traditional history in symbiotic relationship with the victors survived. The co-optative impulse seemed to have been greatest for the Polynesian creation myths. The introduction of the Bible, with its own creation myths—supported, as one might expect, by genealogical scaffolding—presented certain problems for the Polynesians. Their acceptance of Christianity required either the acceptance of its genealogical/aetiological concomitants and the consequent rejection of their own myths, or an attempt to assimilate the two discordant bodies of material. Several attempts at assimilation were in fact made. Some were more obvious than others. These included the introduction of Garden of Eden concepts into Polynesian creation myths, the banishment of evil spirits from a paradise, purgatory, the Flood, and the interpolation of prominent Biblical figures into Polynesian genealogies.[8]

Close scrutiny of available sources has demonstrated some of the processes by which this feedback of extraneous material into traditions occurred in Polynesia. According to Tahitian traditions 'Ta'aroa was the ancestor of all the gods; he made all things . . . [and] proceeded out of himself, entirely alone [and] had neither father nor mother'.[9] Ta'aroa appeared in similar roles in Samoan traditions.[10] Under the names Tangaroa, Tagaloa, or Tanaoa he also appeared as a lesser god in the pantheons of various islands.[11] The widespread incidence of Ta'aroa in Polynesian myths was at one time erroneously attributed to, among other things, an early diffusion of a

[7] Koskinen, *Missionary influence*, 124–5, 176–9, *passim*.

[8] D. B. Barrère, 'Revisions and adulterations in Polynesian creation myths' in G. Highland (ed.), *Polynesian culture history* (Honolulu, 1967), 105–17; idem, 'Cosmogonic genealogies from Hawaii', *JPS* 70 (1961), 419–28; idem, *The Kumuhonua legends: a study of late 19th century Hawaiian stories of creation and origins* (Honolulu, 1969), 1–2; Kelly, 'Some problems', 241–2.

[9] T. Henry, *Ancient Tahiti* (Honolulu, 1928), 336.

[10] T. Monberg, 'Ta'aroa in the creation myths of the Society Islands', *JPS* 65 (1956), 269.

[11] Ibid. 268–9.

Ta'aroa cult by a single invading group.[12] Certainly before the introduction of Christianity in Tahiti, Ta'aroa appeared as a supreme Creator.[13] After Christianity was introduced into Tahiti, however, the Ta'aroa myth was embellished by various Biblical accretions, for example, his creation of a pair of primeval ancestors.[14] Initially Ta'aroa was the family creator god of the Pomare family, which, by the last quarter of the eighteenth century, was beginning to become predominant in the Society Islands.[15] With the ascendancy of the Pomares in Tahiti Ta'aroa became the recognized creator god on the entire archipelago.[16] In the half-century after Cook's visit to Tahiti in 1773 the concept of Ta'aroa as creator god spread throughout much of Polynesia. If the view that Ta'aroa's rise to supremacy paralleled that of the Pomares is accepted, this diffusion must be confined to this fifty-year period. Inter-island communication became much greater with the regular visit of Europeans after Cook's voyages. Tahitians are known to have visited many other islands on European ships. The uniquely Tahitian royal name of Pomare, only assumed by Pomare I in 1791, appeared among the Maori just a few years later.[17] The obvious implication of all this is that this relatively brief period of fifty years was sufficient to permit the widespread absorption of a Tahitian myth into the traditional cosmologies of several other Polynesian islands. This propensity to absorb data from other oral traditions was accentuated by feedback from written European sources.

The Biblical examples cited earlier are easy to analyse because they present in each instance an array of structural details amenable to comparison. The absorption of the odd genealogical or historical detail is more difficult, often impossible, to discern without an extended study of all sources—sources which are often not available in any case.[18] It is not the purpose here to dwell on the impact of literacy

[12] E. S. C. Handy, *History and culture in the Society Islands* (Honolulu, 1930), 115–18, 324–5.

[13] Barrère, 'Revisions', 104–5; Monberg, 'Ta'aroa', 270.

[14] Barrère, 'Revisions', 105.

[15] C. W. Newbury, '*Te hau pahu rahi:* Pomare II and the concept of inter-island government in eastern Polynesia', *JPS* 76 (1967), 477–81.

[16] Monberg, 'Ta'aroa', 277–8.

[17] E. Best, *Tuhoe: the children of the mist* (2 vols., New Plymouth, 1925), II. 532.

[18] For feedback among the Fante, whose traditions, and often their provenience as well, can be compared with independent evidence, see Chapter V. For two studies of the impact of literacy on the content of African oral traditions, see W. L. d'Azevedo, 'Uses of the past in Gola discourse', *JAH* 3 (1962), 29–31, and V. Görög, 'L'Origine de l'inégalité des races: étude de trente-sept contes africaines', *Cahiers d'Études Africaines*, 8 (1968), 295–301.

on oral societies. This problem has recently been studied in a number of different societies.[19] But it is important to emphasize the reverence for the printed word in 'literizing' societies. All societies contain competing elements and these will grasp at every opportunity to canonize in writing supporting traditions—traditions which in the past have proved too malleable to be reliable for these purposes.

Whether the resulting written tradition is based on earlier traditions or is more a product of the moment, and influenced by feedback, it becomes in turn the source of further feedback as the cycle repeats itself. Now that the first tide of literacy has swept in and subsided this cyclical pattern has become increasingly evident. In New Zealand Maori traditions began to be recorded soon after the imposition of British rule in 1841. Sir George Grey (Governor, 1845–55, 1861–8) was particularly assiduous in collecting Maori traditional materials. This collecting was done on a mass scale and appeared in print in an undigested but at the same time synthesized form. Grey's accounts included the three traditional visits to New Zealand, those of Kupe (*c.* 950), Toi (*c.* 1150), and the Fleet (*c.* 1350). William Colenso, who spent over thirty years among the Maori as a missionary, and who has been described as 'the foremost authority on the Maori' of his time, called the tradition of the Fleet 'a mythical rhapsody' and added that, 'while some educated Europeans wholly believed it, the New Zealanders themselves [i.e. the Maori] never did so'.[20] Colenso was referring particularly to the traditions appearing in Grey's *Nga Mahinga a Nga Tupuna*, or *Polynesian mythology*, first published in 1855. Simmons has demonstrated convincingly that this work is 'a patchwork of various traditions designed above all to present Maori settlement as following a coherent pattern where none existed in the original traditions'.[21] Grey's sources were admittedly the most renowned *tohungas* ('wise men') of his time, but each of their accounts, traceable through extant manuscript collections, is a local or regional one. Grey wove these parochial traditions into a coherent and persuasive pan-Maori tradition.[22]

All the components of the orthodox version of early Maori settle-

[19] J. Goody, *Literacy in traditional societies*, *passim*, and sources cited there.

[20] A. H. McLintock (ed.), *An encyclopedia of New Zealand* (3 vols., Wellington, 1966), I. 378; W. Colenso, 'On the Maori races of New Zealand', *Transactions and Proceedings of the New Zealand Institute*, 1 (1868), 404–5.

[21] D. R. Simmons, 'The sources of Sir George Grey's *Nga Mahi a Nga Tupuna*', *JPS* 75 (1966), 177–88.

[22] Ibid. 185.

ment and history noted above, including their dating, derive from Grey's work and from S. Percy Smith's *The lore of the Whare-Wananga*, published from 1913 to 1915. Again, the source for *The lore of the Whare-Wananga* was the testimony of certain *tohungas* which was mostly collected in the 1860s. Most of these testimonies were translated from Maori into English *in situ* and subsequently transcribed several times before publication forty years later.[23] The resulting published account was 'a compilation from different sources and different tribal areas' which, in its synthetic final form, purported to relate a coherent island-wide account of these allegedly epochal events.[24]

When all the individual sources still extant are compared a completely different picture emerges. Only three of the hundreds of genealogies collected dated Kupe to *c.* 950. Those others which mention him at all date him to a period in the fifteenth century. The accounts of Toi follow a similar pattern. Only two Maori areas had traditions of the Toi in question, although at least one other Toi is mentioned in other traditions. Most of the traditions which do mention Toi were recorded after 1870, when feedback from other areas of New Zealand was likely.[25] The genealogies which record Toi place him anywhere from 29 to 42 generations earlier. The standard version of the Fleet, which allegedly settled New Zealand *c.* 1350, is the version which is derived from Smith. It mentions five named canoes as comprising this Fleet and two others which sailed independently but arrived in New Zealand at about the same time. Smith's handling of Fleet traditions bore a marked resemblance to Sir George's. He collected a large number of genealogies from all over New Zealand. Many of these genealogies mentioned the arrival of various canoes. The genealogical depth of these canoe traditions ranged from 14 to 27 generations.[26] The date of 1350, that is 22 generations before 1900, was obtained by averaging all these variant traditions. In fact, only one set of canoe tradition genealogies brackets this mean. All the others are either much shorter or much longer. By genealogical reckoning, the last canoe arrived 325 years after the first.[27] Yet in his desire to postulate a large-scale migration

[23] Simmons, 'The New Zealand myth', 18, 20.
[24] Ibid. 21.
[25] Ibid. 25–6.
[26] Ibid. 28.
[27] Simmons (loc. cit.) speaks of a difference of 550 years, probably through a slip of the pen.

Smith manipulated evidence which most distinctly did not support such a hypothesis in order to create the concept of the 'Great Fleet'. Furthermore, it is not unlikely that Smith's informant for the Kupe and Toi genealogies based his own testimony for their dating on Smith's earlier published writings postulating the arrival of a fleet in *c.* 1350.[28]

The Kupe–Toi–Fleet sequence dated to *c.* 950/1350 has pervaded subsequent Maori traditional accounts as well as general historical accounts of New Zealand.[29] The traditional materials on which Grey's and Smith's works were based showed signs of independent origin and authenticity. Given the widespread literacy in New Zealand today and the fact that Grey's and Smith's works, with their tidy and persuasive chronological/genealogical framework, have been widely disseminated during the past fifty years, it is unlikely that there are many such independently derived traditions still available. The authors of *Nga Mahinga a Nga Tupuna* and *Lore of the Whare-Wananga*, which were largely based on undiluted traditions, distorted their sources by synthesizing the original accounts. Yet these works became in their turn the source for later traditions. Thus, the distorting process has irrevocably altered the sequential transmission of Maori traditions.

Fortunately, the tangled web of the use of Maori traditions during the past century has begun to be critically analysed in all its aspects—from first known recording of the traditions to their latest use. Such an analysis for Africa is at present still exceptional. Even so, there are many instances of recent investigators being referred to printed sources when inquiring about traditions.[30] In Bornu Cohen was told that Palmer 'was the man to consult if I wanted to know anything about Kanuri history'.[31] When a researcher in Karagwe in north-

[28] Simmons, 'The New Zealand myth', 30.

[29] Subsequent works on New Zealand which have accepted the Kupe–Toi–Fleet sequence and dated it to *c.* 950–*c.* 1350 include J. Grace, *Tuwharetoa: the history of the Maori people of the Taupo district* (Wellington, 1959), 19–23; J. Houstoun, *Maori life in old Taranaki* (Wellington, 1965), 13–14, 20–6; W. H. Oliver, *The story of New Zealand* (London, 1960), 24–6; G. L. Pearce, *The story of the Maori people* (Auckland, 1968), 28–31; W. J. Phillips, *Maori life and customs* (Wellington, 1966), 18–19. For a recent example of feedback contamination of Micronesian oral traditions, see R. Mitchell, 'Oral tradition and Micronesian history: a microcosmic approach', *Journal of Pacific History*, 5 (1970), 40n.

[30] Including the writer in his efforts to secure independent traditional information on the early history of the Fante coastal states. For more details, see Chapter V.

[31] R. Cohen, 'Bornu king lists', 47.

west Tanzania sought information on the royal genealogy she was repeatedly told that she could find what she needed in Speke.[32] Speke's genealogy of the Karagwe kings, with its five consecutive Ruhinda/Ntare couplets, bears every aspect of being the result either of a clerical error in transmission or a simple misunderstanding by Speke of the account given him. None the less, it has been hallowed by a century of being in print and available. Furthermore it is the longest recorded genealogy of the Karagwe dynasty.[33] Inevitably therefore it has become the official version of the royal genealogy and has driven other, shorter, variants from the field.[34] Jean Boulègue, who recently conducted fieldwork among the Wolof and Serer of Senegal, also found that the abundance of printed traditional accounts made it difficult to extract new and untainted testimonies from his informants regarding the early history of the states of the area.[35] Examples of this propensity to incorporate the written word into putatively oral traditions, or to base these 'traditional' accounts entirely on printed or written sources can be found wherever literacy has occurred in Africa, not only in areas of European language penetration but of Arabic influence as well.[36]

III THE EFFECTS OF INDIRECT RULE ON THE CHRONOLOGY OF ORAL TRADITION

A modest level of literacy or even an acquaintance with and respect for the written word will often be sufficient to facilitate the absorption of a certain amount of feedback into traditions. For Africa and Polynesia, however, the imposition of indirect rule has aggravated this problem. The advent of literacy in both areas (with the exception of Arabic in parts of Africa) was a concomitant of the imposition of colonial rule. For reasons not germane here this rule often took an

[32] Berger, 'Oral traditions in Karagwe', 3.

[33] Ibid. 2. Speke's list contained 22 *bakama* in 21 generations, certainly an indication, if one were needed, of its spurious nature.

[34] The latest study of Karagwe is I. K. Katote, *The making of the Karagwe kingdom* (Historical Association of Tanzania Paper No. 8) (Dar-es-Salaam, 1970). Katote does not discuss the Karagwe kinglist explicitly, but implies that the longest list of rulers is correct, 21, 29. See also J. Ford and R. de Z. Hall, 'The history of Karagwe (Bukoba district)', *Tanganyika Notes and Records*, 24 (1947), 5–15, 23–4, and Hans Cory, *History of the Bukoba district* (Dar-es-Salaam, 1958), 18–34.

[35] J. Boulègue, 'Le Sénégambie du milieu du XVe siècle au début du XVIIe siècle' (thèse du 3e cycle, Université de Paris, 1969), 22.

[36] For feedback among the Tswana, see Legassick, 'Sotho-Tswana peoples', 91. For the Fante, see Chapter V.

indirect form in which indigenous institutions were retained in principle, however truncated they may have become in function and authority. Whatever political roles traditions may have played in these societies in pre-colonial times they found ample scope for legitimizing functions under the regime of indirect rule. The challenge to maintain position or the opportunity to improve it led the traditional ruling elements of many polities to recast their traditions to suit the new circumstances. They soon learned that the colonial powers, particularly the British, evinced a profound respect for antiquity.

The Maori genealogies illustrate the traumatic impact of British rule and settlement in New Zealand on these genealogies. The Maori realized early that much of their ancestral land would be purchased by the colonial government. Although they never became reconciled to this unpalatable reality many groups none the less sought to profit from necessity. Land purchases inevitably involved disputes regarding ownership of the land. This ownership was predicated on traditional genealogies and could only be resolved through them. The extensive documentation available amply charts the course of this genealogical warfare.[37]

Indirect rule, in its various guises, prevailed throughout most of British Africa and, though to a much lesser degree, in French Africa as well. The tendency of the French to suppress established indigenous dynasties, together with the fact that many areas of French West Africa and French Equatorial Africa had been exposed to Islam and literacy before the advent of colonial rule reduced the impact of foreign rule on the content of the traditions of these areas.

The desire to gain favour with and advantage from their colonial overlords sometimes led polities to tailor their past so egregiously as to seem amusing in retrospect. The Ntem of western Cameroon fell under British control when the Germans were expelled from the area in 1914. In its subsequent administrative arrangements the colonial government in Nigeria placed the Ntem chief under the neighbouring Wiya ruler.[38] At first, this suited the expressed wishes of the Ntem

[37] K. Sinclair, 'Some historical notes on an Atiawa genealogy', *JPS* 60 (1951), 55–65; idem, *The origins of the Maori wars* (Wellington, 1957), 172–3. For a similar Maori example, see H. J. Fletcher, 'A review of the Toi–Kau–Rakau genealogies', *JPS* 39 (1930), 190–1.

[38] M. D. W. Jeffreys, 'Some historical notes on the Ntem', *JHSN* 2/2 (1961), 262–3.

chief since his main desire was to escape the onus of Banyo Fulani domination.[39] In 1924 a list of the Ntem chiefs was drawn up, showing a genealogy of six chiefs in three generations. The fact that the ancestor of the Wiya line was shown as the younger brother of the ancestor of the Ntem line probably reflected the beginnings of Ntem disenchantment with Wiya administrative control. By 1935 the Ntem chief had decided that he wished to be completely independent of Wiya control. To support his application to the British authorities to this effect he submitted a new history of the Ntem chiefdom. The number of Ntem chiefs now rose to 23 in an unspecified number of generations.[40] This new genealogy was submitted specifically to prove that Wiya should be subordinate to Ntem rather than the reverse. Not surprisingly, the administration in British Cameroons did not see fit to disturb the existing administrative structure in the light of the new Ntem genealogy.

IV THE INTERACTION OF STIMULI: THE KINGLISTS OF BUNYORO AND EARLY SCOTLAND

Listing further examples of this almost reflexive response to the perceived opportunities for the political use of the duration of the past would quickly assume the dimensions and character of a catalogue. It will be more useful to study in some detail two important examples of the political uses to which kinglists and 'venerable antiquity' have been put. These two illustrations are drawn from societies in very different stages of literacy but the circumstances which prompted the development of the traditional accounts and the role of 'feedback' are more enlightening in their similarity than in their contrast.

The evolution of the kinglist of Bunyoro provides an excellent illustration of the interacting effect of literacy and political expediency on the development of oral traditions. At the advent of British rule in the interlacustrine region the kingdom of Buganda was the most powerful of the many states in the area, and the one most favoured by the administration of the Uganda Protectorate. Not accidentally, the historiography of Buganda became much more fully developed than that of any other interlacustrine state. During the first quarter of this century two important works on the Ganda

[39] Ibid. 260–1.
[40] Ibid. 266–76. See also idem, 'Further historical notes on the Ntem', *JHSN* 2/3 (1962), 386n.

royal dynasty appeared.[41] The result of these works was a dynastic chronology that extended over 22 generations and 30 reigns before 1884. Information on the royal genealogy of Bunyoro paled in comparison. The longest lists of the *bakama* of Bunyoro in existence in 1930 showed 17 and 15 rulers in 17 and *x* generations and 14 rulers in 11 generations.[42]

From 1935 to 1937 a series of articles on the rulers of Bunyoro appeared in the *Uganda Journal*.[43] The author of these articles was Tito Gabafusa Winyi, the *mukama* of Bunyoro. The information in them was based on his own knowledge and that of his father Chwa II Kabarega (ruled *c.* 1869–1899, died on returning from exile in 1923) and Winyi signed the articles with the anonym K.W. to indicate this dual authorship. The list of *bakama* in these articles quickly superseded all previous lists and is now accepted as the official list of the *bakama* of Bunyoro. It is the list used in studies of interlacustrine history and chronology.[44] Given these factors it is useful to discuss the provenience and characteristics of this kinglist and to compare it with earlier printed lists.

K.W.'s account of the Nyoro dynasty was admittedly drawn up in response to a letter previously published in the *Uganda Journal*.[45] In

[41] Roscoe, *Baganda*, and A. Kaggwa, *Ekitabo kya Basekabaka be Buganda* (London, 1901; rev. eds. 1912 and 1927). The edition of Kaggwa's work used here is *The kings of Buganda* (tr. and ed. M. S. M. Kiwanuka) (Nairobi, 1971). The growth of the Ganda kinglists from the first one of eight names to those of Roscoe and Kaggwa presents interesting parallels to the Nyoro case. For a brief discussion of this evolution, see Kaggwa, *Kings* xxxix-xl, 192–3, and Kiwanuka, 'Sir Apolo Kaggwa and the pre-colonial history of Buganda', *UJ* 30 (1966), 145, 148.

[42] Roscoe, *The Bakitara or Banyoro* (London, 1923), 88, and R. Fisher, *Twilight tales of the black Baganda* (2nd ed., London, 1970), 114–72. J. Gorju, *Entre le Victoria, l'Albert et l'Edouard* (Rennes, 1920), 64; J. Czekanowski, *Forschungen im Nil-Kongo-Zwischengebiet* (5 vols., Leipzig, 1917–27), I. 56. This list was proferred by Daudi Kasagama, ruler of Toro and a scion of the Nyoro dynasty. Czekanowski discussed the merits of the lists of Kasagama, Wilson, and Fisher and concluded that 'the data of Kasagama are the best and most trustworthy list of the rulers of Bunyoro', ibid. 59. The reasons for this conclusion were not stated, but it seems to have been based on the fact that Kasagama's list was the longest of the three. For instance, Czekanowski argued that Fisher had omitted Kasagama's generations 3–8, even though Fisher claimed this his own list was complete and that his third ruler was the son of his second. The relationship of these rulers can be seen more clearly in Table 2, p. 108.

[43] K. W., 'The kings of Bunyoro-Kitara', *UJ* 3 (1935), 155–60, 4 (1936), 75–83, 5 (1937), 53–69.

[44] e.g. Cohen, 'Survey', 182–3, 184; B. K. Taylor, *The western lacustrine Bantu* (London, 1962), 19–20.

[45] K.W., 'Kings', 155.

this letter a Belgian professor had briefly summarized some of the kinglists of Bunyoro which had appeared in print. He deplored their meagreness, noted their contradictory elements, and expressed a hope that 'fuller information' on the Nyoro dynasty might be forthcoming.[46] K.W., in introducing his account, modestly submitted that 'some alterations' in the Nyoro dynastic genealogy were necessary.[47] The extent of these alterations may be seen in Table 2, p. 108, which compares the kinglists of Bunyoro published before K.W.'s account with the latter.[48]

The composite nature of the K.W. list is immediately apparent, especially for the fourth to twelfth *bakama*. The assigning of the same praise name to different rulers makes it impossible to speak with any finality, but apparently only Mpuga Rukidi, Chwa I, and the last several *bakama* are mentioned in all the sources. As the connector of the Nyoro dynasty with the Bacwezi, Mpuga Rukidi would have become a fixture in all Nyoro traditions as the progenitor of the royal dynasty and his ubiquity in the lists is not surprising. Several other *bakama* in K.W.'s list are mentioned in only a single other source. Several names mentioned in the earlier lists are not positively identifiable with any particular name in K.W.'s list.[49] Otherwise, K.W. seems to have used every royal name in the earlier printed sources. Indeed, recourse to the single note by Derscheid could have supplied him with all but a very few names.[50] The resulting Nyoro royal

[46] J. M. Derscheid, 'The Bakama of Bunyoro', *UJ* 2 (1934), 252–3.

[47] K.W., 'Kings', 155.

[48] The numbers represent the ordinal placement of a ruler in a particular source. Kaggwa's and Roscoe's accounts of Buganda mentioned only two early Nyoro rulers. One of them, Winyi or Wunyi, cited as a contemporary of the second Ganda *kabaka*, Cwa, has erroneously been identified with KW_4. Cohen, 'Survey', 188 and chart opp. 190. KW_4 was also cited (see Table 2) as a contemporary of *kabaka* Kaima, who ruled, according to Ganda traditions, six generations later than Cwa. Actually the Wunyi of Ganda accounts should be identified with K.W.'s Mpuga Rukidi (KW_1), who was called Winyi by Bikunya and Wunyi by Gorju. Fisher, *Twilight tales*, 120, described how Mpuga Rukidi was renamed Winyi. Nyoro traditions, of course, do not mention *kabaka* Cwa at all. Gorju followed Fisher, *Twilight tales*, 61 (first published in 1911).

[49] These include B7—Rukidi Olimi Omuitabyaro
R5—Oyo Kabambaiguru (this is perhaps the same as KW_3, whom Roscoe simply called Nyimba)
R8—Isaza Gabigogo (perhaps the same as F8 below)
F8—Isansa. Fisher, Kasagama, and Gorju distinguished between an Olimi and his son and successor Isansa. K.W. made these into one *mukama*, KW16, Olimi III Isansa.

[50] All the royal names (as opposed to praise titles) used by K.W., except

TABLE 2

Printed Lists of the Bakama of Bunyoro, 1902–37

KW 1935/7	J¹ 1902	J² 1902	K 1907	F 1911	G¹ 1920	G² 1920	R 1923	B 1927
1 Mpuga Rukidi (Winyi)	1	1	1	1	1	1	1	1
2 Ochaki Rwangira				2	2			
3 Oyo Nyimba				3	3		2	2?
4 Winyi I Ruhembeka						6		6
5 Olimi I Rukidi Rwitamahanga	2?					7		
6 Nyabongo I Chwa Rulemu						3		
7 Winyi II Rubagiragesa	6?		4			2		
8 Olimi II Ruhundawangeye							6	
9 Nyarwa Omuzikyakyaro			5					4
10 Chwa I Rumomahanga	5		6?	4	4?	4?	3	5
11 Masamba (called Dunego in F and G¹)				5	5			
12 Kyebambe I Winyi Omuzikya						5		
13 Winyi III Ruguruka Macholya			7	6	6		4	3
14 Nyaika						9		
15 Kyebambe II Bikaju		3?	9?			8	7	8
16 Olimi III Isansa	3	5	8/10	7/8	7/8	10		
17 Duhaga 1 Chwa Mujuiga	4	4?	11	9	9	11	9	
18 Olimi IV Kasoma	8		12	10	10	12		
19 Kyebambe III Nyamutukura (called Dubongoza in F and G¹)	9	8	13	11	11	13?	10	
20 Nyabongo II Mugenyi	10	9	14	12	12	14	11	
21 Olimi V Rwabakale				13				
22 Kyebambe IV Kamurasi	11	10	15	14	13	14	12	

Note to Table 2: KW—K.W., 'Kings'.

J¹ —list collected by George Wilson, Deputy Commissioner, Uganda Protectorate, in H. H. Johnston, *The Uganda Protectorate* (2 vols., London, 1902), II. 596–8.

J² —list collected by the Revd. A. B. Fisher, the husband of Ruth Fisher, in ibid. II. 598–9.

K —list produced by Daudi Kasagama, ruler of Toro, for Czekanowski in 1907, in Czekanowski, *Forschungen*, T. 55–6.

F —Fisher, *Twilight tales*, 114–72.

G¹ —Gorju, *Entre le Victoria*, 61–2.

G² —Fr. Torelli's list in ibid. 64; this list was based on 'the chants of the native *aèdes* [bards]'.

B —Petero Bikunya, *Ky 'Abakama ba Bunyoro* (London, 1927), as cited by Derscheid.

genealogy of 26 names spanned 18 generations, which brought it nicely into line with Ganda traditions.

Indeed, there is some indication that K.W. used Kaggwa's Ganda traditional history as a frame of reference for his own work. Oliver has accepted the close correlation between K.W.'s account of Nyoro traditional history and that of Kaggwa for Buganda as evidence in favour of the reliability of K.W.'s account.[51] Oliver was referring primarily to the ebb and flow of fortune in the incessant Ganda–

Masamba, Nyaika, and Duhaga, were mentioned in Derscheid's note. It was not necessary in any case to have a written source for the name Duhaga since it was the name of K.W.'s brother and predecessor.

[51] R. Oliver, 'Traditional histories', 113. Oliver concluded that 'if it [K.W.'s account] was a forgery it would be brilliant'.

Nyoro wars—'generation by generation and province by province it [K.W.'s account] squares with the traditions of Buganda'.[52] This is true in so far as the two bodies of tradition are mutually checkable. In its broad outlines there is a certain internal consistency and thrust in K.W.'s account. It agreed with Ganda traditions when it was expedient to do so, but contradicted them when Nyoro interests demanded. There was no reason for the Nyoro *mukama* to dispute the claims of Kaggwa that Buganda expanded at the expense of Bunyoro. After all the final result of this expansive product was clear to all and could scarcely be denied. It behoved Nyoro traditional accounts to support Ganda claims because these latter admitted that Bunyoro had once been the most important state in the area. In short, Ganda traditions themselves supplied a line of argumentation for Nyoro efforts to regain such territories as the 'lost counties'. On the other hand, K.W.'s account of the establishment of the Ganda dynasty contradicted Kaggwa's account. Kaggwa claimed that the Ganda dynasty sprang from Kintu and antedated the establishment of the Bito dynasty in Nyoro by several generations. The account of the establishment of the Ganda dynasty in K.W., however, called the founder of Buganda Kato and identified him with Kimera, the third *kabaka* in Kaggwa's history. Furthermore, according to Nyoro traditions, Kato was the [younger?] twin of Mpuga Rukidi and was sent by Mpuga Rukidi to rule Buganda as viceroy of Bunyoro.[53] It was obviously not in the best interests of the Nyoro to accept Ganda claims for the priority of the establishment of their own dynasty.[54]

Where Ganda and Nyoro traditions, as exemplified by Kaggwa and K.W., related the same events, they generally agreed with each other—or rather K.W.'s account generally agreed with Kaggwa, differing only when Bunyoro interests required that they do so. With regard to the Nyoro kinglist, however, the pattern is very different. Whereas Kaggwa and Roscoe found it unnecessary to refer to more

[52] Ibid. 113–14. Such close correlation, it need hardly be emphasized, is suspicious in itself. For the 'generation by generation' aspects of this correlation, see Table 3, p. 111.

[53] K.W., 'Kings', 75. See above p. 66.

[54] K.W. further strengthened his argument for Nyoro precedence by claiming that two dynasties had preceded his own. To the first, the Abatembuzi, he assigned twenty rulers, while claiming that 'some of the names of the first kings have been lost'. K.W., 'Kings', 156–7. Only ten years previously Bikunya had ascribed only five rulers to this dynasty, Beattie, *Nyoro state*, 58. Of course all three dynasties were genealogically connected in K.W.'s and later accounts. See ibid. 57, for a schematic presentation of these connections.

than a few Nyoro *bakama* when they reconstructed Ganda traditional history, K.W. constantly referred to Ganda *bakabaka* when constructing his own list of the *bakama* of Bunyoro. Many of these references are patent *obiter dicta*, whose only purpose seemed to have been to establish the principle that for every Ganda *kabaka* there was a contemporary Nyoro *mukama*.[55] Table 3 illustrates the synchronisms with Ganda *bakabaka* mentioned by K.W. The generational calculations necessarily assume the contemporaneity of Mpuga Rukidi and Kato/Kimera since such a contemporaneity is a basic assumption of K.W.'s list. The names of the *bakama* are not repeated here from Table 2; the numbers KW1, KW2 . . . refer to the numbering of *bakama* in Table 2.

The generational discrepancies between the two kinglists start almost at the beginning and reach their maximum divergence as early as the reign of the seventh *mukama*. Such a discrepancy is almost impossible but not necessarily inexplicable. Kiwanuka, in editing Kaggwa's work, suggests that an earlier date for Kimera would obviate the necessity for further ingenious efforts to reconcile the two genealogies. Since, however, we are discussing the provenience and rationale of the Nyoro kinglist, we must, *ex hypothesi*, accept the contemporaneity of Kato/Kimera and Mpuga Rukidi, since this coevality is one of the list's basic premisses. Assuming differential generational lengths for Bunyoro and Buganda rulers because of different modes of succession could conceivably account for the generational differences over the whole length of the two dynasties, but is of no use when dealing with only a small part of this period.[56] Nor is the fact that 'long' reigns were assigned to the early *bakama* by K.W. sufficient, as suggested by some scholars.[57] The practice of assigning long reigns to early rulers is, as we have already noticed, a convention which should be ignored when chronological/genealogical calculations are being made. Still, the acceptance, for the sake of argument, of extremely long reigns for the early rulers of Bunyoro and, by arguing *ex silentio*, the acceptance of short reigns for the

[55] See, e.g., K.W., 'Kings', 77, 83, 56.

[56] E. B. Haddon, 'Kibuka', *UJ* 21 (1957), 115–17, suggested the possibility of differential regnal averages as a solution to this problem.

[57] Haddon, 'Kibuka', 115, followed by J. Sykes, 'The eclipse at Biharwe', *UJ* 23 (1959), 46. George Wilson on the other hand asserted that only ten *bakama* before Kabarega ruled longer than 'nine or ten years', Johnson, *Uganda protectorates*, II. 597. This is in interesting contrast to Nyakatura's statement cited below that *bakama* who ruled less than nine years were not remembered at all.

TABLE 3

Comparative generational and regnal counts—Buganda and Bunyoro

Nyoro *bakama*	Ganda *bakabaka*	Nyoro gen.	Ganda gen.
KW1	Kato/Kimera (75–6)	1/1	1/1
KW2	Kigara (77)	2/2	3/4
KW3	Kiimba (77)	3/2	4/5
KW4	Kaima (78)	4/3	5/6
KW5	Nakibinga/Mulondo (78)	5/4	6–7/7–8
KW6	—	6/5	
KW7	Kimbugwe/Katarega (80)	7/6	11–12/10–11
KW8	—	8/7	
KW9	—	9/8	
KW10	—	10/8	
KW11	—	11/8	
KW12	Kagulu (83)	12/9	18/14
KW13	Kagulu (53)	13/10	18/14
KW14	—	14/11	
KW15	—	15/11	
KW16	Kyabugu (56)	16/12	23/15
KW17	Junju (57)	17/13	24/16
KW18	—	18/14	
KW19	Semakokiro/Kamanya (60)	19/14	25–6/16–17
KW20	Suna (61)	20/15	27/18
KW21	—	21/16	
KW22	Suna/Mutesa II (62–3)	22/16	27–8/18–19
KW23	Mutesa II/Mwanga (62–6	23/17	28–30/19–20[58]

Note: Only those *bakabaka* mentioned by K.W. or Nyakatura are included in this list.

corresponding *bakabaka* could reconcile the generational discrepancies. Doing so, however, would involve a series of improbable assumptions. It is necessary to assume identical ages for Mpuga Rukidi and Kato/Kimera. The two first generations are therefore exactly contemporaneous. For the next three generations in Bunyoro we have seven generations in Buganda. This implies a minimum period of not much less than 150 years. Fifty-year regnal generations in Bunyoro and 21-year regnal generations in Buganda would be possible if ultimogeniture had been consistently practised in the

[58] Numbers in parentheses are page references to K.W.'s articles. The generational calculations for the Ganda *bakabaka* are based on Kiwanuka's calculations in Kaggwa, *Kings*, 195, and differ slightly from Kaggwa's own account, but not for the crucial earliest period.

former and primogeniture rigidly followed in the latter. But then it would be necessary to postulate an abrupt change in Nyoro succession patterns about the time of the reign of Winyi II since from his time to 1900 there were twelve generations in Bunyoro and only eleven in Buganda. This is a series of assumptions which will not bear scrutiny.

A more plausible explanation can be found in the nature of the Bunyoro kinglist itself. It has been assumed throughout this discussion that K.W.'s list of the Nyoro *bakama* both responded to and oriented itself on Kaggwa's and Roscoe's accounts of the *bakabaka* of Buganda. This assumption, while not provable, is strongly reinforced by the structure of K.W.'s account, particularly his extensive use of synchronistic references, even when not called for, and by the very ambience in which this kinglist appeared. The personality-orientation of oral tradition has already been noted.[59] This tendency is exemplified in the Nyoro kinglist by the propensity to disregard the more abstract concept of generations in constructing these synchronisms. Furthermore the common pattern of one-ruler-to-one-ruler is apparent in K.W.'s list. That is, each of the earliest *bakama* was remembered as the contemporary of only one *kabaka*. The only exception of necessity occurs in the reign of Olimi I, who killed his Ganda counterpart in battle. After the time of Winyi II overlapping becomes more common. The implied converse is that each *mukama* had one contemporary *kabaka*—no more, no less.[60] With the one exception noted, this is indeed the pattern for the reigns of the first six *bakama*. In other words, generations were ignored while emphasis was put on reigns, that is, on individuals. From the perspective of reigns there is little discrepancy in the early chronology of the two dynasties. In the later parts of the Nyoro royal genealogy the synchronisms become more circumstantial and overlapping more common. There is then no effort to match up the Nyoro genealogy reign by reign with the Ganda accounts. Nyoro historians recognized that there were several more *bakabaka* during the period after Winyi II, even though the number of generations was almost the same. John Nyakatura, who wrote a history of Bunyoro a decade after K.W.'s articles appeared, attributed this to the fact that in

[59] See Chapter I.

[60] For the lack of overlapping synchronisms in the Asante stool histories, when compared to the Asantehenes, see Chapter VI. The Asantehenes served the same purpose in the compilation of these stool histories as the Ganda *bakabaka* did for K.W.—reference-points to orient his genealogical compass to.

Buganda 'they count[ed] anyone who sat on the throne . . . [even] Mwanga I who spent only nine days as Kabaka', whereas in Bunyoro only *bakama* who had ruled at least nine years were remembered.[61]

In short, the Nyoro list of K.W. bears many of the hallmarks of an originally telescoped kinglist infused with new names at a later date and for specific purposes.[62] The raw materials for this task were all available in the earlier published lists of Nyoro *bakama*. The spread of literacy made it possible to utilize these when the occasion required it.[63]

The above analysis is, of necessity, based partly on speculation, probabilities, and inference. There is, however, one datum which, when taken in conjunction with the circumstances already discussed, impeaches the validity of K.W.'s list on more substantial, definable, grounds. Remember that K.W. was in fact Tito Gabafusa Winyi, *mukama* of Bunyoro. Winyi acceded to the Nyoro throne in 1924. His title, for at least the first ten years of his reign, was not Winyi IV, but Winyi II. He both referred to himself in correspondence and signed several documents during this period, including the Bunyoro Agreement of 1933, as Winyi II.[64] Works on Uganda published during the period and which mention Winyi unanimously refer to him as Winyi II.[65] There is thus every reason to argue that until 1935, when the first of the series of articles appeared in the *Uganda Journal*, Winyi conceived of himself as only the second *mukama* of that name. This is consistent with the information in the kinglists available before that time. None of these showed more than two Winyis before 1924, and most showed only one. In a trice, Winyi II became metamorphosed into Winyi IV. The kinglist in K.W.'s article is apparently the first

[61] Nyakatura, 'Abakama', 55.

[62] For instance, there may have been circumstances in Bunyoro during the early 1930s, besides the appearance of Derscheid's note, which stimulated the need to flesh out the Nyoro kinglists. The investigator who is interested in interlacustrine chronology must try to determine if this is so.

[63] For the extent of Winyi IV's education, see A. R. Dunbar, *A history of Bunyoro-Kitara* (Nairobi, 1965), 136.

[64] See Winyi II to J. R. P. Postlethwaite, 23 July 1928, cited in Postlethwaite, *I look back* (London, 1947), 118; Postlethwaite was DC, Bunyoro, from 1927 to 1928. See also Bunyoro Agreement dd 23 Oct. 1933, and signed 'Tito G. Winyi II', *Uganda Gazette*.

[65] e.g. H. B. Thomas and R. Scott, *Uganda* (London, 1935), 462; 'Tito Gabafusa Winyi II' was made an Honorary Commander of the Order of the British Empire in the New Year's Honours List of 1934. General Notice No. 3, *Uganda Official Gazette*, 5 Jan. 1934, 3.

appearance of the name 'Winyi IV'.[66] Thereafter, of course, it was the official title of the former Winyi II.

This analysis of the Nyoro kinglist should be regarded as both speculative and tentative. My purpose is simply to suggest some of the chronological and genealogical anomalies of the most widely accepted list and to emphasize that K.W.'s work was more a piece of applied research than an unadorned presentation of received oral traditions; for example, he evidently journeyed as far as Rwanda for information.[67] Nor is it unlikely that he consulted some of the printed lists of *bakama*. The largely synthetic list that resulted may just possibly be more valid than any earlier list, although this is both very unlikely and unprovable. In any case any further evaluation of K.W.'s list would require both the fieldwork necessary to provide a more profound acquaintance with Nyoro society and local archival research to provide further context to the development of this list.

The expansion of the Nyoro kinglist may not have affected seriously the perceived duration of the Nyoro state. Other traditions, particularly those of Buganda, testify to the existence of the Nyoro polity at the beginning of the sixteenth century. Normally, though, the expansion of a kinglist entails the prolongation of the time-depth of the polity involved, as the Ntem case illustrates. Still, the means and motivation which resulted in the expansion of the Nyoro kinglist are instructive. The processes there illustrate very aptly how the conjunction of extraneous circumstances can and often did result in the creation of what has often subsequently passed for undiluted and independent oral tradition.

The tendency to use the past for the purposes of the present is not confined to oral or partially literate societies. The historiography of forty completely fictitious rulers of the Scots illustrates the political purposes for which genealogies and kinglists have often been used in literate societies as well. Early Scottish chronicles invariably identified Fergus m. Erc (474–501) as the first ruler of the Scots after their emigration from Ireland.[68] During the twelfth century Scotland began to fall into the political orbit of England and at the same time the chronicles' accounts of the early Scottish kings began to take on a

[66] K.W., 'Kings', 156.

[67] Dunbar, *Bunyoro-Kitara*, 7. I have dealt more fully with Nyoro regnal chronology in my 'K.W.'s Nyoro kinglist'.

[68] T. Innes, *A critical essay on the ancient inhabitants of the northern parts of Britain, or Scotland* (Edinburgh, 1879), 361–3, 367. This work was first published in 1729.

new complexion. At the coronation of William the Lion in 1165 a genealogy was recited which traced the ancestry of the Scottish dynasty back to one Scota, who was identified as a daughter of the Pharaoh at the time of the Exodus.[69] Furthermore, subsequent chronicles tended to place the line of Dalraidic (Scottish) kings before the Pictish rulers, whereas earlier chronicles had correctly shown the two lines to be contemporaneous. This innovation allowed them to place the foundation of the monarchy several centuries earlier.

By the end of the thirteenth century, then, several genealogies of the ancestors of Fergus m. Erc had developed, although all of them still regarded him as the first ruler of the Scots.[70] After 1291 several factors combined to carry this process one step further. In that year Edward I of England claimed the Scottish throne. In seeking to enlist the support of the Papacy in 1301 he advanced the usual tale that the British kingdom had been founded by Brutus the Trojan. The Scottish representatives responded with the story of Scota and claimed that their own monarchy had been established at the same time as the British kingdom and had never been subject to it; the new history was gradually replacing the older, more sober accounts of the origins of the Scottish monarchy.[71]

This transformation was completed with the appearance of John of Fordun's *Scotochronicon*, which was written between 1363 and 1384.[72] Fordun metamorphosed this genealogy into a kinglist and asserted that Fergus m. Feradach, hitherto just another name in the genealogy, had actually founded the Scottish kingdom in 330 B.C.[73] Fordun admitted that, although he had spent much time in searching out 'old records', information on these early rulers was scanty, and in fact he only identified three of his forty-five new rulers by name.[74]

These ancient rulers were not to be denied, however, and in due course they dramatically made their appearance in Scottish historiography. In 1526 Hector Boece published his *Scotorum Historiae*. This

[69] W. F. Skene's introduction to *John of Fordun's Chronicle of the Scottish nation* (Edinburgh, 1872), lxii–lxiii. This work was first published in the fifteenth century.

[70] For these genealogies, see Innes, *Critical essay*, 135–40.

[71] E. L. G. Stones (ed.), *Anglo-Scottish relations, 1174–1328: some selected documents* (London, 1965), 97–100, 113; Innes, *Critical essay*, 334–40, 367–9.

[72] For Fordun, see ibid. 123–30.

[73] John of Fordun, *Chronicle*, 41–2.

[74] Innes, *Critical essay*, 136–7, 382–3; J. B. Black, 'Boece's *Scotorum Historiae*' in University of Aberdeen, *Quatercentury of the death of Hector Boece, first principal of the University* (Aberdeen, 1937), 37.

work contained a detailed account, in the image of Geoffrey of Monmouth, of these rulers, now reduced in number to thirty-nine.[75] Boece not only revealed to the world the names of these hitherto anonymous rulers but also provided a marvellous amount of circumstantial detail regarding their rule.[76] The most interesting and relevant of these details was that no fewer than twelve of these rulers had been deposed, exiled, or assassinated for their tyrannical behaviour. Happily, this new information justified the recent action of the Scottish barons who had killed James III in battle in 1488; their action was thereby retrospectively clothed with the raiment of legitimacy and precedent.[77] Boece claimed that his account of these rulers was derived from newly discovered manuscripts, which regrettably disappeared nearly as quickly as they had appeared. One author, writing soon after Boece, claimed to have consulted them; thereafter they were not seen by any known historian, although several later scholars searched for them. Thomas Innes later demonstrated that, if these sources had ever existed in written form, they were palpable forgeries of a period only shortly before Boece wrote.[78] Truly Boece's account of these Scottish kings was 'very intriguing, very edifying, and very unhistorical'.[79] As christened by Boece they derived their names from names in the earlier genealogies, but much distorted, and from the names of chieftains mentioned in Tacitus.[80]

None the less, despite its obvious artificiality, Boece's account of early Scottish history remained nearly intact for two centuries. The long historiographic lives experienced by these kings can be attributed primarily to their political utility. Half a century after Boece wrote, George Buchanan published his *Rerum Scoticarum Historia.* Buchanan was a more careful historian than Boece and certainly less credulous. But, although he recognized that Boece's rulers were fictitious, he repeated and even embellished his account of them.[81] Buchanan perpetuated the historicity of these rulers, not for their historical value but for their roles as exemplars and precedents.

[75] Innes, *Critical essay*, 36–8; Kendrick, *British antiquity*, 65–8; Innes, *Critical essay*, 140–6.

[76] For an account of these rulers, based on Boece, see Buchanan, *History of Scotland*, I. 149–230, which was first published in 1582.

[77] Innes, *Critical essay*, 149–50; Black, 'Boece's *Scotorum Historiae*', 51–2.

[78] Innes, *Critical essay*, 132–5, and Black, 'Boece's *Scotorum Historiae*', 47–53, discuss Boece's sources.

[79] Ibid. 42.

[80] Innes, *Critical essay*, 145.

[1] Ibid. 209–11; Black, 'Boece's *Scotorum Historiae*', 40, 44.

Buchanan, unlike Boece, was 'a party man' and actively supported the deposition of Mary Stuart in 1567.[82] Boece's account of the fate meted out to unpopular Scottish rulers 1,500 years before provided a very convenient historical precedent and ensured the perpetuation of the memory of them.

When the Stuarts ascended the English throne their apologists could no longer use these early Scottish rulers in the accustomed way and they lay dormant during most of the seventeenth century. Their utility, though diminished, had not yet ended, however. James II (VII), the last reigning Stuart king, though unpopular in England, retained support in Scotland. In 1685 Sir George Mackenzie, king's advocate in Edinburgh, published a new defence of the antiquity of the Scottish monarchy. Ignoring the by then obsolete significance of the twelve deposed monarchs, he emphasized the antiquity that the entire line represented. His argument was peculiarly representative of the common acceptance of an interrelationship between antiquity, legitimacy, and power:

> It seems to me a great injury to our kings to have their line shortened, so as thereby to postpone them to many others . . . Whoever shortens it [the royal line] lessens the influence of our kings and endangers the succession . . . I admire [wonder] that any of the subjects of Great Britain did not think it a degree of *lèse majesté* to injure and shorten the royal line of their kings.[83]

Boece's account had been under intermittent attack since the middle of the sixteenth century but the fitness of his version of the origin of the Scottish monarchy and the weakness of these attacks combined to ensure its perpetuation.[84] With the death of Anne, the last reigning Stuart, in 1714, the necessity to champion Boece against all-comers ended. In 1729 Thomas Innes's *A critical essay on the ancient inhabitants of the north of England, or Scotland* appeared. Innes was a critical historian who valued objective inquiry over patriotic considerations. He argued that the account of Boece, so reminiscent of the now discredited Geoffrey of Monmouth, 'brought reproach on the country'.[85] By exposing the spuriousness of Fordun's

[82] Ibid. 40; Innes, *Critical essay*, 209–11.

[83] Sir George Mackenzie, *A defence of the antiquity of the royal line of Scotland* (Edinburgh, 1685), 10–11.

[84] Mackenzie's tract was written in reply to such attacks. For the critics of Boece, see Kendrick, *British Antiquity*, 85–6, and Black, 'Boece's *Scotorum Historiae*', 43–6.

[85] Innes, *Critical essay*, 6. Innes argued that, even if Fergus mac Erc was reckoned the first king of the Scots the Scottish royal line would be of 'greater

and Boece's sources and the political expediency served by Boece's and Buchanan's accounts Innes demolished whatever credit they still retained. What is important, however, is that they had risen and were fostered and perpetuated in circumstances which rendered their version of the antiquity of the Scottish monarchy, however implausible, very attractive. This genealogical myth was sustained, not by its intrinsic historical plausibility, but because it repeatedly proved to be a potent political tool. The birth, growth, active life, decay, and death in Scottish historiography of the first Scottish kingdom is instructive, if necessarily depressing. It demonstrates that utility often transcends veracity as the propelling force for this kind of tradition.

V THE IMPORTANCE OF TEXTUAL CRITICISM

The uses of royal genealogies and kinglists in Bunyoro and in Scotland illustrate the similar patterns in this regard among both literate and oral or newly literate societies, but the historian's task in assessing the extent of this problem in a newly literate society will perforce be more difficult and his conclusions less secure. He must first recognize, however, that the alarming propensity of partially literate societies to regard oral traditional materials as inferior to written sources has been almost reflexive in its application. Recognition that feedback materials may be co-opted into traditional accounts is essential when working with materials that may claim to be undiluted oral traditions.

In turn the investigator must understand the whole range of problems that the process of feedback implies for his assessment of 'oral' data. For instance, it cannot be assumed that accounts are mutually supportive because they are consistent with each other. In his scepticism the investigator must *a priori* assume that any consistency is the result of recourse to printed, written, or para-literate sources or because of deference to 'official' accounts.[86] Obviously the likelihood

antiquity than any hereditary monarchy of Europe of one uninterrupted race can pretend to', ibid. 5.

[86] Para-literate sources may be defined as verbal testimonies from sources known to be literate, which have been subsumed into traditional accounts at some time in the past. Given the difficulty of detecting even the more blatant forms of feedback, it may be impossible in most cases to evaluate the effect of para-literate testimony, but the possibility of its existence in any given tradition should be borne in mind. The effects of para-literate feedback can be seen in a recent account of the Hanya people of south-western Angola. The investigator recorded his 'astonishment' when a very old, completely unschooled informant in this 'one of the most remote corners' of Hanya country, dated the origin of the

of traditional accounts containing such extraneous matter will vary from locale to locale and from one type of tradition to another. It is less likely to appear in 'eye-witness' testimonies than in accounts of the earliest periods of a society. At the same time the ability to absorb feedback into traditions will obviously directly depend on the level and extent of literacy in a society as well as on the extent of the printed sources available for it.[87] In short, it behoves the investigator to apply with equal rigour the same kinds of textual criticism that he would to a written document when assessing the impact of feedback.

If anything, the importance of applying tests of textual validity is even greater with regard to the particular ambiences under which a traditional account arose and was recorded. Obviously, the determination of these circumstances will not always be possible, but it is always desirable. The Nyoro examples illustrate some of the types of stimuli which encourage the amplification of remembered traditions. The evidence for this case is rather more clear-cut than most others are likely to be. In order to interpret his traditions most properly the researcher should know, to as great an extent as possible, the political and social vicissitudes his society underwent in both the colonial and independence periods. He can in turn usually, and properly, assume that similar circumstances conducive to the changing of traditions obtained in the earlier periods, even though he will not often be able to document this particular assumption.

The reader may be prompted to ask at this point whether, if the arguments advanced here are accepted, there is in fact any point at all in collecting and assessing oral traditions for their chronological

---

local royal line to the time of 'Liaku kao', that is, Diogo Cão, the Portuguese navigator who discovered the Congo river in 1482. A. Hauenstein, *Les Hanya: description d'un groupe ethnique bantou de l'Angola* (Wiesbaden, 1967), 5. My thanks to Joseph C. Miller for this reference. The existence and dating of Diogo Cão would have been learned at the Portuguese schools in the area. As the earliest mentioned of the Portuguese, who now ruled throughout the area, it would not be unnatural for Cão to enter Hanya traditions as a chronological *terminus a quo*.

[87] This may be a facile dichotomy. The impact of para-literate feedback, as exemplified in the previous footnote, would be independent of available printed sources. And even when printed sources are available, their impact may only be cumulative over time. For instance, D. W. Cohen found that in Busoga Y. K. Lubogo's *A history of Busoga*, published in 1960, had 'been read by virtually no one' six years later. Cohen, *The historical tradition of Busoga: Mukama and Kintu* (Oxford, 1972), 30, 205. The influence on the traditions of the Busoga of Lubogo's work and of Cohen's own researches may become more apparent in the next few decades.

materials. Obviously it is important that these historical sources, like any historical source, be collected and evaluated. But any evaluation of them must be based on the recognition that they seldom were designed to be abstract relations of past events—although they may often have been interpreted to be. Even so, such traditions will often contain a core of useful, reliable chronological information. It is regrettable, but none the less most often true, that the chronological aspects of traditions are the elements least likely to be authentic. Societies for whom the past was a prelude of uncertain duration to and justification for the present could only respond to the calendrical biases of twentieth-century western civilization and the political circumstances of foreign rule by meeting it on terms alien to themselves. This necessitated, *inter alia*, using, when possible, literate civilization's own data. Doing so lightened the impossible task these societies felt was imposed on them. Concomitantly, however, it has increased the task of those who will use these materials, and who must work and rework them with increasing sophistication and critical awareness.

CHAPTER IV

Quantification: Data *v.* Method

> . . . we may legitimately expect to be able to use king-lists and genealogies for chronological purposes with increased confidence and greater precision.[1]

> This [African chronology] is a field in which statistical method has simply nothing to offer.[2]

THE quantitative approach to the study of chronology has proceeded over twenty-five centuries from the simple generational calculations of the Greek chronographers to the use of sophisticated statistical techniques by contemporary historians. The most extensive use of statistical methods to infer early chronology has been made by historians of Africa.[3] Statistical analysis can have the effect of dazzling the reader and inducing a belief in its infallibility as an indicator of probabilities. It may be a truism that no statistical inference can be stronger than the quality of the data from which it is drawn, but it is obviously a point that bears constant reiteration. The other chapters of this work discuss in ample detail the nature of the evidence with which the student of the chronology of oral tradition must work. The analysis of this evidence suggests its use, however random, to support statistical inferences of any kind is severely limited.

Nevertheless, a large body of raw data has been gathered in the preparation of this work and, because of the perceptible inclination of the African historian to utilize statistical inference as a tool for

[1] P. C. Gibbons, 'King-lists and chronology: a note on work in progress', *GNQ* 8 (Jan. 1966), 25.

[2] Jones, 'Problems of African chronology', 168.

[3] See, e.g., I. Wilks, 'The growth of Akwapim state: a study in the control of evidence' in J. Vansina, R. Mauny, and L.-V. Thomas (eds.), *The historian in tropical Africa* (London, 1964), 396–408; idem, 'Aspects of bureaucratisation in Ashanti in the nineteenth century', *JAH* 7 (1966), 229–31; Flight, 'The chronology of the kings and queenmothers of Bono-Manso'; Karugire, *A history of the kingdom of Nkore*, 27–30. For an excellent non-African example, see T. R. Trautmann, 'Length of generation and reign in ancient India', *JAOS* 89 (1969), 564–77.

suggesting chronological parameters, it may be useful to analyse quantitatively this 'hard' (that is, documented) material for various kinds of chronological indicators in order to determine the extrapolative value of quantitative analysis. These will include the following categories:

(*a*) average expectation of generation length (unrefined)
(*b*) average expectation of the length of five- and ten-generation sequences
(*c*) limits of a 'fraternal' generation
(*d*) limits of a father/son dual generation
(*e*) expectation of average regnal length in rotating succession systems
(*f*) expectation of average regnal length in promotional succession systems[4]

For two reasons any analysis of this body of data deliberately has been at a very rudimentary level. First, though large and variegated, this near universe of documented succession systems *may* not be representative of the pre-colonial African experience; hence the finer the analysis the less applicable it could validly be. Secondly, in presenting a vast and superficially persuasive array of statistical analyses I would in effect be allowing myself to be hoisted by my own petard. Rather, I have frankly limited myself to presenting those data which emphasize the limitations of 'cliometrics' in an area where the data are incapable of precise analysis. In these calculations I have imposed certain arbitrary standards in those circumstances where the generation is not closely determinable biologically or is non-biological. A dynastic change has been assumed to represent one half-generation in all calculations. Similarly, the succession of a 'cousin' has been seen to represent one half-generation since I found that allocating all cousins to the same generation very often resulted in unacceptably long generations. Husband/wife or wife/husband successions are regarded as constituting a single generation.

[4] A list of the 737 dynasties included in this sample will be found on pp. 136–44. Several statistical tests regarding the incidence of multiple reigns and usurpers, the expected lengths of five- to twelve-generation sequences, and the expected average regnal length in varying succession systems were conducted for this large body of data. The results of these tests will, it is hoped, be presented elsewhere where their presentation would be more appropriate and useful. These data have been utilized in this chapter only to emphasize the necessity for adapting the statistical methods to the quality of the data: to have conducted extensive but inapplicable statistical measurements would have been pointless.

A completely unrefined sample drawn from 737 dynasties from throughout historical time and space, except sub-Saharan Africa, reveals a distribution of generation lengths as shown in Table 4. The tabulations have been grouped into five-year increments running from fifteen to fifty years.

TABLE 4

Distribution of Generational Averages in Documented Dynasties

	Percentage
15–19 years— 27	3·7
20–24 years—118	16·0
25–29 years—263	35·6
30–34 years—217	29·6
35–39 years— 87	11·7
40–44 years— 21	2·9
45–50 years— 4	0·5

This distribution only confirms the longstanding assumptions of most historians. Sixty-five per cent of the dynasties had generational lengths averaging between 25 and 34 years, and 93 per cent fall within the range of 20 to 39 years.

It may be useful to take note of the characteristics of those dynasties forming the excluded fringes of this sample. Only two of the 27 dynasties which had generational averages of under 20 years (and both of these were in the 19-year range) were not Asian dynasties. For several of the other 25 dynasties the evidence is of a dubious nature, in most cases consisting of chronicles of late provenience. The suspicion must be that in some of these dynasties collateral successions have been masked by attributing a father/son relationship to rulers who were of the same generation. Sixteen of the dynasties with 40-year-plus generational averages were European states, principally the small principalities of late medieval and modern Germany. Their ruling families practised what has been described as 'the European pattern' of marriage—that is, marriage at a relatively late age, with fewer children and with a larger proportion of the population remaining unmarried.[5] The British peerage exhibited similar marriage patterns, at least before the nineteenth century with comparable results.[6] While this pattern tended to produce longer generations, the

[5] J. Hajnal, 'European marriage patterns in perspective' in D. V. Glass and D. E. C. Eversley (eds.), *Population in history* (London, 1965), 101.

[6] T. H. Hollingsworth, *The demography of the British peerage* [supplement to *Population Studies*, 18 (1964/5] (London, 1965), 27–8, 51.

decreased fertility and, particularly in the case of the British peerage, very limited succession rights concomitantly resulted in the extinction of a high proportion of ruling lines.[7]

Possible statistical correlations between long regnal generations and brevity of dynastic length because of the lack of proper heirs has not been quantitatively investigated, but the implications of limited eligibility are none the less fairly obvious. The longest dynasty of this group of 16 dynasties endured for 13 generations, but there were four changes of line within this period. The other 15 dynasties spanned from 3 to 11 generations with, in some cases, changes of line. Finally, a factor which may have served to increase artificially the generational averages in several of these cases is the consobrinal succession which occurred and for which, as noted, one half-generation has been assigned. In many instances even this figure has been too low, with the resulting tendency, in dynasties of such brief duration, to skew the mean inordinately.

It is unnecessary to discuss the large bulk of dynasties which fall within the expected parameters. The distribution of this extensive sampling of reasonably firm examples of dynastic succession simply reinforces the informed estimates for African dynasties already made by several historians.[8] An advantage of this large, if unrefined, sample is that it encompasses nearly every possible type of succession system from the widely fraternal succession common in many of the Islamic dynasties to the closely filial, practically, in terms of the age of the father, ultimogenitural, succession patterns in western Europe. The clustering of this sample within the 26- to 32-year range as shown in Table 5 suggests that reasonable parameters of expectation are possible, with the limitations suggested below, particularly if extrapolation must be made from uncontrolled or incomplete data. Over one half of the total sample of dynasties fall within this six-year range and do so with convincing consistency.

Exploring the expected period of time covered by sequences of five and ten regnal generations under varying circumstances can offer

[7] Burke, *Vicissitudes of families*, xiii–xix; idem, *A genealogical history of the dormant, abeyant, forfeited, and extinct peerages of the British Empire* (London, 1883), vii–ix. For the German principalities, few of which were ruled by the same line from foundation to end, and many of which were incorporated into other principalities because of the extinction of the ruling line, see Isenburg, *Stammtafeln, passim.*

[8] e.g. R. Oliver, 'Ancient capital sites of Ankole', 51–2; Jones, 'Problems', 166–7.

TABLE 5

Distribution of 26- to 32-year Generational Averages

26-year average—53 dynasties	(7·2%)
27-year average—58 dynasties	(7·9%)
28-year average—54 dynasties	(7·3%)
29-year average—54 dynasties	(7·3%)
30-year average—38 dynasties	(5·2%)
31-year average—56 dynasties	(7·6%)
32-year average—60 dynasties	(8·1%)

some gross parameters of expectations. These groups of five- and ten-year sequences were chosen to represent 'short' and 'long' sequences within each dynasty and do not have of themselves any unusual validity. Table 6 surveys 40 dynasties, each of which spanned at least 15 generations and for which documentation is reasonably secure. Beyond these criteria these 40 dynasties were selected to encompass as much cultural and geographical diversity as possible and, more importantly, to include several different types of succession systems. Within each dynasty I chose at least six 5-generation sequences and four 10-generation sequences. In this selection all periods of a dynasty were included. Overlap was unavoidable of course, but this has been minimized by spreading the sequences throughout the dynasty. In all cases, however, the first two and last two generations were excluded since they were those most likely to be aberrant in so far as unusually short regnal generations are more likely to occur at those points of a dynasty. The dynasties listed in Table 6 are arranged according to average generational length.

As expected, the degree of range in the ten-generation sequences is much less than for comparable five-generation sequences. The longer the sequence the less effect one or two aberrant cases will have on the mean since counterbalancing factors will tend to cancel out the aberrations. The dynasties marked (*) had rotational systems or systems of very broad eligibility for most of their duration. The lower limits of the samples from these dynasties tend to be higher for both the five- and ten-generation sequences. This supports the contention that such 'generations' can become distended almost beyond recognition and can in fact caricature the commonly held concept of regnal generation as a usable tool. Kirchberg unhappily demonstrates the possible parameters of a system in which fraternal succession is common. There were four lengthy fraternal generations in Kirchberg

TABLE 6

Five- and Ten-generation Sequences in Selected Dynasties

Dynasty	1	2	3	4
Nanchao (937–1260)	76–159	201–238	19·0	24/17
Hafsids of Tunis	106–158	216–230	23·1	32/15
Eastern Chou dynasty	94–176	199–265	24·8	24/21
Samstkhe	97–169	214–284	24·8	30/18·5
Ryazan'	92–150	242–264	24·9	24/17
Kashmir (627–1286)	119–197	170–300	25·4	62/25
Assyria (1365–611)	101–156	250–302	25·7	44/29
Eastern Chalukyas	113–174	261–266	25·7	35/16
Ponthieu	120–148	246–268	25·8	16/16
ʿAbbasid Caliphs	105–233	238–351	26·7	41/19
Dunois	100–190	282–320	26·7	18/16
Chosun	109–207	250–358	27·3	27/19
Shirvan	134–164	264–312	28·2	42/24·5
Laval	104–191	272–340	28·3	22/20
Carcassonne	124–173	263–290	28·5	19/15
Ethiopia (1270–1855)	154–174	300–340	28·5	70/20
Rouci	112–190	226–356	28·7	28/22
Cambodia	94–220	255–282	29·0	48/18
Castile	110–158	249–274	29·1	21/16
Norway (863–1387)	107–167	251–312	29·1	37/18
Tuad Muma*	119–182	274–283	29·2	31/15
Gruyères	134–177	281–318	29·3	18/16
Georgia (786–1258)	149–157	264–278	29·5	18/16
Koryo	114–207	257–331	29·6	35/16
Ahoms of Assam	90–156	206–271	29·9	42/20
Neuchâtel	116–177	252–315	30·6	25/22
Bohemia*	131–194	272–332	30·7	31/15
Angoulême	150–204	254–333	30·8	21/15
Bavaria (1392–1918)	119–191	317–339	31·0	23/17
Bar	123–192	310–318	31·1	20/17
Mecklenburg-Schwerin	112–225	310–342	31·7	27/18
Savoy	142–220	314–366	32·2	41/28·5
Albret	121–190	272–331	32·8	24/20
Astarac	104–192	268–329	33·1	19/18
Cenél nEoghain*	151–242	347–393	23·1	55/16
Mide*	130–202	320–393	33·4	82/32
Denmark	108–230	328–363	34·0	53/32·5
Montmorenci	144–227	305–371	35·5	24/19
Ailech*	147–239	361–380	37·4	42/17
Kirchberg	207–275	492–507	44·4	25/16

Column 1—range in years of selected five-generation sequences
Column 2—range in years of selected ten-generation sequences
Column 3—aggregate generational mean for entire dynasty
Column 4—total number of reigns and total number of generations for entire dynasty

of 71, 64, 71, and 63 years. In three of these instances the son of the last brother succeeded his father. Whatever the expressed ideal in fraternal succession systems, the pattern of the son of the last reigning brother succeeding to the exclusion of older cousins is the one most commonly found throughout fraternal succession systems. If the sons of the last reigning and presumably youngest brother are able to monopolize the succession the likelihood of longer fraternal generations being negated by short ones is less strong. Because of this it is not unlikely that the average regnal generation for some of the Mossi states such as Yatenga and Bussuma is somewhat higher than the thirty years recently suggested.[9]

On the other hand, where succession is more direct it may be possible that the commonly accepted 27- to 30-year estimate for African regnal generations may be slightly excessive. The Asian states included in Table 6 all had rather low five- and ten-generation figures. This was also true for Asian dynasties in the larger sample of 737 dynasties discussed earlier. Almost all the Asian dynasties fell within the lowest one-third of the range of generations in Table 4. Some demographic circumstances in medieval and early modern Asia, such as marriage and fertility patterns, were more closely parallel to those of pre-colonial Africa than to Europe.

The data in Table 6 are more important, however, for what they obviously cannot tell us. The range and distribution of both the five- and ten-generation samples, but particularly the former, illustrate clearly the folly of putting much faith in the concept of generational averages for computing or inferring dates for pre-colonial African history. Even if it were possible to place confidence in certain African genealogies and kinglists it would be rash to calculate the duration of the past from them. Within any dynasty a whole range of circumstances can affect generational averages over time. These include the accidents of birth and death, marriage customs, and the incidence of unrest, warfare, and succession struggles.

But the most important influence on regnal generational averages,

[9] M. Izard, *Introduction à l'histoire des royaumes mossi* (2 vols., Paris, 1970), I. 100–3, II. 242–4. N. Levtzion, *Muslims and chiefs in West Africa* (Oxford, 1968), 199–201, suggests a 38- to 40-year generation for some of the Mossi states. In suggesting a higher average I am not arguing that the chronology of Mossi macro-history, as discussed by Fage, would be affected. Rather, it is not unlikely that the filiation of the remembered *nabas* is in some cases incorrect. See J. D. Fage, 'Reflections on the early history of the Mossi-Dagomba group of states' in Vansina, Mauny, and Thomas, *Historian*, 177–87.

as it is for regnal averages, is the succession system of a dynasty. It has been argued in Chapter I that many succession systems change imperceptibly over time. Sometimes, in fact, the change is more dramatic. An analysis of generational sequences among the Ottoman Sultans starkly illustrates the effects changes in succession patterns can have on generational averages. Before 1603 succession to the Ottoman throne was, without important exception, from father to

TABLE 7

Five-generation Sequences for Ottoman Dynasty

Group A: (all ended before 1603)	Group B: (all straddled 1603)
3–7 122 years (1359–1481)	10–14 103 years (1520–1623)
4–8 123 years (1389–1512)	11–15 82 years (1566–1648)
5–9 118 years (1402–1520)	12–16 121 years (1574–1695)
6–10 145 years (1421–1566)	13–17 135 years (1595–1730)
7–11 123 years (1451–1574)	**Group C: (all began after 1603)**
8–12 114 years (1481–1595)	14–18 186 years (1603–1789
9–13 91 years (1512–1603)	15–19 221 years (1618–1839)
	16–20 228 years (1648–1876)
	17–21 229 years (1695–1924)

son. After 1603 a new pattern rapidly developed in which fraternal succession predominated and there were twenty-five Sultans in only eight generations. Table 7 represents all five-year generation sequences from 3–7 to 17–21. Table 8 illustrates all ten-generation sequences in the Ottoman dynasty from the third to the twenty-first generations. In Table 8 only the first two ten-generation sequences fell entirely before 1603, and the change in succession after that year is not so clearly reflected, although a progression can readily be seen over the last four sequences. The changes in the five-generation cohorts in Table 7, however, are quite dramatic and revealing. It can be seen, for instance, that the four earliest *ten*-generation sequences are approximately as long as the last three *five*-generation sequences. If the Ottomans were an African dynasty for which the last few generations could be dated and were used to extrapolate a chronology for the earlier period—a common practice—the distortion would be well beyond acceptable tolerance. If the first fourteen generations were divided into five-generation segments averaging 225 years each, the resulting date for the foundation of the Ottoman state would be *c.* 970 instead of the actual date of *c.* 1290. An exercise of this kind is not as frivolous as it might seem at first glance; a great deal of pre-colonial African chronology has been inferred in just this fashion.[10]

It cannot be emphasized too strongly that we know almost nothing certain about the early succession patterns in African states. To project recent or present succession practices unchanged into the distant past is to deny African societies the dynamics that existed elsewhere. The pace and extent of the transformation of Ottoman succession practices were unusual but certainly not rare enough to be discounted. In fact it is disturbing that in both Ethiopia and in Kongo, two of the African states about which we know most, fairly dramatic changes in succession practices occurred. Less dramatic but scarcely less profound succession changes have occurred in innumerable other dynasties. Most often these take the form of a change from fraternal

TABLE 8

Ten-generation Sequences for Ottoman Dynasty

3–12	236 years (1359–1595)	8–17	249 years (1481–1730)
4–13	214 years (1389–1603)	9–18	277 years (1512–1789)
5–14	221 years (1402–1623)	10–19	319 years (1520–1839)
6–15	227 years (1421–1648)	11–20	310 years (1566–1876)
7–16	244 years (1451–1695)	12–21	350 years (1574–1924)

to more direct patterns, that is, the opposite of the Ottoman experience. The chronological implications of such changes have been discussed in Chapters I and II. It remains only to re-emphasize that genealogical reckoning which does not consider this debilitating reality is worse than meaningless—it is misleading as well.

It has been observed that the regnal generation of any number of brothers will be equal to the number of years the last brother survives his father.[11] In other words the longest recorded fraternal regnal generation should approximate to the longest recorded reign of a single individual. In fact this is the case. The longest fraternal regnal generation discovered in the present inquiry was 88 years; three brothers ruled the German principality of Bentheim from 1333 to 1421.[12] Surprisingly, the longest known individual reign in history was somewhat longer. The extant Egyptian kinglists credit Neferkare‘ Piopi II of VI Dynasty with a reign of $90 + x$ years and Manetho

[10] Most recently by Karugire, *Nkore*, 27–8.

[11] Vansina, *Kingdoms of the Savanna*, 253.

[12] S. Muller Hz., 'Het oude Register van Graaf Florenz', *Bijdragen en Mededeelingen van het Historisch Genootschap te Utrecht*, 22 (1901), chart opp. 301; Stokvis, *Manuel*, 3, 340–1. J. C. Möller, *Geschichte der vormalingen Grafschaft Bentheim von der ältesten Zeit bis auf unsere Tage* (Lingen, 1879), 186–223.

ascribed a reign of 94 years to this Pharaoh. Improbable though a reign of this length may seem, the available evidence strongly supports, although it does not absolutely confirm, this figure, and it is generally accepted by Egyptologists when they calculate the chronology of the Old Kingdom.[13]

But more important than a consideration of similarity of range is the frequency with which unusually long fraternal regnal generations are likely to occur. Both individual reigns and regnal generations of 70 to 80 years have occurred. But in the body of evidence under analysis—the 737 dynasties—there were about fifteen regnal generations of this length to every such reign. The case of Kirchberg, already discussed, illustrates this point. No Burggraf of Kirchberg held office for longer than 54 years, but there were four regnal generations considerably longer than this. The historian must recognize that generational calculations in a society where fraternal succession was practised extensively are useless, even if the traditional genealogies proved acceptable.

Another matter of some interest is the possible limit of a single father/son dual generation. Cases of a father and a single son ruling for a period of as long as 117 years are known.[14] There are many father/son reigns covering over a hundred years.[15] From before 1795 to 1908, there were only two rulers, father and son, in Burundi, where ultimogeniture was practised.[16] Admittedly these spans are exceptional when measured against the total number of examples available (more than 4,000); they probably represent less than one per cent of the total number of father/son generations, and most such generations fall within a forty- to seventy-year span. The purpose here is only to suggest some maximal numerical parameters for such dual generations. The minimum possibility, zero, while at least as rare, is certainly more obvious.

[13] For the argumentation, see Gardiner, *Egypt of the Pharaohs: an introduction*, 101–2, 436; W. Stevenson Smith, 'The Old Kingdom in Egypt', *CAH*², 52–3; H. Kees, 'Beiträge zur Geschichte des Vezirats im Alten Reich. Die Chronologie des Vezirs unter Phiops II', *Nachrichten* [Jahrbuch] *der Akademie der Wissenschaften, Göttingen*, 4/2 (1940), 39–54.

[14] e.g. Jean II and Guillaume, Barons of Montmorenci, ruled from 1414 to 1531. The previous two rulers, representing two generations, had ruled 89 years, so the four regnal generations spanned 206 years. Stokvis, *Manuel*, II. 111.

[15] I exclude in these calculations the figures for several of the native states of India found in the chronicles. In these accounts one can find many examples of father/son dual generations exceeding 125 years.

[16] Vansina, 'Note sur la chronologie du Burundi ancien', 442.

Under some circumstances the concept of regnal average may be more useful than efforts to compute by generations. This is particularly true in succession systems, such as those of Celtic Ireland, in which succession was broad and father/son succession uncommon. A large number of African systems would fall within this definition. If a well-defined and *consistent* mode of succession can be discerned in these systems some use might be made of the data in the following paragraphs.

Basically there are two types of rotational or circulating succession systems. An individual may become ruler because he is chosen to represent the lineage whose turn it is to succeed in a system where there are several eligible lineages. Such a ruler will be genetically unrelated to his predecessor. If seniority is particularly prized in his society he will probably be elderly and his period of rule will be relatively brief. If, on the other hand, emphasis is placed on more practical political considerations, his lineage may see fit to choose a young but proved representative whose tenure in power will, it is hoped, allow his party to reap for a longer period the benefits associated with office-holding. These opposite possibilities will vary from one political system to another. They will also vary within a single system over time as exigencies dictate. In times of national crisis a mature and well-tested ruler is likely to be chosen. During periods when the monarchical office is weak *vis-à-vis* the magnates young and weak (or perhaps senescent and moribund) rulers will be chosen—rulers incapable of asserting the authority of the office they hold. In short the variety of possibilities is almost endless and all that can, or should be, said with any degree of certitude is that, under 'normal' circumstances regnal lengths in circulating succession systems should tend to be shorter than in filial systems.

To attempt to quantify this assertion in any way would be purposeless, for it is not necessarily the mechanics of the succession system itself which influence regnal length but often unrelated sociopolitical factors. For example, the regnal averages in early Celtic Ireland were rather short. In Ulaid there were 70 reigns between *c.* 480 and 1201 or an average reign of 10·3 years. In Muma there were 41 reigns between *c.* 480 and 978, an average of 12·1 years; in Lagin there were 63 reigns between 443 and 1171, an average of 11·6; in Ailech (later Cenél nEoghain) there were 42 reigns between 425 and 1061, an average of 15·1; and in Ciarraighe Luachra there were 30 reigns between *c.* 730 and 1165, an average of 14·5. In these and the other Irish states of the period the same mode of succession to the throne prevailed. Under the *derbfhine* system sons should not have and seldom did succeed their father, since this would jeopardize the eligibility of other members of the *derbfhine*.[17] But it was not the *derbfhine* system alone which circumscribed the regnal lengths of Irish rulers. In addition, the chaotic political and social situation, in which there were several independent states and a host of lesser polities, caused warfare to be endemic. This situation, exacerbated by the feuds between lineages of the same 'clan', caused the majority of the rulers of Irish states between *c.* 520 and *c.* 1000 to be assassinated or killed in battle. There is no doubt that the succession system was a contributory factor to the brevity of Irish reigns during this period. In more placid times, however, the average regnal length might well have approached the standard for other contemporaneous societies, despite its rotational aspects. Presumably (few birth dates are given in the annals) the tendency in the Irish states was to choose younger, more vigorous, rulers.

Promotion through a series of lesser offices to an apical office may also be practised, as among the Bemba recently.[18] In effect, fraternal succession is the obverse of promotional succession since the paramount office works down to the last brother rather than his working his way up to it. The best example of promotional succession in terms of the continuity of the structure and the length of time for which it can be documented is that of Elam in the second millennium B.C. During the period from *c.* 1850 to *c.* 1500 there were three rulers in Elam; in descending order they were the *sukkalmah* of Elam, the *sukkal* (viceroy) of Elam and Simash, and the *sukkal* (prince) of Susa. Originally the viceroy was the brother or nephew of the *sukkalmah*, while the prince of Susa was his son or nephew. In theory the viceroy would become *sukkalmah* on the death of the incumbent and another brother would become viceroy. The prince of Susa would become viceroy only when the supply of brothers (or, if necessary, cousins) became exhausted.[19] Under this system there were twenty *sukkalmahs*, thirteen viceroys, and twenty-two princes in eleven generations covering three and a half centuries.[20] More importantly, the succession

[17] The intricacies of the *derbfhine* system are most extensively and clearly explained in Hogan, 'The Irish law of kingship', 187–95. But also see Chapter I, note 71.

[18] Roberts, 'Chronology of the Bemba', 221.

[19] W. Hinz, 'Persia, *c.* 1800–1550 B.C.', *CAH*², 5–6.

[20] Ibid. 19.

pattern in Elam demonstrates the uncertainties of promotional systems in practice. Walther Hinz aptly commented that 'it must be emphasized that the clarity with which the *rule* of succession can be inferred from the sources is matched by the rarity of its *working out* perfectly'.[21] Only three times in the twenty successions to the office of *sukkalmah* did the prescribed formula of promotion operate. Nine princes of Susa died before advancing to a higher office while three viceroys died without becoming *sukkalmah*. Seven princes of Susa became *sukkalmah* without having served as viceroy. Only three individuals served in all three offices.[22] Hinz suggests that this high mortality rate may be attributed in part to the widespread practice of incest in the Elamite royal family, but other factors also operated.[23] Some rulers were killed in battle before being able to ascend in due course to a higher office. At other times the vagaries of the system meant that a prince of Susa became *sukkalmah* directly because of lack of appropriate candidates. The analysis of the succession system in Elam illustrates that short reigns and asymmetrical patterns are characteristic of this type of succession system.[24]

These irregular patterns are also reflected in the promotional succession to the Dagomba and Wa skins in northern Ghana as recently studied by Ferguson and Wilks.[25] Although some of the disorientation in the succession patterns of these two states is attributable to the policies of the Gold Coast administration, there were several cases of 'aberrant' successions in the pre-colonial period.

A pattern of short reigns is also apparent in another well-known promotional system—the Papacy. Election as Pope has been, since the Middle Ages, generally the culmination of a long ecclesiastical career. From 996 to date there have been 125 Popes, with an average tenure in office of 7·85 years.

These examples are sufficient to suggest that two assumptions may tentatively be advanced regarding promotional succession systems. Incumbency in office, if the system operates to design, is likely to be shorter than in other types of succession systems. On the other hand,

[21] Ibid. 6. Emphasis added.

[22] Ibid. 11–18, 19.

[23] Ibid. 6–7.

[24] See above, pp. 33–4, and P. M. Fraser, 'The tribal-cycles of eponymous priests at Lindos and Kamiros', *Eranos*, 51 (1953), 32–5.

[25] P. Ferguson and I. Wilks, 'Chiefs, constitutions and the British in northern Ghana' in M. Crowder and O. Ikime (eds.), *West African chiefs: their changing status under colonial rule and independence* (Ile-Ife, 1970), 341–50, 353–63, esp. 358–60. See also J. C. Dougah, *Wa and its people* (Legon, 1966).

such systems will probably *not* function in practice in the same way as they were conceived in theory. Those interested in assessing the chronology of such systems may be able, equipped with an abundance of data, to assess roughly the correlation of design to practice. In the absence of sufficient data, however, the investigator must *never assume* a very high level of correlation.

Emphasis in the present analysis has been on the futility of constructing statistical castles on the quicksand of weak, insufficient, or distorted data. A recent analysis of the Bono-Manso kinglist by Colin Flight illustrates well the pitfalls of such an exercise. The only source for early Bono-Manso chronology has been the kinglist collected by Eva Meyerowitz.[26] This kinglist was collected under peculiar and suggestive circumstances and exact dating was provided in it for each of the rulers of the state.[27] All but one of the early reigns were unusually long, while all but two of the later reigns were rather short. Because of this, and the 'suspicious regularity' of the early reigns, historians have tended to view Meyerowitz's chronological framework rather sceptically. Flight regarded the second part of the Tekyiman kinglist, with regnal lengths for the last twelve rulers of 14, 9, 15, 6, 10, 10, 5, 5, 15, 8, 20, and 28 years, as, *prima facie*, acceptable. He accepted the rather implausible mnemonic dating methods described by Meyerowitz, but argued that it was developed under Muslim influence only at the time that the Bono kinglist changed from very long reigns to reigns of normal length.[28] Accepting the figures for the last twelve reigns as accurate, he extrapolated a suggested chronology for the first eight reigns and arrived at a notional date of 1420/30 for the foundation of the state. In short he accepted all of Meyerowitz's data except the regnal lengths of the first eight Bono-Manso rulers.

While one might therefore quarrel with Flight's uncritical acceptance of some of Meyerowitz's more unlikely theses, the result of his inquiry, which, as Flight notes, 'seems to square well with current thinking' on the chronology of state formation in northern Ghana, actually tends to reinforce the authenticity, if not the accuracy, of Meyerowitz's data.[29] In this sense the results of fieldwork conducted

[26] E. K. L. Meyerowitz, *Akan traditions of origin* (London, 1952), 29–36; idem, *The Akan of Ghana: their traditional beliefs* (London, 1958).

[27] Flight, 'Kings and queenmothers', 259–60. See now Flight–Meyerowitz correspondence in *JAH* 13 (1972), 348–50.

[28] Flight, 'Kings and Queenmothers', 265.

[29] Ibid. 268; Fage, 'Reflections', 77–78.

in Tekyiman in 1969/70 become particularly relevant to the present argument. D. M. Warren, who spent a total of four years at Tekyiman, collected a large body of evidence for Tekyiman traditional history. Two of his informants, the ex-Tekyimanhene Akumfi Ameyaw III, and Kwame Nyame, had also been two of the three major sources of Meyerowitz's data.[30] Both denied ever supplying Meyerowitz's interpreter with a list of the queenmothers of Bono-Manso. Furthermore, when asked for a list of Bono-Manso rulers, both Kwame Nyame and the present Tekyimanhene gave Warren a list of only 23 stoolholders to the present incumbent, whereas Meyerowitz listed no fewer than 37. Even more significantly, these informants claimed to have no knowledge of 12 of the 20 rulers of Bono-Manso (nos. 4–6, 10–11, 13–19).[31] It is possible, though scarcely probable, that Meyerowitz had unique talents for extracting reliable information. More likely the circumstances of her collection of the data influenced its form.[32] Clearly, however, the history of the Bono-Manso/Tekyiman data itself illustrates the extemporaneous form that is characteristic of this kind of traditional evidence.[33] Flight has inferred statistically a chronology for early Bono-Manso from data concerning rulers that contemporary informants claim did not exist.

Trautmann has shown that careful statistical reasoning based on fairly complete and reliable data can provide limited but useful levels of probability when applied with discretion.[34] Even so, we have seen that the parameters established from even well-documented materials do not lend themselves readily to precise analysis. More importantly, however, textual criticism must precede statistical inference in any

[30] D. M. Warren, 'A re-appraisal of Mrs. Eva Meyerowitz's work on the Brong', *Research Review* [Institute of African Studies, Legon], 7/1 (1970), 69; Meyerowitz, *Akan of Ghana*, 103n. Meyerowitz's third major informant, the Krontihene of Tekyiman, had died in the meantime.

[31] Warren, 'Re-appraisal', 69–70. Bono-Manso was the name of the state before the Asante conquest in 1722–3. Its successor stool, much smaller, is called Tekyiman.

[32] The data on Bono-Manso were collected by Meyerowitz's interpreter during her absence and later passed along to her. Meyerowitz, *Akan of Ghana*, 103–4. Meyerowitz's objectivity may have been marred by her passionate advocacy of the separation of Tekyiman and the rest of the Brong-Ahato area from the Ashanti Confederacy.

[33] I am at a loss to explain the absence of feedback from Meyerowitz's works in this more recent Tekyiman testimony. It may be that, though doubtless aware of them, the Tekyiman informants recognized their deficiencies.

[34] Trautmann, 'Length of reign'. But see Chapter II, for comments on one limitation of Trautmann's evidence.

exercise of this kind. Clearly the result of any such exegesis of the chronological aspects of African traditional materials will preclude the need for quantitative exercises which tend to invest the data on which they are based with a validity they do not possess.

EXCURSUS

The following listing represents those dynasties used in the tabulations discussed in this chapter. They are arranged in ascending order by generational average. In most cases all successions in a dynasty have been used when making calculations; however, for many of the Indian dynasties only the period after *c.* 1750–1800 is included since the data for the earlier periods are not trustworthy.

15.0 Seoni
16.3 Hojo Shikken (Japan)
16.8 Kathmandu
17.0 Peshwas (Marathas)
17.5 Cuddapah
17.6 Mac Dynasty (Tonkin)
18.0 Chahamanas of Chandravati
18.1 T'o-pa (Northern Wei)
18.1 Nawabs of Karnatak
18.2 Aghlabids of Tunis
18.3 Yüan Dynasty
18.3 Perlis
18.3 Buwayhids of Iraq
18.4 Atjeh
18.6 Patiala
19.0 Cortone
19.0 Sirmur
19.0 Israel
19.0 Nanchao (first dynasty)
19.1 Hanau-Müntzenburg
19.3 Chahamanas of Naddula
Nanchao (second dynasty)
Zangids of Damascus
19.4 Kajars of Persia
19.8 Kin Dynasty
Fadhli
Seleucids
20.0 Vexin
20.1 Touggourt
Samanids of Transoxiana
20.2 Yazd
20.3 Pataudi
20.5 Buwayhids of Fars
20.6 T'ang Dynasty
Mar'ashi Sayyids
20.7 Zanzibar
20.8 Khairagarh
20.9 Dhrangadra
Seljuks of Kirman
21.0 Banswara
21.1 Gujarat
21.2 Bahawalpur
White Horde
21.3 Ava
Vettavalam
21.4 Karauli
21.5 Former Han
Kashmir
21.6 Baria
Judah
Mataram
21.7 Conaille-Muirthemhne
21.8 Rampur
Fatimids
22.0 Kalachuri dynasty
Khwarizm Shahs
22.2 Burma
Tehri-Garhwal
22.3 Avadh

Isfendiyar-Oghullary
Ortukids of Hisn-Kaifa
22.4 Atjeh (later)
22.5 Arborea
Kashtwar
Trinh dynasty of Tonkin
Urartu
Saka Satraps
Paku Alam
22.6 Sanseverino
22.7 Limbdi
Western Karakhanids
Ya'furids
22.8 Johore
22.9 Ani
23.0 Ming dynasty
Montpellier
Chanderi
23.1 Bar-sur-Seine
Jhind
Hafsids of Tunis
Dungarpur
23.2 Baghal
Dujana
Pesaro
23.3 Fallahiyeh
Seljuks of Rum
Granada
23.4 Benares
23.5 Faenza
Kawardha
Bantam
Oswieçem
23.6 Fabriano
Taungu
Vladimir-Volyn'
23.7 Auxerre
Sidon
Rasulids of Yemen
23.8 Ahmadnagar
Loharu
Nawanagar
Ravenna
Scotland
Kyrene
Dhar
Burdwan
23.9 Lunawada
24.0 Paleologus dynasty
Lorraine
Mudhol
Tripolis
Hammadids
24.1 Bhadrawah
Surakurta
24.2 Farrukhabad
Khitan
Wat'asids of Morocco
24.3 Annam
Khairpur
Malines
Santa Fiora
24.4 Segni
Croatia
24.5 Sung dynasty
Kangra
Shahpura
Koch Hajo
Tao
Melgueil
24.6 Bijapur
Indore
24.7 Alwar
Egypt
Patan
Partabgarh
Morocco (I)
Forli
24.8 Bundi
Savanur
Samtskhe
Vijayanagar
Shaddadids of Ganja
Bawandids
24.9 Ryazan'
Sirohi
25.0 Bhor
Dewas Senior

Donzi
Parma
Nan
Verona
Setupatis of Ramnad
Ghaznawids
Nevers
Schwartzburg-Kaefenburg
25.1 Bharatpur
Tonnerre
25.2 Aversa
Ichalkaranji
Rewa
Lower Yafa'i
Sunth
25.3 Eu
Chahamanas of Sapadalaksa
'Umayyads
Kishangarh
25.4 Holland
Kashmir (II)
La'hij
25.5 Dauphiné
Koch Bihar
25.6 Artois
Bijawar
Nguyen dynasty of Hué
Eastern Karakhanids
Charkhari
Louvain
25.7 Eastern Chalukyas of Vengi
Guines
Jodhpur
Idar
Dax
25.8 Tung Tsin
Maguelone
Pfalz-Zweibrücken
Pico-Mirandola
Ponthieu
25.9 Darband
Pallars (II)
26.0 Couci
Vala
Clann Aeda Buide
Afghanistan
Jawhar
Sikhs
Danta
26.1 Jaipur
Béarn
Bhatgaon
26.2 Chiny
Sachin
Tonk
26.3 Urgell
Halich
Salerno
Ikkeri
Bentivoglio of Bologna
Nassau-Dietz
26.4 Chanda
Rethel
Wankaner
Kedah
(unnamed)
Ryukyus
Majapahit
26.5 Lakhtar
Masserano-Concordia
Narbonne
Guria
Aster
Gramont
26.6 Asturias
Morocco (II)
Baoni
26.7 Ajaigarh
Banganapalle
Bourbon
Dunois
Muli
'Abbasid Caliphs
'Aqrabi
Looz
26.8 Datia
Foligno

Hsi Hsia
Kalsia
Pudukottai
Ur III
Safavid
Radhanpur
26.9 Hohenems
Holland
27.0 Pagan
Hormuz
Pratiharas
Gajapatis
Jogjakarta
Jaisalmir
Cyprus
27.1 Bhavnagar
Faridkot
Mantua
Palas of Bengal
Silesia-Breslau
Besalù
Austrasia
Tanhoun
27.2 Gondal
Joigni
Pallavas
Ayyubids of Hamah
Babylon
Lan Chang
Chhatarpur
Baduspanids
Suzdal'
27.3 Bresse
Chamba
Chou dynasty
Liao dynasty
Chosun
Limburg
Palembang
27.4 Hohenzollern-Haigerloch
Hohenzollern-Sigmaringen
Sachsen-Coburg
Cholas of Tanjore
27.5 Manipur
Stampalla
Najd
Maisur
27.6 Archipelago
Bosporus
Man (II)
Mughals
Najahids
Ortukids of Maridin
Hazaraspids (II)
27.7 Gwalior
Viennois
Kelantan
27.8 Bansda
Ramadan-Oghullary
Kuwait
Mangits of Bukhara
Salgharids of Kirman
Tursan
27.9 Later Han
Craon
Almohads
28.0 Burgundy (II)
Lombards
Miraj Junior
Idrisids
Paramaras of Dhara
28.1 Afrasiyabids
Ghurids
Artanuji
28.2 Dinajpur
Rajkot
Rashtrakutas
Sharvan
Sawantwadi
28.3 Carpi
Western Chalukyas
Kachh
Laval
Salins
Sparta (Eurypontids)
Zayrids of Tunis
Great Poland
Rimini

28.4 Braunschweig-Wolfenbüttel
Sailana
Turenne
ʿAbbasids of Egypt
Barcelona
Eastern Gangas
Tartas
28.5 Carcassonne
Epirus
Ethiopia
Yaʿrubids of ʿUman
28.6 Anhalt-Dessau
Goedens
Trebizond
Valois
ʿAjman
Laurenzana
Orthe
28.7 Forez
Naples
Rouci
Midrarids of Sijilmasa
Wroclaw
28.8 Flanders
Serbia
Clann Aeda Buide
Karts of Herat
Raciborz
28.9 Junagadh
Maler Kotla
Pomerania-Wolgast
29.0 Ali Rajpur
Camerino
La Marche
Balasinor
Labourd
29.1 Castile
Maratha Chhatrapatis
Norway
Porbandar
Sulu
29.2 Pfalz
Silesia-Leignitz
Sparta (Agids)
Tuadh Muma
Smolensk
29.3 Chalons-sur-Saône
Hessen-Darmstadt
Normandy
Brunei
Cambodia
Moncada
Gruyères
Hornes
Lavedan
29.4 Cappodocia
Perche
29.5 Aumale
Vianden
Georgia
Vaudemont
29.6 Koryo
Antiparos
Saarbrucken
Penthièvre
29.7 France
Hungary
Maçon
Orange
Sachsen-Hilburghausen
Waldeck-Eisenberg
Thüringen
29.8 Brittany
Ch'ing
Kurnool
Orchha
Saint-Pol
Akalkot
Tokugawa Shoguns
Ternate
29.9 Ahoms of Assam
Cardona
Hessen-Kassel
Tver'
Veldentz
30.0 England
Ziyarids
Girona

Seljuks
30.1 Neustria
Hohen-Geroldseck
30.2 Tanjore
Tibet
Ottomans
Schwartzburg-Blankenburg
30.3 Ostfrise
Florence
Buhturids of Lebanon
30.4 Ampurias
Pallars (III)
Hainault
Pomerania-Rugen
Montechiarugolo
Mecklenburg-Werle-
Guestrow
30.5 Beaujeu
Tinos-Mykonos
30.6 Burgundy (I)
Coorg
Saluzzo
Thouars
Neuchâtel
Mansfeld
30.7 Bohemia
Saffarids of Sijilmasa
Dulghadir-Ogullary
30.8 Angoulême
Dreux
Forcalquier
Hessen-Rheinfels-
Rotenburg
Portugal
Trengganu
Mecca
Majorca
31.0 Alençon
Mecklenburg-Strelitz
Sweden
Cephalonia (I)
Patani
Man (I)
Bavaria
31.1 Austria
Bar
Diepholtz
Holstein-Gottorp
Cilicia
Sharjah
Kakatiyas of Warangal
Pallars (I)
Barcelona
Pereieslavl'
Polotsk
31.2 Aundh
Sassanids
Hoysalas
Laremne
31.3 Brandenburg
Klettenburg
Rossello
Sachsen-Weimar-Eisenach
Dalriada
Cerigo
Dubayy
Salihids
31.4 Nassau-Weilburg
Rügen
Sandur
Ciarraighe Luachra
31.5 Brienne
al-Hasa
Ashikaga Shoguns
Mazyadids of Hilla
31.6 Narsinghgarh
Saxony
Sitamau
Connacht
31.7 Hanau-Babenhausen-
Lichtenberg
Mecklenburg-Schwerin
Rouergue
Surguja
Umm al-Qaiwain
31.8 Navarre
Weimar
Mengkunegara

31.9 'Abd-al-Wadids of Tilimsan
Champagne
Nassau-Wiesbaden-Idstein
Penthièvre (II)
Samthar
Pagan (I)
32.0 Genevois
Mingrelia
Mölln
Vien Chang
Des Muma
Hawshabi
32.1 Baden-Durlach
Hsia dynasty
Palanpur
'Uman
Rançon
New Valangin
Baigorry
32.2 Brandenburg-Bayreuth
Mecklenburg-Guestrow
Montfort
Nabha
Savoy
Western Gangas
Bikanir
32.3 Monferrato
Vermandois
Barwani
Mag Luirc
Rajpipla
32.4 Baugenci
Ferrara
Krim
Reuss-Köstritz (middle)
Valentinois
Cairbre
Montpellier
Mazowsze-Plock
32.5 Anhalt-Bernberg (II)
Cybò-Malaspina
Golkonda
Württemberg
Germiyan-Oghullary
Macwilliam
32.6 Faucigny
Guastalla
Kärnten
Kolhapur
Reitberg
Bithynia
Brega
Tunis
Kapurthala
Moers
Yaroslavl'
Khandesh
Wertheim
32.8 Albret
Netherlands
Spain
Bernicia
Cephalonia (II)
Hazaraspids (II)
Mazowsze-Czersk
33.0 Darbhanga
Grand-Pré
Sachsen-Altenburg
33.1 Andros
Astarac
Cenél nEoghain
33.2 Aragon
Nassau-Dillenburg
Chaulukyas
Nordgau
33.3 Bourbon (II)
Périgord
Provence
Tuscany
Abu Dhabi
33.4 Foix
Rodez
Torres
Urbino
Pegu
Mide
33.5 Abasgia

33.6 Gerderland
Hyderabad
Nuremburg
33.7 Schwartzburg
33.8 Bentheim
Ladakh
Mecklenburg
Schleusingen
Silesia Glogau
Agilolfs of Bavaria
Holstein-Schauenburg-Pinneburg
Holstein-Rendsburg
Holstein-Sonderburg-Beck
Culenborg
33.9 Cambodia
34.0 Denmark
Reuss-Ebersdorf
34.1 Lippe-Detmold
Meulent
Muscovy
Perak
34.2 Bavaria
Fougères
Hohenzollern-Hechingen
34.3 Bhopal
Fézenzaguet
Scotland (from 1058)
34.4 Marinids
Pitange
Schaumburg-Lippe
34.6 Braunschweig-Luneburg
34.7 Raciborz
Sancerre
34.8 Nalagarh
Leuchtenburg-Waldeck
Sandomierz
34.9 Hessen-Homburg
Pitange (II)
Waldeck-Pyrmont
Ferrara
35.0 Boudounitza
Jaora
Jever
Limoges
Pahang
Venkatagiri
Nio
Jamkhandi
Helfenstein-Weisensteig
35.2 Julich
Hohenzollern (I)
35.3 Jath
Aitonà-Ceros
Bergà
Montescudaio-Guardistallo
35.4 Cerdanya
35.5 Holstein-Senderburg
Montmorenci
35.6 Castellbò
Schwarzenburg-Hohenlandsberg
Maihar
35.7 Tecklenburg
Limpurg-Speckfeld
35.8 Armagnac
Correggio
Rocaberti
36.0 Hessen-Philippsthal-Barchfeld
Kurland
Reuss-Köstritz (Younger)
Reuss-Schleiz
36.1 Hanau
Modena
36.2 Anhalt-Bernburg
Hessen-Philippsthal
Pardiac
Nassau-Liebenscheld
Utrecht
36.3 Baden-Baden
Cambay
Fezzan
36.4 Lippe-Beisterfeld
Toulouse
Waldeck-Bergheim
Pomerania-Stettin
Pomerelia

36.5 Vizcaya
36.6 Piombino
36.8 Matelica
Cenél Fiachrach
Rustamids of Tahart
Shihabids
37.0 Piedmont
37.2 Desana
Schwarzburg-Rudolstadt
Maʿnids of Lebanon
Janids of Bukhara
37.4 Ailech
37.5 Holstein-Sonderburg-Augustenburg
Schwarzburg-Sonderhausen
Pergamon
San Secondo
37.6 Pontus
Uí Maine
37.7 Marwanids
37.8 Shang dynasty
Najran
38.0 Reuss-Selbitz
Bangkalan
38.1 Macedonia
Masserano-Crevacuore
Nurpur
Holstein-Glücksburg
38.2 Hebrides
38.3 Nassau-Bilstein
38.5 Vence
38.6 Bologna (Casali)
38.7 Anhalt-Zerbst
Liechtenstein
38.8 Sifanto
38.9 Holstein-Schauenburg
39.0 Sachsen-Lauenburg
39.1 Berg
39.3 Nassau-Usingen
39.7 Reuss-Greiz
Sachsen-Meiningen
39.8 Novello
Piedmont (II)
40.0 Cleve
40.3 Nassau-Saarbrücken
40.7 Anhalt-Köthen
40.8 Brandenburg-Ansbach
40.9 Siunik
41.0 Baroda
Opole
41.2 Ferrette
41.4 Savona
41.7 Sorbello
41.8 Wartenburg
42.0 Luang Prabang
Tidore
42.2 Semur
42.3 Oldenburg
42.7 Pomerania-Danzig
42.8 Comminges
43.1 Vadagarai
44.3 Reuss-Obergreiz
Krakow
44.4 Kirchberg
45.4 Stampalla
46.5 Reuss-Köstritz (elder)
46.8 Sorbello (II)
48.3 Vaspurakan

CHAPTER V

The Traditional Chronology of the Coastal Fante

> My ancestors brought their independent stool from Techiman [*sic*] and have never been subordinate to any other ruler in this country [Fanteland].[1]

I THE NATURE OF FANTE CHRONOLOGY

THE following two chapters will analyse in microcosm the problems which have already been discussed in broader perspective. The traditions of the coastal Fante and Asante of Ghana differ from each other in their provenience, character, and in the means by which they can be analysed.[2] Nevertheless these traditions display many of the characteristics of creation and content that we have discussed in the preceding chapters. The conclusions which I have reached in these two chapters are not as positive as I had hoped they would be when I undertook research; perhaps, however, the very reasons for this may prove instructive.

The traditional materials for the origin and history of the coastal Fante states are extremely fragmentary; few of them have been published in a systematic way.[3] Paradoxically, however, we possess a continuous series of written data for several aspects of the history of many of the coastal states for a period unrivalled in sub-Saharan

[1] Petition of Ewusi Tsinasi, Chief of Abeadzi, to Governor Hugh Clifford, dd 10 June 1918, NAG/ADM11/1/707. Ewusi Tsinasi's claim epitomizes the traditional claims of most of the Fante stools regarding their migration and their independence 'from time immemorial'.

[2] The term 'Fante' in this chapter is used in a broader sense than usual. The quintessential Fante—in a historical sense—occupy the coast of Ghana and the near hinterland from the Pra river in the west to just west of Winneba in the east. This is roughly the area called Fantee or Fantijn in the European sources for the eighteenth century. For a discussion of whether the Elminans qualify as Fante, see H. M. Feinberg, 'Who are the Elmina?', *GNQ* 11 (June 1970), 20–6. For our purposes Shama and Ahanta west of the Pra are included.

[3] See especially E. J. P. Brown, *Gold Coast and Asianti reader* (2 vols., London, 1929), and Meyerowitz, *Akan traditions of origin*, 63–86.

Africa, with the single exception of the Kongo kingdom. Scattered Portuguese records for the period from 1482 to 1642 have been preserved. Much fuller Dutch, Danish, and English records for the period after *c.* 1600 are available.[4] The particular nature of these records precludes the possibility of a detailed reconstruction of the internal history and political structure of these states.[5] None the less, a skeletal framework of the political history of many of them, particularly their interstate relations, is possible, and a chronology of their stool-holders can sometimes be reconstructed, although never without some doubt and many lacunae. While such a chronological framework is seldom enlightening in itself, it can be useful as a basis of comparison with traditional accounts in order to suggest patterns of distortion.

European observers from the seventeenth to the nineteenth centuries often commented on the contentious spirit with which the Fante seemed to conduct their political life.[6] In any event, stool disputes were endemic among the Fante states in the later nineteenth and twentieth centuries. Most of the oral traditional accounts of the coastal states which purported to deal with matters more specific than migrations and stool origins arose in response to stool, succession, and land disputes. A study of the records of these disputes makes it possible to trace in detail the uses to which Fante traditions were put. The examples studied in this chapter represent only a small portion of the large number available; I have selected them to illus-

[4] I used the records of the Dutch West India Company and the Dutch colonial government in their transcriptions in the Furley Collection (henceforth FC) at the Balme Library, University of Ghana. The English records were used at the Public Record Office, London (henceforth PRO), and the Bodleian Library, Oxford University. The Danish records cover the area from Accra to the Volta and were not consulted.

[5] With the exception of Elmina, the Dutch headquarters, for which a great deal of circumstantial evidence is available. See Feinberg, 'Elmina, Ghana: a history of its development and relationship with the Dutch in the eighteenth century', Ph.D. dissertation, Boston University, 1969, and idem, 'An incident in Elmina–Dutch relations, the Gold Coast (Ghana), 1739–40', *AHS* 3 (1970), 359–72. A comparison of Elmina (Edina) stool traditions with the Dutch records will be treated fully in the author's 'Kingship in Elmina before 1869: a study in feed-back and "traditional stability" ', *Cahiers d'Études Africaines*, 14 (1974), in press.

[6] e.g. W. Bosman, *A new and accurate description of the coast of Guinea . . .* (London, 1705), 165–8, 176–7; H. Meredith, *An account of the Gold Coast of Africa* (London, 1812), 106; B. Cruikshank, *Eighteen years on the Gold Coast of Africa* (2 vols., London, 1853), I. 272–6; W. Mollan, Agent at British Sekondi, responding to questions of the Company of Merchants trading to Africa, 1810, National Archives of Ghana (henceforth NAG), ADM1/2/418. See also K. Arhin, 'Diffuse authority among the coastal Fanti', *GNQ* 9 (1966), 66–70.

trate several aspects of the Fante use of oral traditions. These include the ambiences in which the traditions arose, the importance of changes of succession practices, and, most importantly, the role that feedback from external sources played in the development of these traditions. It is neither practicable nor necessary to attempt a comprehensive survey of the traditions of each Fante state. The traditions of some stools are much fuller than those of others.[7] This is because the extent of 'traditional' material available for any stool is nearly always directly correlated to the extent of stool disputes there. Necessarily, I shall concentrate on those stools for which enough evidence is available to draw reasonable inferences.

It should be emphasized at once that the *chronology* of Fante traditions is not intrinsic, that is, calculated from their own evidence, but seems to be based on a single transcending presumption—that the original wave of Fante migrants had arrived on the coast and developed states there *before* the arrival of the Portuguese in the fifteenth century. This is the chronology that the Fante have developed over the last century, and it is the chronology accepted in most modern accounts of the early history of the area.[8] The current assumption that the Fanta *qua* Fante had arrived and established states on the coast by 1500 is evidently based on a single piece of evidence from Pacheco Pereira, who wrote *c.* 1505. In describing the coastline east of São Jorge da Mina (Elmina), Pacheco Pereira spoke of 'places of fishermen' called 'Fante the Great' and 'Fante the Small'.[9] According to his description these villages lay in the heart of what later became the Fante country. Still, there are no other known references to the Fante as a people or as a political unit until the

[7] I use the term 'state' and 'stool' interchangeably in this chapter, as indeed they are used interchangeably among the Fante. Stool implies 'paramount stool' and each paramount stool is independent of any other stool. This contrasts with Asante, where all the stools recognize the supremacy of the Asantehene. Given the size of many of the Fante polities, the term state probably lacks appropriateness in many cases. In the 1948 census several Fante stools contained fewer than 200 households. Gold Coast, Census Dept., *Report of the census of population, 1948* (Accra, 1950), 98, 150.

[8] e.g. A. A. Boahen, 'Asante and Fante, A.D. 1000–1800' in J. F. A. Ajayi and I. Espie, *A thousand years of West African history* (Ibadan, 1965), 161, 175–6; J. B. Christensen, *Double descent among the Fanti* (New Haven, Conn., 1954), 7; W. E. F. Ward, *A history of Ghana* (rev. 4th ed., London, 1967), 62–3. Boahen, 'Fante diplomacy in the eighteenth century', paper presented at Conference on the Foreign Relations of African States held at University of Bristol, 4–6 Apr. 1973.

[9] D. P. Pereira (ed. D. Peres), *Esmeraldo de Situ Orbis* (Lisbon, 1954), 146.

seventeenth century.[10] In the eighteenth century the Fante began to coalesce into the states which exist today. The last group of Fante to settle in the coastal areas was the Borbor Fante. Their migration from 'the north' may in some way be connected with the conquest of Bobo-Manso (Tekyiman) by Asante in *c.* 1722/3. Such a connection would help account for the persistent Fante traditions of origin from Tekyiman. In 1752 the English on the coast recorded that 'Acriphy, the Public Orator of Abrah [Abura], told us that ever since the Fantees left Arcania, under the Braffoe Imorah, they had been closely connected with the English, who furnished them with arms and ammunition to conquer the country now called Fantee'.[11] Whatever the motives of the speaker were in identifying himself and the Abura Fante so closely with English interests, his statement suggested a recent migration to the coast. Unfortunately, it is not clear whether he was speaking of the Fante *in toto*, or only the Borbor Fante, when referring to this migration.

The states mentioned in the extant Portuguese records, viz. Eguafo, Jabi (later Shama), Abrem, Fetu, and Asebu, are recognized by the Fante themselves as non-Fante states which were subjected by the newly arrived Fante migrants.[12] An analysis of the European records of the seventeenth and eighteenth centuries suggests that the Fante arrived on the coast in significant numbers and began the process of state formation only in the seventeenth century.[13] It is not germane

[10] The 'King of Fantijn' signed a treaty with the Dutch at Kormantin in 1624. K. Y. Daaku, *Trade and politics on the Gold Coast, 1600–1720* (Oxford, 1970), 55, 185. Marees, who was on the Gold Coast *c.* 1600 spoke of 'a small place named Infantin'—probably the same as Pereira's 'Fante'—with the implication that it was then no more than a local place-name. P. de Marees (ed. S.-P. L'Honoré Naber), *Beschryvinghe ende historische verhael van het Gout Koninckrijck van Guinea* (The Hague, 1912), 87.

[11] 'A diary of narrative of transactions with the Fantees from the death of Intuffer King of Warsaw', dd 23 Sept. 1752, Treasury Records, Records of the African Companies, PRO (henceforth T70), 1520. 'Arcania' or 'Akani' was probably the region of Assin and Twifo stools to the immediate north of the Fante area. Acriphy (or the English?) may have used the term Arcania to mean no more than an undefined area north of the immediate hinterland. Its use may also suggest, however, that the Fante migration was a long process and that Acriphy only remembered the last stop along the migration route.

[12] Meyerowitz, *Akan traditions*, 66–75; M. Manoukian, *The Akan and Ga-Adangme peoples* (London, 1950), 13. Eguafo (Great Commany in the Dutch and English records) and Asebu survive as independent stools. Jabi (Yarbiw) is now a sub-stool of Shama, while Fetu and Abrem are under the paramount stool of Oguaa (Cape Coast).

[13] 'The Borbor Fanti', an unpublished paper by E. T. Collins, University of Ghana. For another opinion, see Boahen, 'Fante diplomacy'.

to the present discussion to attempt to evaluate the various strains of evidence regarding the time of the Fante arrival on the coast, beyond emphasizing that there is no contemporaneous evidence of Fante stools in the area before the seventeenth century. The following discussion should make it clear that the Fante conception of their own traditional chronology today is based on their cumulative knowledge of the time and circumstances of the European arrival.

As already noted, the development of Fante stool traditions can be traced through the succession and jurisdictional disputes that occurred incessantly in this century. For analytical purposes the present discussion will concentrate on the traditional accounts of the origins and history of the Anamabu, Oguaa (Cape Coast), and Shama stools. A study of these stool traditions will provide examples of the important factors which helped to shape Fante traditional history.

II ANAMABU STOOL TRADITIONS

During the eighteenth century Anamabu was the most important slaving entrepôt on the Gold Coast. Various small posts had been erected there by the Europeans since before 1650, but most of them had been occupied only very briefly.[14] In 1751 the French attempted to erect a fort near Anamabu but were rebuffed by John Currantee, the most important individual in Anamabu and the broker for the English at the time.[15] The French effort provoked a British response and the Company of Merchants trading to Africa, newly established on the coast, built Fort William at Anamabu between 1753 and 1757.

Some elements of the stool history of Anamabu can be retrieved from the English company records. In 1701 the town seems to have been subject, at least momentarily, to the ruler of Asebu, a non-Fante state located north of the town.[16] Between 1708 and 1821 the English and Dutch records provide the following data about the rulers of Anamabu:

[14] A. van Dantzig and B. Priddy, *A short history of the forts and castles of Ghana* (Accra, 1971), 18; A. W. Lawrence, *Trade castles and forts of West Africa* (London, 1963), 349–50.

[15] J. N. Matson, 'The French at Amoku', *Transactions of the Gold Coast and Togoland Historical Society*, 1 (1955), 47–9; T. Melvil to Committee, 11 June 1751, CO288/45, pp. 269–70; same to same, 11 July 1751, PRO, T70/1517.

[16] Freeman, Peck, and Hicks, Cape Coast Castle, to Royal African Company, 6 Nov. 1701 (o.s.), quoted in Charles Davenant, *The political and commercial works* (5 vols., London, 1771), V. 184–5.

Quaggie Aqua: mentioned as 'Chief Caboceer' or 'Captain' between 1708 and 1715.[17]

Eggin: called the Royal African Company's 'Company Caboceer' at Anamabu in 1728 and 1729. In 1731 he was dashed (given a gift) on being made 'Captain of that Town'.[18]

John Currantee: mentioned as early as 1734 but first described as 'Captain of that Town' only in 1747. Currantee remained 'Captain' of Anamabu until his death, 28 June 1764.[19]

Quassah: described as 'John Currantee's heir' from 1765 to 1769.[20] It is not clear whether this meant heir to his private fortune or to his position as ruler of Anamabu as well.

Amonee Coomah: called 'one of the Principal Caboceers' in 1765; from at least 1767 he was described as 'Principal Caboceer'. In 1774 his title and position changed. He was variously described as being elected 'principal Captain' and 'King', and his stipend was doubled. In 1775 Amonee Coomah was called 'King of Fantee' and was regarded by the British authorities as second in importance only to the Asantehene. In 1801 Amonee Coomah died 'at a very advanced age'.[21]

Antee: called 'heir to Amonee Coomah'; died in 1804 and was succeeded by John Currantee.[22]

John Currantee: succeeded Antee as 'Principal Caboceer' in 1804 and died in 1809.[23]

[17] Minute of Elmina Council dd 4–7 July 1708, FC1701–15, 1707–15, p. 72 (WIC125). Komenda Journal of William Baillie, 20 July 1715 (O.S.), T70/1464; Requisition for presents from Cape Coast Castle Warehouse, 25 July 1713 (o.s.), PRO, C113/34, Box 1, item 13. Items in the Furley Collection will be cited as follows: box number, notebook number, page; followed, where available, by designation of document in the Dutch archives. The Furley Collection is presently being recatalogued and calendared by Albert van Dantzig and Edmund Collins and the designations used here may therefore become obsolete. Caboceer (from the Portuguese 'caboceiro') was the term applied rather ubiquitously and ambiguously by the Europeans on the coast to a multitude of native authorities.

[18] T70/392, f. 49^{v}; T70/394, f. 93^{v}; T70/397, f. 150^{v}.

[19] T70/401, f. 10^{v}; T70/423, f. 48; T70/31, f. 56^{v}. The ledger garrison showed Currantee's death as having occurred on 5 July 1768, T70/988.

[20] T70/989; T70/1022.

[21] T70/988; T70/989, T70/1035 *sub* 19 July 1774; Mill to Committee, 30 Dec. 1775, T70/32, ff. 30–1; T70/1534; Dalzel to Committee, 2 Jan. 1802, T70/34, f. 54; T70/995.

[22] T70/995.

[23] T70/995; T70/1095 *sub* 31 Mar. 1809.

Amooney Coomah: succeeded John Currantee in 1809; still called 'chief of Anamabu' in 1817. Called 'King of Anamabu' in 1811 by the Dutch.[24]

Baffoe: called 'Head Caboceer of Anomabu' from 1818 to at least February 1821.[25]

Amoney: called 'Captain General' in 1820 and 'King' in 1824.[26] Amoney may be the same as Amooney Coomah.

The absence of detailed information on the principal offices in the coastal towns after 1821 makes it impossible to scrutinize the later period. Amoney, however, may have died in 1837.[27] He was succeeded by a series of *amanhin* (paramount rulers) named Amoney or Amonu.

It appears, then, that the first John Currantee or his immediate predecessor was the first *de facto* independent ruler of Anamabu. Although Anamabu was described as subject to 'the King of Fanteen' as late as 1753, this may have implied no more than active membership in the loosely organized Fante confederacy of the time.[28] John Currantee probably was, as Margaret Priestley has surmised, the founder of the dynasty that subsequently ruled Anamabu.[29] The existence of a second John Currantee suggests that this is true. The variant styling of the titles of rulers of Anamabu in the European records makes it difficult to trace the fortunes of this dynasty, but the events of 1774 seemed to mark a distinct advance in the position of the Anamabu stool.

Not unexpectedly, the few traditional accounts of the Anamabu stool that exist today lean heavily on the printed sources available for John Currantee and for the nineteenth century. One account, prepared for a hearing in a stool dispute in 1932, seems to have been uncontaminated by written sources. According to this account, the

[24] T70/1095 *sub* 31 Mar. 1809; Cruikshank, *Eighteen years,* I. 106; White, Cape Coast Castle to Ruhle, Director-General, Elmina, 8 July 1811, FC 1781–1816, 1810–13, 45.

[25] Minute of Cape Coast Castle Council dd 5 Dec. 1818, T70/154, f. 74^{v}: T70/998; T70/1119.

[26] T70/1119; 'Return shewing the supposed number of Men residing at each Place in alliance with the British on the Gold Coast, Guinea', dd 29 July 1824, CO267/61.

[27] J. M. Sarbah, *Fanti customary law* (2nd ed., London, 1968), xxx.

[28] J. Appersley, Anamabu, to the Rt. Hon. the Lt.-Gen. and the Hon. the Principal Officers of His Majesty's Ordnance, dd 9 Mar. 1753, W55/1817, PRO.

[29] M. Priestley, *West African trade and coast society: a family study* (London, 1969), 13–15.

Anamabu stool was founded immediately after 'the dispersal of the different Fanti groups from Mankessim', that is, by traditional Fante chronology, sometime before the end of the fifteenth century. The list of *amanhin* given in this account contained seven Amonus and Kofi Afari I (ruled 1857–65, and an alternative name for Amonu II in most sources).[30] Unlike the accounts for other stools like Shama and Elmina, Anamabu's traditions for the early period before Amonu I, unidentified and undated but possibly to be identified with Amonee Coomah, are almost non-existent. The most circumstantial account is of undetermined provenience but, from internal evidence, was written between 1922 and 1924.[31] It mentioned several rulers before one Kurentsir, to be identified with John Currantee. Kurentsir was described as a wealthy and highly esteemed member of the community, who was elected to the paramount stool because the previous *ɔmanhen* had died without heirs. In this account the Amonu who succeeded *c.* 1765 is confused with the *ɔmanhen* of the same name who died in 1837 and none of the intervening rulers is mentioned. The account of Kurentsir and information on nineteenth-century *amanhin* was certainly gathered from written sources—principally Sarbah's *Fanti customary law*. Anamabu traditions presume an origin for their paramount stool which antedated the arrival of the Europeans but seldom seek to document this assertion by naming Anamabu rulers from printed sources which are few since Anamabu only became important in the eighteenth century with the increase in the slave trade on the Gold Coast.

III OGUAA STOOL TRADITIONS

The paramount stool of Oguaa (Cape Coast) seems, like that of Anamabu, to have been an eighteenth-century creation. The site of Cape Coast was already settled in the middle of the sixteenth century, but the town was part of the inland state of Fetu.[32] Fetu already existed as a state when the Portuguese arrived in 1482.[33] During the seventeenth and early eighteenth centuries Fetu suffered a series of

[30] NAG/CSO1121/31. A similar list is in NAG/ADM11/1/1103.

[31] Typescript 'History of Anamabu' in Kobina Sekyi papers, NAG/Cape Coast, Accession 554/64.

[32] Account of William Towrson of voyages made in 1555 and 1557 in R. Hakluyt, *Principal navigations, voyages, traffiques and discoveries of the English nation*, Everyman Library (8 vols., London, 1910), IV. 82–4, 89.

[33] See a summary of the Portuguese accounts in R. M. Wiltgen, *Gold Coast mission history, 1471–1880* (Techny, Ill., 1956), 2–8, 10–16.

defeats by the Fante and ceased to be an important factor in local politics and Cape Coast, the site of the main English establishment on the Gold Coast after 1664, quickly surpassed the inland state in importance.[34] None the less, the English continued to recognize the juridical primacy of the Fetu stool over Cape Coast by continuing to pay the *ɔmanhen* and *dey* (chief minister) of Fetu the 'rental' for the land on which Cape Coast Castle stood.[35]

The progenitor of all the later *amanhin* of Oguaa, though apparently never *ɔmanhen* himself, was Cudjoe Caboceer, well known from contemporaneous sources.[36] Cudjoe Caboceer was the counterpart of John Currantee of Anamabu in that he was the chief agent of the English and, indeed, the most powerful and wealthiest man in the town. Cudjoe Caboceer served the English companies for nearly half a century before his death in 1776.[37] The evidence for traditional offices in Cape Coast before him is sparse. One Edward (Ned) Barter, a mulatto who had been educated in Great Britain, returned to Cape Coast in 1693 as an employee of the Royal African Company. Barter has recently been described as 'virtually the ruler of Cape Coast'.[38] What role Barter may have had in the traditional structure of the town is unclear. It is unlikely, however, that the Oguaa stool was then independent of Fetu.[39] The first mention in the English records of a 'King' in Cape Coast was in 1740; unfortunately the name of this ruler was not included.[40] In 1749 'the old King', again unnamed, was

[34] D. B. Birmingham, 'A note on the kingdom of Fetu', *GNQ*, 9 (1966), 30–3; Daaku, *Trade and Politics*, 89–93.

[35] Payments entered in Cape Coast Castle Day Books, T70/1009–1119. Again, the paucity of data after 1821 makes it impossible to determine when this payment ceased. It was still being paid as late as 1824, J. J. Crooks, *Records relating to the Gold Coast settlements from 1750 to 1874* (Dublin, 1923), 128. In 1840 Maclean observed that 'The Fetus . . . have long since ceased to have any power or influence', 'State of the forts and settlements' in CO96/171, p. 202. Presumably the British government had also long since ceased paying the stipend. On the office of *dey* in Fetu government, see W. J. Müller, *Die africanische auf der guineischen Gold-Cust gelegene Landsschafft Fetu* (Hamburg, 1673), 67–9.

[36] See especially T. Thompson, *An account of two missionary voyages . . .* (London, 1758), 34, and M. Priestley, 'Philip Quaque of Cape Coast' in P. D. Curtin (ed.), *Africa remembered* (Madison, Wis., 1967), 99–139.

[37] T70/394, f. 52^{v}.

[38] Daaku, *Trade and politics*, 98. See also Bosman, *Description*, 51–2.

[39] James Phipps (RAC Agent-General at Cape Coast) described an incident which occurred in 1712 or shortly after, when Fetu forces besieged Cape Coast Castle and seemed to exercise effective control over the inhabitants of Cape Coast town. Phipps and Bleau to RAC, 30 Mar. 1717 (O.S.), PRO, C113/34, Box 2, item 35.

[40] T70/413, f. 32. The appearance of the term 'King' in the European records

given gifts.[41] In 1753 the missionary Thomas Thompson spoke of the king Amroh Coffi as the brother of Cudjoe Caboceer, and Amroh Coffi seems to have ruled until sometime shortly after 1761.[42] In March 1765 one Mramma was elected, 'as the properest person for being King', but he died within four months.[43] The kingship of Cape Coast evidently lapsed from 1765 into the 1780s. No 'King' was paid from Company funds, nor is there any mention of a paramount ruler in the letters of Philip Quaque written during this time.[44]

When the office was reinstituted it was held by a member of the Aggrey family who was a descendant of Cudjoe Caboceer. Since before 1720 the office of Chief Caboceer or Head Linguister for the Royal African Company and its successor had been the most influential person in Cape Coast. By 1715 one Thomas Awishee was the Company's Head Linguister and he held the office until 1742, when he removed to Anamabu as the Company's chief agent there.[45] In 1729 a certain 'Cudjoe' was listed on the Company's payroll as 'Linguister and Messenger Extraordinary'.[46] In 1742 this individual, now known as Cudjoe Caboceer, became the Company's Head Linguister and retained the post until his death thirty-four years later. Cudjoe Caboceer is the most important figure in Oguaa traditional history. The traditional accounts, discussed below, are based on the relative abundance of printed matter available for Cudjoe Caboceer. In order to evaluate the traditional accounts of the succession and succession practices in the Oguaa stool it is necessary to describe in some detail the succession to the offices that contemporaneous records indicate that Cudjoe Caboceer held. Cudjoe Caboceer evidently never became 'King' of Cape Coast, although he was long the most powerful man in the town. If he held any traditional office, it was probably that of *tufohen*, or captain of the *asafo* companies—

does not, of course, necessarily indicate newly won independence from Fetu by the Oguaa stool. It may reflect only the increasing importance of the town and of its traditional rulers. In fact, the ambiguity of the European nomenclature for the traditional offices will already have been noticed by the reader.

[41] T70/424B, f. 7, *sub* 15 May 1749 (O.S.).

[42] Thompson, *Missionary voyages*, 34; T70/1015, *sub* 23 Nov. 1760.

[43] T70/1022, *sub* 5 Mar. 1765; T70/1026, *sub* 17 Sept. 1768.

[44] Quaque to Society for the Propagation of the Faith, 5 Sept. 1769; SPG Archives, West Africa C/AFR, W, 1, no. 16.

[45] T70/382, f. 52^v; T70/417, f. 14^v; Thomas Awishee is described (under the name of Tom Osiat) by William Smith in 1727 as 'Grand Caboceroe' of Cape Coast and a Christian who was raised and educated in Ireland. Smith, *A new voyage to Guinea* (London, 1745), 124–5.

[46] T70/394, f. 52^v.

a military post also held by his descendants.[47] After 1765 he was apparently able to dispense completely with the *ɔmanhen*, and after Cudjo Caboceer's death in 1776 when the office of 'King' or *ɔmanhen* was re-established, it was held by one of his descendants. The change probably represented a change in ruling line, although the evidence is not unambiguous. Thompson described Cudjoe Caboceer as the [half-]brother of the reigning Cape Coast king and most Oguaa stool traditions agree. The principles of succession, if any, that prevailed before 1765, are simply not known. Cudjoe Caboceer was a member of the Aggrey (or Aggery) family. An 'Aggree, late Captain of Cape Coast', was mentioned in 1715 as having died owing the Royal African Company money.[48] According to tradition, Cudjoe Caboceer and his mother came from Ekumfi-Adanse. She married the then-ruling *ɔmanhen* of Cape Coast and their son—Cudjoe Caboceer's half-brother—was Amroh Coffi.[49] Thus Cudjoe Caboceer's relationship to the Aggrey family may have been through marriage, if the traditional accounts are accepted. The succession after Cudjoe Caboceer ran as follows, according to contemporaneous records:

Aggery described as 'General of the different Companies of Soldiers belonging to this town [Cape Coast]' in 1780. He thus apparently succeeded his father Cudjoe Caboceer as *tufohen*. Aggery died in 1793, when he was called 'the Company's Linguist and Captain of Cape Coast town'.[50]

Botty: Botty 'succeeded his uncle Cudjoe in that station [principal Caboceer] which it is the usage of the Country for the sons not to do'. Botty died in 1789, 'having no Heir'.[51]

[47] On the *asafo* system among the Fante, see A. K. Datta and R. Porter, 'The *asafo* system in historical perspective', *JAH* 12 (1971), 279–97, esp. 284–5, and J. C. de Graft Johnson, 'The Fanti Asafu', *Africa*, 5 (1932), 307–22.

[48] T70/382, f. 52ᵛ; T70/386, f. 14ᵛ.

[49] Brown, *Gold Coast reader*, II. 122–3; information from W. S. Kwesi Johnston, Cape Coast, 19 May 1971. The story also occurred several times in the testimony given at the various stool inquiries held between 1915 and 1944.

[50] Roberts and Council to Company, 24 Dec. 1780, T70/32, ff. 56–56ᵛ, 87ᵛ; T70/1035, *sub* 1 Aug. 1774; Dalzel to Committee, 28 Feb. 1793, T70/33, f. 187ᵛ.

[51] Roberts to Company, 11 July 1780, T70/32, ff. 56–56ᵛ. Botty was probably 'the supposed heir to the Stool so called (or in other words, the crown of the late Cudjoe Caboceer)' mentioned by Philip Quaque in his description of the obsequies of Cudjoe. Quaque to SPG, 17 Jan. 1778, SPG Archives, C/AFR-W, 1, no. 30, reprinted in Priestley, 'Philip Quaque of Cape Coast', 129. Fielde and Miles to Company, 17 June 1789, T70/33, f. 107.

Aboahdo: described as 'the late Captain Aggery's successor' in 1793.[52]

Ando: called 'Captain-General of Cape Coast' in 1795; Ando was evidently still alive in 1817.[53]

Fat Aggery: installed [as successor of Aggery?] in 1794; died in 1800[54].

Aggery: 'Caboceer in place of the late Fat Aggery' in 1800; called 'King of Cape Coast' in 1801 and 'Captain of the Town' the following year. This Aggery died in 1814.[55]

Joe Aggery: Joe Aggery was elected *ɔmanhen* of Oguaa in 1816. He was then described as 'an intelligent and respectable native' and 'a man of authority' in the town. Known in Oguaa tradition as Burupu, he died in 1851.[56]

The most common account of the origin of the Oguaa paramount stool among literate informants is that the ruler of Fetu fled to Cape Coast about 1697 as a result of the war mentioned by Bosman and re-established his authority there.[57] The Oguaa stool is thus seen as simply a continuation of the ancient Fetu state. This tradition is unquestionably based on the printed sources available—that is, Phillips, Bosman, Barbot, Thompson, Claridge *et al.* It is more difficult to sort

[52] Komenda Day Book, *sub* 26 Nov. 1793, T70/1127.

[53] T70/1067, *sub* 25 Dec. 1795; T70/1111, *sub* 18 Nov. 1817. The position Ando held in Cape Coast is uncertain. He often took precedence over the *ɔmanhen* Aggrey. He was probably not the *tufohen*, as suggested by Porter, 'The Cape Coast conflict of 1803: a crisis in relations between the African and European communities', *THSG* 11 (1970), 30–1, since Quamina Adoo was installed as 'Captain of the 4 Quarters of the Town' in 1812 in succession to Coffee Akinny, T70/1101, *sub* 15 Nov. 1812.

[54] T70/1065, *sub* 12 July 1794; T70/1077, *sub* 23 Dec. 1800.

[55] T70/1077, *sub* 23 Dec. 1800; T70/995, *sub* 3 Sept. 1801; Agreement dd 19 Jan. 1802, T70/1081; White and Smith to Committee, 10 Mar. 1814, T70/36, f. 29v.

[56] T70/1109, *sub* 26 Aug. 1816; Smith and Council, Cape Coast Castle, to Committee, 15 Mar. 1817, T70/36, ff. 118, 118v. Gov. Hill to Earl Grey, 4 Nov. 1851, CO96/23, ff. 174, 174v. John Duncan, who visited Cape Coast in 1845, described Joe Aggrey as 'a venerable old man' of over seventy years, who had 'served several years on board a British man-of-war, previously to attaining his sovereignty'. John Duncan, *Travels in western Africa in 1845 and 1846; comprising a journey from Whydah through the Kingdom of Dahomey to Adofoodia in the interior* (2 vols., London, 1847), I. 28, 29n.

[57] Interview with Kwesi Johnston 19 May 1971; Bosman, *Description*, 47–8; this flight actually occurred in 1693. See T. Phillips's account of his voyage in 1693 in T. Astley (ed.), *Collection of voyages and travel* (4 vols., London, 1745–7), II. 401.

out some of the other traditional accounts recorded in this century. Each was influenced by the continuing dispute about whether succession to the Oguaa stool was patrilineal or matrilineal. The 'accepted' version is that before 1856 succession to the stool was patrilineal, as in Fetu, but that with the progressive Fante-izing of the town, matrilineal succession replaced it.[58] In these accounts the succession was usually traced back to before 1700. In fact some traditions claimed that the founder of the stool had visited 'Juan Carlos, King of Portugal' in the sixteenth century, apparently a garbled interpretation of William Towrson's relation of several voyages he made to the Gold Coast in the 1550s in which he mentioned a certain 'Don John'.[59]

Even so, the traditional information for the succession to the paramount stool before 1856 seems to demonstrate some valid recollections. For instance, although the mode of succession and the number and names of the *amanhin* are often disputed, there is a persistent recollection that most of the *amanhin* were members of the Egyr (Aggrey) family. Some accounts mention Boatsi and Essen Andoh as predecessors of Burupu (to whom traditional accounts, for unknown reasons, invariably assign regnal dates of 1801–51 or 1802–52).[60] All descriptions of early succession practices were, of course, extremely partisan. Unfortunately, the contemporaneous English sources help little in solving this problem. Although we know the relationship of Botty and Aggrey to Cudjoe Caboceer, it is not certain to which of the latter's offices each succeeded. Cudjoe Caboceer was never *ɔmanhen*, hence the observation that Botty succeeded because sons could not fails to clarify the issue of succession to the paramount stool itself. Aggrey would naturally have succeeded his father as *tufohen*, because *asafo* offices were hereditary in the male line.[61] No filiations are known for the other Cape Coast *amanhin*[?] of this period. It is likely that succession was broad and loosely

[58] 'Report of 1942 Commission of Enquiry into the dispute over the election of a successor to the paramount stool of Oguaa', p. 1, NAG/ADM11/1/1752. It is also alleged that patrilineal succession gave way to matrilineal succession in Winneba (Efutu) stool in the 1850s. The result, as in Oguaa, was a succession of stool disputes.

[59] 'Report of 1916 Enquiry into the Oguaa Stool dispute', NAG/ADM11/1/629. Hakluyt, *Principal navigations*, IV. 82–4.

[60] e.g. 'Notes of evidence of the 1916 Enquiry', pp. 5–7, NAG/ADM11/1/1765.

[61] De Graft-Johnson, 'Fanti Asafu', 312. According to de Graft-Johnson the office of *tufohen* in Oguaa began to be inherited matrilineally in the twentieth century, ibid.

defined. The fact that Joe Aggrey (Burupu) was wealthy was probably more important than any blood relationship with his predecessors.

This analysis of Oguaa stool traditions suggests that the most important factor in assessing their value is, as for most of the Fante states, the problem of feedback. The chronological structure of most of the traditional accounts is based on a *mélange* of Towrson, Bosman, Barbot, Thompson, and other written accounts. The mention of Boatsi in some accounts may, for instance, reflect no more than a familiarity with Cruikshank's work.[62] The Cape Coasters are proud of their literate heritage, probably the oldest continuous one in Ghana.[63] One such informant, commenting that 'you can't go against the European records', based his account of pre-twentieth-century Oguaa stool history entirely on such sources, even though he had been an active participant in Oguaa stool affairs for forty years. He himself had collected, and was very proud of, an impressive library of European source materials for coastal Fante history.

IV SHAMA STOOL TRADITIONS

The effect of feedback on the traditions of nearly every coastal stool is particularly important in assessing them. It is not possible to elaborate here in greater detail the widespread adaptation of external materials to traditional uses.[64] However, a single representative example of this propensity of Fante traditional historians can illustrate the problem more clearly. Today Shama is a small town at the western side of the mouth of the Pra river and the seat of a paramount stool. The town of Shama already existed when the Portuguese arrived on the coast and the chronicler of the Portuguese expedition which established São Jorge da Mina spoke of a 'Chief of Shama'.[65] There is no other indication, however, that Shama was an independent state before the end of the eighteenth century, and a good deal of evidence that it was not. The 1629 Dutch map showed Shama

[62] Cruikshank, *Eighteen years*, I. 54, mentioned 'Botty, King of Cape Coast'.

[63] During the 1916 Inquiry most of the supporters of patrilineal succession referred to Sarbah's *Fanti customary law*, p. 256, to support their position. See also Petition of E. C. K. Sey, dd 23 Oct. 1939, NAG/CSO1414/31, and testimony at 1916 Inquiry, NAG/ADM11/1/1765.

[64] For a more detailed discussion of the problem of feedback see my 'The problem of feedback in oral tradition: four examples from the Fante coastlands', *JAH* 14 (1973), 223–35.

[65] R. de Pina (ed. A. M. de Carvalho), *Crónica de el-Rei D. João II* (Coimbra, 1950), 13, followed by J. de Barros and D. do Couto, *Da Asia* (12 pts. in 21 vols., Lisbon, 1777–99), I. 162.

as part of Ahanta.[66] Later Shama fell under the control of the state of Jabi, whose capital was situated a few miles north of Shama.[67]

The first mention of an independent ruler in Shama was in 1781, when 'Quouw Koekoem' signed a Pen and Contract (Agreement) with the Dutch as 'King of Chama' and it is likely that the office of Shama *ɔmanhen* had only been created shortly before that time.[68] Jabi (now called Ya[r]biw) has been a substool of Shama for nearly a century. Shama traditions vaguely recall the early primacy of Jabi when they claim that the alleged founder of the Shama paramount stool stopped briefly at Yabiw on his way to the coast.[69] These traditions fail to recognize, however, that Jabi remained an independent state until the latter half of the nineteenth century, albeit during the last years of its existence of little consequence and eclipsed in importance by the Shama stool.[70] Rather, they see the Shama state as a direct successor of Jabi, just as Oguaa traditions consider their stool to have followed that of Fetu.

Succession to the Shama paramount stool is patrilineal, but there were several efforts from the 1920s to the 1940s to change the succession to the female line. Those who supported the change naturally had recourse to genealogies which purported to prove that at one time succession to the paramount stool in Shama had been matrilineal. These genealogies invariably depicted the foundation of the

[66] K. Y. Daaku and A. van Dantzig, 'An annotated Dutch map of 1629', *GNQ* 9 (1966), 15; Marees, *Beschryvinghe*, 94. This work was first published in 1602 and is the earliest extant detailed description of the Gold Coast. See also J. B. Amissah, 'Introducing *Description and historical account of the golden Coast of Guinea* of Pieter de Marees', *THSG* 9 (1968), 121–7.

[67] J. Ogilby, *Africa* . . . (London, 1670), 421. This is a translation of Dapper's work, itself a patchwork of earlier accounts. Report of J. Valckenburg, Director-General at Elmina, dd 1659, FC1658–64; J. Barbot, *A description of the coasts of North and South-Guinea* . . . (London, 1746), 153. Barbot's work was written *c.* 1690, though only published in 1732 and must be used with extreme caution as much of it is derivative.

[68] Pen and Contract dd 10 July 1781, FC1781–1816, 1781–2, 156 (WIC989).

[69] Meyerowitz, *Akan traditions*, 74. Testimony of 'patrilinealists' given at 1922 Stool inquiry, pp. 22–3, NAG/ADM11/1/1464; Notes of Testimony of 1942 Stool inquiry, p. 103, NAG/ADM11/1/1805.

[70] J. S. G. Gramberg, *Schetsen van Afrikas Westkust* (Amsterdam, 1861), 171, mentioned 'the kingdom of Jabio' and noted that Jabi itself was then 'a small village [though] the remainder of [a] once powerful and warlike tribe'. By 1870 Jabi was counted as one of the districts of Shama, Annual Report of the Chama Division for 1870, FC1843–72, 1870–2, 149 (NBKG645). See also minute of J. D. Simons, a former Dutch official at Elmina, dd 1 Sept. 1894 in M. P. 3062/94, NAG/ADM11/1/626.

dynasty as antedating the arrival of the Portuguese.[71] The earlier parts of these genealogies have no obvious historical value and suggest a complete lack of knowledge for the period before the beginning of the nineteenth century. They were developed at least in part as the result of a desire to claim that early rulers of the town had leased the land on which the Portuguese and Dutch built their forts. The story of this event is a consistent refrain, perhaps the only one, throughout recorded Shama traditions.[72]

In 1922 the Abakam Efiana family, which claimed to be the sole stool family in Shama, submitted a petition recounting in great detail the early history and succession to the paramount stool.[73] This memorial contained several interesting statements. For instance, it detailed in great length how a ruling queen of Shama named Abba Bakam (apparently a matronym) invited the Portuguese to build a fort there. Abba Bakam laid the cornerstone of this fort herself and subsequently the Abakam Efiana family allegedly collected the rental for the land on which it stood. The son of this queen and next ruler of the town was, according to the petition, a certain Anquah. It is the appearance of Anquah in this tradition that is of particular interest. The memorialists pointed out in support of their argument that this Anquah had been mentioned in a recent work by a British traveller to the Gold Coast.[74] Bowler had in fact said that 'in speaking of Chama, Bosman refers to a king called Anquah'.[75] Bowler, however, was incorrect and had misinterpreted Bosman badly. Bosman described Shama as 'moderately large and well-peopled, but . . . miserably poor'.[76] Bosman also spoke of Anquah, a particularly sanguinary military leader of the time, but he was then referring to Adom (now represented by Supome, a substool of Shama), a district to the north of and then quite distinct from Shama. Bosman described Adom as 'governed by five or six Principal Men, there being no King'.[77] Anquah was one of these 'Principal Men'. In fine, then, Bosman

[71] See, e.g., the genealogical table proposed by the matrilinealists in NAG/ADM26/5/36, opp. p. 110, and similar tables in NAG/ADM11/1/1805, pp. 65, 129.

[72] Some of the genealogies dated the construction of the fort to 1629. In fact the first fort at Shama was built by the Portuguese about the middle of the sixteenth century. The Dutch captured it *c.* 1638 and largely rebuilt it.

[73] This petition, dd 22 Apr. 1922, is in NAG/ADM11/1/1464.

[74] L. P. Bowler, *Gold Coast palaver: life on the Gold Coast* (London, 1911).

[75] Ibid. 147.

[76] Bosman, *Description*, 20.

[77] Ibid. 23.

described Anquah as a non-king of non-Shama, and Bowler erroneously metamorphosed him into an *ɔmanhen* of Shama. One of the contending parties in Shama, seeking to bolster its own claims by whatever means possible, integrated Anquah into the framework of the stool's traditional history. The balance of the petitioners' historical account was presumably manufactured to fit this new piece of 'hard' (i.e. written) evidence which had come to their attention.

The petitioners may have felt that any account which seemed to support written 'evidence' would appeal to the colonial administration. In any event they, too, thought it unwise to 'go against' the European records. They were not in a position to judge the quality of the information provided by Bowler, but evidently assumed that any datum that had been hallowed by publication was superior to their own traditions, which, of course, had not mentioned Anquah previously. Bowler's book had only been in print eleven years and its circulation in the Gold Coast was probably minimal. The incorporation of information in it speaks well of the enterprise of the Abakam Efiana family. The fact that the deeds attributed to mother and son were separated by a century and a half (*c.* 1550–*c.* 1700) illustrates the customary irrelevance of chronological sequence in traditional accounts.

The handling of Shama traditions is germane to the problems discussed here because it exemplifies several points common to coastal Fante traditions. The propensity to absorb feedback matter into traditional accounts and the alacrity with which this has been done is the most important of these. No traditional account of Fante stool history has been able to escape this tendency where such information has been available. Fortunately, perhaps, the Fante respect for the written word often enables the scholar to detect this propensity easily since most traditional accounts allude to the external sources they have used.

Shama traditions, or at least the lists of the *amanhin* of the town, while of no value for the earlier periods, do exhibit a surprisingly high degree of accuracy for a period of about 100 to 125 years. Contrasted below are a typical traditional list of the Shama *amanhin* and the information about them available from contemporaneous sources.

Kobina Kumah	1781:	Quouw Koekoem
	1791:	Coema Koeokoem
	1798:	Mysang Doedoen

Kobina Segu (destooled)	–1810	Sogoe (destooled)
	1819:	Quamina Abroba
Kobina Issah	1841:1846	Cobbin Isa
Kweku Ebbina	1850:1855	Kwakoe Ebbena
Kojo Freiku	*c.* 1856–:1891	Cudjoe Freiku[79]
Kwow Freiku[78]	1905–1917	Kwow Freiku[80]

(a colon denotes that an *ɔmanhen* was known to have been ruling in the years shown but dates of accession and death or destoolment are not known).

It is remarkable that all of the traditional accounts recalled that Segu had been destooled.[81] None of the accounts mentioned Quamina Abroba, however. Rather they claimed that Kobina Segu, Kobina Issah, and Kweku Ebbina were brothers. While possible, such a relationship among the three is unlikely, given the period of time covered by their reigns. This ability to recall with some precision the names and sequence (often with additional details) of the rulers over

[78] Petition dd 22 Apr. 1922, pp. 9–10, NAG/ADM11/1/1464; Notes of Evidence of 1922 Inquiry, p. 22, NAG/ADM11/1/1464; S. C. Leung (lawyer for Abakam Efiana family) to Commissioner, Western Provinces, 30 Sept. 1921, NAG/ADM 11/1/1464.

[79] An accession date of *c.* 1856 for Cudjoe Freiku is inferred from his statement made in 1884 that he had been *ɔmanhen* 'about twenty-nine years'. Cudjoe Freiku to DC, Dixcove, 2 Oct. 1884, M. P. 1967/84, NAG/ADM11/1/1464. He was ruling in the early 1860s. See C. A. Jeekel, *Onze bezittingen op de kust van Guinea* (Amsterdam, 1869), 12.

[80] 1781 Pen and Contract dd 10 July 1781, FC1781–1816, 1781–2, 156 (WIC989)
1791 Pen and Contract dd 10 Nov. 1791, FC1781–1816, 1790–4, 79 (G223).
1798 Pen and Contract dd 5 Jan. 1798, Furley Photostat Collection (G223).
1810 Elmina Journal *sub* 28 Nov. and 25 Dec. 1810, FC1781–1816, 1810) 6, 55 (Arch. der Kol. 1225).
1819 Elmina Journal *sub* 12 Mar. 1819, FC 1815–1823, 1818–20, 36 (Arch. der Kol. 1227).
1841 Elmina Journal *sub* 24 June 1841, FC1830–47, 1840–7, 45 (NBKG 520); Pen and Contract dd 5 Nov. 1846, FC, Treaties, 1846–69, 11.
1850 Pen and Contracts dd 12 Sept. 1850 and 4 Apr. 1855, FC, Treaties, 1846–69.

[81] This recollection may have been influenced by the fact that the circumstances of Segu's destoolment were rather spectacular. It resulted in the burning of half of the town and the intervention of the Dutch authorities. Segu fled to British Sekondi, a fact some of the traditions remembered, and evidently was extradited back to Shama a dozen years later. See Elmina Journal *sub* 28 and 30 Nov. 1810, FC 1781–1816, 1810–16, 49–51, and Willem Poolman, Director-General, Elmina, to James Chisholm, Cape Coast Castle, 8 Aug. 1822, FC1815–23, 1822, 78–9 (NBKG 661).

a period of a century or somewhat more is also reflected in the traditions of Abrem, Elmina, Dutch Sekondi, and other stools of the area. And there seems to be no question of feedback here. The records which contained the names of the rulers of these states were not available to the traditional authorities. In fact the Dutch records were often not available to the British colonial authorities themselves. The general accuracy of these skeletal traditions for this more limited period, even though the data are meagre, probably delimits more reasonably the uses to which these kinds of oral traditions can be put.

V GENERAL CHARACTERISTICS OF FANTE TRADITIONS

The reader has probably already noticed the similarity of the origins of the stools of Shama, Oguaa, and Anamabu. Each was once subject to states whose capitals were inland. With the advent of European trading companies and the concomitant economic opportunities new centres of traditional authority arose on the coast to oppose and later supersede the older inland seats. Available evidence strongly suggests that the stools of all the coastal towns from Axim in the west to Winneba in the east, with the possible exception of Ahanta (Bushua), only became independent and paramount after the construction of European forts there. These new stools arose in opposition to the inland states (Sekondi/Ahanta, Shama/Jabi, Komenda and Elmina/Eguafo and Fetu, Oguaa/Fetu, Anamabu/ Abura or Asebu) and quickly surpassed them, so that the political continuity of independent stools from pre-European times to the present is confined to a very few stools. The traditions of the coastal states, however, generally simplify or distort these processes by claiming either that their stools had existed as paramount from before the arrival of the Europeans, or that they represented the continuation of older stool dynasties which, for varying reasons, had removed to the coast from the interior. Fante traditions offer little help in determining whether the well-springs of the power of these new stools was essentially traditional in character or whether, as the contemporaneous written accounts suggest, they arose in response to the opportunities created by the presence of the European trading posts, and only later acquired the necessary traditional sanctions.[82]

[82] John Kabes of Komenda, discussed at length in Daaku, *Trade and politics*, 115–27, is an excellent example of the entrepreneur turned traditional ruler. There is an unfortunate lacuna in the letters from Komenda to Cape Coast for the years

Finally, the traditions of Shama vividly illustrate the propensity of Fante traditional accounts to regard the erection of the European forts as chronological *termini a quibus* for the foundations of the various stools. Each of the kinglists provided by the contenders in the endemic Shama stool disputes identified some *ɔmanhen* with the construction of the Portuguese fort there.[83] Similar patterns occur in Winneba, Kormantin, Oguaa, Elmina, Komenda, the Sekondis, Ahanta, and the Dixcoves—that is, in nearly every coastal stool.[84] These trade forts represented visible proofs to the traditional historians that their paramount stools must have existed at some remote date. It was both simple and at the same time reasonable to expand available fragmentary traditions to include the coming of the Europeans and the building of their fort. This permitted the argument that the fort had been built with the sanction of the stool authorities, and that in the past rental had been paid to the stool for the land occupied by the structure. It further created an impression of the erstwhile superiority to the European intruders of the now dependent stools. The migration from the north ('Tekyiman') and the building of the European trading forts are the two ubiquitous chronological linchpins of Fante traditional history, which were fitted adventitiously into the various schemes devised by the Fante stools for their history as the need to do so was perceived.

A final word needs to be said regarding the possibility of genealogical reckoning among the Fante, if only for a period of four to five generations back. The concept of a royal genealogy structured into generational form was alien to the Akan. The insistence of the British that such genealogies be submitted to support claims to the stool only resulted in chaos confounded. Succession patterns among the Fante were too broad to be amenable to genealogical structuring.[85] In some

---

1684 and 1685 in Rawlinson MSS. C. 745–7, Bodleian Library, Oxford. Extant letters for these years might have illuminated the details of the rise of Kabes, who was almost certainly the founder of the paramount stool of Komenda. He was unknown, however, to Komenda traditions until after 1918, when the proceedings of a Komenda/Nkusukum stool dispute were published as a Sessional Paper. The editorial introduction to this paper discussed John Kabes as he was known from the available records. Later Kabes, as Inkabee, entered traditional accounts of Komenda stool history. See Henige, 'Problem of feedback'.

[83] See, e.g., NAG/ADM11/1/1805, 129; NAG/ADM23/5/36, opp. p. 110.

[84] For an analysis of the development of an *ɔmanhen* in Elmina stool traditions to account for the Caramansa of the European records see my 'Problem of feedback' and 'Kingship in Elmina'.

[85] M. J. Field, *Akim-Kotoku: an omen of the Gold Coast* (London, 1948), 113; undated [1914 ?] memo of F. G. Crowther, Secretary of Native Affairs, NAG/

cases (e.g. Anamabu, Dutch Sekondi, Ahanta, and Upper Dixcove) the adoption of a single stool name created additional mnemonic problems. In other stools the succession allegedly rotated among as many as twelve eligible stool families.[86] In still other instances (e.g. Agona and Gomoa Assin) the ruling lines themselves have changed in this century—sometimes more than once. These factors, besides creating likely situations for the distortion of traditions, shattered the patterns of serene, predictable, and quantifiable succession and made genealogical reckoning impossible.

This brief examination of Fante stool traditions in the light of the discussion in previous chapters illustrates in varying degrees of salience several of the points discussed earlier. If the problem of feedback, not surprisingly, has been the most serious of these, it is also very often the problem most easily recognized when assessing a body of Fante traditions. The other modification patterns of coastal Fante stool traditions, such as artificial lengthening and genealogical parasitism, conform to what we have come to expect in terms of both creation and simplification. In examining Fante traditions we are fortunate to have external data for a period long enough to enable us to document the ebb and flow of many aspects of Fante political life. It is hoped that the Fante example, though not typical, can illuminate the kinds of processes which the historian will suspect, but be unable to document, in many other African societies.

ADM11/1/1445, pp. 1–2; J. M. Sarbah, *Fanti national constitution* (London, 1906), 19–20; Christensen, *Double descent*, 45–6.

[86] See questionnaire submitted for 1925 election to the stool of Assin-Fosu, NAG/ADM11/1/355.

CHAPTER VI

Asante Microchronology

> . . . sur la base des mêmes faits, chaque génération refait l'histoire. A la lumière des ses préoccupations dominantes, elle comprend autrement le déroulement des événements, les heurts des hommes et le jeu des forces en présence.[1]

> Owing to a somewhat complicated system of succession, whereby this stool [Mampong] was occupied at various times by descendants of several different kindred groups, it was sometimes found difficult to obtain an authentic history of past events; the natural tendency was to suppress all allusion to persons and happenings not connected with the line at present occupying the stool.[2]

ANY attempt to analyse Asante stool traditions presents a range of problems very different from those for the coastal Fante. The most obvious difference between the two bodies of evidence is the almost complete lack of independent, external evidence for the Asante stools before, at the earliest, 1816. On the rare occasions when an Asante substool[3] came into contact with the Europeans on or near the coast, such as the Juaben emigration of the late 1830s, some non-traditional evidence is available.[4] Necessarily, then, the major task in assessing Asante traditions is one of comparative internal textual criticism, particularly for the period of the eighteenth and early nineteenth centuries. In contrast to the coastal Fante traditions, a large corpus of Asante traditional material has been collected and processed in the last decade. This material must be evaluated both as a product and as a source of oral tradition.

[1] M. Rodinson, *Mahomet* (Paris, 1961), 3.

[2] R. S. Rattray, *Ashanti law and constitution* (Oxford, 1929), 235n.

[3] This chapter is confined, with a few exceptions, to the stools of 'metropolitan' Asante, that is, Asante itself and Adanse. Denkyira and the Brong stools are excluded from consideration since they are outside the area included in the present Asante Confederacy.

[4] A. A. Boahen, 'Juaben and Kumasi relations in the nineteenth century', *Report* of the First Conference of the Ashanti Research Project held 17–20 May 1963 (Legon, 1964), 25–7.

The problems presented by destoolment practices are the first to be considered. Destoolment among the Akan results, in effect, in a form of structural amnesia. Consequently the incidence of destoolment and its effect on Asante stool traditions must be discussed at some length. Among the Akan, the traditions of the stoolholders are recited during the *adae* ceremony, held at forty-day intervals. A ceremony of libation is performed, at which the spirits of the ancestral stoolholders are invoked. These stoolholders are remembered because their stools have been 'blackened' (smoked) and preserved.[5] For various reasons, however, stools of certain chiefs might be disposed of rather than blackened. According to Kyerematen, 'the general principle governing the preservation of black stools is that a black stool is preserved in memory of every ruler who succeeded in retaining his office up to the time of his death'.[6] Thus neither the stools, nor presumably the memory, of destooled chiefs were preserved.[7] There were other reasons why a chief's stool would not be blackened. These included an ignominious death—killed in battle or committed suicide, or because it was later determined that an individual had not belonged to the proper stool family, or because a chief had been of servile origin, or simply because 'they were not good chiefs and did practically nothing good for their subjects'.[8]

Since destoolment represented an important cause for omission from the libation ceremony, it is desirable to concentrate only on this aspect of structural amnesia among the Asante. It is necessary to attempt to determine what impact destoolment might have had on the inferred chronology of Asante stools. Destoolment was rampant throughout both Asante and the Gold Coast Colony in this century; its incidence was great enough to excite the concern of Governor Guggisberg who, in 1923, commented on 'the deposition of a large

[5] For a description of this process, see A. A. Y. Kyerematen, 'The royal stools of Ashanti', *Africa*, 39 (1969), 1.

[6] Kyerematen, *The panoply of Ghana* (London, 1964), 16.

[7] See also Rattray, *Ashanti law*, 146, 166.

[8] Ahinsan Stool history in K. Y. Daaku, 'Adanse', mimeographed copy at Institute of African Studies, Legon (henceforth IAS), 137; ibid. 238n. Nyinahin Stool History, Ashanti Stool History collection (henceforth IAS/AS) at IAS, Legon, 107, p. 6; Kona Stool History, IAS/AS 156, p. 5; Daaku, 'Adanse', 147; W. Tordoff, *Ashanti under the Prempehs, 1888–1935* (London, 1965), 150; Akankade Linguist Stool History, IAS/AS 75, p. 2. Most of the stool histories collected by Daaku in Adanse and Assin contain similar statements concerning the omission of destooled chiefs from the libation ceremony. Although several of the chiefs questioned by Daaku stated that chiefs of servile origin were omitted, others said they were included.

number of chiefs by their people'.[9] The colonial administration was wont to blame the widespread incidence of destoolment on the 'young men'.[10] Authorities on the Asante have generally agreed that this endemic destoolment was the result of the new political and economic conditions of the colonial period. Busia saw it partly as a reaction to the British policy of 'protecting' the chiefs from 'excessive restraint by the people'.[11] The rise of a new economic class with the spread of cocoa farming has also been seen as a contributing factor to this undoubted political turbulence.[12] It has also been argued that the loss of prestige, especially military, by the chiefs under the British rule contributed to their vulnerability to destoolment.[13] Traditional informants usually relate what they see as an increase in destoolments to the inferior quality of recent chiefs.[14] When prompted, they will occasionally agree that cocoa cultivation and the economic revolution it wrought contributed to the malaise.[15]

It cannot be gainsaid that a multiplicity of factors combined to create political unrest under the British colonial administration. It can be argued, however, that the policy of the British regarding destoolment mitigated these factors to some extent.[16] The point to be made here is that there may not have been the large *increase* in destoolments in the twentieth century that has generally been postulated. Those who have remarked on the phenomenon of destoolment have usually contrasted the period of colonial rule with the earlier, allegedly more halcyon, period.[17] Only Rattray argued that

[9] Gold Coast (Colony), *Gold Coast Legislative Council debates, 1923/1924*, 82.

[10] *Colonial reports, Ashanti, for 1920*, 22; Tordoff, *Ashanti*, 195.

[11] K. A. Busia, *The position of the chief in the modern political system of Ashanti: a study of the influence of contemporary social changes on Ashanti political institutions* (London, 1951), 108.

[12] Ibid. 107–8; *Report of the Western Province* [of the Gold Coast Colony] *for the year 1920* (Accra, 1922), 5; Tordoff, *Ashanti*, 192.

[13] Busia, *Position of chief*, 111–12. Busia's observation, ibid. 110, that 'under the British the chief had become a subordinate authority' certainly applied to the earlier period as well, when all stools were subordinate to the Asantehene.

[14] Daaku, 'Adanse', 15–16 (Fomena), 50 (Dompoase), 89 (Bodwesango), 99–100 (Odumasi), 160 (Akwansramu), 201 (Apagya), 328 (Pomposo); Daaku, 'Denkyira', mimeographed at IAS, Legon, 215 (Mudaso).

[15] Daaku, 'Adanse', 16 (Fomena), 160 (Akwansramu).

[16] Certain policies of the colonial administration, e.g. the wholesale replacement of stoolholders by 'non-royals' after the Yaa Asantewa war of 1900, did contribute to the destoolment pattern. Later, however, the British colonial administration took great pains to ensure that 'native customary law' was observed in both enstoolment and destoolment proceedings.

[17] e.g. Busia, *Position of chief*, 21, 37–8; J. N. Matson, *A digest of the minutes*

'destoolments were not, as is so often stated, uncommon in olden days'.[18]

The argument that destoolment was rare in pre-colonial times contains certain contradictory elements. Early Akan society is often characterized as peculiarly democratic, with destoolment as a constitutional weapon at the disposal of a discontented *oman*.[19] At the same time it is argued that, because an abortive destoolment attempt could result in the death of the conspirators, the expedient was seldom resorted to.[20] Apparently the guiding principle was that 'those who elected a chief [i.e. the stool Elders], have also the power to destool him'.[21] An important aspect of this problem is the question of the role and authority of the Asantehene in destoolment proceedings. The evidence here is ambiguous. Warrington observed that, once the Elders had decided on destoolment, 'the Head Chief must also be consulted with regard to any proposal to destool a chief who serves him'.[22] This implies that Head Chiefs, including the Asantehene, exercised veto power but the initiative remained with the stool Elders. Busia took a similar position, but added that the Asantehene could not dismiss a Head Chief.[23] The Chief Commissioner, Ashanti, stated in 1916 that

> they [the Asante people] never enjoyed any 'rights' in destoolment cases and would be amazed and suspiciously incredulous if they were now told that they could now demand the destoolment of a chief as a *right*. Whatever system may have evolved in the [Gold Coast] Colony, the Ashanti rule was simplicity itself: no occupier of a stool (no matter how high or low the stool might rank) could be destooled without the full knowledge and consent *of the person to whom he swore* allegiance [i.e. in former times, the Asantehene].[24]

of the Ashanti Confederacy Council, 1935–49, and a revised edition of Warrington's Notes on Ashanti Custom (Cape Coast, n.d.), 26; Daaku, 'Adanse', 14–15 (Fomena), 50 (Dompoase), 89–90 (Bodwesango); idem, 'Assin-Twifo', *sub* Kushia, 10.

[18] Rattray, *Ashanti law*, 255.

[19] e.g. J. E. C. Hayford, *Gold Coast native institutions* (London, 1903), 33–8; Manoukian, *Akan and Ga-Adangme peoples*, 36; Busia, *Position of chief*, 54, 99.

[20] Personal communication from K. Y. Daaku, 8 Mar. 1971.

[21] R. W. Warrington, 'Notes on an inquiry into Ashanti native custom', dd 15 June 1934, pp. 27–8, NAG/ADM11/1/824; Busia, *Position of chief*, 21, 54, 99; Rattray, *Ashanti law*, 85, 401–9.

[22] Warrington, 'Ashanti native custom', 28.

[23] Busia, *Postion of chief*, 21.

[24] F. C. Fuller to Colonial Secretary, 16 Nov. 1916, NAG/ADM11/1 1308. Emphasis in original. Tordoff, 'The Ashanti Confederacy', *JAH* 3 (1962), 405, concluded that the power, if not the authority, of the Asantehene to destool Head

Fuller here was attacking the principle that the 'young men' could have any role in initiating destoolment proceedings. He was also doubtless influenced by the fact that he regarded the British Government, in the person of himself, the Chief Commissioner, Ashanti, as the legitimate successor to the Asantehenes and legatee to the fullness of their power and authority. He was alarmed at the increasing propensity of the 'young men' to initiate or at least abet, destoolments—a prerogative he saw as his own. None the less, the evidence available for the nineteenth century supports the position that the various Asantehenes could and often did destool subordinate chiefs, as they saw fit, including the *amantoo* (important territorial chiefs around Kumasi) and other Head Chiefs.[25]

Lacking the abundance and continuity of the evidence for the Fante we must perforce proceed by indirection and argue by extrapolation in any assessment of the extent of destoolment in early Asante. For this we have two bodies of evidence available—the information on the Asantehenes themselves, and the accounts of several observers in Asante and Kumasi from 1816 to 1874. There were at least twelve Asantehenes from Osei Tutu (*c.* 1690–1712/17) to Kwaku Dua II (1888). It is certain (in the cases of Kwesi Obodum, Osei Kwame, Kofi Kakari, and Mensah Bonsu) or probable (in the case of Opoku Fofie) that five of these twelve rulers were destooled. It is furthermore not unlikely that a thirteenth Asantehene, another Osei, ruled from *c.* 1712 to *c.* 1717 but was forgotten because of his defeat and death in battle.[26] In other words, as many as six of thirteen Asantehenes in pre-colonial times may have been destooled or forgotten in Asante traditions. The destooled Asantehenes could not all be forgotten—they were too important—and it became necessary in some cases to adopt certain fictions to explain the retention of their stools and their inclusion in the traditions.[27]

Chiefs, varied as the relative positions of the Asantehene and is subordinate chiefs fluctuated.

[25] For instance Dupuis, who did not mention any destoolments in his *Journal*, wrote that the Asantehene exercised 'unrivalled sway' and that 'every king chief, viceroy, or caboceer [was] his absolute and unconditional vassal' and held their offices 'by virtue of an appointment from the court', *Journal of a residence in Ashantee* (London, 1824), xxvi.

[26] Priestley and Wilks, 'The Ashanti kings of the eighteenth century', 85–9.

[27] For the stools of these destooled Asantehenes, see Kyerematen, 'Royal stools', 6–9. In the case of Kwesi Obodum the fiction was maintained that he was allowed to die under a 'regency'; hence his blackened stool is retained. But see J. K. Fynn, 'The reign and times of Kusi Obodum', *THSG* 8 (1965), 32.

Between 1816 and 1874 several visitors from the coast spent time in Kumasi and left accounts of their visits. These accounts are instructive on the question of the incidence of destoolments and the Asantehenes' role in them. The first of these visitors was Willem Huydecoper, an Elmina mulatto sent by the Dutch Director-General as an emissary to the Asantehene in 1816 to anticipate a similar mission planned by the English. During his visit to Kumasi Huydecoper observed at least one destoolment. A certain 'General Bariekie was 'destooled and placed in stocks and in a heavy log'. Later he was made 'ferry master of a small river'.[28]

Shortly after Huydecoper left Kumasi the English mission arrived. An account of this mission, which remained in Kumasi about three months, was written by its head, Thomas Edward Bowdich.[29] Bowdich repeated the story of Bariekie's destoolment and added that the unfortunate chief had hanged himself, presumably in chagrin at being demoted to such a lowly office.[30] When the Bowdich mission left, William Hutchison remained behind as Consul. Hutchison, who remained in Kumasi only a few months, recorded that while he was there 'the stool of Alphia was declared in abeyance'. This stool was then abolished and added to the domains of 'the Caboceer of Preminihia', who was the brother of the former stoolholder.[31]

The case of the destoolment of the ruler of Fomena is of particular interest. The ruler of Fomena, if not yet the Adansehene or paramount chief over all the Adanse stools, none the less occupied one of the oldest and most important stools in Asante.[32] In 1831 'the King of Fomuna' was called 'Kroantje' by J. B. Simons, who passed through the town on his way to Kumasi.[33] Eight years later the

[28] Huydecoper to Daendels, Elmina, 2 Sept. 1816, FC1815–23 (Huydecoper Journal), 31; the same to the same, 28 Oct. 1816, FC 1815–23, 47. In a letter dd 29 Nov. 1816 Huydecoper enclosed a greeting from Osei Bonsu. The Asantehene listed his predecessors who had, like himself, been 'as brothers with the Dutch'. The list omitted Opoku Fofie—perhaps because he had not reigned long enough to establish relations with the Dutch, perhaps because he had been destooled. H. W. Daendels, *Journal and correspondence*, I, *November 1815 to January 1817* (Legon, 1964), 282.

[29] Bowdich, *Mission from Cape Coast Castle.*

[30] Ibid. 73.

[31] Diary of William Hutchison *sub* 25 Nov. 1817 and 28 Nov. 1817, in ibid. 401.

[32] For Adanse, see introduction to Daaku, 'Adanse'; idem, *Trade and politics*, 146–8; Meyerowitz, *Akan traditions of origin*, 93–4; C. C. Reindorf, *The history of the Gold Coast and Asante* (2nd ed., Accra, 1966), 48–9.

[33] Simons, 'Journal of a mission to Ashanti, 1831–2', 12. Typescript in FC.

Methodist missionary Thomas Birch Freeman likewise stopped at Fomena on his first visit to Kumasi. Freeman spent some time with 'the Chief of Adansi, who resides at Fomunah' and whom he called 'Korinchi'.[34] Korinchi was still the ruler of Fomena on Freeman's return to the coast some months later.[35] When Freeman returned to Kumasi two years later and again stopped at Fomena he found that

> Poor Korinchi, my old friend . . . is no longer Chief of Adansi. By some very turbulent conduct in the King's [Asantehene's] presence during the investigation of a palaver between himself and one of his Captains he incurred the displeasure of his Sovereign, has been dishonoured and another Chief placed on the stool of Adansi in his stead.[36]

Freeman reported that Korinchi was living in a small town near Kumasi, evidently an exile. Korinchi/Kroantje was thus ruler of Fomena for a period of at least eight years before he was destooled. Yet there is no trace of him in Fomena stool traditions or in the lists of Fomena stoolholders collected recently by Daaku and Agyeman-Duah.[37] Daaku's informants assured him that 'all the earlier Chiefs died on the stool. It was only after Kwabena Fori [ruling in 1900] that there has been constant destoolment'.[38] Clearly, Korinchi has been omitted from the Fomena kinglists. It is impossible to determine whether this was intentional because he had been destooled or whether it simply reflects an amnesia that is not structural. For our purposes we can assume that at some point in the transmission of Fomena stool traditions the omission was intentional. Certainly, any argument that the elimination of Korinchi from Fomena traditions should be attributed to the fact that he was an ephemeral 'Regent' is implausible.

In 1869 the Basel missionaries Ramseyer and Kühne were captured by an Asante war party at Anum in the Volta region and subsequently spent four years in captivity at Kumasi. By this time the fortunes of Asante had begun to decline and the Asantehene Kofi Kakari was not one of the stronger figures of his line. Still, in commenting on the power of the Asantehene over his chiefs, Ramseyer observed that 'Kari-Kari was persuaded that his whole strength lay

[34] T. B. Freeman, *Journal of various visits to the kingdoms of Ashanti, Akim and Dahomi in western Africa* (London, 1844), 18, *sub* 7 Feb. 1839.

[35] Ibid. 64–5, *sub* Fomena.

[36] Ibid. 110, *sub* 25 Nov.

[37] Daaku, 'Adanse', 14; IAS/AS 89, Adanse Stool History.

[38] Daaku, 'Adanse', 14.

in his power to take life at any moment. One of his highest chiefs was said to have lost his head for daring to suggest that he spent too much money on his wives . . .'[39] The missionaries later described how the Agogohene had been sentenced to death for dereliction of military duty, but managed to escape with a heavy fine.[40] It is not clear from this account whether the Agogohene was destooled as well, but the power to do so clearly fell within the Asantehene's prerogative.

All of these accounts suggest both the ability and the propensity of the Asantehenes to destool chiefs of even the highest rank. There is no hint that the Asantehene merely approved the action of the destooled chief's own stool Elders, although such a fine point could easily have escaped these observers' attention. But in any case, this last distinction is irrelevant; whatever the circumstances of these destoolments, they did occur, and evidently fairly often. Almost every observer commented on them and it may not be unfair to suggest that other destoolments of lesser note or which occurred outside Kumasi itself may not have come to their attention.

Neither the quality nor the quantity of this evidence compares to that for the Fante stools. Nevertheless, it is persuasive; destoolment was a common occurrence among the Asante in pre-colonial times. Stoolholders apparently suffered from being subjected to pressures from both above and below. Whatever may have been the ideological basis of destoolment in Akan customary law, its practice was often a matter of *Realpolitik*. In the only instance where the data are sufficient to check (i.e. Fomena), the traditional kinglist has omitted the destooled chief.[41] There can be little doubt that wholesale telescoping has occurred throughout the traditional lists of Asante stoolholders. The claim that destoolment is a recent phenomenon can be seen, in this sense, as a reaction to the inability to recall past stoolholders at a time when this became important. Any information on these stoolholders is gone for ever, whatever claims one may wish to put forward for the general accuracy of Asante stool traditions. Gone

[39] F. Ramseyer and J. Kühne, *Four years in Ashantee* (London, 1875), 165–6.

[40] Ibid. 240–1. See also J. Beecham, *Ashantee and the Gold Coast* (London, 1841), which was largely based on Freeman's experiences.

[41] A survey of the stool histories for the twentieth century also shows a large proportion of destooled chiefs has been omitted, though many are still remembered. This point, while not truly germane to the present argument since it is conceded that destoolment was common in this century, nevertheless illustrates the consistency with which even recently destooled chiefs are ignored in traditional accounts.

with their memory in most cases is the very evidence of their existence. But it is essential to recognize the probability of omission because of destoolment when evaluating any Asante traditions—particularly when seeking to infer from them any chronological data, such as average tenure in office.

Paradoxically, where external evidence is lacking, 'traditional' evidence abounds. There is now a large corpus of such evidence available for over 200 Asante stools.[42] This extremely useful collection has quickly become a source in its own right and is now often referred to by informants when information about certain stool histories is requested. As such, it must be evaluated by all the normal canons of historical criticism. Regrettably, this is somewhat difficult, since the available versions are heavily, but not admittedly, edited. Nor is the verbatim testimony of the informants accessible. A procrustean bed of conformity in many aspects of these traditions has resulted, and it is impossible to determine whether this is the result of certain characteristics of the stool traditions themselves, or of a desire to develop a self-coherent body of tradition. These include *inter alia* a stereotyped denial that Osei Tutu was killed in battle against the Akyems in *c.* 1712/17, a description of Osei Kwadwo (1764–77) as 'the King who fought in broad daylight', and, in some stool histories, a curious inversion of the sequence of Osei Bonsu's Fante campaign (1807) and his Gyaman war (*c.* 1818). Withal, an analysis of these stool histories can be useful because they do exhibit some features worthy of comment in terms of their chronology.

The most obvious characteristic of these stool histories is their artificial use of stereotyped synchronisms with the Asantehenes and with the series of wars famous in Asante tradition.[43] This has resulted in several anomalies which are inexplicable unless we assume the artificiality of the method. The chronological correlations or synchronisms in the Asante substool histories are, it is important to reiterate, with Asantehenes and with their wars. When a single Asantehene fought several wars, almost invariably a single stool-

[42] IAS/AS 1–215. Most of these were collected by Joseph Agyeman-Duah, formerly an Assistant Secretary in the Office of the Asantehene and a part-time Senior Research Assistant at the Institute of African Studies in Legon.

[43] These include the Denkyira war (1701), Akyem war (*c.* 1715), the conquest of Bono-Manso (Tekyiman) (1722/3), first Gyaman war (*c.* 1740), Sefwi war (*c.* 1745/50?), Anamabu campaign (1807), second Gyaman (Adinkra) war (*c.* 1818), battle of Nsamankow in which Gov. Charles MacCarthy was killed (1824), and Akatamansu (Dodowa) (1826).

holder is recalled as having taken part in all of them. Conversely, wars fought by different Asantehenes are usually remembered as having been fought by different stoolholders.

Let us compare the traditional information contained in the stool histories for two different pairs of wars—the Tekyiman war (1722/3) and the first Gyaman war (*c.* 1740) on the one hand, and the second Gyaman (or Adinkra) war (*c.* 1818) and the Akatamansu campaign (1826) on the other.[44] The first pair was fought in the reign of Opoku Ware (*c.* 1720–*c.* 1750), whereas the second pair was fought in the reigns of Osei Bonsu (1801–24) and Osei Yaw Akoto (1824–38) respectively. This is most interestingly reflected in the Asante stool histories. Eighty-seven stool histories related that their stoolholders fought in both the Tekyiman and Gyaman wars. Only three of these traditions indicate that *different* stoolholders fought in the two wars.[45] All other traditions assign the *same* stoolholder to both wars. Seventy-five stool histories provide details for their stoolholders during the second pair of wars. Forty-six of them claim that the stoolholder who had campaigned in *c.* 1818 had been replaced before 1826.

The demographic implications of these stool traditions are quite startling. Less than 4 per cent of office holders died in the 17–18 years between the Tekyiman and Gyaman wars. In contrast, 61 per cent of the stoolholders died or were destooled between the Adinkra and Akatamansu wars—a period less than half as long as the earlier period. This is clearly aberrant and unacceptable. It suggests that the traditions, in their reflexive correlation of stoolholders' tenure with Asantehenes' reigns, assumed, if anything, that wars fought under a single Asantehene were more nearly contemporaneous than wars fought under different Asantehenes. The result is a patently artificial pattern of stool chronology.

[44] The date of the conquest of Tekyiman is recorded under A. H. 1135 (1722/3) in the Gonja Chronicle, written only a few years later. See N. Levtzion, *Muslims and chiefs in West Africa*, 51, 194–5. The first Gyaman war is dated to *c.* 1740 by the same source. See J. Goody, 'The ethnography of the Northern Territories of the Gold Coast, west of the White Volta', mimeograph, Colonial Office, 1954, and idem, Introduction to J. Goody and K. Arhin (eds.), *Ashanti and the north-west*, Supplement 1 to *Research Review* [Institute of African Studies, Legon] (Legon, 1965), 18–19. E. A. Agyeman, 'A note on the foundation of the kingdom of Gyaman', *GNQ* 9 (1966), 37, dates the death of Abe Kofi, the ruler of Gyaman killed in this war, even later—to 1746. For the date of the second Gyaman war, see Elmina Journal, 28 Aug. 1818, FC 1815–23, 1818–20.

[45] IAS/AS 135, Atwima-Agogo Stool History; IAS/AS 148, Bonwire Stool History; IAS/AS 167, Paakoso Stool History.

TABLE 9

Number of Stoolholders since Osei Tutu

IAS/AS	1	2	3	4	5
96	8	6	2	3	2
201	15	8	4	5	7
121	11	6	2	3	5
95	16	9	4	6	7
5	16	9	5	6	7
111	14	9	5	7	5
137	15	9	4	6	6
164	15	9	4	6	6
75	9	4	—	—	5
199	16	10	3	5	6
80	11	7	3	5	4
17	13	8	3	4	5
106	11	6	5	5	5
212	14	4	—	—	10
77	12	7	5	5	5
175	13	6	2	4	7
186	21	14	9	11	7
200	21	10	3	6	11
134	11	6	1	4	5
98	15	10	—	—	5
99	19	12	6	7	7
190	15	8	3	6	7
173	11	6	3	4	5
1	8	7	5	6	1
76	8	5	[3 ?]	[3 ?]	3
178	8	—	—	—	—
155	23	11	5	8	12
4	6	4	2	2	2
188	14	11	4	7	3
32	11	—	—	—	—
184	14	9	5	6	5
135	14	8	3	4	6
91	10	7	4	6	3
39/40	18	11	5	7	7
54	16	7	4	6	9
58	10	—	—	—	—
105	10	7	3	5	3
133	15	9	2	3	6
148	20	13	11	11	7
174	11	—	—	—	—
117	15	6	—	—	9
70	9	6	—	—	3
170	18	11	2	5	7
154	12	—	—	—	—

TABLE 9 (continued)

IAS/AS	1	2	3	4	5
61	19	9	—	—	10
37	12	7	5	7	5
159	9	6	2	3	3
100	10	6	3	5	4
138	12	5	3	3	7
211	8	—	—	—	—
123	14	10	3	5	4
48	11	8	5	5	3
158	21	15	4	6	6
129	13	7+	—	—	0
57	9	7	3	4	2
36	11	7	3	5	4
103	13	6	4	5	7
102	14	9	3	5	5
145	11	5	5	5	6
30	9	4	3	3	5
176	9	7	3	4	2
22	17	9	—	4	8
26	8	—	—	—	—
107	15	6	1	3	9
166	10	6	2	4	4
131	20	13	6	—	7
206	10	7	5	5	3
122	9	5	3	4	4
163	17	13	2	6	4
28	17	13	6	8	4
120	13	6	4	5	7
193	14	10	3	5	4
52	9	4	1	2	5
43	16	12	5	6	4
41	8	6	3	4	2
161	10	5	4	5	5
191	13	5	—	—	8
50	12	9	2	4	3
185	10	8	4	6	2
128	14	9	4	7	5
149	13	7	—	—	6
124	9	5	3	3	4

Note: Column 1—number of stoolholders from Osei Tutu to 1963.
Column 2—number of stoolholders from Osei Tutu to *c*. 1900.
Column 3—number of stoolholders before reign of Osei Bonsu (*c*. 1801–24).
Column 4—number of stoolholders before reign of Kwaku Dua I (1833–67).
Column 5—number of stoolholders from *c*. 1900 to 1963.

Osei Tutu, and particularly his 'war of independence' against Denkyira in 1701, are cynosures of Asante traditional history, and the Asante stool traditions do not fail to reflect this fact. Table 9 is a tabulation of the number of stoolholders for those stools which allegedly were created by Osei Tutu himself or whose first occupant is remembered as being a contemporary of Osei Tutu.

FIGURE 1

Distribution of Stoolholders, c. *1700–1963* (*column 1 of Table 9*)

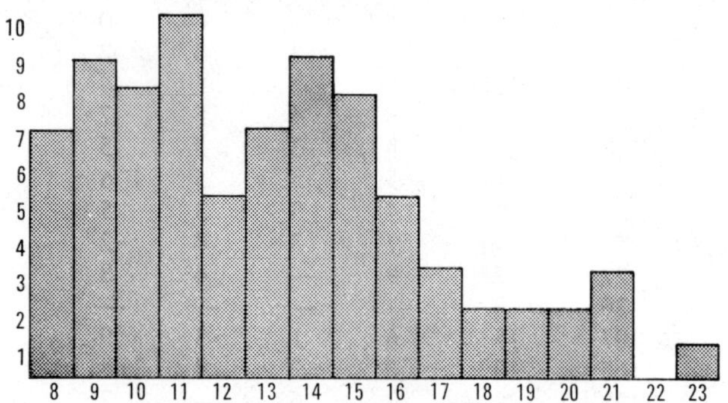

Since the period of time is constant throughout, a 'clustering' effect should result. Unfortunately, neither the range nor the distribution of the figures in this table is encouraging. Figures 1 and 2 are histograms of the distribution of the figures in columns 1 and 2 and illustrate the distribution more clearly. Column 2 is designed to compensate for the possibility of more frequent destoolments under colonial rule, but the range and distribution of the figures in column 2 are not significantly narrower than for the longer period.

Ivor Wilks, using substantially the same material from the Asante stool histories, has argued that the data in these accounts, statistically analysed, can have chronologically predictive uses.[46] He based this on the assumption that 'average length of office [in a given society] tends to constancy'.[47] By postulating an average stool tenure of seventeen years, based on 'dated runs of Kumasi office holders', he extrapolated a 'late sixteenth to late seventeenth century' data for stools having had seventeen to twenty-four incumbents, and proportionately later

[46] Wilks, 'Aspects of bureaucratization', 229–31.
[47] Ibid. 229, and idem. 'The growth of Akwapim', 396–408.

dates for those stools with fewer occupants.[48] This rigid *schema* allowed the positing of a steady growth in the number of Asante stools, since there were some stools with every number of occupants from one to twenty-four.

The above analysis suggests that several of the premisses on which this conclusion is based are fallacious. In the first place, any hope of establishing regnal averages for Asante stools is a chimera. Account must first be taken of the strong, if unprovable and unmeasurable,

FIGURE 2

Distribution of Stoolholders, c. *1700–*c. *1900* (*column 2 of Table 9*)

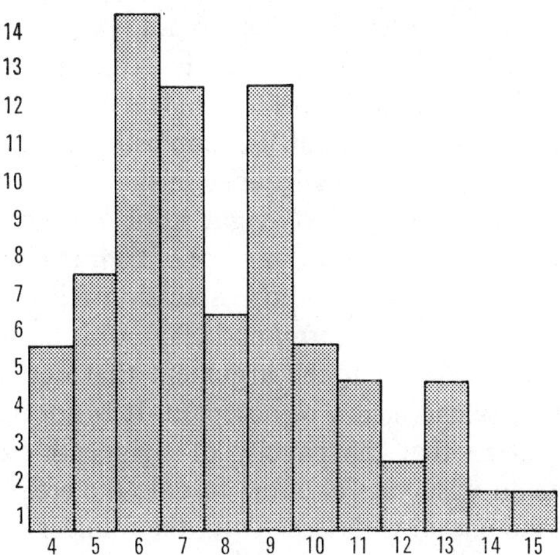

probability of destoolments and fabrication. Secondly, the assumption that 'a stool with $x + 1$ occupants is likely to be older than a stool with x occupants' is gratuitous and unsupported by any kind of evidence.[49] For instance, there is an almost equal likelihood, on the basis of the accounts in these stool histories, that six or nine stoolholders spanned the period from *c.* 1700 to *c.* 1900. Again, the frequency of four and ten is identical. To approach the problem of Asante stool chronology on the basis of average length of tenure is

[48] Wilks, 'Aspects of bureaucratization', 230. G. P. Hagan, 'Ashanti bureaucracy', *THSG* 12 (1971), 43–62, although differing from Wilks's analysis in several details, also accepts unhesitatingly the testimony of the Asante substool traditions regarding the number and names of their occupants.

[49] Ibid. Wilks, 'Aspects of bureaucratization', 229.

impossible, given the nature and quality of the evidence.[50] Nor, obviously, is it possible to assume any consistent pattern of regnal length; if anything, the available data suggest a markedly different conclusion. We might further assume that the length of tenure would tend to vary from one *type* of office to another in Asante.

Given the fact that the distribution itself influences the standard deviation from the mean, the fact that a range of 2σ (5·5–20·3) encompasses 95 per cent of the sample and may be expected to encompass a similar proportion of any further population is meaningless and misleading in this context. It is the measure of dispersion which is significant. To credit any other statistical extrapolations with predictive capacities is to invest the data on which the extrapolations are based with a validity they do not possess. Indeed, as we have seen in Chapter IV, a statistical analysis of these data does no more than confirm the worst fears of the student of traditional history who seeks to use statistics as a tool. The sophistication of the method does no more than mask the inadequacy of the data.

It is noteworthy that only thirty-eight stool histories included in Table 9 show that at least one half or more of their stoolholders antedate the reign of Osei Bonsu, whose accession fell approximately halfway between Osei Tutu's *floruit* and 1900. This disparity cannot be affected by destoolment if the argument that destoolment is a twentieth-century phenomenon be accepted. It is not unreasonable, however, to assume that the paucity of eighteenth-century stoolholders reflects an unsuccessful effort to date the creation of many stools to a period coeval with Osei Tutu, the founder of Asante.

The problem of identifying Osei Tutu as the creator of so many stools is complicated by the confusion between him and Osei Bonsu (Osei Tutu Kwamina) in many unedited traditions. There is evidence that Osei Bonsu created a large number of stools. William Hutton observed that Osei Bonsu 'takes every opportunity of increasing the number of secondary Captains, by dignifying the sons of those who are brought up about his person'.[51] This is not reflected in the stool histories—only sixteen of these state that their stool was founded by

[50] See above, Chapter IV. The lack of consistency in stool tenure can also be seen by comparing the number of incumbents in the stools created by Osei Bonsu. Most of these record from seven to nine incumbents, but range as high as seventeen and as low as four. This for a period only about one half as long as the one under analysis.

[51] Hutton, A *voyage to Africa*, 315–16, quoting Bowdich, *Mission from Cape Coast Castle*, 252n. Hutton was Consul at Kumasi after Hutchison.

Osei Bonsu. Furthermore, Osei Bonsu fought the only other important Denkyira war in Asante history. Several of the stool histories speak indiscriminately of having taken part in 'Osei Tutu's Denkyira war'. It is only when some of these traditions identify the ruler of Denkyira as Kojo Otibo that it becomes apparent that they are speaking of the war of *c.* 1810/15 rather than that of 1701.[52]

In fine, Dupuis's observation that 'the wisdom as well as the valour of Sai Tootoo are themes on which the natives dwell with a national satisfaction' is still reflected in the Asante stool histories.[53] This sentiment is most clearly exemplified in the traditions of the nineteen stools covered by the stool history project which claim Denkyira origin. Only three of these stools admit that their founder came to Asante as a result of the defeat of Denkyira by Osei Tutu. All of the others credit their first occupant with the prescience to see that Osei Tutu was marked for great things. Hence he and his followers emigrated to Asante where lands were given them and a stool established. Subsequently they assisted Osei Tutu at the battle of Feyiase (1701), where the Denkyira ruler was killed. In reading these stool histories one cannot but conclude that Osei Tutu exhibited poor statesmanship in warring against Denkyira. Patience alone would have been rewarded with the emigration or flight to Asante of most of the inhabitants of Denkyira, thereby precluding the necessity for conquest.[54]

A final incongruity of the stool histories is the exceedingly small number of stoolholders alleged to have been killed in the numerous Asante wars. For instance, according to these accounts, only two stoolholders were killed at Feyiase, none in the Adinkra war (admittedly a hard-fought campaign in which 'several important Caboceers' were killed), and only four at Akatamansu, where every piece of

[52] See, e.g., Ashanti Court Record Project at IAS, Legon, IAS/CR 64, 21–5; Daaku, 'Assin-Twifu', *sub* Assin-Ayaase, 5; *sub* Assin-Nyankumasi, 2–3, 5–7, 15; *sub* Ekrofuom, 1, 6; *sub* Amoabeng, 5; W. A. S. Cole, 'Dadiaso', manuscript dd 1932, NAG/ADM11/1/824/1. The Dadiaso traditions recorded that when the contemporary of 'Osei Tutu (*circa* 1700)' died, the stool Elders notified 'Osei Yaw [i.e. Osei Yaw Akoto, 1824–33], then King of Ashanti', because no adult was available to succeed to the stool.

[53] Dupuis, *Journal*, 229.

[54] The traditions of IAS/AS 12 (Dadiesoaba stool), IAS/AS 98 Amoaman stool), and IAS/AS 103 (Nfensi stool) admit that their founders came to Asante after the battle of Feyiase; the traditions of IAS/AS 1, 13, 55, 70, 80, 105, 129, 134, 135, 136, 164, 176, 178, 184, 188, and 199 claim a pre-Feyiase migration. See numerical list of Asante stool histories at the end of this chapter for the identification of these stools and other stools mentioned only by number in the text.

contemporary evidence indicates that the carnage among Asante 'Captains' was great.[55] This problem may be one of editing, but is more probably due to the reticence of traditions of all kinds to recall this sort of detail. Apparently, however, this lack of candour can vary from one account to another. The Akyempim stool is a patrilineal (*mmamma dwa*) stool allegedly created by Osei Tutu. The account in IAS/AS 106 does not impute a death in battle to any of the Akyempimhenes. Other accounts, however, have indicated that three of the first four Akyempimhenes died in battle.[56] Owusu Kaffuor, the third of these stoolholders, is completely ignored in the IAS/AS account.

It is clear that the IAS/AS stool histories contain contradictions, omissions, and chronological distortions. In a few instances we can compare the lists of stoolholders in the IAS/AS series with earlier lists or 'genealogies'. During the period from *c.* 1915 to *c.* 1930 the British colonial administration required that a genealogy showing the nominee's right to the stool be presented before his installation was confirmed.[57] The Oyokohene is the head of the *abusua* (lineage or clan) to which the Asantehene himself belongs. In 1929 Kojo Agyekum was elected Oyokohene and his genealogy was submitted to the colonial authorities in Asante. This genealogy covered seven generations. The list of the stoolholders in this genealogy is presented in Table 10 and compared with the list of Oyokohenes in the IAS/AR collection, which was compiled in 1963. Probable identifications are included in Table 10. The list submitted in 1929 may reflect the tendency mentioned by Rattray to exclude other lineages; or the 1963 list may be unduly lengthened for various reasons. In any case, the two lists are substantially different. Probably neither is correct.

In 1922 and again in 1925 kinglists for Kumawu stool were sub-

[55] For the Adinkra war, see Elmina Journal, 13 Aug. 1818, FC 1815–23, 1818–20, p. 9, and Dupuis, who called it 'the bloodiest campaign they [the Kumasi Muslims] had ever witnessed' and observed that the Asantehene 'had sustained heavy losses in the early part of the war', *Journal*, 98, 115. For Akatamansu see J. Purdon, Accra, to Earl Bathurst, 10 Aug. 1826, CO267/74, quoted in G. E. Metcalfe, *Great Britain and Ghana: documents of Ghana history, 1807–1957* (London, 1964), 103–4.

[56] E. O. Ayisi, 'Academicism in social anthropology', *Research Review* [Institute of African Studies], 5/1 (1968), 41.

[57] For Rattray's comments on these genealogies, which he characterized as 'generally worthless documents', see his *Ashanti law*, 128–9. See below for further discussion on genealogies among the Akan.

mitted.[58] Since the two genealogies were submitted by competing candidates for the stool, they naturally do not agree with each other. The Kumawuhene who submitted the 1925 genealogy was Rattray's informant for the latter's genealogy of Kumawu rulers.[59] Hence a high degree of correlation between his genealogy and Rattray's

TABLE 10

Lists of Oyokohenes

1929 list[60]	*1963 list*[61]
Adu Nontwiri	Odiawuo (contemporary of Osei Tutu)
	Bene Ako
	Taah
	Asare
	Kwabina Ankara
Kobina Asomaning	Kweku Asumani
Kwame Baafi	Baafi
Kweku Nyamah	
Kwasi Boampong	Buapong
	Kwateng
	Nyamoah
	Odwemah
Kwame Agyekum	Agyekum Panyin
Kwame Nkansa	Kwame Nkansah
	Kwame Dapaah
Kofi Dompeh	Kofi Dompeh
Kojo Agyekum	Agyekum II
	Kofi Poku

published genealogy might be expected. Surprisingly, however, neither the names nor the genealogical filiations of the Kumawuhenes in Rattray's genealogy agree completely with the list submitted about the same time that Rattray was collecting his data. For instance, it only showed ten generations for the same period for which Rattray's genealogy showed twelve generations. The discrepancies here can probably be attributed to the hazards of 'genealogizing' discussed later in this chapter.

The usual genealogy was submitted on the election of Kwame Essuman as Dadiesoabahene in 1925. Although the stool is nominally one in which matrilineal succession prevails, the genealogy

[58] NAG/ADM11/1/1308.
[59] Rattray, *Ashanti law*, 217–22, chart opp. 234.
[60] NAG/ADM11/1/1362.
[61] IAS/AS 28.

showed that all but four successions were in the male line. Table 11 compares this 1925 genealogy with that collected in 1963. The wildly discordant patterns of these two genealogies indicate that perhaps remembered figures in Dadiesoaba stool traditions were strung together when the occasion demanded. The identity of eleven of the

TABLE 11

Lists of Dadiesoabahenes

1925 list[62]	*1962 list*[63]
1 Atobra Ahen	3 Atobra Kwesi
2 Nti Panin	1 Nti Panin
3 Piprah Yaw	13 Pepra Yaw
4 Ampratwum Ahinkro	4 Oti Awere
5 Yaw Da	
6 Ampratwum Krapa	2 Nti Kumah
7 Kofi Ako	5 Ako
8 Kobea	7 Kubea
9 Eninkate	6 Ani Kete
10 Kobea Ntehua	10 Kwame Asumin I
11 Kwame Duodoo	8 Kwame Duodu
12 Osei	9 Osei
13 Kofi Nti	11 Kofi Nti Takora
14 Kwabina Sekyere	12 Kwabena Sekyere
15 Kwame Essuman	14 Kwame Asumin II

fourteen or fifteen names implies a common pool of information, while the two sequences of these eleven names—

1–2–3–7–8–9–11–12–13–14–15
3–1–13–5–7–6–8–9–11–12–14

suggests an adventitious application of these data.

In 1921 the Nkawiehene, testifying at a land dispute hearing, could recall only three of his predecessors before the time of the Asantehene Kofi Kakari (1867–74).[64] By 1963 this number had increased to seven, but only one of the seven names agreed with any of the names on the earlier list.[65]

Similar discrepancies appear between a list of Amakom stoolholders presented by the Amakomhene in a jurisdictional dispute

[62] NAG/ADM11/1/1336.
[63] IAS/AS 12.
[64] Testimony of Nkawiehene Kobina Kaffuor, NAG/ADM11/1/1310.
[65] IAS/AS 102.

with Adonten stool in 1924/5 and a list collected in 1963.[66] The earlier list only included the first eight occupants of the stool. Only two of these, numbers 4 and 5, appear in the later list, and then as the first two rulers.

These examples are selective rather than comprehensive. In fact no two lists of stoolholders for any Asante substool which were collected at different times agree with each other. The above analysis is designed simply to illustrate the protean and *ad hoc* characteristics of these stool traditions. Again, the circumstances of their transmission are important in understanding the evanescent nature of these traditions. The IAS/AS stool histories were collected under the Nkrumah government. Under this regime many of the traditional chiefs in Asante were destooled and replaced by individuals whose devotion to CPP policies was deemed more important than provable lineal legitimacy.[67] None the less, these 'parvenus' felt it important to graft themselves on to the stool genealogy. This consideration partly explains the distortions which are so apparent in these stool histories. In like fashion, the 'genealogies' collected during the 1920s were intended to serve legitimizing purposes—either to justify election to the stool or to show priority of settlement in land and jurisdictional disputes with other stools.[68] Even so, these circumstances alone are not sufficient to explain the dimension of the discrepancies between lists of occupants of the same stool. The inevitable conclusion is that the combination of frequent destoolment, lack of knowledge for the earlier period, and the desire to attribute stool foundations to the time of Osei Tutu, while at the same time confusing Osei Tutu and Osei Bonsu, has resulted in a level of distortion too great to be unravelled without the assistance of external, more neutral, data. And these are lacking.

If chronological reckoning on the basis of regnal length is impossible, can generational reckoning be more useful? The structuring of ancestors into a genealogical tree was an innovation of the British colonial administration. The genealogies submitted during the period

[66] NAG/ADM11/1/1338, pp. 39–43; IAS/AS 77.

[67] D. Apter, *Ghana in transition* (New York, 1963), 312–15; K. Kesse-Adu, *The politics of political detention* (Accra, 1971), 53–6. A particularly lucid—and disturbing—account of the role that contemporary political exigencies play on the content of oral tradition is A. F. Robertson, 'Histories and political opposition in Ahafo, Ghana', *Africa*, 43 (1973), 41–58. It should be required reading for anyone proposing to collect historical data in the field.

[68] e.g. Rattray, *Ashanti law*, 128–30, 236; Busia, *Position of chief*, x–xi.

that they were required were sometimes criticized by the British administrators.[69] Yet, since these genealogies were no more than an effort to implement an ill-conceived colonial policy such criticism was as unfair as it was supercilious. The Asante were forced to cope with a conception of kinship that was alien to them. The broad eligibility to Asante stools, the existence of classificatory kinship, and ambiguous kinship terminology foredoomed any attempt to genealogize stool histories.[70] Rattray, who considered these genealogies 'worthless', nevertheless expressed his faith in the concept of Asante stool genealogies by constructing elaborate genealogies for the stools of the seven most important territorial stools of metropolitan Asante (*amantoo*)—Asumegya, Bekwai, Juaben, Kokofu, Kumawu, Mampong, and Nsuta.[71] For the period from Osei Tutu to *c.* 1925 the seven genealogies show depths of five, eight, eight, four, ten, eleven, and eight generations. If we were to assume, for instance, the widely accepted twenty-seven-year generation average, this would result in placing alleged contemporaries anywhere in time from 1638 to 1817. Allowing greater variation in generation averages because of matrilineal succession would only increase the disparities.

In fact the stool histories reflect, however inadvertently, the fact that only synchronisms with Asantehenes or with dated events can provide even a modicum of a chronological framework for Asante substool history. The uses to which this technique has been put, however, may have destroyed any value it might have had. The series of Asantehenes is closely enough dated after *c.* 1700 to provide a satisfactory framework for Asante macro-history. If the means were available to judge the relative merits of the various traditional accounts of the many substools, some internal chronology for the

[69] See Minute of J. T. Furley dd 2 July 1924 *re* Dadiesoaba genealogy, NAG/ADM11/1/1336; Ag Colonial Secretary to Ag Chief Commissioner, Ashanti, 24 Aug. 1933 *re* Bompata genealogy, NAG/ADM11/1/1311; Rattray, *Ashanti law*, 128–30.

[70] Tordoff, *Ashanti*, 51n, states that Prempeh's classificatory grandson was nineteen years older than Prempeh himself. A similar example occurred in Atebubu in 1931, where the chief elected in 1931 was called the grandson of the previous occupant, who had been destooled a year earlier at the age of eighteen, NAG/ADM11/1/1323. On the vagueness of the term *nua* ('cousin', 'sibling'), see Furley to Secretary for Native Affairs, 21 Apr. 1922, NAG/ADM11/1/1470, and J. G. Christaller, *A dictionary of the Asante and Fante language called Tshi* (*Twi*) (Basel, 1933), 353. See also M. Fortes, 'Kinship and marriage among the Ashanti' in A. R. Radcliffe-Brown and D. Forde (eds.), *African systems of kinship and marriage* (London, 1950), 254–61, 278–9.

[71] Rattray, *Ashanti law*, charts opp. 146, 168, 196, 216, 234, 253, and 268.

Asante state might be possible. At present this, too, seems quixotic except for those few stools for which some documentation exists for the nineteenth century. Certainly, however, any proliferation of the type of traditional material now available would only intensify the problems attending the present state of the inquiry.

EXCURSUS

Numerical List of IAS/AS Stool Histories at the Institute of African Studies, University of Ghana, Legon:

1 Asonkwahene Batahene[1]
2 Ankobia
3 Ananta
4 Asrampong
5 Adum
6 Atumpan
7 Asamang
8 Akyawkrom
9 Atipin
10 Lake Bosumtwi
11 Ejisu (origins)
12 Dadiesoaba[1]
13 Chief Goldsmith
14 Asumfuo
15 Gyase
16 Juaben Paramount Stool
17 Akwaboa
18 Ohwim
19 Nkabom
20 Nkabom Linguist
21 Atene Akuapong[2]
22 Nsumankwa
23 Boakye Yam
24 Odurogya Horn
25 Kwadwom
26 Ntahera
27 Abrofoo
28 Oyoko
29 Ntutia
30 Asantehene stool carriers
31 ——
32 Atutue
33 ——
34 Antoa
35 Kaase
36 Mpaboahene Sandals
37 Kodua Topa
38 Akwamu
39 Bantama (I)
40 Bantama (II)
41 Sana
42 Anaminako[2]
43 Safie and Amoanim
44 Kokofu
45 Atene Akoten[2]
46 Gyebi and Banahene
47 Nkonson
48 Kyerema Kobina (Akyeame)
49 Afari
50 Suame
51 Anonomsa[2]
52 Saamang
53 Bremang
54 Bantama-Baamu
55 Obogo Paramount[1]
56 Oyoko-Breman
57 Mentia
58 Baworo
59 Boadu Linguist
60 Esereso
61 Juansa
62 Agogo

[1] Stools of Denkyira origin according to tradition.
[2] Stools created by Osei Bonsu according to tradition.

63 Odumase[2]
64 Mamponten
65 Debooso
66 Duakyeame
67 Achiase
68 Nfanti
69 Asem
70 Fontomfrom Drum[1]
71 Omanti
72 Aboatem
73 Boakye Yam Linguist
74 Feyiase
75 Akankade Linguist
76 Asomfo
77 Amakom
78 Anyinase
79 Asokore Mampong
80 Akumanten[1]
81 Nsenie
82 Ofoase
83 Somi
84 Ayebiakyere
85 Fumesua
86 Ofiri and Manso
87 Sewuah
88 Adwaase
89 Adanse Paramount
90 Obuokrom
91 Baamu
92 Danpoomu[2]
93 Nkaniasohoe[2]
94 Essienimpong
95 Adonten
96 Abenase
97 Hiawu
98 Amoaman[1]
99 Anwomaso
100 Kronko
101 Gyenyaase
102 Nkawie-Kuma
103 Nfensi[1]
104 Mmagyegyefuo
105 Besiase[1]
106 Akyempim
107 Nyinahin
108 Nkarawa
109 Suma
110 Kenyase
111 Adwunakaasi
112 Kumasi Zongo community
113 Kyeneyekenfuo
114 Prempeh Drum
115 Sekyedomase
116 Kumasi Wangara
117 Duase
118 Kotei
119 Pekyi No. 1
120 Pekyi No. 2
121 Aboabogya
122 Okyere-Kurom
123 Kwaso
124 Wawase
125 Asanso
126 Jachie
127 Jachie Linguist
128 Toase
129 Manso-Mim[1]
130 Asantre-Adankwame[2]
131 Ofoase-Adomasa
132 Mamprusi community in Kumasi
133 Boaman
134 Amoako[1]
135 Atwima-Agogo[1]
136 Nkwanta Kessie[1]
137 Ahenkro
138 Kwaduo
139 Adubinsukese
140 Ahwerewamu
141 Atasomanso No. 1
142 Ano Panyin Linguist
143 Ahubrafoo
144 Ampabame
145 Nkofe
146 Kotoko Ameyaw
147 Apagya

148 Bonwire
149 Trede
150 Domi-Keniago[2]
151 Akokofe
152 Kuntenase
153 Adankraja
154 Hia
155 Asoromaso
156 Kona
157 Nnibi
158 Kyidom
159 Koraase
160 Aboaso
161 Sanakoroa Wono
162 Gyamfi Wono
163 Oti Kurom
164 Ahensan[1]
165 Twafuo
166 Offuman
167 Paakoso
168 Asantehene Blacksmith
169 Kwamang
170 Hemang
171 Ntonso
172 Mamesene[2]
173 Asamang
174 Busumuru Fabem Linguist
175 Amakye Bari
176 Nkwanta Essase[1]
177 Atasomanso No. 2
178 Asumfuo[1]
179 Bohyen
180 Enon
181 Akyineyekyenfuo[2]
182 Kyirapatre
183 ——
184 Atwima[1]
185 Taahyen
186 Amansie Abodom
187 Sepe Owusu Ansah[2]
188 Assuowin[1]
189 Krapa
190 Apede Drum
191 Soadoro
192 ——
193 Pramso
194 Asuboa[2]
195 Beposo
196 Derma
197 ——
198 Asankare
199 Akropong[1]
200 Amoaful
201 Abenkyim
202 Potrikrom[2]
203 Twumaduase[2]
204 Nkontonko
205 Pomaakrom
206 Okyerekrom
207 ——
208 Tuobodom
209 ——
210 ——
211 Kwaku Ndwema
212 Akyeresua
213 Seikwa
214 ——
215 Ejisu (II)

Conclusion

Stemmata quid faciunt? quid prodest . . . longo sanguine censeri?[1]

CHRONOLOGY has been defined as 'the science of computing time or periods of time, and of assigning events to their true dates'.[2] Perhaps a recent definition of chronography, the art of the chronologist, as 'the attribution of dates to persons and events for which the dates are not found in the source material' will be more familiar to Africanists.[3] These definitions, in their emphasis on the marriage of mathematics and memory, suggest that the ideal and realizable offspring of this union will be exact dates, on which historical narrative and causative analysis can safely be based.

This quest for exactitude has been characteristic of chronographers of all ages who, like Eratosthenes and Isaac Newton, were often mathematicians or astronomers, who brought to their study of the past a belief that precision was possible as well as desirable. In this quest the unfortunate reality that their data were unsuitable to such exercises was often disregarded.

Although some commentary has been necessary in this work on the general nature of oral tradition as historical evidence, I have focused throughout on its value in determining the length of the past it purported to record. In this regard traditional evidence generally has been found wanting, at least for periods of more than a century before the initial transcription of the tradition. There have been exceptions to this norm, of course, but the fact remains that these have been *aberrant*. The conclusion is inevitable that kinglists and genealogies, the most easily distorted form of time indicators in non-calendrical societies, are in themselves of little value in, for instance, attempting to date the formation of African states. Heavy reliance on these forms of evidence will only, can only, result in faulty conclusions.

[1] 'What good are family trees? . . . what's the advantage in your ancient blood?', Juvenal, Satire viii in *The Satires of Juvenal*, tr. R. Humphries (Bloomington, Ind., 1958), 101.

[2] *Oxford universal dictionary*, 3rd ed. rev. with addenda (Oxford, 1955), 309.

[3] M. Miller, 'Herodotus as chronographer', *Klio*, 46 (1965), 109.

This is not to argue that these data should be discarded out of hand. On the contrary, they should be viewed as being dynamic and analysed accordingly. 'Absolute truth', that is, in this case exact dating, will not result from this kind of analysis. None the less recognition of this reality is preferable to an ingenuous acceptance of exact but wholly unreliable dating.[4] The harm of uncritically accepting and using traditional materials often ramifies as subsequent research accepts the conclusions based on it. Unpleasant realities are optimistically ignored or artfully camouflaged. For this reason the emphasis throughout this work has been on the limitations of the data, in the belief that it is time that we stress the indisputable weaknesses of traditional material for chronological enlightenment (other than for some relative chronology) in place of being beguiled by dubious strengths.

The extensive use of comparative data brings a new dimension to the analysis of the chronological content of oral traditional material by bringing into sharper relief the ways in which its weaknesses manifest themselves. If I have, conversely, ignored or at least minimized Collingwood's dictum it is because I believe that this is a study in which a macro-approach can be more useful.[5] It is hoped that some of the suggestions embodied in this work will be applied by the investigators of particular societies. Most importantly, however, the student of African chronology must recognize that, because of the refractory character of much of the data which he must analyse, 'his work will be imperfect, his vision transient, and his goal still far away'.[6]

I feel that any final word should stress again that this entire study has been devoted to a single aspect of oral traditional data—its chronological content. No one who has worked extensively with oral materials will deny their value as historical sources. Nor indeed, despite the negative aspects of much of the present work, would I deny to oral tradition much valid chronological content. My main purpose has been to suggest probable parameters of reliability in order that the data can be mined and refined in such a way that the residuum will bear critical scrutiny.

[4] A point also made by Jones, 'The problems of African chronology', 162.

[5] See above, pp. 9–11.

[6] F. M. Powicke, *History, freedom and religion* (London, 1938), 13–14.

APPENDIX A

The Assyrian King Lists

TWO nearly complete King Lists of Assyria, known as the Khorsabad and SDAS kinglists, have survived.[1] Both lists were put into their final form in the eighth century B.C.[2] The Khorsabad list is an updated duplicate of an earlier list composed in the reign of Aššur-dan II (934–912). In turn this earlier list was probably based on a eponym list, now lost, from the eleventh century.[3] The Assyrian eponyms, or *limmu*, were annual officials after whom the year was named; hence an eponym list provided a basis for accurately calculating some period of the past.

Except for some minor points the Khorsabad and SDAS lists are identical and in fact may be regarded as two copies of the same original.[4] Unfortunately all the Assyrian King Lists were damaged in the same places. This means that the regnal lengths for the rulers between Erišu I and Šamši-Adad I (*c.* 1815–*c.* 1783) are lacking. Furthermore the eponym list on which the King Lists were presumably based was deficient—or never existed—for the extremely troubled period from Šamši-Adad I to Adasi, his eighth successor in the King Lists.[5] The first thirty-two names in the Assyrian King

[1] The Khorsabad King List was discovered during the 1932/3 season at modern Khorsabad, the ancient Dar-Šarrukin, the capital of Sargon II (722–705). The contents of this King List have been fully described by Poebel, 'Khorsabad'. The SDAS List is owned by the Seventh-Day Adventist Seminary in Washington, D.C. The date of its discovery is unknown, but it was before 1914. The peculiar chain of circumstances through which it reached its present locale are discussed in Gelb, 'Two Assyrian King Lists', 209–10. A third list, known as the Nassouhi list, is less well preserved than these two but parallels them closely.

[2] The Khorsabad list was composed in 738, Poebel, 'Khorsabad', 250. The last name in the SDAS list is Šulmanu-ašarid V, who ruled from 727 to 722 and this list was probably composed in the reign of his successor Sargon II. See also Lewy, 'Assyria, *c.* 2600 to 1816 B.C.', 17.

[3] Hayes *et al.*, 'Chronology'; M. B. Rowton, 'Ṭuppū in the Assyrian King Lists', *JNES* 18 (1959), 220–1; Poebel, 'Khorsabad', 251.

[4] These differences are discussed in Gelb, 'Two Assyrian King Lists', 210–11.

[5] Hayes *et al.*, 'Chronology', 25–6.

Lists were not assigned regnal lengths by those who transcribed the lists and the reasons for this will become apparent from the later discussion. Six of the eight rulers after Šamši-Adad I are described in the King Lists as *ṭuppišu šarruta ēpuš*. The exact meaning of this phrase is in dispute, although most scholars feel that, for chronological purposes, the phrase represents a regnal length of zero value.[6] This zero value reflects the possibility that the ruler in question either reigned for no more than one year or that, possibly, he was a co-regent or contemporaneous contender with his predecessor; for whatever reason, however, he did not hold the office of *limmu*, which an Assyrian king usually held in the first or second year of his reign.[7]

The interpretation of *ṭuppū* in the Assyrian King Lists has implications for the chronological structuring of ancient Near Eastern history. If the King Lists are regarded as complete for the period after Šamši-Adad I, acceptance of zero-value years for the reigns of six of his nearest successors lowers his own date and that of his contemporary Hammurabi of Babylon.[8] However, as we have seen in Chapter I, there is considerable evidence that several Assyrian rulers in the period after Šamši-Adad were omitted.[9] The character of the King Lists for this period (this also being one of the places in which they are physically damaged) precludes any firm judgements since the evidence of the King Lists could support, if interpreted in different ways, dates of 1728–1686 (low chronology) or of 1792–1750 (middle chronology) for Hammurabi. The weight of other evidence, however, supports the earlier date and hence all datation in this discussion is based on the middle chronology.

Since the problems of the Assyrian King Lists after Šamši-Adad I have already been discussed we shall emphasize here the nature of these King Lists for the period before that ruler, whose contemporaneity with Hammurabi is perhaps the best-documented aspect of ancient Near Eastern chronology. Šamši-Adad I is the thirty-ninth name in the Assyrian King Lists. This portion of the lists is given in Table 12. The rulers numbered 17 to 26 were given in reverse order

[6] Rowton, 'Ṭuppū in the Assyrian King Lists', 217–21; idem, 'Mesopotamian chronology and the "Era of Menophres" ', *Iraq*, 8 (1946), 98–101.

[7] Poebel, 'Khorsabad', 77; Rowton, 'Ṭuppū in the Assyrian King Lists', 217–21.

[8] Rowton, 'Ṭūppu and the date of Hammurabi', *JNES* 10 (1951), 201–3. At the time he wrote this Rowton supported the low chronology but later opted for the middle chronology. See his 'Date of Hammurabi', 107–9.

[9] See above, pp. 30–2.

in the King Lists but they have been adjusted to their proper order in the Table. The years 1815 and 1783 can be regarded as the first reasonably firm dates in Assyrian history. This fact, and the peculiar nature of the Assyrian King Lists before the time of Šamši-Adad I make his reign an appropriate point of departure.

TABLE 12

1 Tudia	22 Iakmesi (son of 21)
2 Adamu	23 Iakmeni (son of 22)
3 Iangi	24 Iazkur-ilu (son of 23)
4 KITlamu	25 Ilu-kapkapi (son of 24)
5 Harharu	26 Aminu (son of 25)
6 MANdaru	27 Sulili (son of 26)
7 Imsu	28 Kikkia
8 HARsu	29 Akia
9 Didanu	30 Puzur-Aššur I
10 Hanu	31 Sallim-ahhe (son of 30)
11 Zuabu	32 Ilušuma (son of 31)
12 Nuabu	33 Erišu I (son of 32; ruled 40 years)
13 Abazu	34 Ikunu (son of 33)
14 TILlu (or Belu)	35 Šarru-kin (son of 34)
15 Asarah	36 Puzur-Aššur II (son of 35)
16 Ušpia	37 Naram-Sin (son of 36)
17 Apiašal (son of 16)	38 Erišu II (son of 37)
18 Halu (son of 17)	39 Šamši-Adad I (son of Ilu-kapkapi)[10]
19 Salmanu (son of 18)	
20 Haianu (son of 19)	
21 Ilu-Mer (son of 20)	

The abundance of epigraphic evidence has allowed scholars of ancient Near Eastern history to dissect and evaluate the Assyrian King Lists in ways which will be discussed. This luxury is seldom afforded the historian of African societies who, when presented with a kinglist or genealogy, must accept and analyse it on its own terms. For purposes of diagnosis it may be useful, then, before discussing the nature of the Assyrian King Lists at length, to treat them as if they were kinglists from African states.

The Assyrian King Lists described the first seventeen rulers of Assyria as 'kings who dwelt in tents', suggesting a nomadic period. With this in mind, Arno Poebel, who first analysed the Khorsabad

[10] Poebel, 'Khorsabad', 87–8; Gelb, 'Two Assyrian King Lists', 222–4. Neither King List provides the filiation of Sallim-ahhe and Illušumma but this is known from their own inscriptions, Poebel, 'Khorsabad', 275.

King List, assigned an average regnal length of only ten years to the first fifteen rulers.[11] The next twelve rulers (nos. 16 to 27) were presented in the List as ruling in a father/son succession.[12] Taking them at their face value for the nonce we can assign each of these rulers average reigns of at least twenty-five years. The relationship of the next three rulers (nos. 28–30) is unknown but we may fairly assign them an aggregate regnal period of fifty years. Šamši-Adad's eight predecessors (nos. 31 to 38) again succeeded in father/son order and therefore ruled about 200 years. Therefore, the minimal calculated period during which these thirty-eight Assyrian kings ruled is 150 + 300 + 50 + 200 years or 700 years. In this calculation no genealogical or chronological liberties have been taken with the evidence and the lists have been treated in much the same way as many African kinglists have been analysed. We should, then, on the basis of the data in the lists alone, feel justified in placing the reign of Tudia to *c.* 2500 B.C. In short the Assyrian King Lists for the period before Šamši-Adad I seem, prima facie, to represent a reasonable succession pattern over seven centuries. If Šamši-Adad I had been an African ruler known to have been ruling in 1875, the foundation of his state might reasonably be placed in the twelfth or thirteenth centuries.

Fortunately the Assyrian King Lists need not be assessed in isolation and we can now examine the results of thirty years of scholarship. When the Khorsabad King List was first studied it was assumed to represent what ancient Near Eastern history then lacked —a continuous and precise framework for early Assyrian chronology. Admittedly the incidence of eleven consecutive father/son successions (Apiašal to Sulili) was thought unusual and Poebel suggested that perhaps some collateral rulers had been omitted.[13] Otherwise the sequence of reigns seemed unexceptionable. The identity of the twenty-fifth ruler with the father of Šamši-Adad I was considered but rejected on the grounds that the intervening reigns constituted 'at least ten generations'.[14] In general, the authority and accuracy of the Khorsabad King List and its use as a valuable new chronological tool were accepted.[15]

Subsequent analysis and the discovery of new sources for this period radically altered these sanguine first expectations. Ušpia, the sixteenth name on the List, is known from building records inscribed

[11] Ibid. 260. [12] Ibid. [13] Ibid. 271.
[14] Ibid. 286. [15] Ibid. 251–85 *passim.*

by later rulers and may be regarded, at least provisionally, as a real historical figure who was in some way associated with the foundation of Aššur itself or the gaining of independence from foreign control.[16] However, 'the kings who dwelt in tents' have been shown to be no more than assorted spurinyms, similar to the early Biblical genealogies, or the twelve 'sons' of Jacob. In other words they represented neither a dynasty nor any other sequence of rulers spanning a period of time.[17] The recent discovery of a list of 'ancestors' of the First Dynasty of Babylon confirms this interpretation.[18] The Babylonian genealogy contained many of the same names as this portion of the Assyrian King List. These names evidently represented a kind of inventory of eponyms or at least a common pool of genealogical traditions among the west Semitic peoples.[19]

The group of rulers numbered 17 to 26 in Table 12 has been the subject of interest from the first publication of the Khorsabad King List. This sequence was inserted into the King Lists in reverse order—Aminu was listed first and called the son of Ilu-kapkapi, the next name on the list, and so on up to Apiasal, who was called the son of Ušpia, who was listed many names before him.[20] Poebel thought this series may have represented an ascendant genealogy with some names missing, but still all kings of Assyria.[21] Certain peculiarities of the sequence, however, inevitably invited other interpretations. In the lists Šamši-Adad I was called the son of an Ilu-kapkapi and Ilu-kapkapi was also the twenty-fifth name on the List and was called the father of Aminu. Other evidence suggests that Šamši-Adad I may in fact have had a brother named Aminu, who may have preceded him as ruler of either Terqa or Ekallatum, where he ruled before usurping the Assyrian throne.[22] This evidence has led some to the conclusion that this entire sequence of names was no more than a list of the putative ancestors of Šamši-Adad I, who were inserted into the King List and connected with Ušpia to give Šamši-

[16] Lewy, 'Assyria', 19; G. van Driel, *The cult of Aššur* (Assen, 1969), 1–3. For Ušpia's dating, see below.

[17] On these names, see esp. Kraus, *Könige*, 123–42; Lewy, 'Assyria', 18–19; Oates, *Studies*, 22–4; Malamat, 'King lists', 165–8.

[18] Finkelstein, 'Genealogy', 95–102.

[19] Malamat, 'King lists'. This is an excellent analysis of these and the Biblical genealogies and has a wider application that these. See also Yeivin, *Israelite conquest of Canaan*.

[20] Poebel, 'Khorsabad', 268–9.

[21] Ibid. 269–70.

[22] Kupper, *Nomades*, 208–12; Landsberger, 'Assyrische Königsliste', 34.

Adad a legitimate claim to a throne he had conquered by force.[23] This interpretation is plausible, although the unusual placement of the sequence in the King Lists has caused some scholars to reject this hypothesis.[24] However, its likelihood is strengthened by the circumstances surrounding the creation of this part of the King List—a point to be discussed later.

The artificial character of the names is also apparent in the inclusion of several pairs of rhyming couplets, reminiscent of the Pictish kinglists discussed in Chapter I. Hallo has suggested that the rulers from Apiašal to Ilu-kapkapi ruled simultaneously with the line of kings from Kikkia to Puzur-Aššur II (nos. 28 to 36), who were certainly historical.[25] Either alternative—that these names were not ruling kings or they represented a line ruling outside Assyria—is more likely than that they ruled Assyria during the period allotted them by the Assyrian King Lists. And either alternative would reduce the distance between Ušpia and Šamši-Adad I to a period of two or three centuries.

In sum, only fourteen of the first thirty-nine names in the Assyrian King Lists have escaped at least the imputation of being fictive rulers.[26] Furthermore, epigraphic evidence has shown that at least three rulers of Aššur were not included in the King Lists. Azuzu was governor of the city under Maništusu of Akkad (2306–2292).[27] Zāriqum ruled Aššur for Ur III from before 2048 to after 2042.[28] Ititi ruled Aššur, probably in the period between Azuzu and Zāriqum, as the representative of either Akkad or Ur III.[29] These names were probably omitted because they represented periods of foreign rule.

[23] Ibid. 32–5; Oates, *Studies*, 24; Malamat, 'King lists', 169–70. See also W. G. Lambert, 'Another look at Hammurabi's ancestors', *JCS* 22 (1968), 2.

[24] Lewy, 'Assyria', 20, notes this and argues that these names represent ancestors of Sulili rather than Šamši-Adad I, but this view is generally rejected.

[25] Hallo, 'Zāriqum', 221n. Hallo's argument that this solution 'would harmonize the generations' between Šamši-Adad and Ušpia may, in the light of the earlier discussion of artificial synchronizing and Appendix C, be seen as an argument *against* this solution, which otherwise has many attractions. See also Malamat, 'King lists', 169–70nn.

[26] To this one might add no. 37 Naram-Sin, who was a contemporaneous ruler of Ešnunna who evidently occupied Aššur for a brief time. A. Goetze, 'An old Babylonian itinerary', *JCS* 7 (1953), 59, and Oates, *Studies*, 25, support this identification. Lewy, 'Assyria', 15, argues for two rulers named Naram-Sin during this period.

[27] Ibid. 19; van Driel, *Cult of Aššur*, 3.

[28] Hallo, 'Zāriqum', 220–5; Oates, *Studies*, 28.

[29] Hallo, 'Zāriqum', 220n.

It is clear that the chronological value of the Assyrian King Lists before the reign of Šamši-Adad I is very limited, and equally misleading. This can be demonstrated by the various datings postulated for Ušpia. Ušpia, as we have seen, was an early and important ruler of Aššur who was connected in some way with the founding or independence of the city and who was remembered in several later inscriptions.[30] If the argument that he was responsible for the first foundation of Aššur is accepted it is possible to date Ušpia to before *c.* 2500 since archaeological evidence indicates that the city was in existence well before the Akkadian period.[31] On the other hand it is not necessary to date Ušpia to the time of the actual settlement of the site of Aššur.[32] If he was the ruler who freed Assyria from the yoke of Akkad he must be dated to the end of the twenty-third century. If, however, he is linked to the withdrawal of Ur III control, he could be dated even later. On the basis of genealogical reckoning Hallo has dated him to the twenty-first century—a time when Ur III was in decline.[33] Others would reject so late a date and suggest merely that Ušpia should be dated to 'sometime before the conquest of Aššur by the Third Dynasty of Ur [i.e. before *c.* 2100]'.[34] Whatever time we date Ušpia to, however, we must do it on the basis of events known from other sources and not from the Assyrian King Lists themselves. For on the basis of these Lists it would be necessary to date him to about the middle of the twenty-fourth century.[35] Of all the period before Šamši-Adad I this would be the *least* likely time for Ušpia to have reigned. It falls precisely in the middle of the reign of Sargon of Akkad (2371–2316), who created the greatest empire in the ancient Near East before the eighth century B.C.—an empire which included Assyria. In other words it was a time when Assyria lost her independence, not when it gained or regained it.

It is apparent that, whatever the Assyrian King Lists purported to be for the period before Šamši-Adad I they were not in fact lists

[30] For the building inscriptions of several later Assyrian rulers and their application to early Assyrian chronology, see Lewy, 'Assyria', 24–6; Oates, *Studies*, 27–8nn; Rowton, 'The date of Hammurabi', 107–9; Hayes *et al.*, 'Chronology', 32–4.

[31] Lewy, 'Assyria', 19, and her chronological schema, ibid. 50. Cf. Malamat, 'King lists', 169.

[32] Van Driel, *Cult of Aššur*, 2–3.

[33] Hallo, 'Zāriqum', 221n.

[34] Oates, *Studies*, 28.

[35] A. Parrot, *Archéologie mésopotamienne* (2 vols., Paris, 1953), dated Ušpia to the reign of Naram-Sin of Akkad (2291–2255).

of Assyrian rulers. This can be explained to a great extent by the ambience in which this part of the List developed. Landsberger has deduced that the early parts of the Assyrian King Lists were originally composed under the dynasty of Šamši-Adad I.[36] Šamši-Adad was a usurper, with no known genealogical claim to the Assyrian throne. Furthermore, he was the greatest of the early Assyrian kings and, although his dynasty was short-lived, it was long remembered. Under these circumstances it becomes easier to understand the nature of the distortions which the King Lists contain—certainly the inclusion of Šamši-Adad's alleged ancestors is explicable, although the inclusion of the rulers of the dynasty he overthrew is less so unless the factors prompting what we have called genealogical parasitism were operating.

Under Šamši-Adad I Assyria was a growing power and it is not difficult to believe that any rulers who may have ruled under foreign auspices would be excluded, even if their memory or their monuments had been preserved. The inclusion of the fifteen eponymous rulers seems merely to have been a convention of the time, as typified by the Babylonian genealogy as well. Puzur-Aššur I, who evidently founded a new dynasty in Assyria, can reasonably be dated to the late Ur III period or immediately afterwards (i.e. *c.* 2050–*c.* 1950) and this may be regarded, in the present state of the evidence, as the earliest reasonably certain date in Assyrian regnal history.[37]

The omissions and other distortions in the Assyrian King Lists during the time of troubles followed the reign of Išme-Dagan, the son of Šamši-Adad I, have been discussed earlier.[38] Apparently these omissions were designed to disguise long periods of Kassite and Hurrian domination. The King Lists also fulfilled legitimizing purposes by excluding some collateral rulers during this period. Finally, the Assyrian King Lists displayed the usual tendency to assign father/son relationships in cases where it was doubtful.[39]

Each of the preserved Assyrian King Lists contained over 100 names and spanned about 1,300 years. Within these broad parameters they, both wilfully and unconsciously, presented a wide variety of distortions.[40] Thus a study of the Assyrian King Lists

[36] Landsberger, 'Assyrische Königsliste', 109–10.
[37] Lewy, 'Assyria', 20–1; Oates, *Studies*, 27.
[38] See above, pp. 31–2.
[39] These problems of the Assyrian King Lists are discussed in Chapter II.
[40] See Hallo and Simpson, *Ancient Near East*, 97, 115. For observations of the importance of 'genealogical legitimacy' to the Assyrian kings and the measures

illustrates particularly well the whole spectrum of considerations that are important in analysing a genealogy or kinglist for its chronological value. The character of the distortions, which range from the wholesale inclusion of spurinyms to questionable father/son successions, the circumstances surrounding the composition of large parts of the Lists, and the high level of analysis to which they have been subjected combine to make them convenient and instructive microcosms for the whole study of genealogical and chronological problems in kinglists.

---

they took to ensure it, see R. Labat, 'Assyrologie', *Annuaire du Collège de France*, 56 (1956), 255–6.

APPENDIX B

The Jodhpur Chronicles

JODHPUR, or Marwar, was the largest, wealthiest, and second most populous state in Rajputana.[1] From about the thirteenth century it was ruled by the Rathor Rajputs. As for most of the former Native States of India, evidence for the earliest history of Jodhpur is found, with but a few exceptions, in the *khyats* or chronicles.[2] Most genealogies in chronicles of this kind traced the ruling lines back to the solar or lunar ruling lines of the Purānas.[3] The early parts of these genealogies, which often ran to more than 150 generations, are obviously mythical.[4] Consequently there is no need to discuss them, but only to cite them as examples of the distortive mechanisms of the chronicles.[5] It has been observed by a particularly well-qualified observer that 'there is probably no bardic literature in any part of the world, in which truth is so masked by fiction, or so disfigured by hyperbole, as in the bardic literature of Rajputana'.[6]

Not surprisingly, this observation seems particularly true of their chronological content. The reasons for these distortions can be found in an analysis of the circumstances of the origins of most of these chronicles. The majority were written in the sixteenth and

[1] *Imperial Gazetteer of India* (26 vols., Oxford, 1907–9), XIV. 179–88.

[2] For the bardic chronicles, see L. P. Tessitori, 'A scheme for the Bardic and Historical Survey of Rajputana', *JASB*, N.S. 10 (1914), 373–86; C. von Fürer-Haimendorf, 'The value of Indian bardic literature' in C. H. Philips (ed.), *Historians of India, Pakistan and Ceylon* (London, 1961), 87–93.

[3] For a discussion of the Purānic genealogies, see above, pp. 61–3.

[4] See, e.g., Tessitori, *A descriptive catalogue of the Bardic and Historical Survey of Rajputâna, Manuscripts,* Section I, Pt. 1 (Calcutta, 1917), 12, 54; idem, 'Scheme', 403; idem, 'A progress report on the work done during the year 1917 in connection with the Bardic and Historical Survey of Rajputana', *JASB*, N.S. 15 (1919), 20, 25; idem, 'A progress report on the work done during the year 1918 in connection with the Bardic and Historical Survey of Rajputana', *JASB*, N.S. 16 (1920), 266–7.

[5] See Shah and Shroff, 'The Vahīvancā Bāroṭs of Gujarat', 46–64, for a discussion of the methods of one group of genealogists.

[6] Tessitori, 'Progress report for the work done in the year 1916 in connection with the Bardic and Historical Survey of Rajputana', *JASB*, N.S. 13 (1917), 228.

seventeenth centuries when the Rajput states, including Jodhpur, were under Mughal suzerainty.[7] During the period of Mughal ascendancy the Rajput rulers were a favoured group at court, where many of them lived almost permanently and where they exercised important military commands. In their competition they constantly jockeyed for the favour of the Mughal Emperors. One weapon at their disposal was their allegedly illustrious ancestry. The use of this genealogical arsenal was facilitated and encouraged by the Emperor Akbar (1556–1605), who has been described as 'a believer in genealatry'—his account of his own ancestry bore ample witness to this.[8] Under the impact of these opportunities the *khyats*, which had previously been 'chronicles of contemporary events which were remarkable for accuracy, sobriety, and dispassionateness' were transformed into panegyrics of the antiquity of the dynasty they served.[9] The bases for their new character were the *vamśāvalīs*, which were prose histories of each state. Until the sixteenth century the *vamśavālīs* were 'works of small pretensions and humble proportions' but when they were incorporated into the new *khyats* their lacunae were filled to give them the appearance of antiquity and continuity.[10]

Given these circumstances the contents of the *khyats* are rather predictable. Once the obligatory Purānic connections had been made it became necessary to connect the origins of the Rathor state with an illustrious dynasty of later medieval India. The Jodhpur chroniclers chose the Gāhadavāla dynasty for this signal honour. The Gāhadavālas had ruled Kanauj in the eleventh and twelfth centuries. The last important ruler of the dynasty was killed by Muslims in 1193 although the dynasty lingered on with localized authority for another fifty years.[11] The Gāhadavāla origin of the Rathors (or the Rathor origin of the Gāhadavālas) is, from all available evidence, a creation of the sixteenth-century chronicles.[12] The few extant inscriptions of Rathor rulers made no mention whatever of this connection

[7] Tessitori, *Descriptive catalogue*, 64; idem, 'Progress report for 1915', 228–9; idem, 'Progress report for 1917', 20–2.

[8] Tessitori, 'Progress report for 1918', 263; A. L. Srivastava, *Akbar the Great* (2 vols., Agra, 1962–7), II. 15, 21, 320–3.

[9] Tessitori, 'Progress report for 1917', 26–7.

[10] Ibid. 26.

[11] For the Gāhadavālas, see Niyogi, *Gāhadāvalas*, and *HCIP* V, *The struggle for empire* (Bombay, 1957), 51–5.

[12] Tessitori, 'Progress report for 1918', 263. 'This [connection with the Gāhadavālas] . . . was . . . a novelty of the time, no previous bard of the Rāṭhoras having been aware' of it.

—a reticence which, if such a connection had existed, is inexplicable since one of these inscriptions actually belonged to Siha, the alleged grandson of Jayachandra, the Gāhadavāla ruler killed in 1193.[13] Many modern historians of Jodhpur have accepted the relationship of Siha, the supposed founder of the state, with Jayachandra, despite the fact that the first claim of this relationship was made more than three centuries after the disappearance of the Gāhadavālas in works whose primary aim was to elevate the status of the Jodhpur ruling line in the eyes of its suzerain.[14]

Once the Gāhadavāla connection had been made the chroniclers related the history of the rulers of the state after Siha. It became the bards' task to provide details for the intervening period to the fifteenth century. Apparently this task proved more difficult than one might at first expect. The earliest *khyats* which undertook to trace the royal genealogy invariably took it back only to Salkha, the eleventh ruler in Table 13.[15] Salkha even developed as an eponym for the Jodhpur Rathors, which indicates that at one time he was regarded either as the apical ancestor of the line or at least a very early ruler.[16] Later chroniclers, however, were able to ascertain that the Jodhpur line reached several generations further back to Siha. Table 13 presents a composite kinglist for Jodhpur as recorded in several later *khyats*.[17]

The dates for the deaths of Siha and Dhuhar are known from two inscriptions which are the only supporting data for the accounts of any of the early rulers in the chronicles. And in fact these inscriptions may have been known to the chroniclers who may have constructed

[13] D. R. Bhandarkar, 'Bithu inscription of Siha Rathod', *Indian Antiquary*, 40 (1911, 181; idem, 'The dates for the early princes of the present Jodhpur family', *Indian Antiquary*, 40 (1911), 301.

[14] See, e.g., Bhandarkar, 'Bithu inscription', 181, who felt that the date of this inscription (A.D. 1273) placed this relationship 'beyond all doubt'. He cited the *Ain-i-Akbari* of Abul Fazl, a late sixteenth-century life of Akbar, in substantiation of this position. If nothing else, Abul Fazl's recitation of this myth illustrated the utility and efficacy of the Jodhpur chroniclers' efforts. See also B. N. Reu, *Glories of Marwar and the glorious Rathors* (Jodhpur, 1943), xi–xiii; idem, *History of the Rāshṭrakūtas (Rāthoḍas)* (Jodhpur, 1933), 131–5, 141–3: J. Tod, *Annals and antiquities of Rajasthan* (reprint of 1829/32 edition: 2 vols., London, 1960), II. 8–10; Rajasthan and Ajmer, *List*, 100; A. Adams, *The western Rajputana States: Marwar, Sirohi and Jaisalmir* (London, 1899), 42–3.

[15] Tessitori, 'Progress report for 1917', 21–2.

[16] Ibid. 22.

[17] Reu, *Glories of the Rathors*, xi–lxiv; Tessitori, 'Progress report for 1917', 21n.; P. R. Karan, 'History of the Rathors' in *Sir Asuthosh Mukherjee Silver Jubilee Volume* (3 vols., Calcutta, 1921–7), III/1. 267–74.

the Jodhpur genealogies around them. The inscription of Dhuhar called him the son of Asvatthama (Asthan) but did not specify that Siha was the father of the latter.[18] If the chroniclers used this inscription they inferred this filiation and it has generally been accepted.[19] Dhuhar's inscription was found at some distance from that of Siha.[20]

TABLE 13

1 Siha (died in 1273)
2 Asthan (son of 1)
3 Dhuhar (son of 2; died in 1309)
4 Rayapala (son of 3)
5 Kanhapala (son of 4)
6 Jalansi (son of 5)
7 Chhada (son of 6)
8 Tida (son of 7)
9 Kanharadeva (son of 8) or Salkha
10 Tribhuvamsi (son of 9) or Mallinatha (nephew of 9)
11 Salkha (nephew of 9 or 10) or Viramji
12 Viramji (brother of 11 ?)
13 Chunda (son of 12) *c.* 1385–1424
14 Kanha (son of 13) 1424–5
15 Salla (son of 13) 1425–7
16 Ranamala (son of 13) 1427–38
17 Jodha (son of 16) 1438–88[21]

This could indicate either that the capital of the inchoate state had moved or that Siha and Dhuhar were not dynastically related.

The genealogy and chronology of the Jodhpur kinglist from the death of Dhuhar to the time of Mallinatha and Salkha are particularly confusing. Accepting the evidence of the chronicles forces us to believe that, however they are interpreted for the period after Tida, no fewer than seven generations ruled Jodhpur between 1309 and 1383 when, according to an inscription of 1658, Viramji was killed. It has been observed—rather wryly—that seven ruling generations in seventy-four years is 'somewhat unusual'.[22] Any evaluation of the level of probability for this should bear in mind that several rulers of this period were credited with having had as many as twenty sons. Oddly, some authorities who have argued that the interval of eighty years between the deaths of Jayachandra (1193) and Siha (1273)

[18] Bhandarkar, 'Bithu Inscription', 181; idem, 'Dates for early princes', 301.
[19] e.g. ibid. and *HCIP* VI, *The Delhi Sultanate* (Bombay, 1960), 349.
[20] Ibid.
[21] Many of the *khyats* included Salkha and Viramji, not because they ruled Jodhpur, which seems unlikely, but because they were in the direct line. Conversely, they omitted Tribhuvamsi. The end of the fourteenth century, the threshold of historicity in Jodhpur, was a confused period in the state. There were apparently several contenders and collateral rulers which the chronicles could not accommodate. For a comparison of the major *khyats* see V. S. Bhargava, *Marwar and the Mughal emperors, A.D. 1526–1748* (Delhi, 1966), 177.
[22] *HCIP* VI, *The Delhi Sultanate*, 349.

made it 'perfectly probable' that the former was the grandson of the latter have not been inclined to impeach the credibility of the chronicles for their fourteenth-century genealogy.[23]

Anyone inclined to accept the testimony of the Jodhpur *khyats* regarding the names and number of rulers before Chunda must at the same time recognize that the chronicles have converted a kinglist into an ascendant genealogy.[24] The propensity of Indian chronicles to disguise or omit collateral successions has been discussed in Chapter II. Although primogeniture later became the preferred form of succession among the Rajput states, succession to the throne in the early period was often determined by the nobles of a kingdom and ability—or lack of it—was often the decisive factor.[25] Furthermore Jodhpur seems an excellent example to which to apply Southwold's analysis of succession principles in Buganda.[26] Jodhpur, like all the Rajput states, engaged in constant warfare with the Muslims and with each other during this period. Under these circumstances it is difficult to argue that a long series of minors administered the state, even if the genealogical-chronological evidence could be contrived to allow for this.

The simplistic genealogies, the lack of epigraphic or other 'extra-chronicle' evidence for any of the rulers from Rayapala to Salkha, and the tardy appearance of these rulers in the *khyats*, throw doubt on their very existence. Common sense suggests that, if all of these individuals did rule, they succeeded collaterally and probably represented no more than three generations. This impression is reinforced by the succession to the Jodhpur throne after 1424, when primogenitural preference was stronger than it had earlier been. From 1424 to 1948 there were twenty-nine rulers in twenty-one generations. Fifteen successions were from father to son, although at least one of these was through adoption.[27] Hence, even primo-

[23] Bhandarkar, 'Bithu inscription', 181.

[24] For the opposite operation, that is, converting an ascendant genealogy into a kinglist, see Appendix C.

[25] S. C. Dutt, 'Conception of sovereignty in a medieval Rajput state', *Calcutta Review*, 3rd Ser. 15 (1924/5), 28–33; S. K. Rai, 'A new light on Chunda', *Indian Historical Quarterly*, 11 (1935), 559–63; Bhargava, *Marwar*, 56–7; R. P. Vyas, *Role of the nobility in Marwar, 1800–1873 A.D.* (New Delhi, 1969), 8–10; G. R. Parihar, *Marwar and the Marathas* (Jodhpur, 1968), v–viii.

[26] Martin Southwold, 'Succession to the throne in Buganda' in Jack Goody (ed.), *Succession to high office* (Cambridge, 1966), 104–7.

[27] Reu, *Glories of Marwar*, xi–lxiv; Rajputana and Ajmer, *List*, 100–1; Bhargava, *Marwar*, *passim*.

geniture as a narrowly preferential mode of succession in a polygynous society displayed certain limitations.[28]

The material in the Jodhpur chronicles bears every aspect of having been created to 'command more respect' from the Mughal authorities.[29] When the fragmentary materials in the older sources were found insufficient new genealogies were created taking the ancestry of the Rathors and of the Jodhpur state back to a suitably early period. Two of the figures in the early genealogies were real enough but there is no evidence except the chronicles themselves that they ruled Jodhpur or were ancestors of later rulers of the state. It was only with the accounts of the rulers and events of the late fourteenth century that some verisimilitude entered the chronicles. The careful historian must reject the accounts of the earlier period on their own evidence.

[28] See above, pp. 78–80, for a fuller discussion of adoption to the Indian *gadis*.

[29] Tessitori, 'Progress report for 1917', 25.

APPENDIX C

The Spartan Royal Genealogies

ANCIENT Sparta was a dyarchy. Its two lines of kings, called the Agiads and Eurypontids (or Procleids), were allegedly founded by twin sons of Aristodemos, great-great-grandson of Heracles. Most of the extant information on the early Spartan kings comes from Herodotus and from Pausanias, a second-century A.D. author of a geographical description of Greece. In order to understand the bases and nature of this inquiry into early Spartan regnal chronology it is necessary to quote at length these accounts. When describing the preliminaries of the battle of Thermopylae Herodotus wrote that

> in command of the entire force [of Greeks] was the Lacedaemonian Leonidas [the king of Sparta]. Now Leonidas was son of Anaxandridas, who was son of Leon, who was son of Eurycratidas, who was son of Anaxander, who was son of Eurycrates, who was son of Polydorus, who was son of Alcamenes, who was son of Telecles, who was son of Archelaus, who was son of Agesilaus, who was son of Doryssus, who was son of Labotas, who was son of Echestratus, who was son of Agis, who was son of Eurysthenes, who was son of Aristodemos, who was son of Aristomachus, who was son of Cleodaeus, who was the son of Hyllus, who was the son of Heracles.[1]

Herodotus then described how Leonidas 'quite unexpectedly' became king of Sparta in succession to his brother Cleomenes, who had died 'without male offspring'.[2]

Later Herodotus had occasion to describe the activities of Leotychides, the other Spartan king:

> This Leotychides . . . was son of Menares, son of Agesilaus, son of Hippocratides, son of Leotychides, son of Anaxilaus, son of Archidamus, son of Anaxandrides, son of Theopompus, son of Nicander, son of Charillus, son of Eunomus, son of Polydectes, son of Prytanis, son of Euryphon, son of Procles, son of Aristodemus, son of Aristomachus, son of Cleodaeus, son of Hyllus, son of Heracles. He belonged to the younger

[1] Herodotus, *The Persian wars* (Rawlinson ed.), VII. 204.
[2] Ibid. VII. 204–5.

[Eurypontid] branch of the royal house. All his ancestors except the two[3] next in the above list to himself had been kings of Sparta.[4]

Herodotus' aim was to describe the wars of the Greeks with the Persians in the first quarter of the fifth century and any details on the history of particular states or other periods proceeded from this primary intention. This was reflected in his accounts of the ancestors of the Spartan kings of the time. Only a very few of them are mentioned elsewhere in his work. Nowhere did he purport to be presenting a list of Spartan kings in these passages. Indeed, his account of the ancestors of Leonidas can be seen as no more than an effort to give this king a Heracleid lineage. These ancestors were not described as kings of Sparta, although it may have been Herodotus' belief that they were so. Even less is there any suggestion that they were *all* the rulers of the Agiad line. In this regard it is particularly significant that Leonidas himself had succeeded, not his father but his brother who, by Leonidas' accession, became a collateral and was omitted from this ascendant genealogy. The genealogy of the Eurypontid line, while more substantial, again did not claim to be a kinglist. Its main purpose may have been to legitimize the accession of Leotychides by carefully stipulating that which could not be denied—that his father and grandfather had not ruled before him—while at the same time showing that his remote ancestors *had* ruled.

Six centuries after Herodotus wrote his history Pausanias wrote *Periegesis of Greece*, which has been described as 'the ancient equivalent of our modern Murrays and Baedekers'.[5] In this work Pausanias provided a more detailed account of the early Spartan kings than Herodotus. He used the same genealogy for the Agiad line as Herodotus but transformed it into a kinglist by adding the detail that each of the individuals in the genealogy had ruled and had succeeded his father.[6] For the Eurypontid line, however, Pausanias' kinglist differed considerably from that of Herodotus. The succession in the Eurypontid line was, according to Pausanias, from father

[3] The Rawlinson translation of Herodotus substitutes 'seven' for 'two' in this passage but this is the result of an earlier translation and is rejected by most scholars.

[4] Herodotus, VIII. 131.

[5] J. G. Frazer, *Studies in Greek scenery, legend and history* (London, 1919), 25; Jones, *Sparta*, 2.

[6] Pausanias (ed. J. G. Frazer), *Pausanias' description of Greece* (6 vols., New York, 1898), Bk. III. 2. 1–7; 3. 1–8.

to son throughout.[7] He thus once again went beyond the data in Herodotus.

Since the accounts of Herodotus and Pausanias are the only ones extant it has been observed that the modern scholar has the Hobson's choice of 'either accepting Herodotus and rejecting Pausanias [for

TABLE 14

Herodotus	*Pausanias*
Procles	Procles
Eurypon	Soös
Prytanis	Eurypon
Polydectes	Prytanis
Eunomus	Eunomus
Charillus	Polydectes
Nicander	Charillus
Theopompus	Nicander
Anaxandrides	Theopompus
Archidamus	Zeuxidamus
Anaxilaus	Anaxidamus
Leotychides	Archidamus
Hippocratides	Agesicles
Agesilaus *	Ariston
Menares *	Demaratus
Leotychides	

*Did not rule according to Herodotus.

the Eurypontid list], or the reverse'.[8] Even so, many efforts have been made to synthesize the two accounts into a single, coherent kinglist.[9] It is neither necessary nor desirable to discuss these hypotheses because they fail to consider a third alternative—that Herodotus' genealogy is not a kinglist at all. In a sense this is rather an unpalatable 'solution' because it does not solve the problem by creating a new and better hybrid royal genealogy but suggests instead that it is not possible to construct a complete kinglist for Sparta before *c.* 520. It has recently been suggested that the unusually long regnal

[7] Ibid. III. 7. 1–10.

[8] Den Boer, *Laconian studies*, 67.

[9] e.g. G. Dum, *Die spartanischen Königslisten* (Innsbruck, 1878), T. Lenschau, 'Agiaden und Eurypontiden. Die Königshauser Spartas in ihren Beziehungen zueinander', *Rheinisches Museum für Philologie*, 88 (1939), 123–33; J. Beloch, 'Zur Geschichte des Eurypontidenhauses', *Hermes*, 35 (1900), 255–69; Den Boer, *Laconian studies*, 68–9, 84–8; Chrimes, *Ancient Sparta*, 334–47; Huxley, *Early Sparta*, 117–19.

generation that Herodotus implicitly used for Spartan history reflected his appreciation that regnal generations in Sparta were longer because succession was consobrinal before the middle of the sixth century.[10] In other words, there was more than one Spartan king in each generation. Certainly it is impossible to accept a generation average as high as forty years over a period of fifteen generations, no matter what contingencies are postulated.[11] Certain features of Spartan life such as marriage while still in barracks, and the penalizing of bachelors in various ways suggest a tendency towards shorter generations.

It is not more reasonable, on the principle of Occam's Razor, to argue that Herodotus' genealogy of the Eurypontid line reflected a different tradition from that which Pausanias used? We must remember that it is a genealogy for a ruler who represented either a new line or the 'return' of the original ruling line. The two genealogies might, therefore, have represented contemporaneous lines succeeding to the throne in some kind of rotation. On the basis of these genealogies there would have been at least two rulers in most of the six or seven generations before Leotychides.[12] This would have been the period, of course, when more genealogical details would have been remembered.

Even though any *argumentum ex silentio* from Herodotus' account of the Spartan kings has merit the contention that his genealogies were not kinglists can be supported by other data as well. As we have seen in Chapter II there has been only one documented instance of unbroken father/son succession over fifteen generations. To postulate two such series in a single state over the same period of time beggars the imagination. Certainly the succession patterns in the Spartan royal lines diverged markedly from a lineal profile after

[10] Miller, *Sicilian colony dates*, 172. Miller argues that 39-year generations are more accurate than 40-year ones. See her 'Archaic literary chronology', *Journal of Hellenic Studies*, 75 (1955), 54, and 'Herodotus as chronographer', 115, 115n.

[11] Den Boer, 'Political propaganda', 164, argued that 'it would be far from absurd to put the average distance between the birth of a father and his son in Sparta at 40 years'. He argued that late marriage and infant mortality were common in Sparta. Even so, and one might dispute his first point, as we have seen in Chapter IV, only a very small proportion of dynasties have had regnal generations exceeding forty years. Even for consobrinal succession a 39- or 40-year average is unlikely to have prevailed over the long run. As with extended father/son succession, many contingencies would be operating to reduce the likelihood.

[12] A similar proposal has been made by Miller, *Sicilian colony dates*, 174–5.

c. 500. Miller has argued that succession practices changed from consobrinal to primogenitural preference after the middle of the sixth century.[13] If so, subsequent successions fully illustrated the limitations of primogeniture in practice. It will already have been noticed that, at the very time the Spartan kinglists became historical, the succession was not lineal. The Eurypontid king was, at the closest, a second cousin to his predecessor, while in the Agid line Leonidas had succeeded a brother who had left no male issue.[14] Between *c.* 520 and 219 there were seventeen Agid kings in eleven generations and only eight times did son succeed father.[15] During approximately the same period there were thirteen rulers in ten generations in the Eurypontid line and only six sons succeeded their fathers.[16] In other words the succession patterns for the two dynasties resembled a system in which eligibility to the throne was broad, with some preference being given to sons, if they were available.

A final point of contrast between the two parts (pre-520 and post-520) of the Spartan kinglists is the complete absence of depositions noted for the earlier period. During the later period at least four Spartan rulers were expelled from the throne.[17]

Later historians and chronographers such as Diodorus Siculus and Eusebius provided exact dates for the early Spartan rulers. This dating was done on the basis of one ruler per generation in an effort to span the period between the Persian wars and alleged early synchronisms with Codrus of Athens and, later, with the Trojan war.[18] To do this it was necessary, as we have seen, to postulate a regnal generation of about forty years since the limited number of royal names available precluded the use of a shorter generational period.[19]

[13] Ibid. 175.

[14] Herodotus, VII. 204–5. This pattern, in which collateral succession and documented history coincide, has been more fully analysed, particularly for the Indian states, in Chapter II.

[15] Jones, *Sparta*, genealogical table opp. 189; Chrimes, *Ancient Sparta*, 500–1.

[16] Jones, *Sparta*, opp. 189. There is some doubt regarding the filiation and succession of the last rulers of the Eurypontid line. See Beloch, 'Eurypontidenhauses', 264–7. The number of generations assumes that Demaratus and Leotychides, probably cousins, were of the same generation. For a pedigree of the two dynasties, see also P. Poralla, *Prosopographie der Lakedaemonier bis auf die Zeit Alexanders der Grossen* (Breslau, 1913), 137–65, esp. 144–9, 157–65.

[17] H. W. Parke, 'The deposing of Spartan kings', *Classical Quarterly*, 39 (1945), 108–12.

[18] Den Boer, *Laconian studies*, 8–9.

[19] Even so, as we have noticed in Chapter I, some rulers were fabricated by later historians in order to provide the same number of generations in each ruling line.

Later historians found it easy to accept Herodotus' long regnal generations as well as inferring kinglists from his genealogies.[20]

It is not relevant to discuss here the many ways in which genealogical chronology has been used to date such 'events' in early Spartan history as the reforms of Lykourgos or the Messenian wars. Most of these attempts have assumed, whether explicitly or in the nature of their argumentation, that Herodotus' genealogies, at least up to three generations before Leonides and Leotychides, were kinglists.[21] Whether or not Herodotus believed this, such an assumption is not supported by his presentation of the data.[22] Herodotus relied on a number of sources for his information on the Spartan rulers, including informants in Sparta.[23] Pausanias, either by misinterpreting Herodotus, on whom he relied heavily, or by relying on other, post-Herodotean, sources for his information, became the first historians known to effect this metamorphosis.[24] Yet it is likely that Herodotus, in citing the genealogies of the two Spartan kings almost as *obiter dicta,* did so principally to emphasize their Heracleid ancestry. He traced both genealogies back to Heracles, although neither that legendary hero nor the next several names in the genealogies were ever considered to have been kings of Sparta at all.

It is easy to catalogue the possible chronological implications of the present interpretation of Herodotus' Spartan genealogies. It is more difficult to propose that any one of them is more likely than the others. Perhaps among the Spartans generations really meant reigns.[25] This would serve to reduce the time span covered by the lists by as much as half. Conversely, and more probably, Herodotus was passing along genealogical information that he had received from other sources. Whether he believed that these genealogies were, *pari passu,* complete kinglists is unknown. It is also irrelevant since

[20] For instance, W. G. Forrest, 'The date of the Lykourgan reforms', *Phoenix,* 16 (1963), 167n., in discussing Polydorus of the Agiad line, argued that 'he would be an exceptionally unlucky Spartan king not to be allowed a good 30 years'. See also ibid. 168.

[21] Den Boer, 'Political propaganda', 163; Huxley, *Early Sparta,* 20–1; Prakken, 'Herodotus and the Spartan kinglists', 462, 466, 470.

[22] Ibid. 462, 466, argued that Herodotus believed that his genealogies represented complete kinglists.

[23] For Herodotus' sources, see Jones, *Sparta,* 2; Den Boer, *Laconian studies,* 6–7, 13–14; Prakken, 'Herodotus', 464; Tigerstedt, *Legend of Sparta,* 20.

[24] For Pausanias' sources, see M. Broadhead, *Studies in Greek genealogy* (Leiden, 1968), 94; Huxley, *Early Sparta,* 19; F. Jacoby, *Apollodors Kronika* (Berlin, 1902), 128–37.

[25] As proposed by Broadbent, *Studies,* 96.

in any case they certainly could not have been. In fact, there is no reason to impute to Herodotus the *naïveté* exhibited by some of his successors. It is more likely that the later parts of his genealogies are accurate ascendant genealogies that can provide some generational structuring for Spartan history for about two or three centuries before his time. How many of the names in his genealogies were kings of Sparta and how many Spartan kings who succeeded collaterally (or became retrospectively collateral) were excluded is not known and, barring the discovery of some of the local histories of Sparta known to have been written, it is unknowable as well. Meanwhile it may be best to conceive of the names in Herodotus' genealogies as representing 'generations' or their temporal equivalent—generations in which more than one king may have ruled in each line. For instance, if the information in Pausanias actually represented another valid tradition for the Eurypontids, the six generations before 469 could be labelled Zeuxidamus/Anaxilaus; Anaxidamus/Leotychides; Archidamus/Hippocratides; Agesicles/——; Ariston/——; Demaratus/Leotychides.[26] Posed in these terms some of the chronological framework of proto-historic Spartan history can be preserved.

It is most important, however, to avoid the common error of equating ascendant genealogies with kinglists, with resulting extended father/son succession patterns. As we have seen in Chapter II these often seriously distort the perceived span of a polity. Recognizing that the genealogies of Herodotus were not, and probably never were intended to be, kinglists may permit a new approach to the study of the political development of ancient Sparta.[23]

[26] See Miller, *Sicilian colony dates*, 174–5, for a similar proposal. Herodotus specifically stated that the generational contemporaries of Agesicles and Ariston did not rule.

[27] I have excluded any discussion of the role of Lykourgos in the Spartan genealogies. This famous lawgiver was probably an invention rather than a historical figure. He fluctuated from the genealogy of one royal line to the other and his generational placement changed with changing circumstances as well. See esp. Jones, *Sparta*, 5–6; Den Boer, 'Political propaganda', 165; idem, *Laconian studies*, 12–13, 22; Tigerstedt, *Legend of Sparta*, 378.

Bibliography

INTRODUCTION

The following Bibliography includes many items not cited in the text. It is designed to serve primarily as a serviceable introduction to the wealth of material which addresses itself to the problems discussed in this work. By dividing it into African and non-African sections it is hoped to illustrate that he who wishes to adopt the comparative approach in the area of oral chronology will not lack available materials.

I MANUSCRIPT SOURCES

Public Record Office, London

T70 Series: Treasury Papers, African Companies.

Chancery Masters Exhibits: C113/34–36, Papers of James Phipps.

C.O. 96 Series: Gold Coast, Original Correspondence.

C.O. 267 Series: Sierra Leone, Original Correspondence.

Bodleian Library, Oxford University

Rawlinson MSS. C745–747: Royal African Company, Correspondence from the outforts to Cape Coast Castle, 1680–1699.

National Archives of Ghana/Accra

ADM 11/1 Series: Files 1–1856, Secretariat of Native Affairs files.

CSO Series: Colonial Secretary's Office files (continuation of ADM 11/1 Series, 1931–1940).

BF Series: Book File (continuation of CSO series, 1941–).

LBS 97–111: Land Boundary Settlement transcripts.

National Archives of Ghana/Cape Coast

RAO Series: Regional Administrative Officer, Central Region, files on Native Affairs.

Kobina Sekyi papers.

Balme Library, University of Ghana

Furley Collection of Portuguese, Dutch, and English records [in transcription and semi-translation].

Institute of African Studies, University of Ghana

IAS/AS: Ashanti Stool History Project histories.

II PRINTED SOURCES

African

ABRAHAM, D. P. 'The principality of Maungwe.' *NADA* 28 (1951), 59–83.

ADAMS, W. Y. 'Ethnohistory and the Islamic tradition in Africa.' *Ethnohistory*, 16 (1969), 277–88.

AGYEMAN, E. A. 'A note on the foundation of the kingdom of Gyaman.' *GNQ* 9 (1966), 36–9.

ALMEIDA TOPOR, HÉLÈNE D'. 'Rigueur historique et imprécision de la tradition orale.' *Bulletin de l'Institut Supérieur de Bénin*, 11 (Oct.–Nov. 1969), 46–54.

ALPERS, E. A. 'Dynasties of the Mutapa-Rozwi complex.' *JAH* 11 (1970), 203–20.

AMISSAH, JOSEPH BROOKMAN. 'Introducing *Description and historical account of the golden Kingdom of Guinea* of Pieter de Marees.' *THSG* 9 (1968), 121–7.

APTER, DAVID. *Ghana in transition*. New York, 1963.

ARHIN, KWAME. 'Diffuse authority among the coastal Fanti.' *GNQ* 9 (1966), 66–70.

AVERY, GRETA M. K. 'African oral traditions.' *Africana Research Bulletin* [Institute of African Studies, Fourah Bay College], 1/1 (Oct. 1970), 17–36.

AYISI, ERIC O. 'Academicism in social anthropology.' *Research Review* [Institute of African Studies, Legon], 5/1 (1968), 32–49.

AZAN, H. 'Notice sur le Oualo.' *Revue Maritime et Coloniale*, 9 (1863), 394–422, 607–55; 10 (1864), 327–60, 466–98.

AZEVEDO, WARREN L. D'. 'Uses of the past in Gola discourse.' *JAH* 3 (1962), 11–34.

BARBOT, JEAN. *A description of the coasts of North and South-Guinea; and of Ethiopia inferior, vulgarly Angola; being a new and accurate account of the western maritime countries of Africa.* London, 1746.

BARNES, J. A. 'The collection of genealogies.' *Rhodes–Livingstone Journal*, 5 (1947), 48–55.

—— 'Genealogies' in A. L. Epstein (ed.), *The craft of social anthropology*. London, 1967, 101–28.

BARROS, JOÃO DE, and DIOGO DO COUTO. *Da Asia de João de Barros e Diogo do Couto*. 12 pts. in 21 vols. Lisbon, 1777–99.

BARRY, BOUBACAR. *Le Royaume du Waalo: le Sénégal avant la conquête*. Paris, 1972.

BEATTIE, JOHN. *The Nyoro state*. London, 1971.

BECKINGHAM, C. F., and G. W. B. HUNTINGFORD (eds.). *Some records of Ethiopia, 1593–1646*. London, 1954.

BEECHAM, JOHN. *Ashantee and the Gold Coast: being a sketch of the history, social state and superstitions of the inhabitants of those countries; with a notice of the state and prospects of Christianity among them*. London 1841.

BEIDELMAN, THOMAS. 'Kaguru time reckoning: an aspect of the cosmology of an east African people.' *Southwestern Journal of Anthropology*, 19 (1963), 9–20.

BERGER, RUTH. 'Oral traditions in Karagwe.' Paper read to East African Institute of Social Research, Makerere, June 1963.

BIKUNYA, PETERO. *Ky'Abakama ba Bunyoro*. London, 1927.

BIRMINGHAM, DAVID B. 'The date and significance of the Imbangala invasion of Angola.' *JAH* 6 (1965), 143–52.

—— 'A note on the kingdom of Fetu.' *GNQ* 9 (1966), 30–3.

BOAHEN, A. ADU. 'Asante and Fante, A.D. 1000–1800' in J. F. A. Ajayi and Ian Espie, *A thousand years of West African history*. Ibadan, 1965, 160–85.

—— 'Fante diplomacy in the eighteenth century. Paper presented at the Conference on the Foreign Relations of African States, University of Bristol, 4–6 Apr. 1973.

—— 'Juaben and Kumasi relations in the nineteenth century.' *Report* of the First Conference of the Ashanti Research Project held 17–20 May 1963, pp. 25–33. Legon, 1964.

BOHANNAN, LAURA. 'A genealogical charter.' *Africa*, 22 (1952), 301–15.

BOHANNAN, PAUL. 'Concepts of time among the Tiv of Nigeria.' *Southwestern Journal of Anthropology*, 9 (1953), 251–62.

BOSMAN, WILLEM. *A new and accurate description of the coast of Guinea divided into the Gold, the Slave and the Ivory Coasts containing a geographical, political and natural history of the kingdoms and countries: with a particular account of the rise, progress and perfect condition of all the European settlements upon that coast; and the just measures for improving the several branches of the Guinea trade*. London, 1705.

BOULÈGUE, JEAN. 'Le Sénégambie du milieu du XVe siècle au début du XVIIe siècle.' Thèse du 3e cycle, Université de Paris, 1969.

BOURDILLON, M. F. C. 'The manipulation of myth in a Tavara chiefdom.' *Africa*, 42 (1972), 112–21.

BOWDICH, THOMAS EDWARD. *Mission from Cape Coast Castle to Ashantee, with a statistical account of that kingdom and geographical notices of other parts of the interior of Africa.* London, 1819.

BOWLER, LOUIS P. *Gold Coast palaver: life on the Gold Coast.* London, 1911.

BRADBURY, R. E. 'Chronological problems in the study of Benin history.' *JHSN* I/4 (1959), 263–87.

BREUTZ, P. L. *Die Stamme van die Distrik Ventersdorp* (DNA Ethnological Pubs. 31) Pretoria, 1954.

—— *The tribes of the Mafeking district* (DNA Ethnological Pubs. 32). Pretoria, 1955.

—— *The tribes of the Marico district* (DNA Ethnological Pubs. 30). Pretoria, 1953.

—— 'Tswana tribal governments today.' *Sociologus*, 8 (1958), 140–54.

BRIGAUD, FÉLIX. *Histoire traditionnelle du Sénégal.* Saint-Louis, 1962.

BROWN, EMMANUEL J. P. *Gold Coast and Asianti reader.* 2 vols. London, 1929.

BRYANT, ALFRED T. *Olden times in Zululand and Natal containing earlier political history of the Eastern-Nguni clans.* London, 1929.

BUSIA, KOFI ABREHA. *The position of the chief in the modern political system of Ashanti. A study of the influence of contemporary social changes on Ashanti political institutions.* London, 1951.

CHRISTALLER, J. G. *A dictionary of the Asante and Fante language called Tshi (Twi).* Basel, 1933.

CHRISTENSEN, JAMES BOYD. *Double descent among the Fanti.* New Haven, Conn., 1954.

CISSOKO, SÉKÉNÉ MODY. 'Civilisation Wolof-Sérère.' *Présence Africaine*, 62 (1967), 121–46.

COHEN, DAVID W. *The historical tradition of Busoga: Mukama and Kintu.* Oxford, 1972.

—— 'A survey of interlacustrine chronology.' *JAH* 11 (1970), 177–201.

COHEN, RONALD. 'The Bornu king lists' in J. Butler (ed.), *Boston*

University papers on Africa, II, *African History*. Boston, Mass., 1965, 39–83.

COHEN, RONALD. 'The dynamics of feudalism in Bornu' in ibid. 87–105.

COIFMAN, VICTORIA B. 'History of the Wolof state of Jolof until 1860, including comparative data from the Wolof state of Walo.' Ph.D. thesis, University of Wisconsin, 1970.

CORY, HANS. *History of the Bukoba district*. Dar-es-Salaam, 1958.

CROOKS, JOHN J. *Records relating to the Gold Coast settlements from 1750 to 1874*. Dublin, 1923.

CROWDER, MICHAEL. 'Genealogy and the Tiv.' *Nigeria Magazine*, 63 (1959), 282–301.

CRUIKSHANK, BRODIE. *Eighteen years on the Gold Coast of Africa, including an account of the native tribes and their intercourse with the Europeans*. 2 vols. London, 1853.

CUNNISON, IAN. 'History and genealogies in a conquest state.' *American Anthropologist*, 59 (1957), 20–31.

—— *History on the Luapula. An essay on the historical notions of a central African tribe* (Rhodes–Livingstone Papers, 21). Cape Town, 1951.

CURTIN, PHILIP D. 'Field techniques for collecting and processing oral data.' *JAH* 9 (1968), 367–85.

CZEKANOWSKI, JAN. *Forschungen im Nil-Kongo-Zwischengebiet*. 5 vols. Leipzig, 1917–27.

DAAKU, K. Y. *Trade and politics on the Gold Coast, 1600–1720: a study of African reaction to European trade*. Oxford, 1970.

—— and ALBERT VAN DANTZIG. 'An annotated Dutch map of 1629.' *GNQ* 9 (1966), 14–16.

DAENDELS, HERMAN WILLEM. *Journal and correspondence, pt. I, November 1815 to January 1817*. Legon, 1964.

DATTA, ANSU K., and R. PORTER. 'The *asafo* system in historical perspective.' *JAH* 12 (1971), 279–97.

DAVENANT, CHARLES (ed. Charles Whitworth). *The political and commercial works of that celebrated writer Charles D'Avenant, LL.D., relating to the trade and revenue of England, the plantation trade, the East-India trade, and African trade*. 5 vols. London, 1771.

DERSCHEID, J. M. 'The Bakama of Bunyoro.' *UJ* 2 (1934), 252–3.

DOUGAH, JOHN. *Wa and its people*. Legon, 1966.

DUNBAR, A. R. *A history of Bunyoro-Kitara*. Nairobi, 1965.

DUPUIS, JOSEPH. *Journal of a residence in Ashantee*. London, 1824.

EGHAREVBA, JACOB U. *A short history of Benin.* Ibadan, 1960.

EVANS-PRITCHARD, EDWARD E. *The Nuer.* Oxford, 1940.

FAGAN, BRIAN. *Southern Africa.* London, 1965.

FAGE, JOHN D. 'Reflections on the early history of the Mossi-Dagomba group of states' in J. Vansina, R. Mauny, and L.-V. Thomas (eds.), *The historian in tropical Africa: studies presented and discussed at the fourth International African Seminar at the University of Dakar, Senegal, 1961.* London, 1964, pp. 177–89.

FEINBERG, HARVEY M. 'Elmina, Ghana: a history of its development and relationship with the Dutch in the eighteenth century.' Ph.D. thesis, Boston University, 1969.

—— 'An incident in Elmina–Dutch relations, the Gold Coast (Ghana), 1739–40.' *AHS* 3 (1970), 359–72.

—— 'Who are the Elmina?' *GNQ* 11 (1970), 20–6.

FERGUSON, PHYLLIS, and IVOR WILKS. 'Chiefs, constitutions and the British in northern Ghana' in M. Crowder and Obaro Ikime (eds.), *West African chiefs: their changing status under colonial rule and independence.* Ile-Ife, 1970, 325–69.

FIELD, MARGARET JOYCE. *Akim-Kotoku; an oman of the Gold Coast. London*, 1948.

FINNEGAN, RUTH, 'A note on oral tradition and historical evidence.' *History and Theory*, 9 (1970), 195–201.

FISHER, RUTH. *Twilight tales of the black Baganda.* 2nd ed. London, 1970.

FLIGHT, COLIN. 'The chronology of the kings and queenmothers of Bono-Manso: a revaluation of the evidence.' *JAH* 11 (1970), 259–67.

FORD, J., and R. DE Z. HALL. 'The history of Karagwe (Bukoba district).' *Tanganyika Notes and Records*, 24 (1947), 3–24.

FORTES, MEYER. 'Kinship and marriage among the Ashanti' in A. R. Radcliffe-Brown and Daryll Forde (eds.), *African systems of kinship and marriage.* London, 1950, 252–84.

FYNN, JOHN KERSON. 'The reign and times of Kusi Obodum.' *THSG* 8 (1965), 24–32.

GIBBONS, PETER C. 'King-lists and chronology: a note on work in progress.' *GNQ* 8 (1966), 25.

GOLD COAST (COLONY), CENSUS DEPT. *Report of census of population, 1948.* Accra, 1950.

GOODY, JACK. *The ethnography of the Northern Territories of the Gold Coast, west of the White Volta.* London, 1954.

—— Introduction in idem and Kwame Arhin (eds.), *Ashanti and the*

North-West, Supplement 1 to *Research Review* [Institute of African Studies, Legon] (1965), 1–110.

—— 'Sideways or downwards?: lateral and vertical succession, inheritance, and descent in Africa and Eurasia.' *Man*, N.S. 5 (1970), 627–38.

—— 'Strategies of heirship.' *Comparative Studies in Society and History*, 15 (1973), 3–20.

—— (ed.). *Literacy in Traditional Societies*. Cambridge, 1968.

—— (ed.). *Succession to high office*. Cambridge, 1966.

GORJU, JULIEN. *Entre le Victoria, l'Albert et l'Edouard. Ethnographie de la partie anglaise du Vicariat de l'Uganda*. Rennes, 1920.

GÖRÖG, VERONIKA. 'L'Origine de l'inégalité des races: étude de trente-sept contes africaines.' *Cahiers d'Études Africaines*, 8 (1968), 290–309.

GRAFT JOHNSON, J. C. DE. 'The Fanti Asafu.' *Africa*, 5 (1932), 307–22.

GRAY, RICHARD. 'Annular eclipse maps.' *JAH* 9 (1968), 147–57.

—— 'Eclipse maps.' *JAH* 6 (1965), 251–62.

HADDON, E. B. 'Kibuka.' *UJ* 21 (1957), 114–19.

HAGAN, GEORGE P. 'Ashanti bureaucracy: a study of the growth of centralized administration in Ashanti from the time of Osei Tutu to the time of Osei Tutu Kwamina Esibe Bonsu.' *THSG* 12 (1971), 43–62.

HAKLUYT, RICHARD. *Principal navigations, voyages, traffiques and discoveries of the English nation, made by sea or overland to the remote and farthest distant quarters of the earth at any time within the compasse of these 1600 years*. 8 vols. London, 1910.

HAMMOND-TOOKE, W. D. 'Segmentation and fission in Cape Nguni political units. *Africa*, 35 (1965), 151–66.

HARDING, R. W. *The dispute over the obiship of Onitsha: report of the enquiry*. Enugu, 1963.

HAUENSTEIN ALFRED. *Les Hanya: description d'un groupe ethnique bantou de l'Angola*. Wiesbaden, 1967.

HAYFORD, J. E. CASELY. *Gold Coast native institutions*. London, 1903.

HENDERSON, RICHARD N. *The king in every man*. New Haven, Conn., 1972.

HENIGE, D. P. 'K.W.s Nyoro kinglist list: oral tradition or applied research?' Paper presented at 15th Annual Meeting of African Studies Association, Philadelphia, Pa., 8–11 November, 1972.

—— 'Kingship in Elmina before 1869: a study in "feedback" and the traditional idealization of the past.' *Cahiers d'Études Africaines*, 14 (1974), in press.

—— 'The problem of feedback in oral tradition: four examples from the Fante coastlands.' *JAH* 14 (1973), 223–35.

HORTON, ROBIN. 'African traditional thought and western science.' *Africa*, 37 (1967), 50–71, 155–87.

HUTTON, WILLIAM. *A voyage to Africa, including a narrative of an embassy to one of the interior kingdoms in the year 1820; with remarks on the course and terminus of the Niger and other principal rivers in that country*. London, 1821.

ISERT, P. E. *Voyages en Guinée et dans les îles Caraïbes en Amérique*. Paris, 1793.

ISICHEI, ELIZABETH. 'Historical change in an Ibo polity: Asaba to 1885.' *JAH* 10 (1969), 421–38.

IZARD, MICHEL. *Introduction à l'histoire des royaumes mossi*. 2 vols. Paris, 1970.

JACOBS, Alan H. 'The chronology of the pastoral Maasai.' *Hadith*, 1 (1968), 10–31.

JEEKEL, J. *Onze bezittingen op de kust van Guinea*. Amsterdam, 1869.

JEFFREYS, M. D. W. 'Further historical notes on the Ntem.' *JHSN* 2/3 (1962), 384–92.

—— 'Some historical notes on the Ntem.' *JHSN* 2/2 (1961) 260–76.

JONES, D. H. 'Problems of African chronology.' *JAH* 11 (1970), 161–76.

JONES, G. I. 'Time and oral tradition, with special reference to eastern Nigeria.' *JAH* 6 (1965), 152–60.

K. W. [TITO GABAFUSA WINYI IV.] 'The kings of Bunyoro-Kitara.' *UJ* 3 (1935), 155–60; 4 (1936), 75–83; 5 (1937), 53–69.

KAGAME, ALEXIS. *Un Abrégé de l'ethno-histoire du Rwanda*. Butare, 1972.

—— *La Notion de la génération appliquée à la généalogie dynastique et à l'histoire du Rwanda des Xe–XIe siècles à nos jours*. Brussels, 1959.

KAGGWA, APOLO (tr. and ed. M. S. M. Kiwanuka). *The kings of Buganda*. Nairobi, 1971.

KARUGIRE, SAMWIRI R. *A history of the kingdom of Nkore*. Oxford, 1971.

—— 'Succession wars in the pre-colonial kingdom of Nkore.' *Proceedings of the University of East Africa Social Science Council*, 1 (1969), 52–69.

KATATE, ALOYSIUS G. 'Abagabe b'Ankole.' Typescript in Center for Research Libraries, Chicago, Ill.

KATOKE, I. K. *The making of the Karagwe kingdom.* Dar-es-Salaam, 1970.

KENYO, E. ALADEMOMI. *Yoruba natural rulers and their origin.* Ibadan, 1964.

KERR, ALASTAIR J. *The native law of succession in South Africa.* London, 1961.

KESSE-ADU, K. *The politics of political detention.* Accra, 1971.

KIWANUKA, M. S. M. 'Sir Apolo Kaggwa and the pre-colonial history of Buganda.' *UJ* 30 (1966), 137–52.

KI-ZERBO, JOSEPH. 'The oral tradition as a source of African history.' *Diogenes*, 67 (1969), 110–24.

KYEREMATEN A. A. Y. *The panoply of Ghana.* London, 1964.

—— 'The royal stools of Ashanti.' *Africa*, 39 (1969), 1–9.

LAMPHEAR, JOHN and JOHN B. WEBSTER. 'The Jie–Acholi war: oral evidence from two sides of the battle front.' *UJ* 35 (1971), 23–42.

LAW, ROBIN C. C. 'The dynastic chronology of Lagos.' *Lagos Notes and Records*, 2 (Dec. 1968), 46–54.

—— 'The Oyo empire: the history of a Yoruba state, principally in the period *c.* 1600 to *c.* 1836.' Ph.D. thesis, University of Birmingham, 1971.

—— 'The heritage of Oduduwa: traditional history and political propaganda among the Yoruba', *JAH*, 14 (1973), 207–22.

LAWRENCE, A. W. *Trade castles and forts of West Africa.* London, 1963.

LAYA, DIOULDE. 'Tradition orale et recherche historique en Afrique: méthodes, réalisations, perspectives.' *Cahiers d'Histoire Mondiale*, 12 (1970), 560–87.

LEGASSICK, MARTIN. 'The Sotho-Tswana peoples before 1800' in Leonard Thompson (ed.), *African societies in southern Africa.* London, 1969, 86–125.

LEVTZION, NEHEMIA. *Muslims and chiefs in West Africa: a study of Islam in the middle Volta region in the pre-colonial period.* Oxford, 1968.

LEWIS, I. M. 'Historical aspects of genealogies in northern Somali social structure.' *JAH* 3 (1962), 35–48.

—— 'Literacy in a nomadic society: the Somali case' in Jack Goody (ed), *Literacy in traditional societies.* Cambridge, 1968, 265–76.

LUBOGO, Y. K. *A history of Busoga*. Kampala, 1960.

MANOUKIAN, M. *The Akan and Ga-Adangme peoples*. London, 1950.

MAREES, PIETER DE (ed. S.-P. L'Honoré Naber). *Beschryvinghe ende historische verhael van het Gout Koninckrijck van Guinea*. The Hague, 1912.

MARKS, SHULA. 'The traditions of the Natal "Nguni": a second look at the work of A. T. Bryant' in Leonard Thompson (ed.), *African societies in southern Africa*. London, 1969, 126–44.

MATE KOLE, NENE AZU. 'The historical background of Krobo customs.' *Transactions of the Gold Coast and Togoland Historical Society*, 1/4 (1955), 133–40.

MATSON, J. N. *A digest of the minutes of the Ashanti Confederacy Council, 1935–49, and a revised edition of Warrington's notes on Ashanti custom*. Cape Coast, n.d.

—— 'The French at Amoku.' *Transactions of the Gold Coast and Togoland Historical Society*, I/1 (1955), 47–60.

MAYER, IONA. 'From kinship to common descent: four-generation genealogies among the Gusii.' *Africa*, 35 (1965), 366–84.

MBITI, JOHN S. *African religions and philosophy*. London, 1969.

MELDON, J. A. 'Notes on the Bahima of Ankole.' *Journal of the African Society*, 6 (1906/7), 136–53, 234–49.

MEREDITH, HENRY. *An account of the Gold Coast of Africa with a brief history of the African Company*. London, 1812.

METCALFE, GEORGE E. (ed.). *Great Britain and Ghana: documents of Ghana history, 1807–1957*. London, 1964.

MEYEROWITZ, EVA K. L. *The Akan of Ghana: their traditional beliefs*. London, 1958.

—— *Akan traditions of origin*. London, 1952.

MILLER, JOSEPH C. 'The Imbangala and the chronology of early central Africa.' *JAH* 13 (1972), 549–74.

—— 'Kings and kinsmen: the Imbangala impact on the Mbundu of Angola.' Ph.D. thesis, University of Wisconsin, 1972.

MONTEIL, VINCENT. 'Le Dyolof et al-Bouri Ndiaye. *BIFAN* 28 (1966), 595–636.

MORRIS, H. F. *A history of Ankole*. Kampala, 1962.

MORTON, R. F. 'The Shungwaya myth of Miji Kenda origins: a problem of nineteenth century Kenya coastal history.' *IJAHS* 5 (1972), 397–423.

MORTON-WILLIAMS, PETER. 'An outline of the cosmological and

cult organization of the Oyo Yoruba.' *Africa*, 34 (1964), 243–61.

MOTA AVELINO TEIXEIRA DA. 'Un Document nouveau pour l'histoire des Peuls au Sénégal pendant les XVe et XVIe siècles.' *Boletim Cultural da Guiné Portuguesa*, 96 (Oct. 1969), 781–860.

—— 'D. João Bemoim e a expedição Portuguesa ao Senegal em 1489.' *Boletim Cultural da Guiné Portuguesa*, 101 (1971), 63–112.

MÜLLER, WILHELM JOHANN. *Die africanische auf der guineischen Gold-Cust gelegene Landschafft Fetu*. Hamburg, 1673.

MURIUKI, GODFREY. 'Chronology of the Kikuyu.' *Hadith*, 3 (1971), 16–27.

NENQUIN, JACQUES. 'Notes on some early pottery cultures in northern Katanga.' *JAH* 4 (1963), 19–32.

NØRREGÅRD, GEORG (tr. S. Mammen). *Danish settlements in West Africa, 1658–1850*. Boston, Mass., 1966.

N'SOUGAN AGBLEMAGNON, FÉLIX. 'Du temps dans la culture "Ewe".' *Présence Africaine*, 14–15 (1957), 222–32.

NYAKATURA, JOHN A. 'Abakama ba Bunyoro-Kitara.' Typescript in Center for Research Libraries, Chicago, Ill.

OGEDENGBE, KINGSLEY O. 'The Aboh kingdom of the lower Niger, *c.* 1650 to 1900.' Ph.D. thesis, University of Wisconsin, 1971.

OGILBY, JOHN. *Africa, being an accurate description of the regions of Egypt, Barbary, Libya, and Billedulgerid*. London, 1670.

OLIVER, ROLAND. 'Ancient capital sites of Ankole.' *UJ* 23 (1959), 51–63.

—— 'The traditional histories of Buganda, Bunyoro and Nkole.' *JRAI* 85 (1955), 111–17.

OPPONG, C. 'A note on a royal genealogy — Dagomba.' *Research Review* [Institute of African Studies, University of Ghana], 3 (1966), 71–4.

ORENT, AMNON. 'Refocusing on the history of Kafa prior to 1897: a discussion of political processes.' *AHS* 3 (1970), 263–93.

OTHILY, A. 'Tradition orale et structure sociale.' *Documents du Centre des Recherches Kara* (1968), 126–34.

PALMER, HERBERT R. *Bornu Sahara and Sudan*. London, 1936.

—— (tr.). 'The Kano Chronicle.' *JRAI* 38 (1908), 58–98.

PEREIRA, DUARTE PACHECO (ed. Damião Peres). *Esmeraldo de Situ Orbis*. Lisbon, 1954.

PERSON, YVES-DANIEL. 'Classes d'âge et chronologie.' *Latitudes*, sp. no. (1963), 68–83.

PINA, RUI DE (ed. Alberto Martins de Carvalho). *Crónica de el-Rei D. João II*. Coimbra, 1950.

POGUCKI, R. J. H. *Report on land tenure in Adangbe customary law*. Accra, 1955.

PORTER, R. 'The Cape Coast conflict of 1803: a crisis in relations between the African and European communities.' *THSG* 11 (1970), 29–82.

POSNANSKY, MERRICK. 'Bantu genesis: archaeological reflexions.' *JAH* 9 (1968), 1–11.

PRIESTLEY, MARGARET. 'Philip Quaque of Cape Coast' in P. D. Curtin (ed.), *Africa remembered*. Madison, Wis., 1967, 99–139.

—— *West African trade and coast society. A family study*. London, 1969.

—— and IVOR WILKS. 'The Ashanti kings in the eighteenth century: a revised chronology.' *JAH* 1 (1960), 83–96.

PTÉRIDÈS PIERRE. 'Étiologie et finalité des généalogies éthiopiennes.' *Proceedings of the 3rd International Congress of Ethiopian Studies*. Addis Ababa, 1966, 1. 319–29.

RAMSEYER, FRITZ, and JOHANNES KÜHNE. *Four years in Ashantee*. London, 1875.

RATTRAY, ROBERT SUTHERLAND. *Ashanti law and constitution*. Oxford, 1929.

RAYBAUD, L.-P. 'L'Administration du Sénégal de 1781 à 1784.' *Annales Africaines* (1968), 114–73.

REINDORF, CARL CHRISTIAN. *The history of the Gold Coast and Asante*. 2nd rev. ed. Accra, 1966.

RICHARDS, AUDREY I. 'African kings and their royal relatives.' *JRAI* (1961), 135–50.

ROBERTS, ANDREW D. 'Chronology of the Bemba (N. E. Zambia).' *JAH* 11 (1970), 221–40.

—— *Recording East Africa's Past*. Nairobi, 1968.

ROBERTSON, A. F. 'Histories and political opposition in Ahafo, Ghana.' *Africa*, 43 (1973), 41–58.

ROSCOE, JOHN. *The Baganda: an account of their native customs and beliefs*. London, 1911.

—— *The Bakitara or Banyoro*. London, 1923.

ROUSSEAU, R. 'Le Sénégal d'autrefois: une étude sur le Oualo.' *Bulletin de la Comité des Études Historiques et Scientifiques d'Afrique Occidentale Française* (1929), 133–211.

SABERWAL, SATISH. 'The oral tradition, periodization, and political systems.' *Canadian Journal of African Studies*, 1 (1967), 155–62.

SAMB, AMAR. 'Influence de l'Islam sur la littérature "wolof".' *BIFAN* 30 (1968), 628–41.

SARBAH, JOHN MENSAH. *Fanti customary law. A brief introduction to the principles of the native laws and customs of the Fanti and Akan districts of the Gold Coast with a report of some cases thereon decided in the law courts*. 2nd ed. London, 1968.

—— *Fanti national constitution. A short treatise on the constitution and government of the Fanti, Asanti, and other Akan tribes of West Africa, together with a brief account of the discovery of the Gold Coast by Portuguese navigators; a short narration of early English voyages; and a study of the rise of British Gold Coast jurisdiction, etc. etc.* London, 1906.

SAYERS, E. F. 'The funeral of a Koranko chief.' *Sierra Leone Studies*, 7 (1925), 19–28.

SCHAPERA, ISAAC. 'Kinship and politics in Tswana history.' *JRAI* 93 (1963), 159–73.

SHELTON, AUSTIN J. 'Onojo Ogboni: problems of identification and historicity in the oral traditions of the Igala and northern Nsukka Igbo of Nigeria.' *Journal of American Folklore*, 81 (1968), 243–57.

SMITH, H. F. C. 'The dynastic chronology of Fulani Zaria.' *JHSN* 2 (1961), 277–85.

SMITH, PIERRE. 'La forge de l'intelligence.' *L'Homme*, 10 (1970), 5–21.

SMITH, ROBERT S. *Kingdoms of the Yoruba*. London, 1969.

SMITH, WILLIAM. *A new voyage to Guinea*. London, 1745.

SOUTHWOLD, MARTIN. 'The history of a history: royal succession in Buganda' in I. M. Lewis (ed.), *History and social anthropology*. London, 1968, 127–51.

SYKES, J. 'The eclipse at Biharwe.' *UJ* 23 (1959), 44–50.

TAYLOR, BRIAN K. *The western lacustrine Bantu*. London, 1962.

TEGNAEUS, HARRY. *Le Héros civilisateur. Contribution à l'étude ethnologique de la religion et de la sociologie Africaines*. Uppsala, 1950.

THOMAS, F. M. *Historical notes on the Bisa tribe, Northern Rhodesia* (Rhodes–Livingstone Communication, 8), Lusaka, 1958.

THOMAS, H. B., and ROBERT SCOTT. *Uganda*. London, 1935.

THOMPSON, THOMAS. *An account of two missionary voyages by*

appointment of the Society for the Propagation of the Faith in Foreign Parts, the one to New Jersey in North America, the other from America to the Coast of Guiney. London, 1758, facsimile report, London, 1937.

TORDAY, EMIL. *Notes ethnographiques sur les peuples communément appelés Bakuba ainsi que les peuplades apparantées—les Bushongo.* Brussels, 1911.

TORDOFF, WILLIAM. 'The Ashanti Confederacy.' *JAH* 3 (1962), 399–417.

—— *Ashanti under the Prempehs, 1888–1935.* London, 1965.

VAN DANTZIG, ALBERT, and BARBARA PRIDDY. *A short history the forts and castles of Ghana.* Accra, 1971.

VAN DER MERWE, NIKOLAAS J., and R. T. K. SCULLY. 'The Phalaborwa story: archeological and ethnographical investigation of a South African Iron Age group.' *World Archaeology*, 3 (1971), 178–96.

VANSINA, JAN. *L'Évolution du royaume Rwanda des origines à 1900.* Brussels, 1962.

—— 'The foundation of the kingdom of Kasanje.' *JAH* 4 (1963), 355–74.

—— *Geschiedenis van de Kuba van ongeveer 1500 tot 1904.* Tervuren, 1963.

—— *Kingdoms of the Savanna.* Madison, Wis., 1966.

—— 'Note sur la chronologie du Burundi ancien.' *Bulletin des Séances de l'Académie royale des sciences d'Outre-Mer*, N.S. 13 (1967), 433–42.

—— 'Once upon a time: oral traditions as history in Africa.' *Daedalus* (Spring 1971), 442–68.

—— *Oral Tradition.* Chicago, Ill., 1965.

—— 'The use of oral tradition in African culture history' in Creighton Gabel and Norman R. Bennett (eds.), *Reconstructing African Culture History.* Boston, Mass., 1967, 55–82.

VIDAL, CLAUDINE. 'Enquête sur le Rwanda traditionnel: conscience historique et traditions orales.' *Cahiers d'Études Africaines*, 11 (1971), 526–37.

WADE, AMADOU (tr. V. Monteil). 'Chronique du Wâlo sénégalais (1186?–1855).' *BIFAN* 26 (1964), 440–98.

WARREN, DENNIS M. 'A re-appraisal of Mrs. Eva Meyerowitz's work on the Brong.' *Research Review* [Institute of African Studies, Legon], 7/1 (1970), 53–76.

WEBSTER, JOHN B. 'Research methods in Teso.' *East Africa Journal*, 7 (1970), 30–8.

WILKS, IVOR. 'Aspects of bureaucratisation in Ashanti in the nineteenth century.' *JAH* 7 (1966), 215–33.

—— 'The growth of Akwapim state: a study in the control of evidence' in Vansina, *et al.* (eds.), *Historian in tropical Africa*, 396–408.

WILSON, MONICA. 'The early history of the Transkei and the Ciskei.' *African Studies*, 18 (1959), 167–79.

—— 'The Nguni people' in M. Wilson and L. M. Thompson (eds.), *Oxford history of South Africa, I, South Africa to 1870*, 75–130.

—— 'The Sotho, the Venda, and the Tsonga' in ibid. 131–82.

—— and LEONARD M. THOMPSON (eds.). *Oxford history of South Africa, I, South Africa to 1870*. London, 1969.

WILTGEN, RALPH M. *Gold Coast mission history, 1471–1880*. Techny, Ill., 1956.

WRIGLEY, C. C. 'Some thoughts on the Bacwezi.' *UJ* 21 (1957), 11–17.

Non-African and Comparative

ACHARYYA, N. N. *The history of mediaeval Assam*. Gauhati, 1966.

ADAMS, ARCHIBALD. *The western Rajputana states: Marwar, Sirohi and Jaisalmir*. London, 1899.

ALDERSON, ANTHONY D. *The structure of the Ottoman Dynasty*. Oxford, 1956.

ALLEN, DON CAMERON. *The legend of Noah: Renaissance rationalism in art, sciences, and letters*. Urbana, Ill., 1949.

ANDERSON, ALAN ORR. *Early sources of Scottish history, A.D. 500 to 1286*. 2 vols. London, 1922.

ANGLO, SYDNEY. 'The *British History* in Tudor propaganda.' *Bulletin of the John Rylands Library*, 44 (1961), 17–48.

—— 'The Annals of Tigernach' (ed. Whitley Stokes). *Revue Celtique*, 17 (1896), 6–33, 119–263, 337–420; 18 (1897), 9–59, 150–97, 267–303.

AROKIASWAMI, M. 'The Pallava Nayaks of Kōrtāmpet.' *JASB*, 4th Ser. 5 (1963), 27–36.

ASTON, W. G. 'Early Japanese history.' *Transactions of the Asiatic Society of Japan*, 16 (1889), 39–75.

AUBIN, JEAN. Références pour Lár médiévale.' *Journal Asiatique*, 243 (1955), 491–505.

BANERJEE, A. C. 'Expansion of the Rathor state in Marwar.' *Indian Historical Quarterly*, 28 (1952), 142–6.

BARRÈRE, DOROTHY B. 'Cosmogonic genealogies from Hawaii.' *JPS* 70 (1961), 419–28.

—— *The Kumuhonua legends: a study of late 19th century Hawaiian stories of creation and origins* (Pacific Anthropological Records, 3). Honolulu, 1969.

—— 'Revisions and adulterations in Polynesian creation myths' in Genevieve A. Highland *et al.* (eds.), *Polynesian culture history.* Honolulu, 1967, 105–17.

BARRON, OSWALD. 'The bonny house of Coulthart: an old story re-told.' *Ancestor*, 4 (Apr. 1903), 61–80.

BASHAM, A. L. 'The average length of the generation and the reign in ancient India' in idem, *Studies in Indian history and culture.* Calcutta, 1964, 80–8.

—— 'The Kashmir Chronicle' in C. H. Philips (ed.), *Historians of India, Pakistan and Ceylon.* London, 1961, 57–65.

—— 'Modern historians of ancient India' in ibid. 260–93.

BECHERT, HEINZ. 'Mother right and succession to the throne in Malabar and Ceylon.' *Ceylon Journal of Historical and Social Sciences*, 6 (1963), 25–40.

BEEVOR, R. J. 'Distinction and extinction.' *Genealogists' Magazine*, 4 (1928), 59–62.

BELOCH, JULIUS. 'Zur Geschichte des Eurypontidenhauses.' *Hermes*, 35 (1900), 252–64.

BENEDICT, W. C., and ELIZABETH VON VOIGTLANDER. 'Darius' Bisitun Inscription, Babylonian version, lines 1–29.' *JCS* 10 (1956), 1–10.

BENEDIKTSSON, JAKOB. 'Icelandic traditions of the Scyldings.' *Saga-Book of the Viking Society*, 15 (1957/61), 48–66.

BERG, C. C. 'Javanese historiography: a synopsis of its evolution' in D. G. E. Hall (ed.), *Historians of South East Asia.* London, 1961, 12–23.

—— 'The Javanese picture of the past' in Soejatmoko *et al.* (eds.), *An introduction to Indonesian historiography.* Ithaca, N.Y., 1965, 87–117.

BEST, ELSDON. *The Maori school of learning* (Dominion Museum Monograph, 6). Wellington, 1923.

—— *Tuhoe: the children of the mist*. 2 vols. New Plymouth, 1925.

BHANDARKAR, D. R. 'The dates for the early princes of the present Jodhpur family.' *Indian Antiquary*, 40 (1911), 301.

—— 'Bithu inscription of Siha Raṭhoḍ.' *Indian Antiquary*, 40 (1911), 81–3.

BHARGAVA, VISHESHWAR SARUP. *Marwar and the Mughal Emperors* (*A.D. 1526–1748*). Delhi, 1966.

BINCHY, DANIEL. 'The passing of the old order.' *Proceedings of Congress of Celtic Studies* held at Dublin 6–10 July 1959 (Dublin, 1962), 119–32.

BLACK, J. B. 'Boece's *Scotorum Historiae*' in University of Aberdeen, *Quatercentury of the death of Hector Boece, first principal of the university*. Aberdeen, 1937, 30–53.

BORCHARDT, FRANK L. *German antiquity in Renaissance myth*. Baltimore, Md., 1971.

BORCHARDT, LUDWIG. *Die Mittel zur zeitlichen Festlegung von Punkten der ägyptischen Geschichte und ihre Anwendung*. Cairo, 1935.

—— 'Ein Stammbaum memphitischer Priester.' *Sitzungberichten der Preussische Akademie der Wissenschaften*, Phil.-hist.Kl. 24 (1932), 618–22.

BOSE, NEMAR S. *History of the Candellas of Jejakabhukti*. Calcutta, 1956.

BOSWORTH, C. E. 'The heritage of rulership in early Islamic Iran and the search for dynastic connections with the past.' *Iran*, 11 (1973), 51–62.

BRIGGS, LAWRENCE P. *The ancient Khmer empire*. Philadelphia, Pa., 1951.

BRINKMAN, JOHN A., review of C. L. WOOLLEY, *Ur: the Kassite period and the period of the Assyrian kings*. *Orientalia*, N.S. 38 (1969), 310–48.

BROADHEAD, MOLLY. *Studies in Greek genealogy*. Leiden, 1968.

BROMWICH, RACHEL. 'The character of early Welsh tradition' in N. K. Chadwick (ed.), *Studies in early British history*. Cambridge, 1954, 83–136.

BUCHANAN, GEORGE. *The history of Scotland* (ed. ann. and cont. by James Aikman). 4 vols. Glasgow, 1827.

BUCK, PETER H. (TE RANGI HIROA). *Ethnology of Mangareva*. Honolulu, 1938.

BULL, LUDLOW. 'Ancient Egypt' in R. C. Dentan (ed.), *The idea of history in the ancient Near East*. New Haven, Conn., 1955, 3–33.

BURKE, J. BERNARD. *A genealogical history of dormant, abeyant, forfeited, and extinct peerages of the British Empire*. London, 1883.

—— *Vicissitudes of families*. 3rd Ser. 2nd ed. London, 1863.

BURN, A. R. 'Early Greek chronology.' *Journal of Hellenic Studies*, 69 (1950), 70–3.

BURNEY, HENRY. 'Discovery of Buddhist images with Devanágari inscriptions at Tagoung, the ancient capital of the Burmese Empire.' *Journal of the Asiatic Society of Bengal*, 5 (1836), 157–64.

BURROWS, EDWIN G. *Ethnology of Futuna*. Honolulu, 1936.

—— *Ethnology of Uvea (Wallis Island)*. Honolulu, 1937.

BYRNE, F. J. 'The rise of the Uí Néill and the High-Kingship of Ireland.' O'Donnell lecture, University College, Dublin, delivered 28 Nov. 1969.

—— 'Tribes and tribalism in early Ireland.' *Ériu*, 22 (1971), 128–66.

CADIÈRE, L. 'Tableau chronologique des dynasties Annamites.' *BEFEO* 5 (1905), 77–145.

CALLIOT, A.-C.-E. *Mythes, légendes et traditions des Polynésiens orientales*. Paris, 1914.

CALMETTE, JOSEPH-LOUISE-ANTOINE. *Le Réveil capétien*. Paris, 1948.

CAMPBELL, A. 'Saxo Grammaticus and Scandinavian historical tradition.' *Saga-Book of the Viking Society*, 13 (1946), 1–22.

CASSON, STANLEY. *Macedonia, Thrace and Illyria: their relations to Greece from the earliest times down to the time of Philip son of Amyntas*. London 1926.

Central Provinces District Gazetteers: Chanda. Allahabad, 1909.

—— *Chattisgarh Feudatory States*. Bombay, 1909.

CHADWICK, HECTOR MUNRO. *Early Scotland—The Picts, the Scots and the Welsh of southern Scotland*. Cambridge, 1949.

CHADWICK, NORA K. 'Pictish and Celtic marriage in early literary tradition.' *Scotch Gaelic Studies*, 8 (1955), 56–115.

—— 'The story of Macbeth.' *Scotch Gaelic Studies*, 6 (1947), 189–211; 7 (1951), 1–25.

CHAMCHIAN, MICHAEL. *History of Armenia* (ed. and tr. Johannes Avdall). 2 vols. Calcutta, 1827.

CHANDRA, ABINASH. 'Regal succession in the Māhabhārata.' *Journal of the Uttar Pradesh Historical Society*, 33–46.

CHRIMES, K. M. T. *Ancient Sparta*. Manchester, 1949.

COHN, BERNARD S. 'The pasts of an Indian village.' *Comparative Studies in Society and History*, 3 (1960/1), 241–9.

COLENSO, WILLIAM. 'On the Maori races of New Zealand.' *Transactions and Proceedings of the New Zealand Institute*, 1 (1868), 339–424.

COLLINGWOOD, R. G. *The idea of history*. London, 1946.

CORNELIUS, F. 'Chronology: Eine Erwiderung.' *JCS* 12 (1958), 101–4.

CULLEY, R. C. 'An approach to the problem of oral tradition.' *Vetus Testamentum*, 13 (1963), 113–25.

—— 'Oral tradition and historicity' in J. W. Wevers and D. B. Redford (eds.), *Studies on the Ancient Palestinian World*. Toronto, 1972, pp. 102–16.

DASCALAKIS, AP. *The Hellenism of the ancient Macedonians*. Thessalonika, 1965.

—— 'L'Origine de la maison royale de Macédonie et les légendes relatives de l'antiquité' in *Ancient Macedonia: papers read at the 1st International Symposium of the Institute for Balkan Studies. Thessaloniki, 26–9 Aug. 1968*, 155–61.

DAXCURANCI, MOVSES (tr. C. F. J. Dowsett). *The history of the Caucasian Albanians*. London, 1961.

DECHARME, PAUL. *La Critique des traditions religieuses chez les Grecs des origines au temps de Plutarche*. Paris, 1904 [repr. Brussels, 1966].

DEK, A. W. E. *Genealogie van het vorstenhuis Nassau*. Zalbommel, 1970.

DEN BOER, W. *Laconian studies*. Amsterdam, 1954.

—— 'Political propaganda in Greek chronology.' *Historia*, 5 (1956), 162–77.

DER NERSESSIAN, SIRARPIE. *The Armenians*. London, 1969.

DEVAHUTI, D. *Harsha: a political study*. Oxford, 1970.

Diccionari biografic. 3 vols. Barcelona, 1969.

DIKSHIT, D. P. 'The early Western Chalukyas' chronology reconsidered.' *Orissa Historical Research Journal*, 15 (1967), 1–27.

DILLON, MYLES, 'Lebor Gabála Érenn.' *Journal of the Royal Society of Antiquaries of Ireland*, 86 (1956), 62–72.

DONALDSON, GORDON. *Scottish kings*. London, 1967.

DUM, G. *Die spartanischen Königslisten*. Innsbruck, 1878.

DUTT, SABIMAL CHANDRA. 'Conception of sovereignty in a

mediaeval Rajput state.' *Calcutta Review*, 3rd Ser. 15 (Apr. 1925), 27–34.

EDZARD, D. O. *Die 'Zweite Zwischenzeit' Babyloniens*. Wiesbaden, 1957.

EGERTON, FRANK N., III. 'The longevity of the Patriarchs: a topic in the history of demography.' *Journal of the History of Ideas*, 27 (1966), 575–84

EMORY, KENNETH P. 'Development of a system of collecting, alphabetizing, and indexing Polynesian pedigrees. II. The Bishop Museum Polynesian pedigrees collection.' Paper presented at World Conference on Records and Genealogical Seminar, Salt Lake City, 5–8 Aug. 1969.

FAROUGHY, ABBAS. *Histoire du royaume de Hormuz depuis son origin jusqu'à son incorporation dans l'empire persan de séfévis en 1622*. Brussels, 1939.

FERGUSSON, JAMES. *The man behind Macbeth*. London, 1967.

FINKELSTEIN, J. J. The genealogy of the Hammurapi dynasty.' *JCS* 20 (1966), 95–118.

FINLEY, MOSES I. 'Myth, memory and history.' *History and Theory*, 4 (1965), 281–302.

—— 'The Trojan War.' *Journal of Hellenic Studies*, 84 (1964), 1–9.

FIRTH, RAYMOND. 'Succession to the chieftainship in Tikopia.' *Oceania*, 30 (1960), 161–80.

FISCHER, A. 'Kahtān.' *Encyclopaedia of Islam*, III. 628–30.

FISCHER, J. L. 'Genealogical space.' *Oceania*, 30 (1960), 181–7.

FLEET, J. F. 'The Kauthem plates of Vikrama-ditya V.' *Indian Antiquary*, 16 (1887), 15–24.

FLETCHER, H. J. 'A review of the Toi-Kau-Rakau genealogies. *JPS* 39 (1930), 189–94.

FORBES, ALEXANDER KINLOCH. *Râs Mâla. Hindoo annals of the Province of Goozerat in western India*. London, 1924.

FORDUN, JOHN OF. *John of Fordun's Chronicle of the Scottish Nation* (ed. W. F. Skene). Edinburgh, 1872.

FORREST, W. G. 'The date of the Lykourgan reforms in Sparta.' *Phoenix*, 17 (1963), 157–79.

FOX, JAMES J. 'A Rotinese dynastic genealogy: structure and event' in T. O. Beidelman (ed.), *Translation of Culture*. Tavistock, 1971, 37–77.

FOX, RICHARD G. *Kin, clan, raja and rule: state-hinterland relations in pre-industrial India*. Berkeley, Calif., 1971.

FRANKFORT, HENRI, SETON LLOYD, and THORKIL JACOBSEN. *The Gimilsin Temple and the Palace of the Rulers at Tell Asmar* (University of Chicago Oriental Institute Pubs. XLIII). Chicago, Ill., 1940.

FRASER, P. M. 'The tribal-cycles of eponymous priests at Lindos and Kamiros.' *Eranos*, 51 (1953), 23–47.

FRAZER, JAMES G. *Studies in Greek scenery, legend and history; selected from his commentary on Pausanias' Description of Greece.* London, 1919.

FREEDMAN DAVID NOEL. 'The chronicler's purpose.' *Catholic Biblical Quarterly*, 23 (1961), 436–42.

FREEMAN, EDWARD A. 'Pedigrees and pedigree-makers.' *Contemporary Review*, 30 (1877), 11–41.

FÜRER-HAIMENDORF, CHRISTOF VON. 'The value of Indian bardic literature' in Philips (ed.), *Historians of India*, 87–93.

FUSSNER, FRANK S. *Tudor history and the historians.* New York, 1970.

GADD, CYRIL J. 'The cities of Babylonia.' Fascicle in *CAH*[2].

GAI, G. S. 'Shiggaon inscription of Amoghavarsha I.' *Epigraphica Indica*, 35 (1963), 85–8.

GAIT, EDWARD A. *A history of Assam.* 3rd rev. ed. Calcutta, 1963.

GANGULY, D. K. 'The Purānas and their bearing on the early Indian dynasties' in D. C. Sircar (ed.), *Bhārata war and Purānic genealogies.* Calcutta, 1970, 121–40.

GARDINER, ALAN. *Egypt of the Pharaohs.* Oxford, 1961.

GARDINER, K. H. J. 'The Samguk-sagi and its sources.' *Papers on Far Eastern History*, 2 (Sept. 1970), 1–42.

—— 'Some problems concerning the foundation of Paekche.' *Archiv Orientální*, 37 (1969), 562–86.

GASSEL I. 'Fonction de la tradition dans la mutation radicale' in G. Balandier (ed.), *Sociologie des mutations.* Paris, 1970, 113–26.

GEERTZ, H. and G. 'Teknonyny in Bali: parenthood, age-grading and genealogical amnesia.' *JRAI* 94 (1964), 94–108.

GELB, IGNACE J. 'Two Assyrian King Lists.' *JNES* 13 (1954), 209–30.

GHOSHAL, U. N. 'The dynastic chronicles of Kashmir.' *Indian Historical Quarterly*, 18 (1942), 195–207, 302–41; 19 (1943), 27–38, 156–72.

GILL, WM. WYATT. 'The genealogy of the kings of Rarotonga and Mangaia, as illustrating the colonisation of these islands and the

Hervey group.' *Annual Rpt. of the Australasian Association for the Advancement of Science*, 2 (1890), 627–37.

GIORGADZE, G. G. 'The order of succession to the throne in the Old Hittite kingdom.' *Vestnik Drewney Istorii*, 14 (1969), 67–83 (in Russian with English summary).

GOETZE, ALBRECHT. 'The Kassites and Near Eastern chronology.' *JCS* 18 (1964), 97–101.

—— 'An old Babylonian itinerary.' *JCS* 7 (1953), 51–72.

—— 'On the chronology of the second millennium B.C.' *JCS* 11 (1957), 53–61, 63–73.

—— 'The predecessors of Šuppililiumaš of Ḫatti and the chronology of the Ancient Near East.' *JAOS* 72 (1952), 67–72.

—— 'The problem of chronology and early Hittite history.' *Bulletin of the American Schools for Oriental Research*, 122 (1957), 18–20.

GOLDMAN, IRVING. *Ancient Polynesian society*. Chicago, Ill., 1971.

GOLSON JACK. 'Archaeology, tradition, and myth in New Zealand prehistory.' *JPS* 69 (1960), 380–402.

GOODY, Jack, and IAN WATT. 'The consequences of literacy' in Jack Goody (ed.), *Literacy in traditional societies*. Cambridge, 1968, 27–68.

GOPAL, B. R. 'The Kadambas of Goa.' *Journal of Karnatak University* (Dharwar), 4 (1968), 164–77.

—— 'The Kadambas of Hangal.' *Journal of Karnatak University* (Dharwar), 3 (1967), 99–115.

—— 'The Sindas of Reñjeru.' *Journal of Ancient Indian History*, 2 (1968/9), 84–93.

GORDON, CYRUS H. 'Fratriarchy in the Old Testament.' *Journal of Biblical Literature*, 54 (1935), 223–31.

GRAAF, H. J. DE. *Geschiedenis van Indonesie*. The Hague, 1949.

GRAAF, J. J. DE. 'Later Javanese sources and historiography' in Soejatmoko, *Introduction to Indonesian Historiography*. Ithaca, N.Y., 1965, 119–36.

GRACE, JOHN T. *Tuwharetoa: the history of the Maori people of the Taupo district*. Wellington, 1959.

GRAY, JOHN. *I and II Kings: a commentary*. London, 1964.

GREEN, LOUIS. *Chronicle into history: an essay on the interpretation of history in Florentine fourteenth-century chronicles*. Cambridge, 1972.

GRIFFIN, LEPEL H. *The law of inheritance to chiefship as observed by the Sikhs previous to the annexation of the Panjab*. Lahore, 1869.

GRUMEL, VENANCE. *La Chronologie*. Paris, 1958.

Gujarat District Gazetteers: Bhavnagar. Ahmedabad, 1968.

GUREVICH, A. YAKOVLEVICH. 'Space and time in the *Weltmodell* of the old Scandinavian peoples.' *Mediaeval Scandinavia*, 2 (1969), 42–53.

GURNEY, O. R. 'Anatolia, *c.* 1600 to 1380 B.C.' Fascicle in *CAH*^{2}.

GÜTERBOCK, HANS. G. 'The predecessors of Šuppiliiumaš again.' *JNES* 29 (1970).

HAJNAL, J. 'European marriage patterns in perspective' in D. Glass and D. E. C. Eversley (eds.), *Population in history*. London, 1965, 101–43.

HALBERT, R. W., and J. B. W. ROBERTSON. 'Chronology of Maori tradition.' *Historical Review* (Whakatane), 11/12 (Dec. 1963).

HALLO, W. W. 'Zāriqum.' *JNES* 15 (1956), 220–5.

—— and WM. KELLY SIMPSON. *The ancient Near East: a history*. New York, 1971.

HANDY, E. S. C. *History and culture in the Society Islands*. Honolulu, 1930.

HANNING, ROBERT W. *The vision of history in early Britain from Gildas to Geoffrey of Monmouth*. New York, 1966.

HAYES, W. C., M. B. ROWTON, and F. H. STUBBINGS. 'Chronology: Egypt, Western Asia, the Aegean Bronze Age.' Fascicle in *CAH*^{2}.

HEIDEL, WILLIAM ARTHUR. 'Hecataeus and the Egyptian priests in Herodotus, book II.' *Memoirs of the American Academy of Arts and Sciences*, 18 (1935), 49–134.

HENDERSON, ISABEL. *The Picts*. London, 1967.

HENIGE, DAVID P. 'Oral tradition and chronology.' *JAH* 12 (1971), 371–89.

HENQUEL, J. 'Histoire ancienne de Wallis des origines à 1836.' *Bulletin de l'Information du Territoire des îles Wallis et Futuna*,' (Jan. 1967), 14–17.

HENRY, TEUIRA. *Ancient Tahiti*. Honolulu, 1928.

HERODOTUS. *The Persian Wars*. (Rawlinson ed.) in *The Greek Historians*, ed. F. R. B. Godolphin. 2 vols. New York, 1942.

HINZ, WALTHER. 'Persia, *c.* 1800–1550 B.C.' Fascicle in *CAH*^{2}.

HIRTH, FRIEDRICH. *Ancient history of China*. New York, 1908.

HOGAN, JAMES. 'The Irish law of Kingship, with special reference to Ailech and Cenél Eoghain.' *Proceedings of the Royal Irish Academy*, 40, sect. C, no. 3 (1932), 186–254.

HOLLINGSWORTH, T. H. *The demography of the British peerage* [supplement to *Population Studies*, 18 (1964/5)]. London, 1965.

HOWORTH, HENRY H. 'Harald Fairhair and his ancestors.' *Saga-Book of the Viking Society*. 9 (1914/18), 1–252.

HUXLEY, GEORGE LEONARD. *Early Sparta*. London, 1962.

Imperial Gazetteer of India. 26 vols. Oxford, 1907–9.

INNES, THOMAS. *A critical essay on the ancient inhabitants of the northern parts of Britain, or Scotland, containing an account of the Romans, of the Britains betwixt the walls, of the Caledonians of Picts, and particularly of the Scots* [The Historians of Scotland, 8]. Edinburgh, 1879.

ISENBURG, WILHELM KARL, PRINZ VON. *Stammtafeln zur europäischen Staaten*. 2 vols. Berlin, 1936–7.

JACOBSEN, THORKILD. *The Sumerian king list*. Chicago, Ill., 1938.

JACOBY, FELIX. *Apollodors Chronik. Eine Sammlung der Fragmente*. Berlin, 1902.

JAURGAIN, JEAN. *La Vasconie*. 2 vols. Pau, 1898–1902.

JOHNSON, JAMES W. 'Chronological writing: its concepts and development.' *History and Theory*, 2 (1962), 124–45.

—— 'The Scythian: his rise and fall.' *Journal of the History of Ideas*, 20 (1959), 250–7.

JOHNSON, MARSHALL DUANE. *The purpose of the Biblical genealogies with special reference to the setting of the genealogy of Jesus*. Cambridge, 1969.

JOHNSON, VAN L. 'Early Roman chronology and the calendar.' *Classical Quarterly*, Feb. 1969, 203–7.

JONES, A. H. M. *Sparta*. Oxford, 1967.

JONES, FRANCIS. 'An approach to Welsh genealogy.' *Transactions of the Cymmrodorian Society* (1948), 303–466.

JOSEPHUS. *The antiquities of the Jews* in Flavius Josephus, *Complete works*. Grand Rapids, Mich., 1960, 23–426.

—— *Flavius Josephus against Apion* in ibid. 607–36.

JUDGE, H. G. 'Aaron, Zadok, and Abiathar.' *Journal of Theological Studies*, 7 (1956), 70–4.

JUILLET, JACQUES. 'Esquisse généalogique de la maison de Foix.' *Bulletin de la Société ariégeoise des sciences, lettres et arts*, 21 (1965), 119–20.

KALHANA. *Kalhana's chronicles of the kings of Kashmir* (ed. M. A. Stein). 2 vols. London, 1900–2.

KANE, PANDURANG VAMAN. *The history of Dharmaśastra literature*. 5 vols. in 7: Poona, 1930–62.

KARAN, P. R. 'History of the Rathors' in *Sir Asuthosh Mukherjee Silver Jubilee Volume* (4 vols., Calcutta, 1921–7), III, pt. 1, 255–336.

KARVE, I. 'Succession in a matrilineal royal house', *Bulletin of the Deccan College Research Institute*, 20 (1960), 364–8.

KEES, HERMANN. 'Beiträge zur Geschichte des Vezirats im Alten Reich. Die Chronologie des Vezirs unter Phiops II.' *Nachrichten [Jahrbuch] der Akademie der Wissenschaften, Göttingen*, 4/2 (1940), 39–54.

KELLEHER, JOHN V. 'Early Irish history and pseudo-history.' *Studia Hibernica*, 3 (1963), 113–37.

—— 'The pre-Norman Irish genealogies.' *Irish Historical Studies*, 16 (1968), 138–53.

—— 'The rise of the Dál Cais' in Etienne Rynne (ed.). *North Munster studies*. Limerick, 1967, 230–41.

—— 'The Táin and the Annals', *Ériu*, 22 (1971), 107–27.

KELLY, LESLIE C. 'Some problems in the study of Maori genealogies.' *JPS* 49 (1940), 235–42.

KENDRICK, Thomas D. *British antiquity*. London, 1950.

KENT, ROLAND G. *Old Persian: grammar, texts, lexicon*. New Haven, Conn., 1950.

KING, L. W. *Chronicles concerning early Babylonian kings, including records of the early history of the Kassites and the country of the sea, I, Introductory chapters*. London, 1907.

KOSKINEN, AARNE A. *Ariki the first-born. An analysis of a Polynesian chieftain title*. Helsinki, 1960.

—— *Missionary influence as a political factor in the Pacific islands*. Helsinki, 1953.

KRAUS, F. R. 'Könige die in zelten Wohnten. Betrachtungen über der Kern der assyrischen Königsliste.' *Mededelingen der koninklijke Nederlandse Akademie van Wetenschappen*, Afd Letterkunde, nieuwe reeks, 28 (1965), 123–42.

KUPPER, JEAN-ROBERT. *Les Nomades en Mésopotamie au temps des rois de Mari*. Paris, 1957.

LABAT, RENÉ. 'Assyrologie.' *Annuaire du Collège de France*, 56 (1956), 255–6.

LAESSØE, J. 'Literacy and oral tradition in ancient Mesopotamia' in *Studia Orientalia Ioanni Pedersen*. Haun, 1953, 205–18.

LALINDE ABADÍA, JESUS. 'La sucesión filial en el derecho visigodo.' *Anuário de História de Derecho Español*, 32 (1962), 113–29.

LANDSBERGER, BENNO. 'Assyrische Königsliste und "Dunkles Zeitalter".' *JCS* 8 (1954), 31–73, 106–33.

LAURING, PAULE. *Reges Daniae. Danske kongen på mønter og medaljer*. Copenhagen, 1961.

LAVAL, HONORÉ. *Mangareva: l'histoire ancienne d'un peuple Polynésien*. Brain-le-Comte, 1938.

—— *Mémoires pour servir à l'histoire de Mangareva. Ère chrêtienne, 1834–1871* (ed. P. O'Reilly and C. W. Newbury). Paris, 1968.

LAVONDÈS, H. 'Observations on methods used in assembling oral traditions in the Marquesas' in G. Highland *et al.* (eds.), *Polynesian culture history: essays in honor of Kenneth P. Emory* (Honolulu, 1967), 483–500.

LEACH, EDMUND. *Political systems of highland Burma*. London, 1954.

LENSCHAU, THOMAS. 'Agiaden und Eurypontiden. Die Königshauser Spartas in ihren Beziehungen zueinander.' *Rheinisches Museum für Phililogie*, 88 (1939), 123–46.

LEVI DELLA VIDA, G. 'Nizār.' *Encyclopedia of Islam*, III. 939–41.

LEWY, HILDEGARD. 'Assyria, *c.* 2600 to 1816 B.C.' Fascicle in *CAH*².

—— 'On some problems of Kassite and Assyrian chronology.' *Mélanges Isidore Lévy* [*Annuaire* de l'Institut de Philologie et d'Histoire Orientales et Slaves, 13 (1953)], 241–91.

LEYSER, K. 'The German aristocracy from the ninth to the early twelfth century: a historical and cultural sketch.' *Past and Present*, 41 (Dec. 1968), 25–53.

LUKMAN, NIELS. 'British and Danish traditions. Some contacts and relations.' *Classica et Mediaevalia*, 6 (1944), 73–109.

MACGOWAN, JAMES. *A history of China from the earliest times to the present*. London, 1897.

MACKENZIE, SIR GEORGE. *A defence of the antiquity of the royal line of Scotland*. Edinburgh, 1685.

MACLAGAN, MICHAEL. *'Clemency' Canning*. London, 1962.

MACNEILL, EÓIN. *Celtic Ireland*. Dublin, 1921.

—— 'The pre-Christian kings of Tara.' *Journal of the Royal Society of Antiquaries of Ireland*, 57 (1927), 153–4.

MAC NIOCÁILL, GEARÓID. 'The "heir designate" in early medieval Ireland.' *Irish Jurist*, N.S. 3 (1968), 326–9.

MAGIE, DAVID. *Roman rule in Asia Minor.* 2 vols. Princeton, N.J., 1950.

MAHALINGAM, T. V. 'The early Pallava genealogy and chronology.' *Proceedings of the 26th International Congress of Orientalists*, 3/2 (Delhi, 1964), 693–9.

MAJUL, CÉSAR ADIB. 'Succession in the old Sulu sultanate.' *Philippine Historical Review*, 1 (1965), 252–71.

MAJUMDAR, R. C. 'The Bhārata war' in D. C. Sircar (ed.), *Bhārata war and Purānic genealogies.* Calcutta, 1970, 11–17.

MALAMAT, ABRAHAM. 'King lists of the Old Babylonian period and Biblical genealogies' in W. W. Hallo (ed.), *Essays in memory of E. A. Speiser.* New Haven, Conn., 1968, 163–73.

MALONEY, CLARENCE. 'Dynastic drift: a process of cultural universalization' in *Professor K. A. Nilakanti Sastri Felicitation Volume*, Madras, 1971, 89–107.

MANKAD, D. R. *Purānic chronology.* Anand, 1951.

—— 'Solar genealogy reconsidered.' *Journal of Oriental Studies* [Baroda], 15 (1965/6), 350–73.

MANUEL, FRANK E. *Isaac Newton, historian.* Cambridge, Mass., 1963.

MARINATOS, SP. 'Mycenaean elements within the royal house of Macedonia' in *Ancient Macedonia: Papers read at the 1st International Symposium of the Institute for Balkan Studies. Thessaloniki*, 26–28 Aug. 1968, 45–52.

MARQUART, J. 'Chronologische Untersuchungen.' *Philologus*, Supplement to Vol. 7 (1899), 635–720.

MARSH, HENRY. *Dark Age Britain: some sources of history.* Newton Abbot, 1970.

MASTER, F. S. *The Mahi Kantha directory.* 2 vols. Rajkot, 1922.

MEEK, THEOPHILUS J. 'Aaronites and Zadokites.' *American Journal of Semitic Languages*, 45 (1929), 149–66.

MENDL, B. 'Les derniers Přemyslides: la fin d'une dynastie Slave.' *Revue Historique*, 179 (1937), 34–62.

MESKILL, JOHANNA M. 'The Chinese genealogy as a research source' in M. Freedman (ed.), *Family and kinship in Chinese Society.* Stanford, Calif., 1970, 139–61.

METCALF, T. R. *The aftermath of revolt: India, 1857–70.* Princeton, N.J., 1964.

MÉTRAUX, ALFRED. *Ethnology of Easter Island.* Honolulu, 1940.

—— 'The kings of Easter Island.' *JPS* 46 (1937), 41–62.

MILLER, MOLLY. 'Archaic literary chronography.' *JHS* 75 (1955), 54–8.

—— 'Herodotus as chronographer.' *Klio*, 46 (1965), 109–28.

—— *The Sicilian colony dates: Studies in chronography, I.* Albany, N.Y., 1970.

MISHRA, Y. *Early history of Vaiśālī.* Delhi, 1962.

MITCHEL, FORDYCE. 'Herodotos' use of genealogical chronology.' *Phoenix*, 10 (1956), 48–69.

MITCHELL, ROGER. 'Oral tradition and Micronesian history: a microcosmic approach.' *Journal of Pacific History*, 5 (1970), 33–41.

MÖLLER, JOHANN CASPAR. *Geschichte der vormalingen Grafschaft Bentheim von der ältesten Zeit bis auf unsere Tage.* Lingen, 1879.

MONBERG, T. 'Ta'aroa in the creation myths of the Society Islands.' *JPS* 65 (1956), 243–81.

MONTGOMERY, J. A. *A critical and exegetical commentary on the Books of Kings.* New York, 1951.

MORAES, GEORGE MARK. *The Kadamba Kula: a history of ancient and mediaeval Karnataka.* Bombay, 1931.

MULLER HZ., S. 'Het oude Register van Graaf Florenz.' *Bijdragen Mededeelingen van het Historisch Genootschap te Utrecht*, 22 (1901), 90–357.

MUNZ, PETER. 'History and myth.' *Philosophical Quarterly*, 6 (1956), 1–16.

—— 'The purity of the historical method: some sceptical reflections on the current enthusiasm for the history of non-European societies,' *New Zealand Journal of History*, 5 (1971), 1–17.

—— 'The skeleton and the mollusc: reflections on the nature of historical narrative.' *New Zealand Journal of History*, 1 (1967), 107–23.

MURTHY, A. V. NARASIMHA. *The Sevunas of Devagiri.* Madras, 1971.

NEWBURY, C. W. '*Te hau pahu rahi:* Pomare II and the concept of inter-island government in eastern Polynesia.' *JPS* 76 (1967), 447–514.

NEWTON, ISAAC. *Chronology of ancient nations amended.* London, 1728.

NILSSON, MARTIN PEHRSSON. *Cults, myths, oracles and politics in ancient Greece.* Lund, 1951.

NIYOGI, ROMA. *The history of the Gāhadavālas.* Calcutta, 1959.

NOORDUYN, JACOBUS, 'Origins of south Celebes historical writing' in Soedjatmoko, *Introduction to Indonesian historiography*, pp. 137–56.

OATES, DAVID. *Studies in the ancient history of northern Iraq*. London, 1968.

OBERMANN, JULIUS. 'Early Islam' in Robert C. Dentan (ed.), *The idea of history in the ancient Near East*. New Haven, Conn., 1955, 237–310.

OBEYESEKERE, GANANATH. 'Gajabahu and the Gajabahu synchronism: an inquiry into the relationship between myth and history.' *Ceylon Journal of Humanities*, 1 (1970), 25–56.

O'BRIEN, M. A. (ed.). *Corpus Genealogiarum Hiberniae*. Dublin, 1962.

Ó'CORRÁIN, DONNCHADH. 'Irish regnal succession: a reappraisal.' *Studia Hibernica*, 11 (1971), 7–39.

Ó CUÍV, BRIAN. 'Literary creation and Irish historical tradition.' *Proceedings of the British Academy*, 49 (1963), 233–62.

OLLOSSON, M. *Gilead, tradition, and history*. Lund, 1969.

OLMSTEAD, ALBERT T. *A history of Assyria*. New York, 1923.

O'RAHILLY, THOMAS F. *Early Irish history and mythology*. Dublin, 1957.

ORBAND, RICHARD. 'Les tombeaux des Nguyen.' *BEFEO*, 14 (1914), pt. 7, 1–10.

OWENS, J. M. B. 'Christianity and the Maoris to 1840.' *New Zealand Journal of History*, 2 (1968), 18–40.

PARANAVITANA, S. 'Matrilineal descent in the Sinhalese royal family.' *Ceylon Journal of Science*, 2 (1933), 235–40.

PARGITER, FREDERICK E. 'Ancient Indian genealogies and chronology.' *JRAS* (1910), 1–57.

—— 'Ancient Indian genealogies: are they trustworthy?' in Bhandarkar Oriental Research Institute, *Commemorative Essays*. Poona, 1917, 107–13.

—— *Ancient Indian historical tradition*. London, 1922.

—— 'Earliest Indian traditional "history".' *JRAS* (1914), 267–95.

—— 'The northern Pañcāla dynasty.' *JRAS* (1918), 229–48.

—— *The Puranic text of the dynasties of the Kali age*. London, 1913.

—— 'Sagara and the Haihayas, Vasiṣṭha and Aurva.' *JRAS* (1919), 353–67.

—— 'Viśvāmitra and Vasiṣṭha.' *JRAS* (1913), 885–904.

—— 'Viśvāmitra, Vasiṣṭha, Hariśćandra and Sunahśepa.' *JRAS* (1917), 37–67.

PARIHAR, G. R. *Marwar and the Marathas (1724–1843 A.D.)*. Jodhpur, 1968.

PARKE, H. W. 'The deposing of Spartan kings.' *Classical Quarterly*, 39 (1945), 106–12.

PARR, C. J. 'Maori literacy, 1843–1867.' *JPS* 72 (1963), 211–34.

—— 'A missionary library: printed attempts to instruct the Maori, 1815–1845.' *JPS* 70 (1961), 429–50.

PARSONSON, G. S. 'The literate revolution in Polynesia.' *Journal of Pacific History*, 2 (1967), 39–57.

PATHAK, V. *History of Kośala up to the rise of the Mauryas*. Delhi, 1963.

PAUSANIAS (ed. and tr. by J. G. Frazer), *Description of Greece*. 6 vols. New York, 1898.

PEARCE, G. L. *The story of the Maori people*. Auckland, 1968.

PEARCE, SUSAN M. 'The traditions of the royal king-list of Dumnonia.' *Transactions of the Honourable Society of Cymmrodorion* (1970), 129–39.

PELLER, SIGISMUND. 'Births and deaths among Europe's ruling families since 1500' in D. V. Glass and D. E. C. Eversley (eds.), *Population in History* (London, 1965), 87–100.

PHAYRE, ARTHUR P. *History of Burma, including Burma proper, Pegu, Taungu, Tenasserim and Arakan, from the earliest times to the end of the first war with British India*. London, 1883.

PHILIPS, C. H. (ed.). *Historians of India, Pakistan and Ceylon*. London, 1961.

PHILLIPPS, W. J. *Maori life and customs*. Wellington, 1966.

PIDDINGTON, RALPH. 'A note on the validity and significance of Polynesian traditions.' *JPS* 65 (1956), 200–3.

—— 'Synchronic and Diachronic Dimensions in the study of Polynesian Cultures.' *JPS* 60 (1951), 108–21.

PLUMB, J. H. *The death of the past*. Boston, Mass., 1971.

POE, DISON HSUEH-FENG. 'Imperial succession and attendant crisis in dynastic China: an analytic-quantitative study through the five-element approach.' *Tsing Hua Journal of Chinese Studies*, N.S. 8 (1970), 84–152.

POEBEL, A. 'The Assyrian King List from Khorsabad.' *JNES* 1 (1942), 247–306, 460–92; 2 (1943), 56–90.

PORALLA, PAUL. *Prosopographie des Lakedaemonier bis auf die Zeit Alexanders der Grossen*. Breslau, 1913.

PORTER, J. R. 'Pre-Islamic Arabic historical traditions and the early historical narratives of the Old Testament.' *Journal of Biblical Literature*, 87 (1968), 17–26.

PRADHAN, SITA NATH. *The chronology of ancient India.* Calcutta, 1929.

PRAKKEN, D. W. 'Herodotus and the Spartan kinglists.' *Transactions of the America Philological Association*, 71 (1940), 460–72.

—— 'A note on the Megarian historian Dieuchidas.' *American Journal of Philology*, 62 (1941), 348–51.

—— *Studies in Greek genealogical chronology.* Lancaster, Pa., 1945.

PRITCHARD, JAMES B. *Ancient Near Eastern texts relating to the Old Testament.* Princeton, N.J., 1955.

Punjab State Gazetteers: Simla Hill States. Lahore, 1908.

PUSALKER, A. D. 'Pre-Bhārata war history from the Purānas.' *Quarterly Review of Historical Studies*, 7 (1967/8), 8–22.

RAI, SAILAJA KINKAR. 'A new light on Chunda.' *Indian Historical Quarterly*, 11 (1935), 559–563.

RAJPUTANA and AJMER. *List of ruling princes, chiefs and leading personages.* Delhi, 1938.

RAMA RAO, M. 'New light on the Viśnukundins.' *Proceedings of the Indian History Congress*, 27 (1965), 78–82.

RANK, OTTO (ed. Philip Freund). *The myth of the birth of the hero and other writings.* New York, 1964.

RAYCHAUDHURI, GOPALCHANDRA. 'The early history of the Kachwāhas of Amber' in D. R. Bhandarkar (ed.), *B. C. Law volume*, Pt. 1. Calcutta, 1945, 683–94.

—— 'Guhilot origins' in B. C. Law (ed.), *D. R. Bhandarkar volume.* Calcutta, 1940, 311–16.

RAYCHAUDHURI, H. *Political history of ancient India from the accession of Parikshit to the coronation of Bimbisara.* Calcutta, 1927.

REDFORD, DONALD B. 'The Hyksos invasion in history and tradition.' *Orientalia*, N.S. 39 (1970), 1–51.

REU, BISHESHWAR NATH. *Glories of Marwar and the glorious Rathors.* Jodhpur, 1943.

—— *History of the Rāshṭrakūṭas (Rāṭhōḍas).* Jodhpur, 1933.

ROBERTON, J. B. W. 'A culture nomenclature based on tradition.' *JPS* 78 (1969), 252–8.

—— 'The early tradition of the Whakatane district.' *JPS* 75 (1966), 189–205.

—— 'The evaluation of Maori tribal tradition as history.' *JPS* 71 (1962), 292–309.

—— 'The role of tribal tradition in New Zealand prehistory.' *JPS* 66 (1957), 247–63.

—— 'The significance of New Zealand tribal traditions.' *JPS* 67 (1958), 39–57.

RODINSON, MAXIME. *Mahomet.* Paris, 1961.

ROGERS, MICHAEL C. 'The thanatochronology of some kings of Silla.' *Monumenta Serica*, 17 (1960), 335–48.

ROWTON, M. B. 'The date of Hammurabi.' *JNES* 17 (1958), 97–111.

—— 'Mesopotamian chronology and the "Era of Menophres".' *Iraq*, 8 (1946), 94–110.

—— '"Ṭuppū" and the date for Hammurabi.' *JNES* 10 (1951), 184–204.

—— '"Ṭuppū" in the Assyrian King Lists.' *JNES* 18 (1959), 213–21.

SANFORD, EVA M. 'The study of ancient history in the Middle Ages.' *Journal of the History of Ideas*, 5 (1944), 21–43.

SAXO GRAMMATICUS. *The first nine books of the Danish History of Saxo Grammaticus.* Tr. Oliver Elton. London, 1893.

SCHNABEL, PAUL. *Berossus und die babylonish-hellenistische Literatur.* Berlin, 1923.

SEN, B. C. 'Early Indian approach to history and some problems of its reconstruction.' *Journal of the Bihar Research Society*, 54 (1968), 1–15.

SÉVIN, FRANÇOIS. 'Recherches sur les rois de Bithynie.' *Mémoires de littérature tirés des registres de l'Académie des Inscriptions et Belles-Lettres*, 12 (1740), 316–30; 14 (1743), 21–37.

SEZNEC, J. *The survival of the pagan gods: the mythological tradition and its place in Renaissance humanism and art.* New York, 1953.

SHAH, A. M. and R. G. SHROFF. 'The Vahīvancā Bārots of Gujarat: a caste of genealogists and mythographers' in M. Singer (ed.), *Traditional India: structure and change.* Philadelphia, Pa., 1959, 40–70.

SHARMA, D. (ed.). *Rajasthan through the ages. I.* Bikanir, 1966.

SHARP, ANDREW. 'Maori genealogies and canoe traditions.' *JPS* 67 (1958), 37–8.

—— 'Maori genealogies and the "fleet".' *JPS* 68 (1959), 12–13.

SHAWCROSS, WILFRED. 'Archaeology with a short, isolated time scale: New Zealand.' *World Archaeology*, 1 (1969), 184–99.

SHKLAR, JUDITH. 'Subversive genealogies.' *Daedalus*, 101 (1972), 129–54.

SIMMONS, D. R. 'A New Zealand myth: Kupe, Toi and the "Fleet".' *New Zealand Journal of History*, 3 (1969), 14–31.

—— 'The sources of Sir George Grey's *Nga Mahi a Nga Tupuna*.' *JPS* 75 (1966), 177–88.

SIMMONS, STEPHEN D. 'Early Old Babylonian tablets from Harmal and elsewhere.' *JCS* 13 (1959), 71–93; 14 (1960), 23–32, 49–55, 75–87, 117–25; 15 (1961), 49–58, 81–3.

SINCLAIR, KEITH. 'Some historical notes on an Atiawa genealogy.' *JPS* 60 (1951), 55–65.

SINHA, S. 'State formation and Rajput myth in tribal central India.' *Man in India*, 42 (1962), 35–80.

SIRCAR, D. C. 'The Guhila claim of Solar origin.' *Journal of Indian History*, 42 (1964), 381–7.

—— 'The Guhilas of Kiśkindha.' *Our Heritage*, 11 (1963), 1–69.

—— 'The myth of the Great Bhārata war' in idem (ed.), *Bhārata war and Purānic genealogies*. Calcutta, 1970, 18–27.

—— 'Problems of Kusana and Rajput history' in idem (ed.), *Prācyavidyā Taraṅginī. Golden Jubilee Volume of the Dept. of Ancient Indian History and Culture*. Calcutta, 1969, 153–217.

—— *Studies in the society and administration of ancient and mediaeval India*, I, *Society*. Calcutta, 1967.

SIRJEAN, GASTON. *Encyclopédie généalogique des maisons souveraines du monde*. 1 vol. to date: Paris, 1956– .

SISAM, KENNETH, 'Anglo-Saxon royal genealogies,' *Proceedings of the British Academy*, 39 (1953), 287–348.

SKØVGAARD-PETERSEN, INGE. 'Saxo, historian of the Patria.' *Mediaeval Scandinavia*, 2 (1969), 54–77.

SMITH, R. MORTON. *Palestinian parties and politics that shaped the Old Testament*. New York, 1971.

—— 'On the ancient chronology of India.' *JAOS* 77 (1957) 116–29, 266–79.

SMITH, SIDNEY. 'Yarim-Lim of Yamḫad.' *Rivista degli studi orientali*, 32 (1957), 155–84.

SMITH, WILLIAM ROBERTSON. *Kinship and marriage in early Arabia*. 2nd ed. London, 1903.

SMITH, W. STEVENSON. 'The Old Kingdom in Egypt.' Fascicle in *CAH*[2].

SOBREQUES I VIDAL, SANTIAGO. *Els barons de Catalunya* (Biografies Catalanes, 3). Barcelona, 1957.

SOLLBERGER, EDOUARD. 'The rulers of Lagaš.' *JCS* 21 (1967), 279–91.

SPOHN, GEORG R. 'Armenien und Herzog Naimes. Zur bayerischen Stammessage im Mittelalter und bei Peter Harer.' *Zeitschrift für bayerische Landesgeschichte*, 34 (1971), 185–210.

SRIVASTAVA, ASHIRBADI LAL. *Akbar the Great*. 2 vols. Agra, 1962–7.

STEIN, BURTON. 'Early Indian historiography: a conspiracy hypothesis.' *Indian Economic and Social History Review*, 6 (1969), 41–59.

STEINER, FRANZ. *Taboo*. Harmondsworth. 1967.

STENTON, FRANK M. 'Lindsey and its kings' in *Essays in history presented to Reginald Lane Poole* (ed. H. W. C. Davis). Oxford, 1927, 136–50.

STERN, S. M. 'Ya'qūb the coppersmith and Persian national sentiment' in C. E. Bosworth (ed.), *Islam and Iran*. Edinburgh, 1971, 535–56.

STEVENSON, J. H. 'The law of the throne—Tanistry and the introduction of the law of primogeniture.' *Scottish Historical Review*, 25 (1927/8), 1–12.

—— 'The prince of Scotland.' *Scottish Historical Review*, 22 (1924/5), 81–94.

STINESPRING, W. F. 'Eschatology in Chronicles.' *Journal of Biblical Literature*, 80 (1961), 209–19.

STOKES, JOHN F. G. 'New bases for Hawaiian chronology.' *Annual Report of the Hawaiian Historical Society*, 41 (1933), 23–65.

STOKVIS, A. H. M. J. *Manuel de généalogie et de chronologie de tous les états du globe*. 3 vols. Leiden, 1888–93.

STONES, E. L. G. (ed.). *Anglo-Scottish relations, 1174–1328: some selected documents*. London, 1965.

STRATHMANN, ERNEST A. 'Ralegh on the problems of chronology.' *Huntington Library Quarterly*, 11 (1948), 129–48.

STURLUSON, SNORRI (ed. Lee Hollander). *Heimskringla*. Austin, Texas, 1964.

SUGGS, ROBERT C. 'Historical traditions and archeology in Polynesia.' *American Anthropologist*, 62 (1960), 764–73.

SUKHABANIJ, KACHORN. 'Proposed dating of the Yonok-Chiengsaen dynasty.' *Journal of the Burma Research Society*, 43 (1960), 57–62.

TAQAISHVILI, E. 'Les Sources des notices du Patriarche de Jérusalem Dosithee sur les rois d'Aphkhazie.' *Journal Asiatique*, 210 (1927), 357–70.

TE HURINUI, PII 'Maori genealogies.' *JPS* 67 (1959), 162–5.

TESSITORI, L. P. *A descriptive catalogue of the Bardic and Historical Manuscripts, Section I, pts. 1 and 2; Section 2, pt. 1.* Calcutta, 1917–18.

—— 'A progress report on the work done during the year 1916 in connection with the Bardic and Historical Survey of Rajputana.' *JASB*, N.S. 13 (1917), 195–252.

—— 'A progress report on the work done during the year 1917 in connection with the Bardic and Historical Survey of Rajputana.' *JASB*, N.S. 15 (1919), 5–79.

—— 'A progress report on the work done during the year 1918 in connection with the Bardic and Historical Survey of Rajputana.' *JASB*, N.S. 16 (1920), 251–79.

—— 'A scheme for the Bardic and Historical Survey of Rajputana.' *JASB*, N.S. 10 (1914), 373–410.

THAPAR, ROMILA. *A history of India.* Harmondsworth, 1966.

—— 'Image of the barbarian in ancient India.' *Comparative Studies in Society and History*, 13 (1971), 408–36.

THIELE, EDWIN R. *The mysterious numbers of the Hebrew kings.* Rev. ed. Grand Rapids, Mich., 1965.

THOMAS, HOMER L. and ROBERT W. EHRICH. 'Some problems in chronology.' *World Archaeology*, 1 (1969), 143–56.

THOMSON BASIL H. *Diversions of a prime minister.* Edinburgh, 1894.

THOMSON, WILLIAM J. 'Te Pito te Henua or Easter Island.' *Annual Report* of the U.S. National Museum for 1889, 447–552.

TIGERSTEDT, E. N. *The legend of Sparta in Classical Antiquity.* Stockholm, 1965.

TOD, JAMES. *Annals and antiquities of Rajasthan*, 2 vols. London, 1960. Reprint of 1829–32 edition.

TOEPFFER, JOHANNES. 'Astakos.' *Hermes*, 31 (1896), 124–36.

TON THÂT HÂN. 'Généalogie des Nguyen avant Gia-Long.' *Bulletin de l'Association des Amis de Vieux-Hué*, 7 (1920) 295–328.

TOUMANOFF, CYRIL. 'Chronology of the kings of Abasgia and other problems.' *Le Muséon*, 69 (1956), 73–90.

—— 'La Noblesse géorgienne: sa génèse et sa structure.' *Rivista araldica*, 54 (1956), 260–73.

—— *Studies in Christian Caucasian history*. Georgetown, Md., 1968.

TRAUTMANN, THOMAS R. 'Length of generation and reign in ancient India.' *JAOS* 89 (1969), 564–77.

VAN DRIEL, G. *The cult of Aššur*. Assen, 1969.

VAN SETERS, JOHN. 'The conquest of Sihon's kingdom: a literary examination.' *Journal of Biblical Literature*, 91 (1972), 182–97.

VENKATA RAMANAYYA, N. *The Chalukyas of L(V)ēmulavāda*. Hyderabad, 1953.

VENKATACHELAM, KOTA. *Chronology of ancient Hindu history*. 2 vols. Gandhinagar, 1957.

VERMA, O. P. 'A discrepancy in the Yadava genealogy.' *Nagpur University Journal* (Humanities), 16 (1965), 32–6.

—— *The Yādavas and their times*. Nagpur, 1970.

VIVIAN, S. P. 'Some statistical aspects of genealogy.' *Genealogists' Magazine*, 8 (1934), 482–9.

VYAS, R. P. *Role of the nobility in Marwar (1800–1873 A.D.)*. New Delhi, 1969.

WALKER, R. J. 'Proper names in Maori myth and tradition.' *JPS* 78 (1969), 405–15.

WARDER, A. K. 'The Pali Canon and its commentaries as an historical record' in Philips (ed.), *Historians of India*, 44–56.

WEERTH, O. 'Zur Genealogie des lippischen Fürstenhauses.' *Mitteilungen aus der lippischen Geschichte und Landeskunde*, 6 (1908), 81–98.

WEGENER, W. *Die Přemysliden*. Göttingen, 1957.

WEIDNER, ERNST. 'Bemerkungen zur Königsliste aus Chorsābād.' *Archiv für Orientforschung*, 15 (1945/51), 85–102.

WEST, THOMAS. *Ten years in south-central Polynesia: being reminiscences of a personal mission to the Friendly Islands and their dependencies*. London, 1865.

WIDENGREN, G. 'Oral and written literature among the Hebrews in light of the Arabic evidence, with special regard to prose narratives.' *Acta Orientalia*, 23 (1959), 201–62.

WILBERFORCE-BELL, HAROLD. *A history of Kathiawad*. London, 1916.

WILLIAMS, H. W. 'The Maruiwi myth.' *JPS* 46 (1937), 105–22.

WOLSKI, J. 'Les Achémenides et les Arsacides. Contribution à l'histoire de la formation des traditions iraniennes.' *Syria*, 43 (1966), 65–89.

WÜSTENFELD, F. *Genealogische Tabellen der arabischen Stämme und Familien.* 2 vols. Göttingen, 1852.

YAZDANI, G. *The early history of the Deccan.* 2 vols. London, 1960.

YEIVIN, SH. *The Israelite conquest of Canaan* [Publications de l'Institut historique et archéologique néerlandais de Stamboul, 27]. Istanbul, 1971.

Concepts of Time

The following bibliography is designed to allow the reader to supplement the rather sketchy attention paid to the concept of time in the present work. It is not intended to be comprehensive, however, but only to indicate the diversity and range of the materials on this important problem.

BASHAM, A. L. 'Ancient Indian ideas of time and history,' in D. C. Sircar (ed.), *Prācyavidyā-Taraṅginī.* Golden Jubilee Volume of the *Department of Ancient Indian History and Culture.* Calcutta, 1969, 49–63.

BEIDELMAN, T. O. 'Kaguru time reckoning: an aspect of the cosmology of an East African people.' *SWJA* 19 (1963), 9–20.

BEKOMBO, M. 'Note sur le temps: conceptions et attitudes chez les Dwala.' *Ethnographie*, 60/1 (1966), 60–4.

BOHANNAN, Paul. 'Concepts of time among the Tiv of Nigeria.' *SWJA* 9 (1953), 251–62.

BOUAH, N. 'Calendriers traditionnels et concept de temps.' *Bulletin d'Information et de Liaison des Instituts d'Ethno-Sociologie et de Géographie tropicale*, I (1967), 9–26.

BRANDON, S. G. F. *History, time and deity.* Manchester, 1965.

BROWN, TRUESDELL S. 'The Greek sense of time in history as suggested by the accounts of Egypt.' *Historia*, 11 (1962), 257–70.

CASSIN, ELENA. 'Cycles du temps et cadres de l'espace en Mesopotamie ancienne.' *Revue de Synthèse*, 55/6 (1969), 241–58.

CHAIX-RUY, J. *Saint Augustin, temps et histoire.* Paris, 1956.

CHÂTELET, F. 'Le Temps de l'histoire et l'évolution de la fonction historienne.' *Journal de Psychologie normale et pathologique*, 53 (1956), 355–78.

CHILDS, B. S. 'A study of the formula "until this day".' *Journal of Biblical Literature*, 82 (1963), 279–93.

COLLINGWOOD, R. G. 'Some perplexities about time.' *Aristotelian Society Proceedings*, 26 (1925/6), 135–50.

DRETSKE, F. I. 'Particulars and the relational theory of time.' *Philosophical Review*, 70 (1961), 447–67.

DUCHESNE-GUILLEMIN, JACQUES. 'Espace et temps dans l'Iran ancien.' *Revue de Synthèse*, 55/6 (1969), 259–80.

EGERTON, FRANK N., III. 'The longevity of the patriarchs: a topic in the history of demography.' *Journal of the History of Ideas*, 27 (1966), 575–84.

EISENSTEIN, ELIZABETH L. 'Clio and Chronos: an essay in the making and breaking of history-book time' in *History and the concept of time*, 36–64.

ELIADE, MIRCEA. *Cosmos and history*. New York, 1959.

—— 'Mythology of memory and forgetting.' *History of Religions*, 2 (1963), 329–44.

FAUBLÉE, JACQUES. 'Espace et temps dans la tradition malgache.' *Revue de Synthèse*, 55/6 (1969), 297–327.

FILLIOZAT, JEAN. 'Le Temps et l'espace dans les conceptions du monde indien.' *Revue de Synthèse*, 55/6 (1969), 281–95.

FINLEY, J. H. *Thucydides*. Cambridge, Mass., 1942.

FINLEY, M. I. 'Myth, memory and history.' *History and Theory*, 4 (1965), 281–302.

GUREVIČ, A. JA. 'Vremja kak problema istorii kul'tury [Time as a problem of culture history].' *Vosprosy Filosofii*, 3 (1969), 105–16.

HALLOWELL, A. I. 'Temporal orientations in western civilization and in a pre-literate society.' *American Anthropologist*, 39 (1937), 647–70.

HÉBERT, J.-C. 'Le Comput ancien des années malagasy, Jour de nouvel an et cycles d'année.' *Bulletin de Madagascar*, 16 (1966), 29–62, 109–39.

History and the concept of time. Beiheft 6 (1966) to *History and theory*.

HULSTAERT, A. 'Le Temps pour les Mongo.' *Bulletin de l'Académie royale des sciences d'Outre-Mer*, 2nd Ser. (1969), 227–35.

JOHNSON, JAMES WILLIAM. 'Chronological writing: its concepts and development.' *History and Theory*, 2 (1962), 124–45.

KHARE, R. S. 'The concept of time and time-reckoning among the Hindus: an anthropological viewpoint.' *Eastern Anthropologist*, 20 (1967), 47–53.

KRACAUER, SIEGFRIED. 'Time and history' in *History and the concept of time*, 65–78.

KUBLER, GEORGE. *The shapes of time: remarks on the history of things*. New Haven, Conn., 1962.

LECLANT, JEAN. 'Espace et temps, ordre et chaos dans l'Égypte pharaonique.' *Revue de Synthèse*, 55/6 (1969), 217–39.

LEYDEN, W. VON 'Antiquity and authority: a paradox in the Renaissance theory of history.' *Journal of the History of Ideas*, 19 (1958), 473–92.

—— 'History and the Concept of Relative Time.' *History and Theory*, 2 (1962), 263–85.

—— 'Spatium Historicum.' *Durham University Journal*, N.S. 11 (1950), 89–104.

LORD, ALBERT B. *The singer of tales*. Cambridge, Mass., 1960.

LOVEJOY, A. O. *The reason, the understanding and time*. Baltimore, Md., 1961.

MAINGOT, E. 'Histoire de la mesure du temps.' *Aesculape*, 46 (1963), 2–46.

MANUEL, FRANK E. *Isaac Newton, historian*. Cambridge, Mass., 1963.

MBITI, J. 'Les Africains et la notion du temps.' *Afrika* [Bonn], 8 (1967), 33–8, 41.

MEYER, HEINRICH. *The age of the world: A chapter in the history of the enlightenment*. Allentown, Pa., 1951.

MEYERSON, I. 'Le Temps, la mémoire, l'histoire.' *Journal de Psychologie normale et pathologique*, 53 (1956), 333–54.

MOMIGLIANO, A. 'Historiography of written and oral traditions' in idem, *Studies in historiography*. London, 1966, 211–20.

—— 'Time in ancient historiography' in *History and the concept of time*, 1–23.

MOREY, ROBERT V. 'Guahibo time-reckoning.' *Anthropological Quarterly*, 44 (1971), 22–36.

MUILENBURG, J. 'The Biblical view of time.' *Harvard Theological Review*, 54 (1961), 225–52.

NEEDHAM, JOSEPH. 'Time and knowledge in China and the West' in J. T. Fraser (ed.), *Voices of time*, New York, 1966, 92–135.

OHNUKI-TIERNEY, E. 'Concepts of time among the Ainu of the northwest coast of Sakhalin.' *American Anthropologist*, 71 (1969), 488–92.

OTTO, E. 'Zeitvorstellungen und Zeitrechnung im alten Orient.' *Studium generale*, 19 (1966), 743–51.

PANOFF, M. 'The notion of time among the Maenge people of New-Britain.' *Ethnology*, 8 (1969), 152–66.

PEPIN, J. 'Le Temps et le mythe.' *Les Études Philosophiques*, 17 (1962), 55–68.

POCOCK, D. F. 'The anthropology of time reckoning.' *Contributions to Indian Sociology*, 7 (1964), 18–29.

PUECH, H.-C. 'La Gnose et le temps.' *Eranos-Jahrbuch*, 20 (1951), 57–113.

STARR, CHESTER G. 'Historical and Philosophical Time' in *History and the concept of time*, 24–35.

THOMAS, L. V., and D. SAPIR. 'Le Diola et les temps: recherches anthropologiques sur la notion de durée en Basse-Casamance.' *BIFAN* 29 (1967), 331–424.

TOULMIN, S., and J. GOODFIELD. *The discovery of time*. London, 1965.

VERNANT, J.-P. 'Aspects mythiques de la mémoire et du temps' in idem, *Mythe et pensée chez les grecs*. Paris, 1966, 51–94.

VIDAL-NACQUET, P. 'Temps des dieux et temps des hommes.' *Revue de l'Histoire des Religions*, 157 (1960), 55–80.

WHITROW, G. J. *The natural philosophy of time*. New York, 1963.

Index